FOR GOD AND COUNTRY?

BINAH YITZRIT FOUNDATION

SERIES IN ISRAEL STUDIES

FOR GOD AND COUNTRY?

Religious Student-Soldiers in the Israel Defense Forces

Elisheva Rosman-Stollman

CENTER FOR MIDDLE EASTERN STUDIES

UNIVERSITY OF TEXAS AT AUSTIN

Cover Photograph: © 2013, Elisheva Rosman-Stollman.
Religious soldier wearing ritual fringes (tzitzit).
Copyediting, cover and text design: Kristi Shuey
Series Editor: Wendy E. Moore

Library of Congress Control Number: 2014941358
ISBN: 978-0-292-75851-3 (cloth)
ISBN: 978-0-292-75852-0 (paperback)

Chapter 2 is based in part on Elisheva Rosman-Stollman's
article published in *Armed Forces & Society* (2008).

This book was made possible by generous support
from the Binah Yitzrit Foundation.

For Aviad

And for Tamar, Yaacov, Michael, Avital, and Meir

When truly brothers,

men don't sing in unison

but in harmony

Shorts 1972–1973, W. H. Auden

TABLE of CONTENTS

ACKNOWLEDGEMENTS

As this book goes to press and I reflect on the numerous stages of its gestation there are so many people I want to thank. While I cannot name them all here, I do wish to acknowledge those whose contributions were most salient.

First and foremost, a heartfelt thanks is due to the young men and women who agreed to participate in this study. Without their cooperation, the interviews that serve as the basis for this study would never have taken place. Due to our confidentiality agreement, their names are not mentioned here, but I thank each and every one of them for graciously allowing me into their lives at a difficult and stressful period, and for their candid and thoughtful conversations.

I also thank the interviewees who are named in this study: rabbis, heads of study programs, officers, and others. Despite very busy schedules, they were willing to find the time to discuss (and sometimes rediscuss) their life's work, and I am deeply grateful.

This project began as a doctoral dissertation written under the supervision of Stuart A. Cohen of the Department of Political Studies at Bar-Ilan University. As always, I am indebted to him for his guidance at the time, but even more for the advice and assistance he has continued to offer ever since.

I was fortunate to receive funding for the translation of the relevant parts of the original Hebrew manuscript from the Argov Center for the Study of the Jewish People at Bar-Ilan University and from the Schnitzer Foundation for Research on the Israeli Economy and Society. I thank them for their generosity and for believing in the project. I also thank Rick Goldberg for his assistance.

This book would not have come into being were it not for Esther Raizen at the University of Texas at Austin. I first met Esther when she invited me to teach in the Department of Middle Eastern Studies as a Schusterman Scholar during her time as department chair. My year in Austin helped me consolidate some of the ideas discussed here and introduced me to new concepts and discourse that influenced my thinking. Esther also graciously invited me to submit the manuscript to the publications program at the Center for Middle Eastern Studies and offered support and reassurance during the long process leading up to publication. I also thank the various anonymous readers of the manuscript, and those who revealed themselves, specifically Ron Hassner at the University of California at Berkley and Robert Eisen at Columbia University, for improving the manuscript. Any errors are, of course, my own. Thanks also to the staff at the Center for Middle Eastern Studies, especially Wendy Moore and Kristi Shuey.

My students in Bar-Ilan University's Conflict Management Program and at the Department of Middle Eastern Studies at the University of Texas at Austin during my year as a visiting scholar helped test and reexamine the ideas discussed here. I am grateful for their insights and input and hope they see traces of our class discussions in the text. Family and friends shared their experiences with me understanding full well that they might find themselves within these pages. My thanks to the extended Stollman-Shor-Be'eri clan, and especially to my in-laws, Sara and Shafer Stollman.

Judith Loebenstein-Witztum not only translated most of the original Hebrew sections into English, but also graced me with her insightful remarks as an informed but nonspecialist reader. Special thanks are due to Tory Tanaka and to Esther Schwartz, who made sure the text was comprehensible to a non-Israeli and nonacademic audience. I cannot thank both of you enough.

I would not have been able to complete this book without the help and support of my family. Our children, Yehonatan, Daniel, Na'ama, Yael, and Adva, are always happy to put my work in perspective and give it context. My grandparents, Elayne and Norman Rosman, have taught me about priorities and greedy institutions in ways no academic text could have.

This book is dedicated to my husband, Aviad Stollman, the most knowledgeable and perceptive reader I could ask for. To paraphrase the Talmudic story of Rabbi Akiva and his wife (BT Nedarim 50a), "yours and mine, is his"; I could not have undertaken such an extensive research project without his active help and support. The book is also dedicated to my siblings, Tamar, Yaacov, Michael, Avital, and Meir. In many ways, the tale told here is their story. It is also a tribute to our parents, who courageously taught us all to use a spindle. Thank you, Abba and Ema, for this. And for everything else.

June 2013
Be-Derech Efrata, Israel

FOR GOD AND COUNTRY?

INTRODUCTION

During the summer of 2005, Israel dismantled settlements in the Gaza Strip during the Disengagement (Hitnatkut). The manpower sent to evacuate the civilians living in these settlements consisted of soldiers; men and women of the Israel Defense Forces (IDF).

In what was considered a great surprise to the Israeli public, fewer than seventy soldiers refused to carry out their orders. The Israeli public, as well as the media, had assumed that religious soldiers, loyal not only to the IDF but also to their religious denomination, would refuse to take part in the Disengagement for religious reasons, leading to mass insubordination in the ranks, chaos, and perhaps even civil war. Had these expectations been fulfilled, they would prove what many both in Israel and the world believe: that religious soldiers answer to their rabbis rather than their commanding officers, that these rabbis have no qualms when giving their followers orders that contradict those of their officers, and that these soldiers are therefore suspect in all military matters. It is thus better for the IDF to reject religious soldiers, and it is certainly unwise for it to accept them into the officers' corps where they might one day stage a coup or worse. Furthermore, public debate centered around preservice study programs, where young men and women study for a set period of time before and during military service—especially the Hesder and Mekhinot programs—and called for their disbandment since they were perceived as hotbeds of potential mutinous ideas.

Surprisingly for those who feared the worst in the months leading up to the Disengagement, these fears were not confirmed. Quite the opposite—most religious soldiers did not disobey orders or cause disturbances. Few soldiers from preservice study programs were involved in the evacuation of civilians from their homes, and those who did participate were not insubordinate. In turn, this angered certain parts of the Religious Zionist sector, the social group to which these soldiers belong in their civilian life. These segments opposed the Disengagement and had hoped that if religious soldiers disobeyed their orders, given their numbers in the IDF, the operation would be thwarted. Some religious soldiers who participated actively in the Disengagement were made to feel like pariahs in social situations when on leave, and in general remained uneasy in the wake of the occurrences.

While this result of the Disengagement was hardly surprising for those who have been following the actions of religious soldiers in the IDF in general—and especially those of the preservice study programs—the situation itself highlights a pivotal issue in civil-military relations in Israel: the expectation of complete military loyalty from soldiers who belong to another similarly intense system, and the premise that such a condition is fundamentally impossible. Additionally, though the Disengagement highlighted conflicting loyalties, it has become clear in the years that followed that it was far from the most problematic situation such soldiers found themselves in. It did, however, serve as an excellent test case for the relationship in question.

Discussion of the Disengagement and civil-military relations in Israel brings another point to light. When non-Israelis discuss the IDF, they inevitably think of the Palestinian-Israeli conflict. Non-Israelis are often not aware of the fact that in Israel the Palestinian-Israeli issue is viewed as mostly a political one, with the IDF perceived as a minor player in it. Most Israelis believe the IDF should not be involved in policy-making, and the political positions of soldiers—especially rank and file soldiers—are irrelevant and to be put aside when in uniform. When discussed domestically, the social issues concerning the IDF are the most heatedly debated by Israelis. As recent publications in Hebrew prove,[1] when talking about the IDF, Israelis are mostly worried about the social construct of their armed force and its effect on society: Should the IDF continue to be conscription-based? What effect would an all-volunteer force have on the IDF and Israeli society? Is the IDF still prepared for battle in an era when conscripts are constantly connected to their smartphones and Facebook? Is the conscription of women something to be encouraged? What will happen to the composition of the IDF if conscription of Haredi (ultra-Orthodox) Jews is enforced? Is there a need for a better form of "sharing the burden" of conscription than the one in use presently? Are religious soldiers a potential fifth column? Can they be trusted in battle and in general?

In other words, most non-Hebrew speakers are largely ignorant of the civil-military issues Israelis—in academia, the military barracks, and on the street—deem most important when discussing their armed forces. While it very well may be that Western readers want to focus on the political situation in the Middle East and feel that this is the most pressing of topics in the region, the people who actually live in Tel Aviv and Haifa are preoccupied with other matters—one of which is civil-military relations. This volume introduces the English-speaking reader to one of the issues most heatedly discussed by Israelis as part of civil-military relations: that of religious soldiers in the ranks. As a result, a rounder, multidimensional picture of the Israel Defense Forces and of Israeli society emerges.

Rather than dealing in depth with national or ethnic minorities, as done in studies such as Rhoda Ann Kanaaneh's *Surrounded: Palestinian Soldiers in the Israeli Military* (2009) and Alon Peled's *A Question of Loyalty: Military Manpower Policy in Multiethnic States* (1998),[2] this book explores the potential points of friction between religious soldiers and the military, offers a number of possible ways various armed forces manage these points of friction, and then concentrates on the Israeli case—specifically on the case of religious Jewish student-soldiers.[3]

The Israeli case offers a unique opportunity to inquire into the relationship between individuals "caught" between seemingly conflicting loyalties and the rival systems to which they belong. The specific historic and social conditions in Israel regarding the IDF—together with the nature of the civil-military boundaries in it, its mode of conscription, and its treatment of religion—have allowed for the creation of mediating structures that help religious individuals maneuver between their conflicting systems. These structures are preservice religious study programs that allow their members a year (or more) of religious study before being actively conscripted, and then support them during their time in uniform. Such a mode of service allows its members to regulate the demands of both their social group and the IDF, communicate with both systems on their own terms, and, in general, empowers them as they attempt to deal with dominating systems that usually care very little about the individual needs and wants of their members.

Previous scholarship in English that examines similar topics discusses the military service of minorities, cultural minorities, and certain aspects of the military service of religious Orthodox Jewish soldiers in Israel: for example, Ronald Krebs's *Fighting for Rights: Military Service and the Politics of Citizenship* (2006) and Stuart A. Cohen's *The Scroll or the Sword?: Dilemmas of Religion and Military Service in Israel* (1997). Others, such as Mady Wechsler Segal and Christopher Dandeker, have examined minorities in other militaries. Ron Hassner has written extensively on religion's place in war and the military. However, despite the noted exception of the scholarship of Stuart A. Cohen, no scholarly work has examined the relationship between more than one factor mentioned above. Furthermore, no comprehensive discussion of the mediating structures in such situations can be found. In a world where religion does not seem to be losing its influence and individuals belong to more than one greedy structure, this topic has become relevant and merits discussion. The current study endeavors to fill this lacuna by expanding the theoretical structure available in order to include the case of preservice study programs and also by offering an in-depth and comprehensive look at these programs—both long overdue in current scholarship.

The social group focused on here is Religious Zionism. This social group, as described in Chapter 3, wishes to live in a liberal, democratic state while continuing to practice their religion to the fullest extent. Like other social groups, Religious Zionism has demands and expectations that it places on its members. It dislikes competing loyalties and pressures its members to avoid them. Likewise, the IDF is suspicious of competing loyalties on the part of its members. The IDF and Religious Zionism can be seen as what Lewis Coser termed "greedy institutions," as discussed in Chapter 1. However, while Coser depicted greedy institutions as given institutions, this work broadens his original definition to include a spectrum of frameworks: when discussing a framework or system, it can be classified as "more" or "less" greedy and placed on a continuum. Likewise, it may be more greedy in certain characteristics and less so in others. This is a more fluid definition than Coser's and fits modern society better since conflicting loyalties are more of a norm now than in the past.

The preservice study programs for religious student-soldiers can be seen as mediating structures between greedy institutions, and this study begins by explaining the theoretical basis for mediating structures and the larger— or super—structures in play. The book examines the relationship between individuals, superstructures, and mediating structures or frameworks from the point of view of political studies and sociology. Although the concept of mediating institutions is not new and was coined by Peter L. Berger and John Neuhaus over two decades ago, it was not applied outside an American and social welfare context. This book tries to broaden its application to non-American cases and to wider contexts; demonstrating its importance to today's society.

After establishing a theoretical basis, Chapter 2 first briefly examines four armed forces (Iran, the United States, India, and Turkey) while noting the following points: the nature of the boundaries between the civil and military spheres; the nature of the military (conscription-based or volunteer-based); and whether or not the armed force in question has a predisposition toward a certain religion. The presentation of these four cases helps us to see the Israeli case in context. It allows us to understand that the dilemmas in Israel in this regard are not unique, but rather it is the Israeli attempt to deal with them that merits attention. Although analyzing the comparative programs in other countries in depth is important, the focus of this book is the Israeli case. This study does not attempt to offer a comprehensive answer to the question of why the Israeli model was not adopted elsewhere. The outlines sketched in the second chapter will hopefully encourage further research on comparable cases, and future studies will continue to try to solve the puzzles raised here.

After setting the theoretical basis and the context, Chapter 3 also briefly discusses the universe of mediating structures in the Israeli case. Since studies on the Military Rabbinate and the reasons it became what it is today—such as the one written by Aharon (Roni) Kampinsky (2007)—are available, this topic is not discussed in detail. It is outlined at the end of this chapter, as are the treatment of non-Jewish and other cultural minorities, other special arrangements made within the IDF for specific groups, and the bureaucratic mechanisms developed in the IDF to deal with the relevant cases.

Chapters 4, 5, 6, and 7 discuss each of the preservice study programs that form the core subject of the book. While they only give brief historical backgrounds to each, these chapters try to give readers a feel for what each study program values, what kind of students they attract, and how these factors impact their relationship both with the IDF and Religious Zionism, as well as with their students. These chapters also attempt to supply readers with the background to understand how each study program endeavors to support its students during their military service and what their students expect of them; preparing readers for the discussion in Chapter 8 of mediation in practice.

Chapter 8 discusses the practical manifestations of mediation through the preservice study programs using three cases: disobeying orders due to religious convictions (including the Disengagement of 2005); coed service and the opening of various field postings to women; and the Stern Initiative to disband Hesder units. Each of these cases demonstrates a situation where individuals seem to have found themselves caught between their loyalty to the IDF and their religious convictions. It is important to note that the Disengagement is not discussed separately, but as part of the general dilemma of insubordination due to religious convictions. Contrary to the widespread feeling that the Disengagement was an isolated and singular occurrence, Chapter 8 frames it in its more realistic context: although important, it's by no means a unique situation. Religious soldiers were confronted with similar experiences during the past decades and were able to cope with the situation with varying degrees of success. Far more problematic is the reality created by coed service. While the public in Israel became aware of this issue only recently, and the international community is still largely unaware of this topic, the probability of insubordination resulting from mixed gender service in field postings is far higher than it was during the Disengagement. Chapter 8 attempts to explain this reality and to examine the effects of mediation on each case presented. Contrary to views outside of Israel, the student-soldiers discussed in this book are far more concerned with these issues than with political ones. They fear finding themselves in complex religious situations more than complex political ones and encounter them more often. Again, while in uniform they are not expected to take a political stand as much as a religious one.

Chapter 9 broadens the discussion of mediation through the study programs by examining more general problems students encounter and the strategies used by students and the programs when dealing with these challenges. While most students did not anticipate the dilemmas discussed in Chapter 8 before conscription, they were aware of the problems discussed in Chapter 9, although they usually did not realize the extent of these challenges. Chapter 9 looks at problems on a personal level (where each soldier must contend with his or her quandary alone rather than as part of a large group, as in the cases in Chapter 8), such as a deterioration in religious observance, as well as the strategies used to cope with these problems—with or without the help of the study programs.

Chapter 10 looks at the situation from the point of view of the students' commanding officers, as well as senior IDF officers. Since study programs can be seen as "belonging" to the Religious Zionist social group and therefore representing it to a certain extent, and since they are civilian frameworks intervening in the military sphere, it is only fair to present the military point of view and understand how the IDF sees the situation at hand. Therefore this chapter examines the military's perception of the study programs and their students from the vantage point of the officers who are in the field and see the direct results of mediation, as well as that of senior officers who see the "big picture" and are able to understand the wider implications of mediation.

Chapter 11 discusses the role the study programs play in the communication of messages from each of the players (the students, the IDF, and Religious Zionism) to the others. As Berger and Neuhaus note, mediating structures play an important part in the understanding and transferring of messages between individuals and public institutions. This case is no different. Students use the mediating structures as a venue for communication and impress their views, demands, and wishes on the larger structures they belong to using the mediator of their choice. At times, they choose to communicate directly, and Chapter 11 explores this option as well.

Likewise, the superstructures use the mediators in order to communicate their own demands and requirements both to each other and to the individuals in question. The mediators themselves have independent messages they would like to make clear and also have their own agendas. In addition, there are tensions between the various study programs, and Chapter 11 illustrates these to the extent that they illuminate the relationship between the mediators and the other players.

Finally, Chapters 12 and 13 turn to observing the implications of the Israeli case, conclusions that can be drawn from it, as well as points for further research and discussion. Building on the observations of the previous chapters, Chapter 12 focuses on analyzing the Israeli case: the uses and dimensions of mediation as well as its limits. Chapter 13 concludes with general observations, as well as thoughts on the theoretical implications that can be deduced from the previous chapters both in general and for civil-military relations in Israel. This final chapter also raises questions for further research. Relations between religion and the military is a neglected field, and while recent years have produced a growing number of relevant studies, there is still much to be learned about this relationship. The questions and puzzles presented in this book will hopefully tempt others to continue this research.

PART I

STRUCTURES AND INSTITUTIONS

CHAPTER 1
GREEDY INSTITUTIONS, MEDIATING STRUCTURES, AND EMPIRICAL EXAMPLES

Can one be completely and truly dedicated to two structures simultaneously? How can a person who belongs to a certain framework be equally loyal to another at the same time? This dilemma is heightened when the question concerns a structure as uncompromising as a military organization: Can an individual serve both the military and another system at the same time?

Systems such as the military, which require absolute loyalty and prevent those who belong to them from being part of another parallel system, are not theoretical constructions. They are recognized in scholarship as greedy institutions (Coser 1974). The degree of greediness demonstrated by this kind of institution may fluctuate, but the fundamental demand for exclusivity results in its inability to recognize any demands put forward by rival systems. Accepted scholarship understands that members of such institutions are expected to serve but one master and cannot belong to any rival institutions.

A greedy institution, unlike a total institution (Goffman 1961), does not necessarily have physical boundaries. A total institution, such as an orphanage, leper colony, or prisoner of war camp, defines its members and serves as the central and only institution in their lives. It will not allow its members to be part of general society. By contrast, a greedy institution is portable. Its members belong to it and feel its presence always. However, it is not confined to a specific time or place, as is a total institution. It is not removed from general society by means of a wall, a fence, a body of water, or any other physical boundary—unlike Goffman's total institution. And although it is not as noticeable, it still demands complete loyalty from its members, seeking to be the only axis around which their lives revolve.

Despite this accepted scholarly definition, however, in today's modern society there are individuals who belong to more than one greedy institution. Though it seems impossible geometrically, their lives are able to revolve around more than one axis simultaneously. A working mother might feel that each of the systems of which she is part—the workplace and family—require 100 percent of her time and talents, and neither will settle for less. A doctor who is a member of a religious community, a civil servant who belongs to a religious or ethnic minority—they too operate within two seemingly conflicting systems, demanding their complete time and undivided loyalty. How is this possible?

This book will first suggest that, contrary to previous definitions, in modern society the "greediness" of larger institutions (like "totality") is a continuum and not a fixed point, and second, that one possibility of regulating rival pressures is through a mediating structure. An institution or framework can be more or less greedy depending on its demands on its members. Some frameworks are greedier than others, and the degree of greediness affects the ability of members to maneuver between structures in their personal and public lives. A mediating structure can take the form of any institution that stands between an individual person and larger systems. It attempts to protect the individual from the tyranny of a larger system (Berger and Neuhaus 1996). How and to what extent mediating systems regulate such pressures—and thus enable greedy frameworks to share members—will be examined. To better understand the theoretical issue, an emphasis will be placed on the roles played by mediating structures in the relations between religion and the military—particularly those between Religious Zionism and the Israel Defense Forces.

GREEDY INSTITUTIONS AND MEDIATING STRUCTURES

Generally speaking, modern society understands the need to protect individuals from pressures that result from being caught between two rival institutions. Modern Western societies do not expect, for example, that one work all day and have no time for one's family. They thus try to regulate these pressures, sometimes by legislation. In the twentieth century it became expected that persons would operate within more than one system simultaneously: family, workplace, community, nation, and so on. To enable this, mechanisms were created to facilitate the regulation of the demands made on the individual in order to protect him or her and prevent individuals from being torn between the various systems. While this does not completely eliminate tensions, as long as none of the systems involved demands totality, insoluble situations do not arise (Coser 1974, 2–3). For instance, in a well-ordered workplace, employers are aware that they cannot demand that their employees dedicate the entirety of their time to work. The time that an employee must spend working is clearly defined, and employees are entitled to holidays, personal time, and sick leave. If an employer requires an employee to work beyond the agreed time, remuneration is expected.

There are, however, institutions that do not recognize the need for the regulation of demands. These greedy institutions demand exclusive loyalty. Coser maintained that greedy institutions do not come to terms with the fact that their members also have other obligations. Someone who belongs to a greedy institution is expected to dedicate himself to this institution completely, ruling out the possibility of being part of any other system. As in the metaphor mentioned in the previous section, one cannot revolve around more than one axis. A greedy institution expects to be that axis and will not accept competition (Coser 1974).

Contrary to total institutions (Goffman 1961), greedy institutions do not necessarily rely on a physical separation of their members from society. Rather, they tend to rely on conceptual, emotional, and cultural forms of separation of the individual. Those people belonging to a greedy institution do not necessarily live apart from the rest of society. They might, however, be distinguished by unique dress codes, special rules of behavior, different cultural codes, and the like. In other words, greedy institutions rely mainly on the commitment of the individual and on their primarily symbolic separation from the rest of society. Prominent examples of greedy institutions are religious sects, the family (especially for women), and ideological sects such as revolutionary groups (Coser 1974).

Coser emphasized that a greedy institution is always exclusive, both in the sense that it demands exclusive loyalty and in the sense that it excludes non-members, differentiating between those who belong to it ("us") and the rest of society ("them"). Accordingly, a greedy institution attempts to portray itself as a beneficial system that will profit those who belong to it and promote their interests. The separation between the individual and society at large is, in this case, achieved by emphasizing the superior status of one who belongs to the institution; being one of "us."

According to Coser, usually, conflicts between a greedy institution and its competitors are minimal. This is due either to the fact that a greedy institution has already diffused rival systems, or because the number of rivals has been vastly reduced (Coser 1974, 7). In the case of religious sects, for example, a sect will attempt to separate a follower from his or her family in order to weaken the family's rival claims. Alternately, there are employers who try to bring an employee's family into the fold of the workplace with the aim of lessening the family's demands. Thus a company might offer child care on location, or organize social gatherings so that its employees form social contacts within the workplace that extend outside it: their coworkers become their social group and there is no need for ties outside of it.

Even in situations where it appears that an individual belongs to two greedy institutions, previous research has shown that such situations are merely *perceived* as problematic but are not truly so. Specifically, one of the systems was not strictly a greedy institution, and therefore it acquiesced to the "real" one. The idea that an individual might actually belong to two truly greedy systems simultaneously, and will have to independently prioritize between them, was thought to be impossible.

The twenty-first century has indicated this view needs modification, as reality proves that there are many situations in which greedy institutions might come into conflict. Furthermore, formerly less-than-greedy institutions are becoming greedier. Even institutions that once restrained themselves or were restrained by society (such as the aforementioned employer) are now putting forward unrestrained demands. For example, in the modern high-tech job sector, employees are expected—as a matter of course—to be completely devoted to their workplace. The employer expects the employee (whether a man or a woman) to work overtime on a large scale, at the expense of private life and family. Previously effective regulating mechanisms have been damaged. The same can be said for prestigious law firms, as well as other employers.

Reality has changed, and people are still able to manage their various obligations relatively well. This makes the question even more significant: How can an individual belong to two greedy frameworks simultaneously and respond to all of their demands? Will these frameworks make a deliberate effort to avoid collision? In other words, the model depicted by Coser demands modification.

Since Goffman, Coser, and previous scholarship based upon them did not consider the possibility of a real conflict between two or more truly greedy institutions, and since in the modern world the reality of many conflicting demands is not at all a unique one, these questions are becoming increasingly significant. Answering these questions using a test case allows us to relate to many other dimensions of the situation. Since, when we observe the world around us, we witness cooperation and coexistence—to varying degrees of success—between greedy institutions, the obvious question is: When and how does coexistence occur?

As mentioned above, this book posits that a mediating structure is an important mechanism enabling greedy frameworks to coexist. Past scholarship—with a few noted exceptions—has neglected this field.[1] What, then, is a mediating structure?

The term "mediating structures" originated from a completely different field of scholarship and was developed by Berger and Neuhaus (1996). Analyzing the dichotomy modernization created between the public and private spheres, Berger and Neuhaus deduced that individuals are distanced from public structures. As the public sphere belongs to all, it belongs to no one. Individuals do not feel as strong a connection to the public sphere as they do to their own personal sphere and to matters that relate to them personally. Berger and Neuhaus illustrated that members of a democratic society need a structure that can mediate between the private domain and the public sphere (Berger and Neuhaus 1996; Berger 1976).

They note that a mediating structure, defined as any structure standing between the individual and general society, allows the individual to continue to believe in private values and beliefs and even transfer these principles into the public realm. In other words, belonging to a smaller community can help individuals feel a sense of belonging toward the public sphere as well as to their personal social constructions. The mediating structure allows the individual to navigate and understand the public sphere using a personal and familiar set of beliefs and values. These beliefs and values are projected onto the greater institutions, lending them legitimacy and making them less public, less alien, and closer to the individual's private belief system.

The opposite also holds true. The mediating structure additionally serves the greater structures and channels their messages to the individuals using private terms and preconceptions. For example, a workers' union can help a member deal with the state, understand labor laws, construct an opinion regarding issues of wages, insurance, pension, and so on. Through membership in the union, the worker feels less alienated from the wider labor policies of the state, is able to communicate messages to the state regarding these issues, and also is able to receive messages from the state transferred through the mechanism of the union. Should the state wish to change relevant legislation and gauge public sentiment, it can do so by speaking to the union representatives. An agreement reached with a union is equal to an agreement reached with each of its members personally.

Furthermore, understanding broader policy and social issues through one's smaller group or association is easier than it would be for an individual alone. For example, Berger and Neuhaus demonstrate how a neighborhood is a mirror for social policy. Public policy, especially in its social manifestations, can be observed as it is implemented in individual neighborhoods. Through the mirroring of public policy in one's neighborhood, an individual can understand this policy, agree with it, demand changes, or object to it.

A good illustration of this idea is the way U.S. citizens understand federal and state economic policy through their retirement programs. Many citizens do not read financial papers or reports. The human resources division in a company translates the main messages of economic policy and the effect these will have on the lives and retirement plans of staff and then explains it to them in newsletters, meetings, and private responses to questions. Depending on their understanding, employees can object, strike, and apply pressure to receive answers to unsatisfactory situations, or they can agree to the present situation. In this way, the human resources division serves as a mediating institution.

In its most basic form, the mediating institution or structure stands between the individual and his or her private life and the greater structures of public life (Berger and Neuhaus 1996, 158). However, the larger—or super—structures also have a vested interest in the creation of mediating structures. Superstructures need legitimacy. They do not create values of their own, but need values in order to justify their existence. If they do not base their legitimacy on shared values, these structures will have to resort to the use of force when attempting to assert their power over their members. A mediating structure can renew the social contract between citizens and their public structures by translating personal values from the citizen to the public structures (bottom-up), and by transmitting messages from the greater structures of government to the citizens (top-down) (Berger 1976, 404). For example, a department of transportation in a certain state does not create values; it is a product of public administration. However, a youth movement that teaches its members to be loyal to the state and obey the law—for example by framing jaywalking or biking without a helmet as moral offenses, since these go against state law—is in fact strengthening the legitimacy of the state and, unwittingly, the legitimacy of the department of transportation. Members of the youth movement understand their state through the value system taught by their movement and therefore accept the state's legitimacy.

Despite the example given above, the mediating structure can be used for a variety of utilities that need not be confined to positive ventures.[2] Organized crime groups such as the mafia or street gangs can be considered mediating structures. This also holds true for anti-democratic or racist organizations. As Berger and Neuhaus point out, the Ku Klux Klan is as much a mediating structure as an organization promoting women's rights. Furthermore, a mediating structure does not necessarily focus on issues of poverty, education, and health. It can be equally utilized in order to deal with any form of interaction between citizens and their government. Americans United for Separation of Church and State, the London Citizens network, Media Bloggers Association of America, a local school's parent group, and a homeowners' cooperative can all be considered meditating structures. These examples demonstrate the basic idea of the mediating structure: the attempt to guard the liberty of the individual to the best of its understanding from the greater structures of modern society that encourage uniformity of individuals—if not outright uniform treatment—and to allow those individuals and the larger structures to communicate and comprehend each other better (Berger 1976). It is a framework or structure into which any substance may be poured.

When looking at the more modern interpretations of mediating structures, it seems that scholarship has assigned this mechanism a role consisting purely of social welfare. As of the 1990s, the concept has primarily been employed to understand the welfare state. While this is certainly an important area of study, confining mediating structures to it is regrettable. Mediating structures are a valuable tool for understanding many mechanisms of modern society, notably the relationship of the military and religion.

Based on this idea, we can visualize the construction of mediating structures not only between individuals and a single public structure, but between a number of public structures. This means that, under certain conditions, a mediating structure is able not only to assist a single individual living in modern society, but also to enable coexistence of greedy institutions and the individuals who belong to more than one of these institutions simultaneously. This idea will help us understand how tolerance and even cooperation can exist between larger structures that compete for the loyalty of the same individual.

Using Figure 1 as a basic model of the relationship between an individual and a greedy institution that demands his or her loyalty, we can construct a more complex model, as in Figure 2:

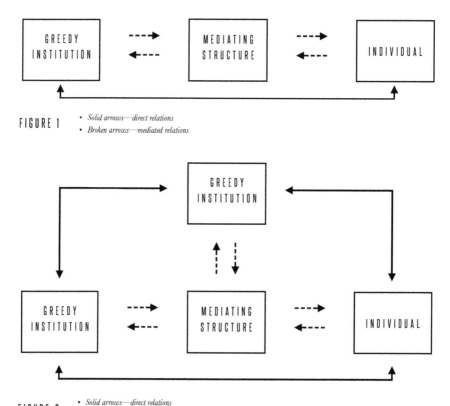

FIGURE 1
- *Solid arrows—direct relations*
- *Broken arrows—mediated relations*

FIGURE 2
- *Solid arrows—direct relations*
- *Broken arrows—mediated relations*

While Figure 2 depicts a model with only two greedy institutions, in theory there may be an infinite number of greedy institutions using one or more mediating structures in their dealings with each other and with a given individual.

As illustrated in the basic model (Figure 1) and its expanded version (Figure 2), communication between the actors occurs through the mediating structure, but also directly between the frameworks. When is direct communication chosen and when do the systems prefer to use the mediating structure as a go-between? In order to further explore this question, we must turn to a more defined example— that of the military and religion. Let us first clarify that these are indeed greedy institutions and determine to what extent and in what ways they are greedy.

RELIGION AND THE MILITARY AS GREEDY INSTITUTIONS

Like other examples previously noted, religious frameworks and military systems are perceived as inflexible formations that demand complete loyalty from their members. Let us begin by looking at religious systems. Beyond spiritual commitment and complete identification, many religions require external forms of practice, such as dietary laws, dress codes, and a strict timetable governing the believers' days, weeks, months, and so on. While most believers are not necessarily required to be confined within a physical space,[3] they are constantly reminded of the presence of their religion in their life by the fulfillment of commandments and requirements throughout their daily routine. While more easily discerned in law-based religions such as Judaism and Islam, this presence of religion in the daily life of a religious individual is recognizable in every religion. In other words, belonging to a religious framework is not membership in a tangible structure that can be entered and exited like a building.[4] It is carried by the members as they walk through life; a constant presence. Some religions are more greedy than others, emphasizing our previous observation that greedy structures are better observed as more or less greedy on a continuum, with law-based (or orthoprax) religions such as Islam or Judaism being be more greedy and non-law-based (or orthodox) religions such as various denominations of Christianity being less so.

Membership in a specific religion also makes the lines between those belonging to the group and those outside of it very clear. The perception is that it usually benefits the believer to belong to this religion, while those who are outside the group are to be pitied. Indeed, in its truest form, religion does not even recognize that any aspect of a believer's life can exist outside of it (Liebman 1983). It strives to include within its boundaries all facets of life and bluntly ignores any outside pressures, since it does not see itself as one of many structures acting within a society. All is part of the religious sphere of influence and nothing is outside its jurisdiction (Blackham 1966). However, for pragmatic reasons of survival or for other ideological reasons, and sometimes because it is forced to do so, it is possible for a religious system to sanction itself or concede part of what it sees as its rightful sphere of influence to secular institutions. These concessions will always be explained in religious terms and given religious significance. For example, the existence of a secular state challenges any religion. Therefore a religion must either explain the secular state in religious terms or include it within the religious sphere in some way. Judaism has addressed the issue of a secular Jewish state—Israel—in a plethora of ways; these range from trying to actively undermine it to completely ignoring its existence (as do some radical ultra-Orthodox sects), to seeing it as a manifestation of the beginning of Redemption and the coming of the Messiah—a miracle and proof of divine providence (as defined by parts of Religious Zionism). The second approach ignores the reality of a secular structure, no matter the cost. Since the secular state is incompatible with the religious framework these ultra-Orthodox groups adhere to, it is impossible for their approach to accept the state's existence. The third approach includes the secular state within the religious framework and sees it as part of a religious set of norms and ideas, giving it a dimension of holiness. It may not be a theocracy governed by God's law (halakha), but it can be seen as the beginning of a holy process and the fulfillment of the divine promise of redemption. Therefore the state is obviously part of the complex framework of Judaism and cannot be seen as without religious significance.

In other words, religion does not accept other institutions and will not share its members with another structure. When confronted with rivals, it will either ignore them or attempt to incorporate them into the religious system. In this sense it is a greedy institution, even if a very large and fluid one. For this reason it is better to see it as a greedy structure or framework, rather than an institution. While institutions are usually more tangible organizations, religion cannot be contained within a single administration and is better described in broader and less defined terms. It is also better, as mentioned above, to observe a given religious system as more or less greedy—to be placed on a continuum—rather than in a fixed position.

Is this also the case with the military system? Can it too be seen as greedy? Obviously an armed force has more tangible boundaries. It does not rely solely upon the emotional-cultural-social commitment of its members—as do most religions in the modern world—but rather uses coercion and physical separation of its members from society as a way of ensuring loyalty. Put simply, a military adheres to Coser's definition of a greedy institution. However, since it has recognizable physical boundaries, it is closer to Goffman's definition of total institutions: "a place of residence and work where a large number of like-situated individuals, cut off from wider society for an appreciable period of time, together lead an enclosed, formally administrated round of life." This definition describes military life well.

Nevertheless, the fact that soldiers in modern militaries move back and forth between their barracks and the civilian world—studying in universities, flying on civilian planes, attending meetings and conferences, and enjoying recreational facilities all while in uniform—shows these boundaries to be more flexible. The modern military structure has become less confined to its bases. Soldiers continue to belong to the military regardless of their physical whereabouts, whether physically in uniform while moving in civilian spheres, or on leave and still psychologically bound to the military. It is as though they carry the military structure with them wherever they go. They are seen by society as belonging to the military, and they recognize themselves as soldiers even when off base. They will only truly leave the military system upon discharge. Therefore, it would appear that the modern military is less total and more greedy than it at first seems: less confined to a physical space, and more a portable institution to be taken along with members as they move between spheres.

The military remains a separate entity that is very different from the civilian world and demands much from its members, however. It has its own judicial system, its own norms of behavior, and it does not adhere to civilian notions of fairness. Ultimately the military reserves the right to order its members to die for a cause it (and not necessarily the member) deems worthy. These characteristics emphasize the greedy nature of a military system.

Like religion, the military must contend with rival structures, and therefore a given military system can be seen as more or less greedy. A soldier is never completely removed from the society he or she serves. Soldiers continue to have family ties and obligations and nonmilitary social connections. Democratic armed forces especially must remember that military service creates conflicts between a soldier's military and civilian roles and address the issues these conflicts create (Janowitz 1959, 89–90). Cell phones and the Internet connect soldiers with their civilian network of social ties in a way previously unknown to the military. Family becomes an even stronger factor when the armed force in question is a professional force employing married personnel and parents, rather than young conscripts. Families, friends, and civilian connections all make demands for soldiers' time and attention and compete with the soldiers' loyalty to the military.

Even if the military structure refuses to share its members with competing frameworks, it must recognize them if it is to ensure its members are not distracted by conflicting loyalties. For example, ignoring the fact that a soldier has a child who is hospitalized can cause the soldier to devote all of his or her mental energy to devising schemes for how to contact home and hear medical updates. This focus will distract the soldier from military roles and responsibilities. In such situations the military is willing to allow the soldier regular contact with the child's caregiver in order to ensure that the soldier stays focused on his or her military job, thus acknowledging that others have claim to the soldier's time and attention.

Furthermore, housing a soldier's family on the base where he or she serves, and having the child at a military hospital under the care of military personnel, is a way to include the family—the competing framework—within the military system and thus reduce its claims upon the soldier. This form of behavior is reminiscent of the way Religious Zionism views the state of Israel in the previous example.

Clearly both the military and religion can be framed using the terminology of greedy structures. Therefore it is no surprise that when an individual belonging to a religious framework becomes a soldier, a series of problems arise.[5] These problems can be divided into two separate levels of difficulty. On the first level, an ideological quandary comes to light. True to their greedy nature (regardless of their position on the more or less greedy spectrum), both religion and the military do not tolerate a reality where an individual belonging to them is committed to a potentially threatening rival authority. Each system views such members with suspicion: Are they a fifth column? Can they be trusted? What will happen if they are forced to choose between loyalties? For example, what will happen if their religious authority claims the military is a heretical institution, or if the military demands that they transgress a religious commandment? These points naturally relate to the degree of greediness of the systems in question.

On the second level, one sees a more practical dilemma. Daily life in uniform and the rigid military schedule make religious observances difficult. Commandments dealing with dress, prayer, and dietary requirements do not always sit well with military life. The military requires its members to conform with regard to conduct and dress. It is a basic tenant of the barracks that soldiers are supposed to resemble each other visually in all external characteristics. Conversely, certain religions have dress requirements in order to set believers apart from society and make believers visually recognizable (heightening the feeling of "us" vs. "them" as in other greedy institutions).[6] Sikhs wear turbans and do not cut their hair. Orthodox Jews cover their heads and wear ritual fringes sometimes visible outside their clothing, to name but two examples. It is no surprise, then, that these commandments have the potential to clash with the military principle of uniformity.

Similarly, military norms do not always sit well with religious sensibilities. Soldiers, regardless of the military force they belong to, are known for coarse and immodest behavior that is not acceptable in civilian society. For a religious person, behavior such as drinking and the use of pornography and profanity are highly offensive. While the military does not necessarily encourage such behavior, it is found within barracks in any armed force. A believer who struggles to live a godly life will find such behavior difficult to tolerate.[7]

Consequently, interaction between the military and religion is fraught with tension. It is not uncommon to find armed forces that oppose religious observance of any kind, as well as religions that will not allow believers to enlist. Yet there are many religious individuals who do serve in uniform and armed forces that accept them in the ranks. Obviously, then, reality shows that belonging to religious and military groups simultaneously is possible. How?

When examining various militaries in the twenty-first century, it becomes clear that a variety of tactics are used by both soldiers, religious frameworks, and the military to allow a form of coexistence. One prominent tool employed is erecting a mediating structure, or a series of such structures, to serve as a go-between. Communicating indirectly, through the mediating structure, allows the various actors to find a way to work together rather than force the individuals in question to choose sides. As we will see in Part II, the Israeli case utilizes mediating structures to a large extent. Nevertheless, this is not the only model found, as the following chapter will show. Armed forces may ignore their religious soldiers and their needs, they may be willing to accommodate these soldiers somewhat, and they might allow the soldiers in question complete religious freedom. In order to understand the range of behavior in these circumstances, the next chapter will describe five possible models of treatment of religious soldiers.

CHAPTER 2
MILITARY ATTITUDES TOWARD RELIGIOUS SOLDIERS:
FIVE CASE STUDIES

The potential difficulties religious soldiers pose to the military can be examined within the context of a number of case studies. By reviewing a sample of armed forces and the way they relate to the needs of religious soldiers, this chapter asks whether we can discern a pattern that explains how different military forces might react to religious soldiers. The answer to this question will clarify the relationship between religion and the military in general, and will also elucidate the Israeli case and put it within a broader context.

To construct a theoretical classification, two variables should first be considered: the kind of religion practiced, and the type of military force studied. What sorts of demands does the religion in question make on its believers, and what is the personnel makeup of the armed force in question? These variables will allow us to categorize our case studies better.

Some religions are characterized by what can be termed as "external" obligations, which hold the believer to a certain code of behavior. These obligations might include various dietary regimens (vegetarianism; a prescribed way of slaughtering animals or preparing food; a prohibition on consuming certain animals, foods, and beverages); requirements concerning external appearance (such as covering one's head, the growing of facial hair, and various definitions of modesty in dress); prayer at preordained times, and other manners of conduct. These kinds of requirements are found mainly in law-based, [1] or orthoprax religions, and these religions are more likely to come into collision with the military than religions with "internal" commandments (usually termed "orthodox"),[2] which have no outward manifestations and are observed within the believer's heart and mind. When a believer who must dress in a certain way and must follow a set daily routine and dietary regimen becomes part of a homogenous military system, it is inevitable that mutual irritants will arise.

Naturally, this is not a clear-cut classification, and it is better to speak of a relativist definition. In other words, a religion or denomination can be seen as having more commandments than one faith, but less than another. For example, Catholicism can be seen as having more commandments than Unitarianism but fewer than Sikhism. Therefore, a religion can be placed on a spectrum showing it to have more or fewer external commandments than comparable religions or denominations.

Our second variable is the makeup of the manpower in the armed force itself. Most armed forces of democratic states in the West are volunteer-based. Citizens enlist of their own volition for a defined period of time and are remunerated for their service. There are, however, states in which military service is compulsory and based on legislation, and citizens are conscripted. There are also militaries whose personnel are comprised of a combination of the two: the lower ranks being conscripts, while officers and noncommissioned officers (NCOs) are volunteers. It seems reasonable to assume that the relation between a military and a given religion is affected by the composition of the armed force. In a military based on conscription, the conscription of religious soldiers cannot be avoided. In a volunteer-based military the organization can choose not to accept religious soldiers and thus avoid the problem altogether.

In addition, it should be taken into account that if a religion is officially recognized as part of the military's identity, then the attitude toward this religion can be assumed to be relatively positive. If no religion is given preference, the attitude toward religious soldiers might differ.

Besides the type of religion and the makeup of the military manpower, another set of more general variables should be considered. If the civilian sphere can oblige the military to behave according to civilian norms, we can expect to see the military mirror civilian trends of behavior toward religious soldiers, and vice versa. Therefore, any comparison made and models constructed must take into account the balance of power between the military and civil systems.

In addition, the nature of the boundaries between the military and the civilian sphere must be considered. The nature of these boundaries indicates if and when the military can influence the civilian sphere and vice versa. In order to typify these boundaries, we will use the typology constructed by Luckham (1971), who describes these boundaries as integral, permeable, or fragmented. In the case of integral borders, the separation between the military and the civil sphere is well defined and there is no irregular transition or contact between the two. If the borders are permeable, it is difficult to discern where the military ends and civilian mechanisms begin. The separation is unclear and the relations between the military and civilian society are unregulated and difficult to control. When the borders are fragmented, interaction between the military and the civilian sphere is unrestricted in some areas, while in others the relations are regulated. For example, in the Israeli case, the IDF radio and the military censor are a fair demonstration of regulated interaction between the military and civil society. Both the radio and the censor have clearly defined tasks, and their mandated activities are mapped out. On the other hand, the presence of military correspondents who accompany commanders in the field is a case of unregulated interaction. Is the military correspondent a civilian if he is accompanying a fighting force? What is his role if the unit is fired upon? How does he treat the soldiers he is with, and how do they treat him? Does this relationship change if it is common knowledge that he served as a combat soldier in the past? These questions demonstrate how the borders between military and civilian spheres can be blurred or, at the very least, be difficult to recognize.

These variables allow us to examine a large range of possible cases that can be placed along the following spectrums (the definition of the military's religion and the type of manpower enlisted) or assigned a specific classification (the nature of the borders between the spheres and the balance of power between them):

FIGURE 3

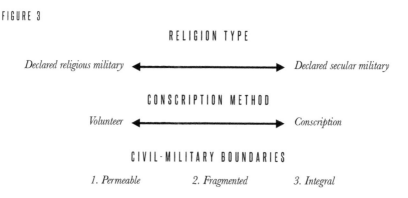

RELIGION TYPE

Declared religious military ⟵⟶ *Declared secular military*

CONSCRIPTION METHOD

Volunteer ⟵⟶ *Conscription*

CIVIL-MILITARY BOUNDARIES

1. *Permeable*   2. *Fragmented*   3. *Integral*

The combination of these sets of factors creates a large number of possible models. However, not all actually exist in practice, and therefore not all can be analyzed. From among the various combinations, five possible practical manifestations, reflected in the following five case studies, can be discerned. Iran is a conscription-based, Shi'i Muslim military, where civil-military boundaries are permeable; Israel is a conscription-based, Jewish military, with fragmented civil-military boundaries; Turkey is partially conscription-based and partially a volunteer force, defined as secular with integral civil-military boundaries; India's armed forces are volunteer-based, and have no declared religion, though unofficially Hinduism is given preferred status, and its civil-military boundaries are integral; and the United States is an all-volunteer force, with no defined religion and integral civil-military boundaries. These case studies are detailed in the following table:

TABLE 1

CASE STUDY CHARACTERISTICS

	IRAN	ISRAEL	TURKEY	INDIA	UNITED STATES
CONSCRIPTION/ VOLUNTEER	*Conscription*	*Conscription*	*Conscription | Volunteer Officers' Corps*	*Volunteer*	*Volunteer*
CIVIL-MILITARY BOUNDARIES	*Permeable*	*Fragmented*	*Integral*	*Integral*	*Integral*
DEFINED RELIGION	*Defined | Shi'i Muslim*	*Defined | Jewish*	*Defined | Secular*	*Undefined (de facto Hindu)*	*Undefined*

The cases presented here, therefore, represent conscription-based militaries, volunteer-based militaries, and combined personnel. These cases also cover the existing types of borders between the military and civil society according to Luckham. They also cover the spectrum of militaries with a defined religion, without a defined religion, with a de facto religion accepted, and with an armed force that is defined as secular. As mentioned above, we cannot present every possible model, since they do not exist in practice, but those that can be represented by a case study appear in this comparison.

In order to understand the individual cases, we shall first offer a short description of each military while presenting pertinent historical elements. We shall follow with a discussion of the religious soldier's ability to observe religious commandments while in uniform, as well as the existence of a mediating structure (as defined in Chapter 1). The Israeli case will be presented in detail in the second part of the book.

THE IRANIAN ARMED FORCES

Due to a paucity of updated material, little has been written about the Iranian military following the 1979 revolution. The aspects that have been discussed in recent scholarship relate to Iranian military capabilities regarding nonconventional weapons and the Iranian military's relationship with the Iranian Revolutionary Guards Corps (IRGC). Even less has been written concerning the individuals within this military system.

The Iranian military is based on mandatory conscription for males. Army units are made up of conscripts, while navy and air force personnel volunteer for these posts.[3] Most of the soldiers are from rural-tribal backgrounds, and some do not speak Persian, the language used in the military. There are also some who are illiterate. It may be concluded that the majority come from a traditional social group where religion is both important and has cultural significance (Cordesman 1994; Hassan 2007).

Officers are selected according to their degree of religiosity, and lessons on religion and faith by senior clergy are routinely held during the officers' training course. The third year of officer training is dedicated to religious instruction as well as courses about the Islamic world in general. Arabic is also taught so that the officers are able to read the Quran in the original language (Hashim 2001; Zabih 1988).

A distinction should be made between the regular Iranian forces (army, navy, and air force) and paramilitary forces made up of ideologically driven volunteers (the Revolutionary Guard and the Basij). The IRGC is in fact a separate military force with its own navy and air force. Its designated mission is to ensure the military's loyalty to the Islamic Republic. As of the 1990s, they also oversee domestic security and the security of the border regions. While the Iranian regime does not entirely trust the armed forces to be loyal, the Revolutionary Guards' loyalty is more certain. However, it seems that this perception is changing and that the Iranian leadership is willing to trust the Iranian army more now than in the past (Eisenstadt 1996, 41–42). Understanding the need to appease the military, the clerics have made an effort to cater to the military's interests and needs in terms of monetary benefits and modern weapons (Hashim 2001, 40–41).

The Imperial Iranian Army was considered loyal to the shah. Consequently, purges and intensive religious indoctrination of the army began immediately after the revolution in 1979. Clergy were attached to military units in order to oversee this process of Islamification of the armed forces. Initially, their task was to convey Ayatollah Khomeini's message to the troops. Following the new regime's adjustment period, purges, and the stabilization of the army, their task was redefined to ensure the military's loyalty and ideological soundness (Rose 1984); similar to the role played by the commissars in the Red Army.[4]

In addition to this function, a section of the army's Ideological-Political Directorate (Modiriyate Aghidati va Siyasi Artesh) is attached to each unit of the army and the Revolutionary Guard. The directorate is responsible for ensuring the military unit's loyalty to the laws of Islam and to the republic. The sections and subunits of the directorate are headed by clergy. At first, after the revolution and the purges in the army, the directorate's personnel had to restore order in the military, to enforce discipline—which had become lax—and to persuade the soldiers to fight "for Islam." After this first stage, however, the official reason given for the presence of the directorate's representatives within army units was the need to educate soldiers about Islam (Zabih 1988). Evidently the military is dominated by the religious system through the directorate. It is weaker than the religious system and its leaders realize this.

The Iranian military system is based on legal justification in Muslim law. Various Quranic verses and Shi'i traditions can be interpreted in a way so as to lend military service and the defense of the Iranian homeland the status of a religious imperative. Section 144 of the constitution of the Iranian republic states that the members of the armed forces must be believers who observe religious commandments. The armed forces must be *maktabi*, meaning truly Muslim (Entessar 1988). Obeying a military commander is described as a religious duty: discipline must be maintained not out of fear of one's commanding officer or actual punishment, but out of a feeling of commitment to Allah as well as solidarity with Muslim soldiers against the infidels (Zabih 1988, 136–137).

Thus it is clear that the observance of the commandments of Shi'i Islam do not pose a problem in the Iranian army. Despite the fact that it is a law-based orthoprax religion with many external commandments, observance does not clash with military obligations. Friday prayers are organized by the Defense Ministry's Department of Services and Public Relations. Soldiers may also receive Shi'i Islam religious instruction, and they attend a four- to six-week political-ideological course within military facilities as part of their service (ibid.). While this is not the same as instruction in a traditional religious study institution (madrassa), a soldier who wishes to study religious texts would not find it difficult to do so during his time in uniform.

Although there are no sources available to support this assertion, it is reasonable to assume that food in the Iranian army is suitable for religiously observant soldiers. Likewise, it can be assumed that keeping the Ramadan fast is encouraged, if not obligatory. The definition of the Iranian army as a Muslim armed force allows its soldiers to observe Islamic rituals and obligations, at least the Shi'i versions thereof.

On the other hand, it is not entirely clear to what extent religious freedom is accorded to non-Muslims in the Iranian military: May a Christian, Jewish, Bahá'í, or Zoroastrian soldier observe his holidays? It is also unclear whether pressures are brought to bear on Sunni soldiers due to their minority status in a Shi'i-dominated country.

It is likewise difficult to gauge the Iranian military's relationship with the government in terms of a mediating structure (see Chapter 1). The Iranian regime—with its totalitarian characteristics—has no need for mediating structures. Since the regime already uses a fair amount of coercion to assert its authority, it need not make an effort to cooperate with mediating structures; thus the conditions enabling the formation of mediating structures are not favorable to begin with (Berger and Neuhaus 1996,160).

On the other hand, the Ideological-Political Directorate can be viewed as a mediating structure to a certain extent. While it serves as a mechanism for intimidation for non-Shi'i and nonreligious soldiers, it does attempt to assist religious Shi'i soldiers who wish to continue practicing their religion. In any case, the directorate is more a tool of the religious establishment, whose primary goal is to keep the military under control ideologically. While it does technically serve as a mediating structure, this is not its chief raison d'être.

The Iranian case is one where the military system is weak in relation to the religious system and thus poses no threat to the religious system. Subsequently, it may be compared to the Red Army and to the armed forces of other totalitarian regimes in which political ideology replaces religion, such as those in China and North Korea.

THE TURKISH MILITARY

Of the cases presented here, the Turkish military is the most similar to the Israeli case. This similarity is due primarily to the fact that both Islam and Judaism are law-based orthoprax religions and thus share a similar attitude toward the secular world.[5] Additionally, these are also two democracies that sustain a conscription-based military.

The relationships between the regime, the military, and Islam in Turkey are complicated. The population is mostly Muslim, and Islamic tradition is an important part of their identity (Carkoğlu and Toprak 2000, 3; Yavuz 2003, 21–23). All religious institutions are controlled by the state. For instance, mosques are run by the government and imams receive their salary from the state. Thus, the regime has control over what happens in religious institutions. While Turkey's citizens take pride in their country's secular nature, on a more individual basis many of them fulfill religious obligations to a certain extent (Jenkins 2001, 59–69; Toprak 2005, 22, 33–35). The election of Recep Erdoğan, the head of an Islamic party, in 2003 and again in 2007, and the attempt to allow women to cover their heads in state universities emphasize this point.

Turkey's military is involved in the country's political life. The armed forces are under the direct command not of the minister of defense, but of the prime minister. Like Turkish society, the military views itself as a defender of secularity and of the heritage of Atatürk—the founder of modern Turkey. The military coups in 1960 and 1980 clearly demonstrated that the armed forces had continuously been involved behind the scenes, although it is important to note that power was always returned to civil society after "order" was restored.

While it is usually not openly involved in government, it is not uncommon for the armed forces to pressure the government to act in the way the generals think best. The Council for National Security (Millî Güvenlik Kurulu or MGK), the existence of which is based on the 1961 constitution, allows the military to "reprimand" the civilian government. At the same time, the armed forces are strongly opposed to any attempt to interfere in their affairs, particularly to political interference in appointments and promotions.[6] MGK powers have been curbed as a result of Turkey's wish to join the EU. To join the European Union, Turkey must make certain reforms such as bringing the military under stricter civilian control. However, the military still exerts much influence in the political sphere.

Despite the picture depicted by the previous paragraph, the boundaries between the military and the civil sphere in Turkey are quite integral: there is no civilian meddling in the military sphere. The military judiciary is internal and is not influenced by civilian powers. Additionally, senior officers are able to translate their military reputation to lucrative civilian employment upon retirement, and most focus on the private sector and do not become involved in politics (Jenkins 2001).

Turkey is among the shrinking number of countries in which there is conscription. No exemptions are available on religious or conscientious grounds, and religious and ethnic minorities must also serve.[7] Public opinion regarding compulsory military service is usually positive.

Most Turkish soldiers are from a rural background and are not highly educated. They are usually conservative and their religious observance includes much folk religion. Soldiers from an urban background are generally less religious and more liberal.[8] Given the preponderance of rural conscripts, religio-cultural elements are found in the Turkish military, and the attitude toward Islam is not necessarily negative. For instance, the infantry's battle cry is "Allah! Allah!" Navy ships carry a copy of the Quran, and the crew cries "bismillah" (in the name of God) before firing (Jenkins 2001, 28). However, a general prayer recited before meals in the mess substitutes a more secular Turkish word, Tanrı, for Allah—the name of God in Islam.[9] It appears that the military accepts the premise that religion can function as a uniting element and prevent dissolution. Religion must, however, be kept in its place (Shankland 1999).

Like in Israel, there are those in Turkey who see military service as a religious commandment. Specifically, the obligation to serve in the Turkish military is equal to Muslim religious obligations in general, and, if one is in uniform, it serves as an exemption from performing other religious commandments (Senior Turkish military sources A, B). A similar frame of thought can be found in Judaism: when one is fulfilling one religious commandment, he or she is exempt from fulfilling other obligations at the same time.

A number of religious minorities reside in Turkey. The largest minority group is the Alevis. Smaller religious groups include Christians, Jews, and Dönmeh. The extent of religious freedom awarded to these minorities while in uniform is unclear. However, it seems that whatever the reactions to their religious differences may be, they are not positive. Reports from various human rights organizations show Alevis petitioning for political asylum in other countries in order to escape military service, claiming they are subject to abuse upon conscription due to their religious beliefs.[10]

Officers are considered to be in an elite social group in Turkey. The Turkish military, like the American one, maintains a strict hierarchy between officers and enlisted personnel (Vaner 1987). The induction process into the officers' corps is long and difficult. It includes an in-depth examination of the candidate and his family. Even a cadet whose extended family is involved in political or religious activity may be disqualified. Candidates are asked to supply family photos in order to see whether the father grows a beard and the mother covers her hair. A candidate considered too religious or too involved in religious organizations will be disqualified (Jenkins 2001).

Graduates of the state-sponsored religious high school system, known as İmam Hatip schools, are not able to become officers. Only graduates of military or science high schools are eligible for officer training. In 2004, some 84,000 students enrolled in İmam Hatip schools and constituted 2.37 percent of the student body in Turkey (Eligur 2010, 124–127). Since the 1990s, the military has been wary of these schools, seeing them as hotbeds of Islamism and trying to curb their activity. Graduates are traditionally given jobs as imams in recognized mosques and are state employees. Some turn to the study of law (ibid.). Since some parents feel a diploma from an İmam Hatip school can stymie the advancement of their sons in the job market, they avoid sending their children to this school system for high school. Instead, they choose to ensure their children receive a good secular education in preparation for the future.

One military source explained that the reason for not accepting İmam Hatip graduates to the officers' corps was due to the fact that the graduates themselves were not interested in this option (Senior Turkish military source A). They prefer to complete their service as quickly as possible and go on to becoming imams. Since they are religious to begin with and military life does not allow for proper observance of commandments, they are not interested in a military career. Obviously there is no reason for them to become officers.

The Turkish military also pays attention to the political and ideological interests of its officers. An officer suspected of problematic sympathies (political or religious) is promptly discharged. Between 1995 and 2000, 745 officers and NCOs were dismissed by the Supreme Military Council due to their perceived ideological agendas—most often Islamist (Jenkins 2001). According to the military system, it seems that the difference between a pious officer and a fundamentalist/Islamist one is his public behavior. An officer who acts or speaks out in favor of a Muslim theocracy will be a candidate for dismissal. Officially, the reason given for discharge on ideological or religious-ideological grounds is "insubordination" or "insubordinate behavior." This is not just a technicality. Dismissal for these reasons is considered a dishonorable discharge and the officer or NCO will receive no pension or compensation. Additionally, his chances of finding suitable employment in the civilian sector are low (Jenkins 2001).

In the past decade, officers and NCOs who were discharged from the military due to their religious beliefs have turned to the European Court of Human Rights (ECHR) and petitioned it to force the military to allow them to appeal the decision to release them from service. (At present, there is no way to appeal decisions reached by the Supreme Military Council.) For example, a petition presented by six members of the Turkish military (four NCOs and two officers) in 1998 was finally rejected in 2003 by the ECHR.[11] Among other points, the petition cited the fact that the wives of the plaintiffs were not allowed to enter the military base they lived on because they wore head scarves in their ID photos. This was seen as discriminating against the plaintiffs for reasons of religious belief. In its defense, the state—representing the military—presented intelligence reports proving the plaintiffs' membership in various branches of the Muslim-mystic Nakşibendi sect, as well as their missionary efforts while in uniform. Furthermore, these reports claimed that the soldiers had "an antisocial character," were "insubordinate," and disobeyed orders to bring their wives to social events or participate in events where men and women were present in the same room. In other words, the state posited that the reason for the dismissal of these soldiers was not their religious beliefs, but their religious "external" behavior. Their behavior clashed noticeably with the expectations of their military role and was therefore unacceptable; a military cannot afford to have insubordinate members in its ranks.

The court saw the situation in a somewhat different light. Although it agreed that an individual soldier's right to religious freedom must be upheld, it recognized that a military framework is not the same as a civilian one. When the plaintiffs chose a military career, they were aware of the unique system of rules upheld by the military and that this system is not the same as the one used in a democratic, civilian system. What is considered fair and just in one system is not always so in the other.

The court also addressed the fact that the military in Turkey regards the Nakşibendi sect as Islamist and therefore as threatening to the state. Since the military system regarded the plaintiffs' loyalty to this sect to be superior to their loyalty to the military, it felt it could no longer benefit from their service and dismissed them. The court stressed it did not see the dismissal as stemming from the soldiers' beliefs, religious behavior, or the head scarves worn by their wives. Rather, it was a direct result of their refusal to follow the military code of conduct. For this reason, the petition was dismissed.

From similar rulings, it seems that this is precisely the way the Turkish government presents the situation: officers belonging to a religious sect are suspected of having dual loyalty and therefore are not trustworthy as far as the military is concerned. Without complete loyalty to the military system, there is no justification for allowing such a soldier to remain in the ranks as a career officer, and he is promptly dismissed.

However, it is impossible to know if this is the true reason for the soldiers' discharge. It is equally plausible that the military is overreacting to what it perceives as a religious threat and that it is also blowing this threat out of proportion (Jenkins 2001, 28–29).[12]

While it is able to avoid officers and NCOs suspected of religious extremism in its ranks to a certain extent, the Turkish military must still contend with enlisted men considered extremist. Due to conscription, the military is sure to have graduates of İmam Hatip schools, as well as other soldiers with religious backgrounds. How are these soldiers treated?

Prayer is allowed in the Turkish military, but as a practical matter it is impossible to pray five times a day, as required of an observant Muslim. The Turkish military schedule does not allocate time for prayer. As long as a soldier prays on his own time, without affecting his military duties, the military will allow it. In other words, it is possible to find time for three prayers (in the morning, during lunchtime, and before bed), but not five, especially if one is a conscript and is therefore subject to a very rigorous and structured military schedule. In recent years, Islamist conscripts have insisted on praying five times a day. When prayer is performed at the expense of military duties, the soldiers are punished. As a Turkish senior military source pronounced: "If you worked for [a] private business and wanted to pray five times, would they let you? No! It is the same." A soldier must realize that his main loyalty is to the military system and that his military duties come first. If his religious duties do not conflict with his military ones, he should have no trouble fulfilling them (Senior Turkish military source A). Nevertheless, while this may be the official position of the military, it is not necessarily the way it treats its soldiers. As evidenced by the petitions to the ECHR, the tolerance level for religious behavior seems rather low.

A number of other rules and regulations affect soldiers' ability to maintain a religious lifestyle. It is not possible to grow a beard or moustache in the Turkish military. There are no provisions made for fasting soldiers; not even during the month-long fast of Ramadan. "As long as you can do your job when you are on duty, no one minds if you are fasting. Defending the country is most important." And as long as fasting does not interfere with the defense of the country, it is permitted. But a fasting soldier will not be accommodated. It is his personal choice to fast, and is a private matter the military framework need not address (Senior Turkish military source A).

Despite the official position, it seems that in the field, officers can make certain decisions in order to accommodate their soldiers if they so wish. For example, an officer who is sympathetic toward his fasting conscripts can change the training schedule around so that classes are held during the fast rather than actual maneuvers. However, when this is done, it is an independent initiative and not sanctioned by the system itself.

On the other hand, where the Turkish military views religious observances as primarily cultural (not religious) observances, allowances are made. Friday prayers are held publicly for those interested. (These prayers are usually conducted by an İmam Hatip graduate, as there is no position of military imam or chaplain in the Turkish military.) During Ramadan, breakfast is held early so that those fasting may eat before the fast begins, and supper is held late enough for those fasting to break their fast with their comrades. Pork is not served, and the reasons given for this are not necessarily religious but in part cultural: "99 percent of Turks will not eat pork. It is not tradition. It is forbidden by our religion and not part of our tradition" (Senior Turkish military source A). Religious holidays are observed. Since most Turks are Muslim, these holidays are celebrated on the national level as well, and it is natural for soldiers to be granted a day off in honor of the festivities.

When examining the Turkish case, in matters of holiday observance and of diet, a religious Muslim soldier may continue his religious observances. However, in matters of prayer and fasting during Ramadan, his observance can be severely compromised. Since Islam has many external commandments, and the Turkish military does not wish religion to be visible in the public sphere, both systems seem set on a collision course.

In general, it seems safe to assert that the main difficulty with regard to the existence of religious soldiers in the ranks is a psychological one. Since most of the troops are Muslim, and many observances are also cultural, it should not be terribly difficult to accommodate religious soldiers to a certain degree. However, the Turkish military finds it hard to accept that a soldier can be equally and simultaneously loyal to his religious beliefs and the military system. The rules of play are ambiguous, not always clear to the individuals, and the system can change them at will. A religious soldier may find himself climbing the ranks, only to be abruptly dismissed when he is no longer seen as pious but as Islamist. He will forever be suspected of dual loyalty and treated accordingly.

Perhaps all those concerned would benefit from a mediating structure of some sort. Should such a structure be situated within the military sphere—such as chaplains in the U.S. military, as will be discussed in the next section—it could regulate pressure more successfully than an external civilian structure, as a civilian structure would automatically be suspected of Islamism. Since the boundaries between the civilian and military spheres are integral, this would be difficult in any case.

The Turkish model is a unique one. A comprehensive comparison between it and the Israeli case is overdue and would further our understanding of the relationship between religion and the military.

THE UNITED STATES MILITARY

Like many modern Western militaries, the U.S. armed forces deals with the needs of religious soldiers through the offices of chaplains. The U.S. military includes many religious denominations and minorities, including law-based ones as well as some that are lesser-known in the Western world, such as Wiccans, Hindus, and Buddhists. Atheists and their concerns are also addressed. Not all denominations have chaplains, however, and in general there is a shortage of them.

Because of the diversity of religious groups involved on the one hand, and the fact that a chaplain is ordained by a specific denomination on the other, a chaplain stationed at a particular base cannot be expected to serve the religious needs of the entire group of soldiers on that base. In other words, chaplains are entrusted with the general spiritual well-being of the troops, whether or not they have the same religious affiliation. Therefore, it is the chaplain's duty to introduce a soldier from another denomination or religion to a lay leader on base who can address the soldier's religious needs.[13] At times, the chaplain will put a soldier in touch with civilian religious authorities. For example, U.S. troops in Hong Kong who wish to attend religious services are instructed to go to the city itself.

The U.S. military has not always utilized chaplains in this way; their definition and scope of responsibility have evolved over the years. As early as the eighteenth century, in the Continental Army, the chaplains' role was to preserve the religiosity of the troops. They were to promote moral behavior and discourage negative habits such as drinking and gambling (Drazin and Currey 1995, 4–6, 8; Slomovitz 1999, 4). This model is similar to that of the Iranian military, as discussed previously. Colonial chaplains were only of Protestant denominations. Catholic chaplains were appointed in 1776. It was only much later that Judaism, Islam, and other religions were able to introduce their own chaplains.

Over the years chaplains were given additional duties, such as ministering to the injured and providing final rites to the dying. Today chaplains are expected to assist soldiers in obtaining the religious services they are entitled to within the bounds of military law. Essentially, it is the chaplain's duty to protect every soldier's right to religious freedom, whether they adhere to a certain faith or are atheists. They are not to focus only on the soldiers of their own faith, but on the general population in uniform. Chaplains are forbidden to postulate and must "forget" the basic assumption of any religion that other beliefs are "mistaken." They are to treat all troops equally and make sure their religious needs are met. As the guidelines for United Catholic Church chaplains state:

> As a chaplain, your job is to enable the troops to be at peace with themselves and with their God (not yours). . . . In summary, if you remember that your first responsibility is neither to the Church nor to the government, but to the welfare of the men and women entrusted to your care, you will make a fine chaplain. (United Catholic Church 2002)

Chaplains are also charged with meeting the religious and emotional needs of soldiers' families, and in many ways they function as de facto psychologists and social workers. In many cases U.S. soldiers have children and spouses, but any tensions in the home are not considered the official responsibility of one's commanding officer. These problems affect a soldier's performance, however, and therefore must be addressed. It is not uncommon for officers to approach a chaplain and request that he or she speak to a certain soldier about that soldier's personal issues. These issues might include anything from the soldier's relationship with a child to weight problems that must be addressed in order for the soldier to pass a fitness qualification test. Recent prolonged overseas tours of duty in the war zones of Iraq and Afghanistan have added to such problems and have only exacerbated the need for such a role.

It is in this capacity that a chaplain serves as a one-man mediating structure. The chaplain is in the field to support the troops and mediate between them and the larger structures of the military and their religion. However, a chaplain does not mediate between these two larger structures. Put differently, a chaplain is not concerned about the relationship between religious systems and the military; he or she is only interested in the relationship between the soldiers and these structures.

The U.S. military also has a loose connection to various external religious organizations that support religious soldiers. The largest of these, the Jewish Welfare Board (JWB), was founded in 1917 and supports Jewish chaplains and lay leaders (JWB website January 2010). However, it appears that despite this organization's work, there is insufficient information within the military about how to contact Jewish lay leaders, and there is little awareness regarding the rights of religious Jewish soldiers in general.

Special arrangements for Muslim soldiers began much later. The first Muslim chaplain in the U.S. military was appointed only in 1994 (*Defence Journal* 1999). The organization supporting Muslims in the U.S. military—the American Muslim Armed Forces and Veterans Affairs Council (AMAF and VAC)—describes itself as "serving as a bridge between Muslims and the various branches of the military." The council responds to Muslim soldiers who approach it with reports of alleged discrimination and brings requests made by Muslims before the U.S. Defense Department (AMAF and VAC website January 2010).

American military regulations address religious freedom in an official document published in 1988 and certified as current in 2009 (Department of Defense Directive 1300.17). Generally, the directives favor granting requests related to religion when feasible. For example, Article 3.2.7.3 specifically permits the wearing of a skullcap for Jews when no other military headgear is worn and specifies the requirements of such a skullcap.[14] However, the U.S. military does not involve itself in a soldier's religious observance and confines itself to making accommodations when possible. As mentioned above, followers of law-based religions, such as Islam and Judaism, are in a more sensitive position than followers of most other religions due to the aspects of their faith dictating daily behavior. Devoting resources to provide kosher or halal food, or permitting soldiers to refrain from physical activity while they are fasting, requires far more effort than granting requests allowing prayer once per week, for example. Therefore, allowing observant members of orthoprax law-based religions to serve in the military can be interpreted as willingness to accommodate various faiths.

American Muslim soldiers are allocated time to pray on Fridays and are not served pork at meals. In addition, during Ramadan, Muslim soldiers are officially excused from physical training and permitted to change their daily schedule to accommodate the traditional evening meal. Nevertheless, some Muslim soldiers report being unable to pray five times a day, as required by their religion.[15]

In the last decade, American Muslim soldiers have found themselves in a problematic position due to their religious affiliation. Since 9/11, the 2003 attack where a Muslim-American soldier threw grenades into a tent at a U.S. military base in Kuwait, as well as the 2009 shooting in Fort Hood, Texas, by a Muslim-American soldier, these soldiers are regarded with more suspicion than in the past. Conversely, other Muslims in the U.S. and the world have accused these soldiers of collaborating with infidels against their fellow believers. Fatwas issued by Muslim clergy supporting Muslim Americans who enlist grapple with these issues.

Meals Ready to Eat (MREs) that are compatible with Muslim and Jewish dietary laws are available. While such special arrangements undoubtedly help Jewish and Muslim soldiers, problems still arise owing to the relatively small number of these soldiers in the U.S. military. It seems that chaplains and support organizations cannot guarantee that religious individuals will be able to practice their faith to the fullest extent in the U.S. armed forces. While they may attempt to mediate between a religious individual and the military system, they are relatively weak, and their influence is limited.

Some religious sects, such as Quakers, Mennonites, and Jehovah's Witnesses, oppose military service. Since the abolition of the draft in the United States, there is no conflict between the two sides. It is interesting to note that, nevertheless, some followers of these sects do serve in the U.S. military. Despite having the right to maintain their faith, their decision to serve obliges these soldiers to make certain concessions. For example, soldiers who are Jehovah's Witnesses are not allowed to refuse medical treatment including blood transfusions, even though these are forbidden by their religion.[16] The U.S. military forces them to accept treatment their religion forbids.

In spite of the heterogeneity of the troops' religious beliefs, U.S. headlines in recent years have drawn attention to cases of religious intolerance toward soldiers. For example, in 2005 there was an instance of religious coercion of non-Evangelical Christian soldiers at the Air Force Academy in Colorado Springs. Among other grievances, cadets complained that they were pressured to attend religious services and that prayers were held before meals. Personal conversations and correspondence with U.S. soldiers and veterans depict a complicated situation where much seems to depend on the relationship that the soldier and commanding officer present have with the chaplain or lay leaders on base. Although the written directives are clear, reality is sometimes different. Nevertheless, it is the directives that set the tone and highlight the military policy on all religious matters.

The feeling given by these directives is one of accommodation. The U.S. military makes a tangible attempt to accommodate its religious soldiers irrespective of their religion or lack thereof. Despite the wish for accommodation, the U.S. military system can claim it is incapable of helping every soldier observe every religious commandment. Soldiers are aware of the situation prior to recruitment. Since it is an all-volunteer force (AVF), the U.S. military can demand soldiers make religious concessions when, in its view, religious observance obstructs their duties as soldiers. A Jehovah's Witness, therefore, can be ordered to receive a blood transfusion.

If the United States had a conscription-based military, soldiers could object to such orders since serving was not their choice. They might reasonably argue that because the military uprooted them from their environment and religious community, it must supply a comparable situation. As U.S. military service is voluntary, however, and soldiers knew before they enlisted what a military career would hold for them in terms of religion, whatever the military can do for these soldiers is pure accommodation; it is not an obligation on the part of the military.

Nevertheless, most Americans consider themselves religious people, and the U.S. military, too, tends to adopt a sympathetic view toward religious faith. It is this approach that allows for the presence of chaplains and lay leaders on bases. The willingness to accommodate religious soldiers to some degree indicates that religion and faith are not regarded as negative factors. Generally speaking, however, religion is considered to be a private matter. While all are free to believe in whatever religion they choose, Americans (civilians and soldiers alike) usually yield to the reigning secular ethos and refrain from parading religious practices in the public domain, particularly if prescribing to a minority religion.

The American case highlights the difference between mediating structures and chaplains. Although chaplains can be considered one-man mediating structures, they clearly belong to one of the parties involved—the military system. Since the boundaries between the military and the civilian sphere are integral in the United States, there is no other option: the chaplains must belong to one framework or the other, and there can be no crossover. While the well-being of religious soldiers is the chaplains' major concern, chaplains are officers in uniform and are expected to be officers first. Therefore, despite the degree of mediation that takes place though chaplains, religious individuals must manage to a large extent on their own. Without knowledge of their rights and the military's responsibilities toward them, they will be unable to take a proactive stance and their needs will not be met.

The American model parallels the situation in the militaries of Western democratic countries such as Australia, the United Kingdom, Canada, France, Germany, and New Zealand. These militaries employ chaplains with similar functions to those described here.

THE INDIAN ARMED FORCES

The modern Indian military has its roots in the colonial Indian armed forces, and its structure has remained the same in many ways. The British Raj preferred to recruit soldiers mainly in ethnically and/or religiously homogeneous regiments— the Sikh Regiment and the Dogra Regiment, for example. Some of these regiments still exist in the independent Indian military. The Indian infantry includes homogeneous regiments (termed "one class" on the basis of ethnic or religious-ethnic affiliation) and heterogeneous regiments, some of which contain homogeneous divisions or companies (fixed class). While some homogeneous units were created in order to appease groups within Indian society, most are a result of the British model of the past (Khalidi 2001).

The Indian military is volunteer-based. Recruits must meet minimum physical requirements, pass a written exam, and attain required scores on high school matriculation exams (Official Indian army website November 2013). Military service in India is a key to social mobility and can elevate the social and economic standing of a soldier's family. A military career is usually lifelong and is therefore important in a society where rates of unemployment are high. In recognition of this, the state has a set quota for lower castes and scheduled tribes in military academies in order to help them enter the military system (Khalidi 2001).

Social-ethnic-religious tensions in India have spilled over into the military. Following independence and the division of India and Pakistan in 1947, the Indian armed forces began to question the allegiance of Muslim officers and soldiers, who were seen as a possible fifth column. For example, Kashmir Muslims were categorically rejected from military service. Officially, underrepresentation of Muslims in the military in the twenty-first century is attributed to inefficiency in recruitment offices in Muslim regions and the low quality of Muslim education.

In contrast to the underrepresentation of Muslims, Sikhs play a very prominent role in the Indian military. Sikhs serve in two homogeneous regiments as well as in other homogeneous military platoons and companies (Ahmed 1999). In 2002, 20 percent of Indian officers were Sikhs, despite the fact that Sikh soldiers were involved in violent incidents (the most famous being the clash between the Indian military and Sikhs at the Golden Temple and the assassination of Indira Gandhi during the 1980s).

Assigning soldiers to homogenous units allows the Indian military to ensure that ethnic groups will not be stationed near civilian populations of the same ethnicity. In this manner the troops' social ties need never interfere with their military duties. For example, Sikh units will not be stationed in Punjab, where the population is predominantly Sikh; Gurkha units cannot be stationed on the border with Nepal. Serving in a homogenous unit also encourages loyalty to the military unit rather than to the military framework as a whole. Soldiers who serve with people who are similar to them in culture, ethnicity, and religion can rely on these characteristics as a common denominator in battle too. Similar to the traditional British model,[17] loyalty is not exclusively based on serving the same nation while in uniform, but to a large degree it is based on personal affiliation with a preexisting social group.

What of the treatment of religious soldiers? While not recognized as chaplains,[18] the Indian military employs the services of religious teachers who are given junior commissioned officer (JCO) rank. They are charged with leading prayers for interested soldiers. Religious teachers "wear dress appropriate to the occasions and customary to their religions"—not uniforms.[19]

The Indian armed forces have no policy regarding special arrangements for religious soldiers on holidays or fast days and deals with religious requests on a case-by-case basis. Muslim and Sikh soldiers are permitted to grow beards in the military. Sikhs may wear their religious head covering, a turban, and are provided with military turbans. They are also permitted to wear other religious articles required by their faith; something completely unthinkable by U.S. military standards. This policy is not reserved just for religious minorities, but can been seen in the treatment of ethnic minorities as well. For example, the dress uniforms of Naga soldiers resemble traditional Naga dress.[20]

The extent to which Muslim and Sikh soldiers are able to eat the meat served in Indian military mess halls is unclear. As noted, religious Muslim soldiers can only eat halal meat. Meat-eating Sikh soldiers cannot eat meat slaughtered by members of other religions (halal or kosher, for example). Some Sikhs, like Hindus from certain castes, are strict vegetarians. Military food is not vegetarian. It is also not clear whether military kitchens provide alternatives to beef for meat-eating Hindus and alternatives to pork for Muslims. Homogeneous units (one class and fixed class) might avoid some of these problems, since they feed fewer denominations from the same kitchen.

Although it has no defined religion, the Indian military has Hindu characteristics, and it appears that preference is given to the majority religion, Hinduism. Minorities have complained that when senior officers speak of the military's values, they base their ideas solely on Hindu sources. Moreover, Hindu sects (but not others) are permitted to distribute printed material and religious articles to soldiers (Khalidi 2001). In other words, the military has become a legitimate forum for Hindu religious activities.

On at least one level, the ethnic-social-religious traditions of soldiers are taken into account. Each infantry unit has its own battle cry, appropriate to the background of its soldiers. For example, the battle cry of the two Sikh regiments appeals to one God, while the battle cry of the Hindu Dogra Regiment appeals to a Hindu Goddess.

The Indian military and civilian spheres are separate and equal in power, and the boundaries between them are integral (Luckham 1971). One need only observe the fact that service duration is seventeen years and that soldiers do not serve close to home to realize the nature of these borders. The Indian model views homogeneous units as a privilege. Accordingly, ethnic or ethno-religious groups strive for homogeneous military units for their members. For Sikhs, serving in their own unit also allows them to wear uniforms that conform to the demands of their religion. If all soldiers in a unit wear a turban, the concept of uniform dress so important to the military is still upheld. At the same time, this model is certainly influenced by the caste system and the assumption that soldiers will never be able to bond sufficiently with members of castes and socio-ethnic groups other than their own. Heterogeneous units will never attain proper unit cohesion, according to such thinking. It is therefore impossible to expect soldiers from different backgrounds to fight and die for each other on the battlefield; hence the need for homogenous units (S. Rosen 1996). However, the primary motivation for creating homogeneous units appears to be sociopolitical; it is a way of assuring that ethnic groups will not be posted in their home states and forced to act against the interests of their communities.

At the same time, homogenous units are in a better position to help their members cope with the military system. While religious teachers are not chaplains and are unable to mediate between religious soldiers and the greater structures of the religious and military establishments, homogeneous units are in a better position to voice the needs and demands of ethnic or religious groups. Two examples of this are the authorization for unique ethnic-religious dress and the adoption of culturally based battle cries. It is also possible that they solve complex religious dietary problems. Having to deal with only Hindu restrictions in the mess is infinitely easier than trying to accommodate Sikh and Muslim requirements in the same kitchen and vice versa.

By establishing a homogeneous unit and granting it allowances, the military can signal it understands the special needs of a certain group. The group, in turn, can voice the concerns of its members in the military through the homogeneous unit. However, not all ethnic and religious groups in India can expect to be allowed to maintain a homogeneous unit, and the Muslim minority is a case in point.

THE INTERNATIONAL CONTEXT AND THE ISRAELI CASE

The cases depicted thus far present a complex picture of four possible relationship models between modern militaries and religion. The Iranian case illustrates relations between a powerful religious system and a much weaker military one. The military system is completely subservient to the religious one, and therefore there is no incentive to create true mediating mechanisms. Obviously the boundaries between the military and religious spheres are permeable, to use Luckham's terminology, where it is difficult to discern where one system ends and the other begins. As a result, religious soldiers who prescribe to the majority religion—Shi'i Islam—have no trouble practicing their religion. However, religious soldiers who belong to minorities, or nonreligious soldiers who do not wish to practice any religion while in uniform, are the injured party in this model. Their needs are not considered. As the Iranian military is conscription-based, these soldiers will always be present within the force, even if their religious needs are not taken into account. Another problem embedded in this case is the fact that military abilities are handicapped due to excessive religious meddling in military affairs: a soldier who is brilliant but secular—or a member of another religion—will be unable to join the officers' corps; the military system is not free to act according to its interests, but must first consider the religious dimension. In other words, contrary to the assumption at the beginning of this chapter, having a defined religion does not guarantee religious tolerance. It promises only tolerance for that religion, and in this case it also ensures religious coercion.

Conscription plays an important part in the Turkish model as well. Due to conscription, one would expect the military system to at the very least recognize its religious soldiers and address their needs in some way. These soldiers did not choose to serve, and are forced out of their religious observances by law. They do not wish to cease practicing their faith, and the military sphere cannot ignore this and expect there to be no consequences. Furthermore, the integral boundaries between the military and the civilian spheres in Turkey prevent civilian frameworks from assisting these soldiers even unofficially. Coupled with the fact that the Turkish military is inclined to suspect anything connected to religion, clearly there will be no attempt at mediation between the military and religious systems in this model.

The Indian and American models, on the other hand, make certain attempts to mediate between the spheres. At first glance, since both militaries are volunteer forces and both have no defined religion, it would seem that neither is likely to construct any mediating structures: If soldiers are well aware of the situation they are volunteering for and for all practical purposes have forfeited their right to practice their faith fully, why accommodate them? Those whose religious observances are important to them will not enlist, and, if they do, should not expect the right to make religious demands.

Surprisingly, perhaps, these armed forces actually consider the needs of religious soldiers and are willing to accommodate them to various degrees. Furthermore, in the Indian military, although it has an unofficial preference for Hinduism, there is a conscious attempt to mediate through the use of ethno-religiously homogenous units. As previously discussed, these units allow the military to accommodate both religious and ethnic needs of soldiers.

Even after examining these cases—volunteer forces with no defined religion or an official preference for a certain religion, and conscription-based forces secular or religious—the relationships between the religious and military systems prove to be complex and difficult to comprehend. It is not easy to discern a pattern of military system behavior vis-à-vis religion and religious soldiers.

In order to clarify the spectrum of cases further, a closer look at the Israeli military is in order. The Israeli case is one of a conscription-based military that defines itself as a Jewish force. The boundaries between the military and civilian spheres are fragmented according to Luckham's classification and Lissak's subsequent work (Lissak 1991), meaning that in some places the boundaries are clear and in others they are not. As Lissak demonstrated, the fragmented boundaries permit mediating structures to move with relative freedom between the military and religious systems, allowing the mediators to support the individuals with more success. Were the boundaries integral, there would be no chance of such support. The Israeli case, therefore, is unique and helpful in understanding the challenges related to religious soldiers in the military sphere and the way they are treated within it. This model will be examined further in Part II.

PART II

BEING A SOLDIER AND A RELIGIOUS JEW: DILEMMAS AND SOLUTIONS

CHAPTER 3
MILITARY SERVICE FROM IDEOLOGICAL, HALAKHIC, AND VALUE PERSPECTIVES

The subject of this chapter is not the history of the Religious Zionist yeshiva or the comprehensive ideology of Religious Zionism vis-à-vis the State of Israel. Rather, this chapter delineates the main lines of the controversy between Religious Zionism and the IDF regarding military service and highlights the chief points of friction that will be described later in this study. After introducing the subject, this chapter will then explore each of the areas of tension: practical issues, tension revolving around conflicting values, and, finally, identity conflicts.

By definition, Religious Zionism is a political-religious movement committed to finding practical solutions to halakhic problems that arose as a result of the foundation of the State of Israel (Ravitzky 1993; Schwartz 1999). The very willingness to define itself as Zionist—in stark contrast to other Jewish religious sectors—indicates the movement's commitment to ensuring the coexistence of Zionism and Orthodox Judaism.

During the prestate (Yishuv) period, and even more so after the foundation of the state, rabbis affiliated with Religious Zionism employed both traditional halakhic language in their writings and teachings and revived phrases related to Jewish sovereignty that had not been in use for millennia (such as "king" or "obligatory war"). The revived terms allowed rabbis to frame the new situation in traditional language and to ease the acceptance and absorption of this new reality.[1] Indeed, many rabbis of Religious Zionism viewed—and still view—the State of Israel as a holy entity that symbolizes "the dawning of our redemption" (*reshit tzmihat geulatienu*). Accordingly, these rabbis see the revival of Israel as a miracle. Contrary to the ultra-Orthodox (Haredi) sector and its view of the state, the framing of the state in traditional terms has allowed Religious Zionism to incorporate the state into a religious set of values and concepts. It is therefore not a completely secular entity; to a certain extent its various facets have a religious dimension. This view—which underlies *mamlakhtiyut*, or the acceptance of the sovereignty attitude within Religious Zionism—allows the Religious Zionist sector to treat the state as a generally positive entity and to engage with it.[2]

Since the military is part of the state apparatus, it, too, is awarded a religious status and is not seen as a strictly secular system. As a result, Religious Zionism does not view service in the IDF as acceptance of the state's superior authority or as the submission of the believer to the military's demands. Rather, service is seen as a true religious obligation. As Judaism is not a pacifist religion and recognizes war as a legitimate means for specific, clearly defined ends, under certain circumstances it sees military service as a religious obligation (mitzva). This attitude may not have been clear and unanimously agreed upon initially, but it seems to have been wholeheartedly adopted following the 1967 war at the latest.[3]

Nevertheless, military service was never taken for granted by Religious Zionist leaders, and the problems faced by a believer in uniform were always calculated when examining the issue of service. The Religious Zionist sector created mediating structures between its members and the IDF to address the problems associated with religious soldiers without forfeiting the principle of military service as a religious obligation.[4] These structures took the form of various educational yeshiva programs. Religious Zionism posited that strengthening elements related to Torah studies prior to military service would help believers in uniform for a number of reasons. For example, studying would bolster them in the battle against secularization. It would strengthen the ties between the religious lives of these youngsters as civilians and their service as soldiers and help them deal with problems they would encounter during service.

While it took some time to construct the mediators, and the process is still an ongoing one, it is obvious that Religious Zionism developed an ideological infrastructure encompassing military service in the IDF—and indeed the IDF itself—in a religious frame of thought. Within this framework, military service and the military are conceived of as a means to a religious aim: the saving of human life, and the defense of the Jewish population in Israel from those who would destroy it (as Maimonides posits in his *Laws of Kings and Their Wars*, 5:1: to deliver Israel from an enemy who has attacked—*ezrat Yisrael miyad tzar*). While in and of itself the IDF is not a halakhic entity, this view allows Religious Zionist rabbis to see it through the halakhic prism and relate to it accordingly.[5]

Thus, the military system becomes part of the comprehensive framework of religious values and therefore not a threat to the religious world. But despite the positive way military service is presented by most of Religious Zionist society, conflicts and tensions exist between the IDF and this sector. The rivalry between the two can be seen on several levels. The first and most fundamental level is the competition for the individual's loyalty. As in the dilemma of the greedy institutions presented in the first part of this study, here too each of the institutions in question is concerned that the other will steal, so to speak, individuals whom they view as belonging to their sphere of influence. On the second level, a person serving in the IDF who wishes to continue fulfilling religious commandments comes face to face with practical difficulties when trying to observe religious obligations. These difficulties must be addressed. Both of these aspects concern any religious soldier, whether a member of the IDF or another armed force.

In Israel's case, two additional levels of rivalry are involved. Religious Zionism and the IDF compete for the individual's time. Service in the military takes place at a time when a religious youth would ideally be dedicating his time to advanced Torah studies at a yeshiva, a religious seminary. Religious Zionist society preserves a traditional approach that assigns great importance to Torah studies, and the timing of military service is such that it coincides with a time when the individual should be studying Torah (S. Cohen 2004; S. Cohen 2001, 186–187).

In addition, many IDF conscripts, from all walks of Israeli society, undergo personal and behavioral transformations during their military service; the effects of which can also be seen in religious observance. The Religious Zionist sector is concerned that life in the military will cause young religious people to forsake their religion. Life in an environment full of "temptations" and promiscuity, without the guidance of teachers and rabbis, might lead these young people astray. Additionally, the difficulties in fulfilling practical commandments (such as prayer) at a time when one must keep to the military's timetable might discourage Religious Zionist youths from meeting such obligations. On yet another level, the atmosphere in the IDF—so different from that of their civilian lives—might bring about moral and social changes in these youngsters. The competition is in fact over influencing the individual's identity, and Religious Zionism feels threatened by service in the IDF.[6]

Put differently, tensions between the IDF and Religious Zionism fall into four categories, two of which are relevant to any religious soldier: that of authority (one's loyalty to religion versus loyalty to the military) and that of practicality (a conflict between life in uniform and fulfilling religious commandments). Two additional categories are unique to Religious Zionism and the IDF: the apparent clash between two values (Torah study versus military service, both competing for the same time frame); and the struggle to influence identity (the military system as an environment within which one might abandon one's religious obligations and social values is a threat to the continuity of Religious Zionism as a sociocultural group). Since the issue of loyalty has already been discussed in Chapter 1, we can turn to a discussion of the three additional dilemmas: one practical, one value-based, and one concerning questions of identity.

HALAKHIC AND PRACTICAL PROBLEMS DURING MILITARY SERVICE

Military service within a secular framework presents an observant soldier with many practical challenges on a daily basis. Such problems exist whether or not the religious individual can utilize mediating structures during his or her service. Some problems arise because a soldier's time is no longer his own, but rather belongs to the military. Military routine demands training and operational exercises. Many times such activities can be neither halted nor postponed. Since many religious obligations are time-bound, such as prayer, holidays, and fasts, this creates scheduling conflicts for the observant soldier. For example, can a soldier pray three times a day as required by Jewish law? Will he be able to pray in a quorum (minyan) at least on Monday, Thursday, and Saturday, when the Torah scroll is read during prayers in the morning? Will the soldier be able to fast the six fasts in the Jewish calendar? Will he or she be able to observe Shabbat (Saturday, the Jewish day of rest when no work can be done) properly?

Not all difficulties are caused because of a direct conflict between military life and halakha. Some can be caused primarily by social constructions. At times, a soldier's commanders and comrades are unaware of the limitations imposed upon him by his beliefs. They may ask him to perform certain tasks or join them for social events without understanding such actions can conflict with religious obligations. Conversely, the soldier may wish to be an integral part of his unit socially and find himself in problematic situations. For instance, rotating a tank turret in order to open the hatch and receive warm food for the crew on Shabbat, spending time with friends in a tent where music is playing on Shabbat, or going out to a restaurant that is not kosher are all problematic situations for a religious soldier who wants to fit in.

The first two examples are situations that cause an Orthodox Jewish soldier to be party to desecration of the Sabbath. While it is permissible to rotate the tank turret on Shabbat for reasons of war, doing so in order to bring in a hot meal is questionable. Since there is food in the tank, there is no immediate need to open the hatch, and the crew is not in any danger if they do not receive a hot meal. However, should the religious soldier refuse to do so, the rest of the crew would be understandably upset. Why should they have to eat K rations due to one soldier's religious beliefs when a perfectly good hot lunch is waiting just outside?[7] In most cases, the relationship between members of a tank crew is quite close. The religious member of the crew certainly does not want his comrades to suffer on his account. Furthermore, the rest of the crew quite possibly does not understand the dilemma their religious friend is facing. Can a solution be found so that this soldier can be considerate of his fellow crew mates without forgoing his religious convictions? Although such problems are primarily caused by social circumstances, not necessarily military ones, this example demonstrates how they lead to halakhic predicaments—some of which can be severe.

Furthermore, the atmosphere in military units sometimes brings about other problems. These situations may not cause religious soldiers to transgress their religious commandments, but they might make them very uncomfortable. For example, they may be exposed to behavior or language that they are not used to or that would be unacceptable in their social group, such as recounting sexual escapades, profanity, and objectification of women. In this sense, religious soldiers are part of a cultural minority. Even if they are assimilated in Israeli society, many forms of social conduct in secular Israeli society are not found in Religious Zionist society and vice versa. Spending all day, every day, in an environment that is very different from what they are used to can be difficult for religious soldiers (as for any individual placed in a similar situation).

The Sabbath

Observing the Sabbath (Shabbat) is a sine qua non for any religious Jew. Shabbat begins on Friday night at sundown and is over on Saturday night when three stars are visible. During this time, an Orthodox Jew refrains from a plethora of activities categorized as "work." These activities are detailed and expounded on in halakhic literature and include not only literal work and labor but also writing, using the telephone, turning electricity on and off, cooking, and transporting objects outside a certain perimeter (*eruv*). But more specifically, this entails treating the day differently and observing the atmosphere of rest that it requires. The day also includes special prayers, festive meals, and the lighting of candles before the day officially begins.

In the military, a soldier must sometimes desecrate the Sabbath. In general terms, it is not always possible to fulfill the religious obligation to honor the sanctity of the day as required by the very detailed laws of Shabbat. At times, it is possible to observe the general concept of Shabbat as a day of rest, but military life dictates the transgression of specific commandments and particulars related to actions on the Sabbath. For example, the troops in the IDF rest on Saturday, and no maneuvers take place. However, routine duties such as guard duty and the carrying of one's personal weapon—sometimes outside the *eruv*—must continue.

Combat situations are less of a problem. Most of the IDF's activities are seen by halakhic authorities as being carried out in order to save lives (*pikuah nefesh*; a categorization allowing one to transgress almost any commandment if it will save a life). During combat situations, which certainly fall within the category of *pikuah nefesh*, clearly there is a halakhic license to desecrate the Sabbath should the need arise.

However, many halakhic issues crop up when *pikuah nefesh* is not necessarily apparent. For instance, what should happen on Shabbat in the case of a soldier in the Intelligence Corps who monitors enemy broadcasts and is supposed to keep an accurate record of the information collected? While obviously an important job by military standards, is it clearly within the category of *pikuah nefesh*? Even if it is, perhaps not all aspects of it may be undertaken. May the soldier use a pen? Perhaps he should use a "Shabbat pen" (with ink that disappears after twenty-four hours)? May he keep records in the usual manner, or must he change something in his regular behavior (such as write with his weaker hand) to honor the Sabbath (*be-shinui*)? And so forth. The soldier must decide whether this is *pikuah nefesh* and whether a change in his performance in order to observe the sanctity of the Sabbath will adversely affect his ability to carry out his military duty.[8]

Military training courses give rise to other questions. During the Sabbath, may one study written material relating to the course (since reading is permitted) or prepare for exams? This might be considered using the Sabbath in order to prepare oneself for secular activities (*hakhana mi-kodesh le-hol*). Furthermore, in this situation a soldier might also be tempted to write, which is a prohibited action on the Sabbath. Perhaps it is better to abstain from nonreligious studies altogether on Shabbat. On the other hand, if he is unprepared, how will this soldier be able to perform the job he is being trained to do? Will this not affect his ability to save lives in the future (Rabinovitch 1993, 155–156)?

Dilemmas such as these arise every Sabbath when a soldier is on base. Even if he is there only to perform guard duty, the way in which he is supplied with food and drink must be considered. How should a guard duty list be drawn up? If he is to join a patrol, how can this be done? May he turn off the engine of the patrol car, and, if so, how? Other questions are related not only to matters of halakha, but also to social interactions. For instance, if another soldier's parents visit on the Sabbath and want to share the food they have brought with a religious soldier, can he eat with them so as not to cause offence, even though the food arrived through desecration of Shabbat? All these problems and many like them are an inseparable part of life in the military.

In addition to these problems, there are others that are related to the Sabbath atmosphere. When secular soldiers listen to music in a room or in a tent, should a religious soldier leave in order to avoid benefiting from his friends' violation of the Sabbath (Rimon 2007, 156–174)? These problems vary in seriousness and number from unit to unit, but they are always present in some form. Shabbat observance tensions associated with military life are inevitable, unavoidable, and myriad. Similar dilemmas exist elsewhere, such as in the medical world. However, while an individual who is considering becoming a doctor or nurse can understand the halakhic implications of such a choice and decide whether or not he or she is prepared to undertake these dilemmas, a soldier in a conscription-based military doesn't have this luxury and cannot avoid addressing such predicaments.

Religious Dietary Restrictions

Orthodox Judaism has a set of strict dietary rules called kashrut. These include permitted foods (a specific list of permitted animals and animal products and the manner in which permitted animals are slaughtered) and forbidden foods (such as pork), but also rules for cooking and consuming milk and milk products versus meat and meat products. Milk and meat may not be eaten during the same meal or cooked together. It is also imperative to wait a certain amount of time after eating meat before eating dairy products. A derivative of these rules is that Orthodox kitchens have at least two sets of dishes and cooking utensils in order to separate dairy from meat.

Officially, IDF kitchens are kosher. Meat and milk utensils and cooking products are separated, and all rules pertaining to permitted animals and foods are upheld. However, a soldier who keeps kosher is still faced with a number of problems. There is a difference between kitchens in organized, permanent bases and those in the field or in small outposts. Kashrut supervisors and professional staff serve in the kitchens of large, permanent bases, and in these kitchens kashrut lapses are relatively minor. For example, meat and milk crockery and cutlery get mixed together, and cabbage and rice are not properly checked for worms and insects. Sometimes a soldier unfamiliar with kashrut laws might use the kitchen improperly, or a cook who is not fully cognizant of the rules might cause some issues concerning cooking on the Sabbath, but these are exceptions.

Most kashrut problems in the IDF arise in small outposts and temporary camps, or in various social contexts. Kitchens in outposts are not always kosher and need to be made so every time a new unit is posted there. When there is no regular cook in an outpost, soldiers cook for themselves, and the chance of ensuing problems is very high. Soldiers unaware of kashrut cannot be expected to be sufficiently competent in observing the rules, and while most Israeli soldiers are aware of the more major rules, they are ignorant of the subtleties.

When elite units train and spend time in the field, or at the end of special exercises such as a final navigating exercise or survival training, rather than eat only K rations, it is customary to eat in soldiers' homes along the way or at their kibbutz dining halls. While this does not happen every day, it occurs often enough in these units to merit mention. Obviously most of the hosting kitchens in these cases are not kosher. Members of the unit who keep kosher therefore find themselves in an awkward situation. On the one hand, they cannot eat in these homes, and on the other, they don't want to offend their friends. As interpersonal relationships in elite units are usually very close, and training encourages members to form strong social bonds, these problems are significant.

Similarly, soldiers bring food from home to share with their comrades and go out to eat together on various social occasions (for example, going out on the town, or celebrating the completion of a training course). The food in these cases is not always kosher. Sometimes even pork makes an appearance on the menu. Apart from the kashrut aspect, many religious soldiers find it difficult to deal emotionally with the presence of pork at social gatherings for historical-cultural reasons. Such situations have the potential to create tension between soldiers who keep kosher and those who do not.

Prayer

Orthodox Jews must pray three times a day: morning, noon, and night. It is preferable to pray in a minyan, or quorum, a group of ten adult males. Three times a week (Monday, Thursday, and Saturday) the morning prayers include reading a portion of the Torah from a Torah scroll. On Saturday the Torah is also read from during afternoon services. This reading can only be done in a quorum. Naturally, procuring a scroll and being able to pray with a minyan is no easy feat while in uniform, and a soldier's ability to do so hinges on where he serves. A soldier training or in the field will have more difficulty arranging these things than a soldier serving on a large base where many religious soldiers are present.

According to General Staff Regulations, the military schedule must include time for prayer. These regulations cannot always be observed, however. Due to their training timetables, soldiers in elite units are not always given enough time to pray, especially in the morning when prayers are the longest. In addition, when on operational duty, it is difficult to find time to pray three times a day.

Moreover, sometimes allotting time for prayer comes at the expense of nonworshipers. Prayer times in the morning usually coincide with morning barrack inspection. Thus, the unit must prepare its barracks (cleaning the living quarters as well as the unit's common gear and weapons) shorthanded as their religious comrades pray. This can give the impression that the religious soldiers are shirking their duties, thus creating resentment (yet another example of a halakhic problem that brings about social difficulties). As a result, some religious soldiers prefer to wake early to pray on their own time rather than antagonize their friends. Consequently, they sleep less, which can be exceptionally difficult for them during training.

Even if a soldier does manage to pray three times a day, in many cases he is unable to pray in the required quorum. Even if he were lucky enough to serve with another nine men who favor communal prayer, it would not always be possible to gather them all at the right time.[9]

Additionally, during the usual morning prayers one must pray with phylacteries (*tfillin*), which gives rise to a variety of questions: When should one lay the *tfillin*? How should they be brought to the field? Can they be carried on the Sabbath so they can be used during the week? There are similar issues with respect to Torah reading, and the concomitant halakhic difficulties are numerous.

Fasts, Holidays, and Time-Bound Commandments
Judaism has six main fasts. Four of them (the Seventeenth of Tamuz, the Fast of Gedalia, the Tenth of Tevet, and the Fast of Esther) last from dawn until the stars can be seen. For the remaining two (the Ninth of Av and Yom Kippur), the fast begins at sunset and ends when the stars come out (approximately twenty-five hours). General Staff Regulations allow a soldier to abstain from physical activity while fasting.

There are other prohibitions related to fast days. During Yom Kippur and the Ninth of Av, a religious soldier not only abstains from food and drink, but is not permitted to wash and wear leather shoes, such as the regulation army issue boots. There are other times during the Jewish calendar when one is not supposed to have one's hair cut, and men are prohibited from shaving facial hair. Understandably, this affects the religious soldier's appearance and mars the military form that the system prizes. In spite of their effect on the soldiers' physical appearance, General Staff Regulations permit religious soldiers to follow these commandments, and a soldier who is not allowed to do so may lodge a complaint and demand that his religious obligations be taken into consideration.

Holidays present a different set of challenges. On the festival of Sukkot, for example, a religious soldier is obligated to eat his meals in a *sukka* (special outdoor temporary hut) and to pray part of the morning service while holding a *lulav* (palm frond with accoutrements). Here, again, field maneuvers and combat operations are not conducive to observance. Providing scrolls for public readings on various holidays, the special and far more stringent rules of kashrut on Passover, blowing the shofar (ram's horn) on the High Holydays, and other traditions are not easily compatible with normal military routine. A religious soldier living within the restricted environment of the military system must depend on its authorities—officially, the Military Rabbinate—to supply his or her needs. However, inefficiencies, misunderstandings, ignorance, competing demands, and the exigencies of military life often result in less than optimal conditions for fulfilling these requirements of religious observance.

Modesty

The issue of modesty can also be divided into two categories: service in the military alongside female soldiers or instructors, and exposure to other soldiers' personal conduct. Direct contact between men and women, especially physical contact, is problematic from a halakhic point of view. Women who dress immodestly (wearing tank tops, shorts, etc.), coed dwellings in which both sexes share common bathrooms, and shared guard duty or lookout duty not only make a soldier raised in religious society feel extremely awkward, but they are also prohibited by halakha.

A situation no less awkward is created when a male soldier is being trained by a female instructor who must come into physical contact with him during training. This occurs during various infantry training courses, such as medic training and sniper training. Not all religious soldiers observe the prohibition to abstain from any form of physical contact with a member of the opposite sex—even when no romantic or sexual meaning is intended (such as shaking hands)—but this can be problematic for the religious soldier who does.

In addition to problems created by the nature of military service itself, there are other issues that arise from the conduct of nonreligious soldiers serving in proximity to religious soldiers: the use of profanity and vulgar language, sexist and rude comments about women, the exhibition of nude posters in the soldiers' rooms, etc. This sort of conduct makes a soldier who grew up in Religious Zionist society, where such behavior is considered unacceptable, extremely uncomfortable. Coming face to face with conduct of this kind is difficult mainly from a cultural point of view.

The problems described here do not include those that are created by performing actual military duties such as guarding beaches used by women in swimsuits (this relates to issues of modesty) or sites like the ski resort on Mt. Hermon (which is open on Shabbat, and thus a desecration of the Sabbath) that soldiers are required to guard in order to protect vacationers. These problematic issues are more easily dealt with halakhically.

Moreover, these problems are not exclusively related to service in the military: every citizen may find himself in a situation where he has to deal with issues pertaining to the *eruv* and the correct time for laying *tfillin*. However, a citizen can take steps to avoid such circumstances and has a fundamental advantage over a soldier: his time is his own, and therefore he can better prepare himself for such situations. These problems are more extreme during military service. A soldier must manage a variety of factors that do not exist in civilian life, and since he has to follow the military's schedule as well as his orders, his ability to solve problems of this sort independently is limited.

Portraying service in the IDF as a religious commandment provides certain solutions for the practical issues described above. If it is in the interest of both the IDF and Religious Zionism to deal with the problems—and a genuine effort is made toward this purpose—most predicaments can be solved. The scope of this study does not allow us to illustrate the halakhic solutions in depth, but these continue to be found and discussed in various public forums and produce a wealth of publications, specifically halakhic responsa (She'elot Utshuvot or SHOOT).[10] Soldiers also turn individually to rabbis for solutions to problems they encounter, and this will be discussed in detail below. One must add that numerous practical problems recur and religious soldiers learn to deal with many of them during the course of their service. This detracts neither from the difficulties involved nor from the necessity of coping with them. They are real dilemmas that must be faced, but halakha provides tools for grappling with them, and these can be used when the parties involved are willing to do so.

A COLLISION OF VALUES

Torah study versus military service

Service in the IDF poses a unique problem for classic Jewish culture. Judaism views Torah study as a religious commandment. Every Jew is obligated to engage in study of the Torah. Throughout Jewish history, yeshivot, formal institutions dedicated to the study of Torah, were formed.[11] According to time-honored tradition, ideally every Jew should dedicate his life to the study of Torah, and young men especially should devote their time exclusively to religious studies. This should be the case particularly during childhood (from the age of five or six) and at the very least until marriage. Those with the greatest aptitude should continue studying intensively their entire lives.

Over time this tradition gained further validation. The period of the Volozhin yeshiva (which flourished in Lithuania in the nineteenth century) is considered the yeshivot's heyday. The Volozhin yeshiva, seen today as the model for all yeshivot, was founded by Rabbi Hayim of Volozhin. According to Stampfer's study of the

Lithuanian yeshiva, the most important impetus in its founding was the "sincere desire to help young men realize the ideal of Torah studies" (Stampfer 2005, 43). Students would come to Volozhin after having already mastered the skills required for studying the Talmud and its commentaries.

The yeshiva was essentially an educational institution. In the context of nineteenth-century Enlightenment, it was also a response to modernization (ibid. 2–20, 389–390). Additionally, going to study at a yeshiva was perceived in a way as a rite of passage for young Jewish adolescents. Being cut off from their families and joining an all-male institution symbolized the transition from childhood to adulthood. The student would leave his parents' home and go into exile, so to speak, in order to gain knowledge (*gala lemakom shel torah*). Entering the yeshiva was also a symbol of gaining a form of independence, which would oblige the student to take responsibility for his actions.

Following the discussion in the first chapter, it should be noted that the framework of the yeshiva is comprehensive and exclusive, and it does not allow for the existence of a parallel framework in its students' lives. A student is under the authority of the heads of the yeshiva and its teachers. He is separated from his home, family, and life in the outside world (Stampfer 2005, 390). The yeshiva demands absolute loyalty and cannot accept a situation in which it has to compete with any other institution; it is thus compatible with the sociological definition of a "greedy institution" used previously. Therefore, quite separately from its function as a mediating structure (which will be discussed below), the yeshiva is in and of itself a greedy institution (S. Cohen 1993, 13).

In light of the cultural and traditional expectation that young Jewish men continue studying Torah—especially in the case of gifted students—the friction between Religious Zionism and the IDF is clear.[12] The need to produce a religious leadership proficient in Torah for Religious Zionist society and to allow gifted Torah students to continue their studies brought about a conflict of interest between the IDF and the Religious Zionist sector.

This dilemma is not new. Following the Holocaust, when most of the reserves of future Torah scholars had been destroyed, the fear of losing even more future scholars due to the Yishuv's need for fighting men was heightened.[13] At the time of the establishment of the State of Israel in 1948, when it became apparent mandatory conscription would be instituted, the Religious Zionist sector was concerned that brilliant Torah scholars would defect to the ultra-Orthodox sector so that they could circumvent conscription and continue their studies. As David Ben-Gurion, Israel's first prime minister, had granted deferments to ultra-Orthodox Torah scholars as early as 1947, this was seen as a possible loophole for those who wished to study rather than serve.[14] Religious Zionism thus risked losing its elite students and never building a worthy spiritual leadership. Therefore, both tradition and reality encouraged Religious Zionism's demand to retain control over the lives of youngsters facing conscription. The IDF, as well as the general Israeli leadership, has always realized such a demand cannot be ignored.

Consequently, this dimension of the conflict between the IDF and the Religious Zionist system focuses on a time in a youngster's life that both consider to be of the utmost importance (Drori 2001, 762–763). Each side would like the young men in question to dedicate this time in their lives to it exclusively, without interruptions or distractions: the IDF demands complete devotion to training from its troops, and the tradition of religious study bans any distraction from the study of Torah.[15] This is the cause of a more serious problem when military service itself is viewed as a religious principle, as in the case of Religious Zionism in Israel. If both religious study and military service are divine obligations and occupy the same time slot in a person's life, how can one choose?

Both sides attempt to defuse the tension between them through the use of yeshivot and programs for Torah study, as will be shown below. The ability to continue to study Torah, albeit in a more limited framework that allows for military service, has been enabled by a number of basic assumptions made by the Religious Zionist sector, both halakhic and ideological, that provide answers to the question: How can one permit military service when this comes at the expense of Torah studies? Over the years, substantial Rabbinic literature has been composed with the aim of solving this question. The answers given by the rabbis of the Religious Zionism sector permitting service in the IDF relate to the following considerations.[16]

Israel Is in a State of Obligatory War

The mainstream of Religious Zionism holds the view that from the moment of its founding, the State of Israel has been in a state of religiously ordained or obligatory war, *milhemet mitzvah*, and that such a war takes priority over Torah studies. As has been explained at length in Yehezkel Cohen's study (1994), halakha permits military service at the expense of Torah studies (and of any other religious commandment) at the time of an obligatory war. There are three possible categories of obligatory war. The only one still pertinent to modern times is a war waged in order to "deliver Israel from an enemy who attacks them" (*ezrat Yisrael miyad tzar*, Maimonides, *Laws of Kings and Their Wars*, 5:1)—to save Jews from danger. In obligatory war, all must set out to battle, including brides and grooms on their wedding day, as is found in the Mishna of Tractate Sota, 8:7. The rabbis of the Religious Zionist sector maintain that the State of Israel is indeed in a state of obligatory war. As Rabbi Aharon Lichtenstein, the head of the Har Etzion yeshiva, puts it, those who are opposed to the conscription of yeshiva students must remember "the simple truth that a Jewish soul can only exist within a Jewish body," and this body must be protected (Lichtenstein 2002, 34).

This commandment is given further weight when the issue of protection is bound together with the commandment of living in Israel and settling it (as is explained in detail in Rabinovitch 1993, 9–22). Therefore, "one cannot overestimate the value of the religious commandment of serving in the military in Israel, which comprises two religious commandments—each of which is equal to all other commandments": saving Israel from its enemies and keeping the Land of Israel under the control of the people of Israel (E. Melamed 2002).

Nevertheless, although most Religious Zionist rabbis agree that military service is a religious commandment, they disagree as to whether it is indeed a positive action or if it is merely a necessary evil one must contend with as a result of reality. While some rabbis see military training as a positive achievement and one that the soldier must undertake with enthusiasm and conviction (Shilat 1988; Wolansky 1997), others take a more skeptical view. In their opinion, military service is necessary, but there is nothing positive about it. Wolansky illustrates through the use of religious sources that in a time of need such as obligatory war, soldiers must realize that they are the only thing standing between the enemy and their people, and that it is their religious duty to be prepared for the moment of battle to the very best of their ability. What can be more positive and noble than such an undertaking? Conversely, others, such as Lichtenstein, posit that a yeshiva opposes Plato's view that military training builds character and good citizenship. One must pray for a time when there will be no need for conscription and all will be free to devote their lives to Torah. In the meanwhile, if Israel is to survive as a state, there is no choice but to prepare for war (Lichtenstein 2002).

Additional rabbis are able to see positive elements within military training. Rabbi Tzfaniya Drori, the head of the Hesder yeshiva in Kiryat Shmona, for example, notes that while Torah study is always the focal point of Jewish life, military training teaches young men constructive principles and behavior that will follow them for their entire lives. For instance, he notes that soldiers learn the value of time and how to use it optimally. This skill can be utilized not only for war, but also for study. Accordingly, a young man who returns to study after military service is a far better student who is able to concentrate more and utilize his time to the fullest. A true Talmid Hakham (Torah scholar) can only be one who has gone through military training and mastered such skills (Drori 2001, 777).

Clearly, there are many schools of thought on the religious attitude toward military service, even in a time of obligatory war. However, it is safe to say that mainstream Religious Zionist rabbis all view this service as a religious obligation stemming from the fact that Israel can be classified as being in the religious category of obligatory war.

"Thou shall not stand idly by your brother's blood," "Shall your brothers go to war while you sit here?," and Draft Evasion as a Desecration of God's Name.
Most of Religious Zionist society does not hold that Torah studies exempt one from serving in the military in the case of obligatory war. Likewise, it does not accept the view that it is preferable for some sectors of society to shoulder the burden of military service in order to enable others to study Torah, as does the ultra-Orthodox sector in Israel. This view is based on the idea that a person who does not serve in the military, and therefore does not make the attempt to save others from danger, is hereby transgressing explicit halakhic commandments. The most common examples used by the Religious Zionist sector are "Shall your brothers go to war while you sit here?," from the story of the tribes of Reuven, Gad, and half of the tribe of Menashe, who were ordered to set out to war with the rest of the Israelite tribes, even though the battle was not for their land (Numbers 32), and the commandment "thou shall not idly stand by your brother's blood" (Leviticus 19:16). The latter forbids a person to stand by when someone is about to be killed. He must help the person in danger; failure to do so is a sin. This assistance includes military service, which protects all citizens of Israel.

According to Moses's address to the tribes of Reuven, Gad, and half the tribe of Menashe (who wished to settle on the eastern bank of the Jordan River before the other tribes reached the Land of Israel after the Exodus), it is unfair for some of the Israelites to claim their land and settle down while others must still fight. Religious Zionist rabbis use this example as a model for modern times. As Rabbi Cherlow, the head of the Hesder yeshiva in Petach Tikva explained, "It is a serious moral transgression to trust to others to protect you and not take part in the partnership of [those going out to] war" (Cherlow n.d.). Rabbi Cherlow goes on to add that service in the military engenders social cohesion, which is of great importance in the Israel of today from both a halakhic point of view and a social one.

Other similar arguments in favor of service in the IDF posit that shirking the burden of military service brings about *hilul ha-shem*, the desecration of God's name (Lichtenstein 2002, 19; cf. Z. Melamed 1986, 333). *Hilul ha-shem* is a halakhic term that refers to any action causing dishonor or shame to God's name, or behavior that might bring—even indirectly—the public to disrespect the Torah. As described in Babylonian Talmud (BT) Tractate Yoma (86a), if a Torah scholar behaves immorally, the public links his immorality to his studies. This not only causes embarrassment, as it were, to the Torah itself and to God, but also to the colleagues of the said immoral scholar. The text gives another example for *hilul ha-shem*: "One whose friends are ashamed of his reputation" (ibid.). Despicable behavior has implications, and if a Torah scholar is considered by the public to be a bad person, it is understood that the public will see the entire community of Torah scholars in the same light.

In a similar vein, those who utilize this argument in connection with conscription feel that young men who use religious study as a way to avoid conscription cause the public to view the entire community of scholars as imposters: studying Torah in order to avoid having to go to battle and all that this includes. They enjoy security due to those who serve, but refuse to shoulder the same burden. Therefore, receiving a deferment in order to study Torah, as do most members of the ultra-Orthodox sector, is considered negative behavior that affects the social group (the "friends") of those who behave in this way. Thus, those who use this argument in the context of service in the IDF see avoiding conscription as behavior which brings about *hilul ha-shem*.[17]

*Military Service as Civil Behavior (*Derekh Eretz*), and as a Civic Duty*

To quote Rabbi Shmuel Haber, the head of the Hesder yeshiva in Karnei Shomron: "Saving lives [. . .] is one of the central deeds of loving-kindness (*hesed*) at the national level which a person can do for the good of the people of Israel" (Haber 2005). In other words, serving in the military, in Haber's view, is a way of doing good according to the most basic meaning of the term.

Rabbi Cherlow explicitly points out the element of civic duty in relation to service in the IDF:

> Some of the aspects of the status of a king [the crowning of whom is an affirmative commandment—*mitzvat as'e*—according to Maimonides] are given to the government in his absence. The military is part of the commandment of appointing a king and forming a political entity, and we fulfill this commandment partially by obeying the State's law regarding conscription. (Cherlow n.d.)

There are also those who view service in the IDF not only as a religious obligation, but also as an act of loving-kindness toward the rest of the people of Israel:

In our circumstances [those of the State of Israel at the present], service in the IDF is the most outstanding expression of a much more comprehensive value: that of acts of loving-kindness (*gmilut hasadim*), the most outstanding *hesed* is the very protection of another's life. (Lichtenstein 2002, 23)

Or, as Rabbi Haber puts it, a person who wants to be a true Torah scholar must "bear the burden" and take part in the trials and tribulations of his society. There is no doubt that such a scholar will serve in the military together with the rest of the people of Israel, as this is "the heaviest burden which is borne by almost every family in Israel" (Haber 2005). Thus, to begin with,

anyone who is involved only in study, without simultaneously carrying out other commandments with the same dedication, cuts off the branch on which he is sitting [. . .] and it cannot be that the result of this very same [act of] study will prevent him from reaching the ultimate level of acting with *hesed* toward the public; we think at this time that the [true] act of *hesed* is *ezrat Yisrael miyad tzar.* (Haber 2005)

Put differently, rabbis from the Religious Zionist school of thought see military service as a way of supporting the community to which the students of Torah belong. They cannot remove themselves from the community for the sake of study, as it is morally wrong and indicates a serious flaw in one's value system as a religious person. A true scholar would never see study as more important than acting with *hesed* toward his community.

There are halakhic counterarguments to the issues depicted here, raised mainly by the ultra-Orthodox camp. However, the view prevailing in the Religious Zionist camp at the beginning of the twenty-first century is: "It is the *straightforward* halakhic view [that religious youngsters must serve in the IDF], and any other opinions are those that must be explained and apologized for" (emphasis in the original, Shilat 1988, 50).

The Ramifications of the Halakhic and Ideological Aspects of the Arguments
The formation in 1965 of the Hesder yeshiva system—which for the first time enabled the combination of Torah study with service in the military—raised a halakhic debate as to how this arrangement should be treated.[18] Rabbis disagreed whether the yeshiva embodied an option that should be considered ideal (*lekhathila*; meaning that this was the option that must be acted upon ex ante), or whether it is ex post facto (*bedi'avad*; meaning that this is a permissible solution that came about following circumstantial pressures, but is not the ideal first choice). Presently,

those who view the Hesder option as ideal are a majority, and thus one should undoubtedly study and then interrupt one's studies and enlist. Most of the heads of the Hesder yeshivot view this option as the optimal one, and see the Hesder yeshiva student as the epitome of the ideal Torah student (Drori 2001, 766); they do not feel that this is a compromise.[19] It should nevertheless be noted that there is also a minority who view Hesder yeshivot as an ex post facto solution, rather than an optimal one.[20]

Two other programs for men were established later: the Shiluv program and the Mekhinot. Unlike the Hesder yeshivot, there was no halakhic debate about whether these programs were ideal solutions or acceptable only after the fact. The programs were based on an unquestioning acceptance of the halakhic view concerning the moral and religious obligation to serve a full-length term in the IDF. These two programs maintain that Torah studies cannot be at the expense of military service and cannot exempt yeshiva students from service which equals— both in terms of the time served and the nature of service—that of other soldiers. This view will be discussed in detail in Chapter 4.

Women's Military Service: Halakhic and Social Dilemmas

Both Religious Zionism and ultra-Orthodoxy were opposed to the idea of the conscription of women even before the founding of the State of Israel. The passing of the legislation establishing mandatory conscription heightened the public debate concerning female conscription; this has been described by the former MK (member of the Knesset, Israel's parliament) Dr. Zerah Wahrhaftig, a member of the Ha-Poel Ha-Mizrahi political party and one of the signatories of the Declaration of Independence (Wahrhaftig 1988, 238–261). While ultra-Orthodox opposition was based mainly on halakhic reasons, the Religious Zionists opposed female conscription mainly on grounds related to their worldview. The ultra-Orthodox community is of the opinion that halakha forbids female conscription, while Religious Zionists view it as creating problematic situations from a moral point of view, leading to behavior incompatible with the Religious Zionist way of life. Coed life in uniform is not the same as riding a bus with the opposite sex or sitting in a mixed class in a university. Unlike civilian life, where individuals return to their homes and their social rules of conduct at the end of the day, soldiers do not have this luxury. As MK Moshe Una (Ha-Poel Ha-Mizrahi) remarked during the debate in the Knesset:

> A military and civil framework are not comparable and one does not
> have to be an ultra-Orthodox [individual] from [the ultra-Orthodox

neighborhood of] Mea She'arim to oppose [female] conscription. (Protocols of the First Knesset 1949, 1522)

The religious parties were joined on this point by representatives of the Muslim and Christian minorities, who wished to exempt the women of their communities from mandatory conscription. By the end of the debate, a compromise was reached: religious Jewish women and non-Jewish women would be able to "solemnly declare" that service in the military is contrary to their religious beliefs and would receive an exemption from military duty. All other women would be subject to the draft.

The religious parties remained opposed to female conscription in general, but they accepted this compromise and stayed in the coalition (Wahrhaftig 1988, 244). The agreed-upon declaration that religious women sign affirming that they are unable to serve in the military due to "religious and moral considerations" is still used as a way to exempt religious females from military service, including those belonging to the Religious Zionist sector.

The IDF itself has always accepted that a woman may declare herself unable to serve in the military due to her observance of the Sabbath and adherence to kashrut. Approximately 70 percent of female graduates of the Religious Zionist educational system exercise their right to declare their incompatibility with military service due to religious considerations; most of these women go on to National Service (Lasloi and Rich 2001, 81), as discussed further in the next chapter.

In practice, the opposition to female conscription was a battle fought mainly by the ultra-Orthodox camp, since even as the political debate raged on the floor of the Knesset, women from the Religious Zionist camp were serving in the IDF, usually in religious frameworks in the NAHAL battalion during the period of Israel's foundation (Rosenberg-Friedman 2005). However, as far as presenting a united front in the Knesset was concerned, the Religious Zionist sector joined the ultra-Orthodox cause. The Religious Kibbutz Movement, on the other hand, opposed the stand taken by the religious parties, and the executive council of the Ha-Poel Ha-Mizrahi organization called upon its female members not to take advantage of the declaration and to continue enlisting in the NAHAL's religious units. Even after the subsequent Chief Rabbinate's ruling that female conscription is absolutely prohibited from a halakhic point of view, the Religious Kibbutz Movement continued to encourage its women to enlist in the IDF, considering it a matter of principle. They were not alone in this: in spite of the Chief Rabbinate's ruling, young religious women continued to enlist in the IDF, joining units that were not limited to the NAHAL, while attempting to deal with the attendant halakhic problems.

In the eyes of most of the Religious Zionist camp, women serving in the military pose a problem due to several halakhic and social considerations:

- A woman is prohibited from participating in battle, since this goes against her nature and abilities.
- Due to modesty considerations, a woman should not wear men's clothing (Deuteronomy 26:5). This includes equipment used exclusively by men, such as weapons.
- In Jewish Orthodoxy, the conduct expected of women is usually based on the verse "A princess's honor is within"—*kol kvuda bat melekh pnima* (Psalms 45:14), which serves as a catchphrase meaning "conduct becoming a respectable [Jewish] woman." This verse serves as the basis for every requirement that women not be involved in public life and that they conduct themselves in a modest fashion. One might phrase this as a requirement to refrain from unsuitable behavior, and this is expected of every Jewish woman, religious or otherwise. As such, a respectable woman should not enlist in the military, where the general codes of behavior and lack of modesty are incompatible with the behavior expected from a woman (Sela 2012; Budaie-Hyman 2012).
- A woman should be under her father's authority until her marriage (*marut aviha*), following which she should be under her husband's authority. She cannot be under the authority of a strange man (such as a military commander), especially not as a married woman.

Some of these prohibitions (being under male authority, *kol kvuda*) are also relevant for women who wish to join the National Service program, and some rabbis see them as preventing women from joining any public service program whatsoever, whether in uniform or not.

A booklet published by the Ne'emnai Torah Va-Avoda Movement and the Religious Kibbutz Movement, which support conscription, addresses these arguments in order to allow young women to view the halakhic sources on the subject independently. The booklet illustrates the halakhic arguments permitting service both in the IDF and in the National Service program. The main argument is that in a time of obligatory war, women, like men, are obligated to take part in the military effort (as discussed above). The legal opinions presented in this pamphlet refer to the view that it is preferable for women to serve in special units for religious women, similar to those of the Hesder program (Y. Cohen 1994, 26;

Shaviv 1994, 79–89), and certainly as far away from combat as possible. On the other hand, other rabbis (such as Rabbi Min Ha-Har 1983, 68–78) rule that women should not enlist in the military at all. True, ostensibly women are required to take part in obligatory war. However, their actual role on the battlefield is unclear from the religious sources. In any case, even if it were accepted that they should serve in uniform, present conditions in the IDF concerning codes of modesty are completely unsatisfactory. Additionally, most of the posts filled by women in the IDF are not vital, but rather secretarial jobs. For all the above reasons, these rabbis posit that women should request an exemption from military service (see, for instance, Aviner 2000 Part I, 342–355).

In light of the public debate and prevailing public opinion, approximately 70 percent of women from the Religious Zionist sector declare they cannot serve in the IDF "for reasons of religion and conscience" and are given exemptions (Lasloi and Rich 2001, 81).[21] Most of these women serve a year or two in the National Service program in a variety of posts.[22] About 1 percent of women who sign the declaration do not serve at all (Lasloi and Rich 2001, 81).[23] At present, there are still members of religious society who prohibit women's service in the National Service program for halakhic reasons,[24] or hold that women may serve for one year only.[25]

ISSUES OF IDENTITY

In twenty-first-century Israel, service in the IDF is still perceived as a rite of passage and a formative experience (Ben-Ari and Levy-Schreiber 2001; S. Cohen 2004, 2). Young people, both religious and secular, anticipate their enlistment and prepare themselves for it. In this sense, there is no rivalry or competition between the two systems in question: Religious Zionism and the IDF. The Religious Zionist framework does not question conscription of males and does not officially sanction conscription for females who choose this option. The competition is instead over forming the identity of the student-soldier. The lack of any kind of supervision over a religious soldier and the inability to maintain a desirable religious and social environment are a source of great unease for the religious establishment in regard to the military's influence over a religious individual's identity and behavior. On this level, anxiety takes two forms. One stems from the view of the military as a corrupting environment, which potentially enables religious soldiers to abandon their religious obligations. The other is rooted in the ramifications of the social interaction between young people from the Religious Zionist sector and other segments of Israeli society.

The Military as a Corrupting Environment

The fear of erosion of personal religious values during service in the military prevails mainly among the leadership of the Religious Zionist camp, but students, too, are concerned about moral "deterioration" during their time in uniform.[26] This view is not unique to Religious Zionist society, as the establishment of secular and mixed Mekhinot proves. Israeli society as a whole realizes military service may have an adverse effect on individual conduct, but Religious Zionism fears this possibility perhaps more than most.

The military's influence over soldiers as far as religious observance is concerned is also a source of apprehension in the Religious Zionist sector, since the IDF presents an opportunity for these youths to abandon their religious obligations. The greatest concern is not only that the individual is influenced by the military's problematic environment, but that the next generation of Religious Zionist society will be affected. The IDF may be the cause of its estrangement from a religious lifestyle, and, as such, is a threat to the existence of the Religious Zionist sector.

In spite of these grave concerns, rabbis from the Religious Zionist camp have written little on these issues. Part of the attempt to thwart secularization can be seen in the trend to point religious male conscripts—and recently also female conscripts—toward programs that combine studies in a yeshiva framework. The underlying assumption being that Torah studies will enrich these soldiers—as has been the case for those before them—but, no less importantly, will encourage them to maintain a Religious Zionist lifestyle during and after their military service. Joining such programs consciously sets up the yeshiva as competing with the military's influence over the conscript, but this is not necessarily a bid to undermine the IDF's authority. The argument, at least as it is presented, is that the problem lies mainly with a

> conflict of values, lifestyle, and a feeling of a contradiction between the yeshiva and basic training, especially since the IDF is overwhelmingly secular. The danger is not so much that students will abandon their religion or their commitment to the Torah and their religious obligations [. . .] the main danger is one of erosion—the loss of subtlety, nobility, and a blunting of religious and moral sensitivities which might arise from exposure to the rough aspects of reality. (Lichtenstein 2002, 20)

This is also the message perceived by the students and will be discussed in detail in the following chapters.

It should be emphasized that the "deterioration" is not necessarily caused merely by being in a secular environment. As pointed out in Rabbi Lichtenstein's opinion cited here, there are elements inherent to the military itself that bring about a moral deterioration for religious and secular soldiers alike. The military system in and of itself, by definition, is morally corrupting. Teaching young men and women to kill and be prepared to be killed in war is not acceptable behavior according to civilian morals and values. In a military setting, these ideas are the basis on which the system is built. The fact that the IDF felt the need to establish an ethical code indicates that it is aware of this issue.

The problematic nature of the military affects Israeli society as a whole, but the argument set forth by the rabbis is that young people from Religious Zionist society find it somewhat more difficult to navigate the system. In order to face this difficulty, there are two approaches espoused by the heads of the preservice study programs. One attaches a degree of sanctity to service in the IDF and sees it as a necessity that also has positive aspects. The other approach accepts that service in the military is necessary, but views it mainly as problematic. This approach, led by Rabbi Lichtenstein, sees service in the IDF as a necessary evil.

The rabbis of the Hesder yeshivot do not present the yeshiva as a way of "inoculating" their students against the negative influence of service in the IDF or as a way of serving in a sheltered environment. These might be laudable side effects, but according to the rabbis, they are not aims in themselves. As Rabbi Lichtenstein puts it: "Hesder does not offer only a religious shelter for those who are apprehensive of the routine of military life—although indirectly is does usually, in part, serve as such" (2002, 14). According to most of the rabbis of the Hesder program, first and foremost these yeshivot enable serious study. Since the student is in the yeshiva during most of his military service, and when he is in the IDF he serves in a unit with his fellow Hesder students, it is hoped that the military's influence will be minimal (Lichtenstein 2002; Shilat 1988).

On the other hand, the problematic aspects of service in the military, such as the rough and vulgar behavior encountered by the yeshiva students, are seen as a price that must be paid for being able to participate in the service. This is also considered a way to engender a change in society and to bring the people of Israel closer to the "right" values. As Rabbi Avraham Yitzchak Kook puts it in his famous—and widely studied in the Mekhinot—paper, *Ma'amar Ha-Dor*, it is hard to see how "dignified and dear [people] disgrace and lower themselves until they themselves forget their honor and dignity." And part of the reason one should serve in the IDF and face such behavior is in order to change it.

Unlike the approach of the Hesder program, the Mekhinot and the Shiluv programs are not in favor of religious soldiers serving in separate units. Their hope is that studying before military service will enable the student to withstand the pressures and difficulties encountered by religious soldiers during their service in the military. One could say that this is in stark contrast to the Hesder program. Metaphorically speaking, it is known that on her eighteenth birthday the princess will see the spindle. The Hesder program prefers to minimize all possible contact between the princess and the spindle; even hoping she will avoid seeing one and thus escape her fate of becoming Sleeping Beauty. The Mekhinot and Shiluv programs take another view. These programs allow the princess to be aware of the spindle and the curse set upon her, so that at the moment of truth she will know to be careful not to prick her finger, and thus not meet her foreseen fate: becoming Sleeping Beauty. In most cases, these programs are in favor of explaining the spindle's nature and teaching caution. Having said this, not every program is of the opinion that the princess should also be taught how to spin.

In other words, Religious Zionism sees the IDF as a potentially corrupting environment with respect to morals, values, and the general observance of a religious way of life. It takes this issue very seriously. One way to confront this difficulty is through preservice study programs that either ensure the young men will not encounter a serious threat to their way of life or attempt to prepare them for this encounter and give them tools for managing the dissonance they will encounter.

Cultural Encounters: Religious Zionism as a Cultural Minority
Since the foundation of the State of Israel, the IDF has played a part in the social arena, encompassing roles beyond its definition as a defense force, and has been involved in issues such as immigration, education, and maintaining settlements, as well as functioning as a social melting pot. All this has an effect on forming the soldiers' identity. As put in the Israeli Democracy Institute's project on the military and society in Israel:

> The IDF indirectly contributes to Israeli society by exerting a moral influence on youngsters during their military service. A young adult leaves the military having become acquainted with, and having become accustomed to living with, the multicultural characteristics of Israeli society [. . .]. Experiences of this kind to a certain degree shape a soldier's personality and he emerges from the army equipped to deal with civilian life. (Nevo and Shor 2002, 6–25)

In the military, youngsters from Religious Zionist society come across a conceptual world different from that in which they grew up. Most Religious Zionist youth grow up exposed to Hollywood, Facebook, and Western consumerism, to various extents. In the twenty-first century they are Internet savvy, understand technology, and are certainly a part of Western-oriented Israeli society for better and for worse. In this respect it's not possible to compare them to the Amish in the United States, or even to ultra-Orthodox youth in Israel itself. However, even though these are usually not youngsters raised in a cloistered and exclusively religious society, the process they undergo during military service is significant.

The severe impact of the direct encounter with secular society upon youngsters from the Religious Zionist sector has already been discussed (S. Cohen 2004; Tor-Paz 2005). Language, general behavior, and the attitude toward women all cause shock and distress for religious youth. A soldier from the Hesder program serving in a mixed unit (composed of secular and religious soldiers) describes it thus:

> I shall begin by describing my unit, for those who are unfamiliar with such things. Secular society is hedonist, and behavior is not motivated by values and morals. Stealing someone else's personal equipment happens on a regular basis. The argument against this is: "Don't steal something that will make the owner start searching for it or get too annoyed." This means that you can finish all of someone's candy or take his batteries, but don't take his electric shaver (or you can take it, use it, and not put it back, or put it where it still might fall or something like that). Women are treated like sexual objects. I don't even want to think of some of the words they use for women. For them, "girlfriend" means something completely different from what we [in Religious Zionist society] mean. Halakha doesn't permit me to expound on this topic. The language used, the way they talk, and what they talk about fall somewhere between pure foolishness and things that halakha forbids us to discuss. I don't want to expand upon this. (Tzviran 2005)

This, of course, is a subjective view, and possibly not applicable to every unit of the IDF. However, research shows that to a large degree this is representative of the sentiments of Religious Zionist conscripts when they find themselves in the military.[27] Youngsters from Religious Zionist society find themselves in a state of culture shock when they enlist.[28] Such an encounter, which is harsh enough as it is, is sometimes exacerbated by the rigid nature of the military environment. This observation does not mitigate the difficulty encountered by every conscript when trying to adapt to the military environment; one should, however, take into consideration that a unique dimension comes into play in the case of Religious Zionist conscripts.

* * *

Recent years have witnessed significant changes in the relationship between the IDF and Israeli society in general, and between the IDF and Religious Zionist society in particular. Despite these changes, in its present form, the IDF still reflects the consociational nature associated with Israel.

A consociational democracy recognizes the existence of minorities but generally refrains from regulating disputed social issues. When regulation is unavoidable, however, the relative size of the minority is taken into consideration (Lijphart 1969, 207–225). Accordingly, the IDF has tried to avoid unilateral and compulsory regulation in issues pertaining to religion. An obvious example is the IDF's view that the drafting of yeshiva students is a matter best left to the political echelon and is not analogous to conscientious objectors, who are dealt with through the military-legal system. While in the past this was the accepted view of Israeli politics and Israel was described as a consocialist state (Horowitz and Lissak 1990), today this view is challenged and scholars do not automatically accept this definition (for example: Peres and Ben-Rafael 2007). Whatever the case may be, the IDF still reflects the consocialist nature once more obviously detected in Israel.

Given this sensitivity, as the presence of religious soldiers in all IDF units— and especially field units—has increased, both the military's and their own view of their status has changed (S. Cohen 1997). This new consciousness tracks more general changes in the arranged structure of Israel and in the relations between the IDF and Israeli society (Nevo and Shor 2001; 2001b; 2002; 2002b). The IDF is no longer seen as a sacred institution that is immune to outside assessment. There are criticisms and demands for accountability.

Religious Zionist attitudes toward the IDF and military service have also evolved. The desire to be part of the military establishment and reach higher ranks has grown among Religious Zionist youth, but voices critical of the military have also multiplied. In some Religious Zionist circles this criticism has taken on a political cast in the context of the IDF's functioning in the Territories and especially in light of its central role in the evacuation of Jewish settlers from Gush Katif in Gaza and from northern Samaria in the summer of 2005.

One of the premises of this book is that mediating structures are the main mechanisms that enable coexistence and even cooperation between greedy institutions. In the case of the IDF and Religious Zionism, there are a number of mediating structures, but this situation is not unique. The IDF maintains separate arrangements for several different sectors of Israeli society. These arrangements entail service in homogeneous units and/or special conditions of service: for example, the NAHAL program for children of agricultural settlements (NAHAL Bnei Meshakim), the Atuda program for professional school students (similar to the ROTC program in the U.S. military), the Herev Druze Battalion, the Bedouin reconnaissance unit, the NAHAL Haredi Battalion (Netzah Yehuda), as well as special programs for outstanding musicians and athletes, and options of SHALAT and deferring service in the military.[29] Each of these arrangements did not necessarily develop due to security reasons, but rather grew out of political and social considerations (Nevo and Shor 2002, 29–30).

In each of these cases, the military had to create a bureaucratic framework able to address the paperwork and logistics of the group in question. In the case of Religious Zionism, the military office responsible is the Department of Yeshiva Students (Mador BENISH) in the IDF's Manpower Division (AKA). (From 2006 to 2008, the Manpower Division was known as the Human Resources Division.)

Separate from Mador BENISH, there is also an internal military intermediary that is unequivocally part of the IDF itself and whose job it is to mediate between the military system and its religiously observant soldiers of any stripe. This is the Military Rabbinate. As noted earlier, the chaplain phenomenon is not unique to the IDF, nor is it new. It is an accepted feature of Western militaries such as that of the United States, where there are chaplains of many denominations. Chaplains typically are responsible for the religious needs of all religious soldiers in their unit, regardless of denomination. This is not the case in the IDF, where non-Jewish soldiers receive religious services from civilian clergymen of their own faith—although the head of the Military Rabbinate's public relations unit is formally responsible for providing for their religious needs (IDF Spokesperson's Office 2005).[30]

Accordingly, military chaplains in the IDF are known as military rabbis and are part of the Military Rabbinate. Following General Staff Regulations, the Military Rabbinate must address the religious and halakhic needs of soldiers in the IDF. It is mandated to respond to the demands of soldiers interested in contact with a religious figure in various situations, and thus it deals with the religious spiritual needs of soldiers as well (Michaelson 1982, 88; Kampinsky 2007). It is possible that the original goal was for the Military Rabbinate to also address any tensions between the IDF as a greedy institution and Religious Zionism and its soldiers.[31]

In the past, despite the official role of the Military Rabbinate, soldiers from Religious Zionist society did not take it very seriously (see, for instance, Harel

1999; Schiff 2004). Religious soldiers who studied in one of the preservice Torah frameworks (to be described below) tended to rely more on their rabbis and teachers from these institutions than on the Military Rabbinate (Guttel 2000). When faced with a halakhic dilemma, they usually turned either to their rabbis from their Torah study programs or to civilians.[32]

Since the appointment of Brigadier General Rabbi Yisrael Weiss as chief military rabbi (2000–2006), and more so during the service of his successors Rabbis Avi Rontzki (2006–2010) and Rafi Peretz (2010–), the status of the Military Rabbinate, as perceived by the graduates of the yeshivot, the Mekhinot, and other programs dedicated to Torah studies, has been much improved. Due to his experience as the former head of a yeshiva, Rabbi Rontzki was attuned to the mindset of these soldiers. He is also considered a Torah scholar of some standing. In recent years, students—and especially Hesder students—have commented that the various preservice Torah study programs encourage their graduates to consult the Military Rabbinate. For instance, Rabbi Eliezer Sheinwald, a former teacher at the Golan Hesder yeshiva who is also a deputy brigade commander (res.) and the current head of the Modi'in Shesder yeshiva, has stated unequivocally that he and his yeshiva encourage students to turn to the Military Rabbinate for assistance and halakhic rulings during their military service (Sheinwald, first interview). However, the change has not been dramatic, and usually the graduates of the study programs still prefer to consult their own rabbis.[33] In this respect, the Military Rabbinate does not function as a significant mediating structure, at least in comparison to preservice study programs.

The structures accommodating specific types of soldiers during their service in the IDF depicted in the following chapters have certain characteristics. These programs all "accompany" their members a full cycle: from before their induction into the IDF, during their service, and, to varying extents, after their discharge. This is unlike some other programs where support is not given as part of a comprehensive program. They are all voluntary frameworks in the sense that their members enter and use their services voluntarily. These programs target a very specific social group—members of Religious Zionism—and aim to support and accompany the members of this group during their military service; they are not open to other groups (like secular or mixed Mekhinot). And, finally, they are outside the military sphere and originate from within the Religious Zionist framework. When assessing their actions, these programs have proven to be effective mediators between Religious Zionism and the IDF.

In the following pages, we shall discuss each of the study programs. After a general presentation of each program, the courses of study, the demographics of the students, and the manner in which the programs prepare their students for military service, we shall discuss what students expect from the institutions they attend. In doing so, we shall be able to better understand whether these programs indeed function as mediating structures between the students and the superstructures (Religious Zionism and the IDF).

Following the challenges illustrated in this chapter, a number of formal solutions have been fashioned. Each solution addresses the three issues discussed here (practical problems, halakhic and value-based difficulties, and identity formation) differently. The Hesder yeshivot, the Shiluv program, the religious Mekhinot, and the Gar'in program take these three aspects seriously and try to address the challenges therein—each in its own way—which will be described in the following chapters.

The next four chapters survey the basic characteristics of the study programs that are the focus of this book, as well as their philosophical-educational approach. They also include a general survey of student expectations from their study programs—what prompted them to join a specific program and what they expected from their study program after their induction into the IDF. After surveying the programs and understanding the way they function, the ninth chapter of the book will consider a more detailed discussion of their roles as mediators.

CHAPTER 4
THE HESDER YESHIVOT

As of 2010, there were forty-three Hesder yeshivot in Israel. In 2003 almost four thousand students in active service (SHARAP) and unpaid service (SHALAT) attended these institutions (Brun, first interview).[1] According to more recent numbers, approximately 1,700 young men are inducted every year through the Hesder program (Hager-Lau, second interview). While participating in the Hesder program, students attend the yeshiva for approximately eighteen months and then enlist for active service for another eighteen months.[2] After their active service, the students return to their yeshiva for twenty-six months of unpaid service, completing the five years of the program. The various stages of this program have evolved over the years, and the course outlined here is the one followed today.[3] Following the changes regarding the induction of the ultra-Orthodox community discussed in the wake of the 2013 elections, Hesder service is to be lengthened by one month, but this change has yet to be legislated formally.

Two administrative bodies have been established to deal with the yeshiva students. The military has created the Mador BENISH, or Mador Bnei Yeshivot (the Department of Yeshiva Students in the IDF's Manpower Division), and the yeshivot themselves have the Igud, or Igud Yeshivot Ha-Hesder (the Association of Hesder Yeshivot). These offices address all the technical aspects of the Hesder program, such as registration, military stationing, and so on. At the time the main body of research for this study was conducted, the head of the Igud was Rabbi Avraham Brun. As of 2008, this post has been filled by Mr. Eitan Ozeri. There are no parallel administrative offices for the other study programs.

The official functions of the Igud are to coordinate all technical matters of conscription between the IDF and the yeshivot and to distribute funding from various government sources among the yeshivot. The Igud reports to the IDF the number of Hesder students who will be drafted each year and actively participates in determining the students' military assignments, subject to the military's requirements. The head of the Igud may also address problems that Hesder students encounter during their service. His position and personal ties afford him relatively easy access to army officials, and problems are usually solved efficiently (see below).[4]

For their part, the yeshivot recognize the Igud's importance in their relationship with the IDF: "The military does not want to have to deal with each yeshiva separately; to construct programs, to establish relationships, etc."

(Lichtenstein, first interview). It seems, accordingly, that all the involved parties favor giving the Igud a relatively free rein. The heads of the yeshivot would rather concentrate on teaching Torah and educating their students, leaving the administrative aspects to the Igud. The military benefits by accepting soldiers into predetermined posts and by not having to work out rules and regulations with each individual yeshiva. All the heads of the yeshivot interviewed stated that the Igud's role is purely administrative; in no way does it influence curriculum or internal yeshiva affairs.

THE NATURE AND STRUCTURE OF THE HESDER PROGRAM

The Hesder yeshiva program was established in 1965. The first yeshiva to follow this program was the Kerem Be-Yavneh yeshiva, which was headed by Rabbi Chaim Goldwicht. The identity of the true spiritual father of the Hesder program is disputed. According to the more well-known version of the program's history, Rabbi Goldwicht devised the concept, even if he was not in favor of the program initially (S. Cohen 1997, 106–109). According to another version, the late Rabbi Yehuda Amital, later the head of the Hesder yeshiva of Har Etzion, was the progenitor. In this version, he suggested the idea to Rabbi Goldwicht because Kerem Be-Yavneh was affiliated with the Religious Zionist Bnei Akiva youth movement, the members of which wanted to enlist as one group (gar'in). Since the yeshiva had the proper connections, Rabbi Amital felt it fitting to start the program there (Amital, first interview). So that the yeshiva students would be entitled to unpaid service (SHALAT), the program was based on the central concept of the NAHAL Bnei Meshakim, thus allowing them to attend yeshiva and to serve in the military in a homogenous unit, with the hope that this would maintain a religious atmosphere and facilitate the students' religious observance.

Whichever version one adopts, the Hesder course of service was officially recognized in 1968. Shortly after that, Hesder soldiers began to serve in the Armored Corps rather than in the NAHAL Battalion, apparently in line with the IDF's manpower requirements for this force (Amital, first interview).

In the following years, other yeshivot were established. The first ones were established immediately after the Six Day War: Har Etzion in the Gush Etzion region and Yeshivat Ha-Kotel in the Old City of Jerusalem. As mentioned above, by the end of the first decade of the twenty-first century there are forty-three Hesder yeshivot with over four thousand students (Ozeri, first interview).

Each of these yeshivot forges its own educational path. Some share conceptual and educational ideals; some disagree over a broad range of issues from the way one should view military service and extended service within the officers' corps to the definition of a desirable curriculum and the proper age of marriage for a yeshiva student.

Some yeshivot focus on a particular message. The Hesder yeshiva in Yerucham, for instance, has an obvious social agenda. Politically, the Har Etzion yeshiva is considered to lean to the left of the political map. Those in Mitzpe Ramon, Kiryat Arba, Or Etzion, and the Golan are considered to be more closely affiliated with the Merkaz Ha-Rav yeshiva and the teachings of Rabbi Kook. The preceding is merely a sampler of the multitude of ways in which the Hesder yeshivot differ from each other and by which each institution gives voice to its unique character.

With respect to differences in their attitudes toward army service, the Golan yeshiva promotes the importance of military service and volunteering for officer training, while the Har Etzion yeshiva sees military service as a necessary evil; an obligation to be carried out so that one can then return to studying with a clear conscience. The Hesder yeshivot in Shiloh and Karnei Shomron consider the idea of the Hesder program an ideal to be followed ex ante (*lekhathila*), while the yeshiva in Mitzpe Ramon views military service in the Hesder program as a solution following the pressures put upon yeshiva students to serve in the IDF, and it is to be done ex post facto (*bedi'avad*).

In order to become an official Hesder yeshiva, qualifying for a part of the budgetary pie, the custom has been for a new institution to pass a sort of "admissions committee" made up of several representative heads of the existing institutions. In the past the approval of this committee was a requirement for recognition as a Hesder yeshiva by the relevant ministries of the Israeli government (the funding sources) and by the IDF. In the past decade, it became possible to request government recognition without passing muster in the committee; however, yeshivot candidates still generally seek endorsement from the committee (Amital, first interview). Without such approval, study programs have encountered difficulties obtaining government funding through the Igud.

In addition to government funding, the budget of the Hesder yeshivot is also made up of tuition paid by the students' parents and donations. Monthly tuition in a Hesder yeshiva is paid for by the students' parents during the entire time spent by the student in the Hesder program. Not all students pay full tuition—some receive full scholarships—and a student's acceptance is not conditional upon his financial status.[5]

It is thus clear that the percentage of the yeshivot's budget based on governmental sources varies from one yeshiva to another, according to both the ability of each yeshiva to procure donations and the tuition paid by its students. However, the accepted estimate for a Hesder yeshiva budget is approximately one-third from tuition, one-third government funding, and the final third from donations.

PROGRAM CHARACTERISTICS AND MILITARY SERVICE AS A HESDER STUDENT

Students at a yeshiva are typically not all the same age, and in this sense, studies at the yeshiva are of an intergenerational nature. Due to the length and structure of the program, students are either pre- or postservice, and there are some students who stay on to study after the end of their five years. The yeshivot take educational advantage of the age range, making it customary for an older student (postservice) to study with a first-year student as a study partner (*havruta*) during the independent study session, held in the evening (*seder erev*). This older study partner is termed a *havruta boger*. In addition to the educational benefits, this custom reinforces the bonds between different levels of students, fosters the integration of the younger students into the yeshiva's culture, and is an informal conduit for tips about what to expect from one's stint in the IDF. As we shall see, in interviews students cited both the educational and social importance of the *havruta boger* custom.

Three of the yeshivot examined in depth here, Or Etzion, Mitzpe Ramon, and Petach Tikva, are located next to or within a high school yeshiva, and there is close cooperation between the two institutions. For instance, Petach Tikva Hesder students study once a week with the high school students. The students at the Hesder yeshiva in Yerucham teach twice a week at an elementary school close to the yeshiva. It is apparent that "intergenerational" study is a cardinal educational principle of the Hesder yeshivot.

The military assignments of the students are determined primarily by the manpower requirements of the IDF in coordination with the Igud. In comparison with draftees who enlist immediately at the end of their high school studies or those who study in parallel preservice study programs, Hesder students have fewer options for where to serve. A Hesder student deemed physically fit for active combat may choose between serving in the infantry or volunteering for the Paratroopers Brigade. Student-soldiers who volunteer to serve as paratroopers may do so only if they leave the Hesder program.

Specific military placement for each soldier is decided according to a preexisting agreement between the Igud and the IDF, and each year different infantry brigades receive students from a different yeshiva. For instance, in

2002, conscripts from the Petach Tikva yeshiva were placed in the Mechanized Infantry Corps,[6] in 2003 in the Golani Brigade, and in 2004 in the NAHAL Brigade (Petach Tivka yeshiva 2004). Rabbi Brun did not describe in detail how this placement was carried out and would only say that it was guided by the desire to prevent students from a given yeshiva ending up in the same infantry unit year after year, in order to avoid creating a strong link between a specific yeshiva and a unit. Such a link could bring about a situation in which students who wished to reach a certain unit would choose to study in a specific yeshiva, knowing this choice would enable service in the unit of their choice (Brun, first interview).[7]

Students whose medical profile deems them unfit for infantry service instead serve in the Artillery or the Armored Corps, according to the IDF's needs. Placement is determined in a similar fashion to placement in the infantry, as described above. For instance, in 2003 noninfantry combat students from the Golan yeshiva were placed in the Artillery Corps, and those from Har Etzion were placed in the Armored Corps. Students with a low or poor medical profile are placed in auxiliary and supportive roles, such as Military Intelligence or NCOs in the Military Rabbinate (Brun, first interview). The Hesder students who participated in this research took the issue of placements for granted and did not seem troubled about which exact unit they would serve in, especially in comparison to Mekhinot students, who spent time considering options for service venues. That said, it appears that conscripts with a low medical profile attempted to raise their ranking in order to be given a higher combat rating, and motivation to serve in the infantry is pronounced.[8]

After conscription, Hesder students stationed in infantry units serve in separate platoons (Bnei Yeshivot or BENISH units) within a heterogeneous company made up of other religious and nonreligious soldiers who do not belong to the Hesder program. Following the 2005 initiative of then head of the IDF's Manpower Division, Major General Elazar Stern, some of the yeshivot allow their students to be stationed in heterogeneous units—at least twelve Hesder soldiers are placed in a "regular" platoon with other religious and nonreligious soldiers.[9]

Hesder soldiers serving in the Armored Corps serve in homogenous units until their training is complete. Service within homogenous Hesder units enables the unit to set a daily schedule, including prayer times, and takes into account various religious limitations, such as observing fast days. After completing their training, however, Armored Corps Hesder soldiers are dispersed among the combat units and do not serve together. Noncombat soldiers also do not serve in homogenous Hesder units.

CURRICULUM AND FACULTY

The Hesder yeshivot heads interviewed for this study viewed the yeshiva as a place for Torah study and the nurturing of talented Torah scholars. For them, Hesder is a framework that enables the integration of Torah study with the national need for army service (for example, Weitzman, first interview).[10] They also each emphasized unique features of their own yeshiva. Rabbi Weitzman believed that the role of his yeshiva was to create a community whose members "know what Torah is" and feel a very strong bond to its values while being involved in Israeli society (first interview). By contrast, Rabbi Rabinovitch asserted unequivocally that "as in every generation, the role of the yeshiva is to cultivate Torah scholars." However, the yeshiva must "enable these Torah devotees to also fulfill the commandment of defense of the country and its people" (Rabinovitch, first interview). Rabbis Cherlow and Lichtenstein made a distinction between the educational objectives they set for the individual students and those for the yeshiva—and the country collectively. When considering each individual, the yeshiva should nurture each student, helping him crystallize his identity and sense of self. On the more collective level, the yeshiva is supposed to help create a cadre of citizens who will contribute to the life of the state and the nation by working in the community and embodying moral and Torah values in whatever field they choose to work (Lichtenstein, first interview; Cherlow, first interview).

Rabbi Sugarman of the Golan yeshiva spoke of the importance of placing the role of the yeshiva within the larger context of expanding the settlement of the Golan and strengthening religious life in the area (Sugarman, first interview). Rabbi Blumenzweig noted the role of the yeshiva given its location in the development town of Yerucham:

> In society [in general] there is a feeling that a person donates three years of his life [during military service] to society, and after that he is allowed to look out for his own interests. Here [at the yeshiva] the principle is in some sense entirely the opposite: *Maybe* there is a time when you are preoccupied with yourself [and studying], but after that, throughout your life, you have to find a way for you to give to Am Yisrael.[11] This doesn't end after three years, even after five years [. . .]. Just as we educate [our students] towards prayer and we educate for Torah and to observe the mitzvot—we must educate them towards contributing and [when choosing a profession] to work with others [rather than choose a profession based on how lucrative it is]. (Blumenzweig, first interview)

As mentioned above, this yeshiva's students teach two hours a week at the nearby primary school and participate in other voluntary activities in the community, such as teaching seminars for high school students and taking part in summer camps for children.

In keeping with the general objectives of the Hesder yeshivot, the faculties are composed of rabbis who are themselves Torah scholars. All the yeshiva heads commented upon the importance of the scholarly standing of any rabbi chosen to join the faculty. However, not all the yeshiva heads are looking for the same qualities in potential faculty members. For instance, in Har Etzion, Yerucham, and Ma'ale Adumim, the yeshiva heads emphasized the desire for diversity among the teaching staff. Rabbi Drukman, on the other hand, thought that it was important for each faculty member to hold views "compatible with the yeshiva" and did not mention diversity.

In most of the yeshivot, military service in some form or another was a job requirement, except for the Mitzpe Ramon yeshiva, where the entire approach toward military service is different. Rabbi Drukman of Or Etzion also admitted that military service had never been an actual requirement when hiring faculty, although all the rabbis, past and present, had served in the military: "Whoever comes to us, whoever's worldview is in line with ours, surely served in the military" (Drukman, first interview). The interviewed yeshiva heads further asserted that the identification of a faculty member with the idea of Hesder was important from an educational perspective. Most emphatic on this matter was the head of the Golan yeshiva. Rabbi Sugarman maintained that it is crucial that the faculty believe in the importance of military service and:

> not give the students the feeling that military service is ex post facto (be'diavad) and barely permissible (be'dohak). No, not at all. I would absolutely not accept someone like that [as a member of the faculty]. This has to do with our basic attitude [to military service]. (Sugarman, first interview)

Some of the yeshiva heads said that if someone had been exempt from service due to health issues or for other technical reasons, this would not disqualify him from teaching at a yeshiva. However, such a person's identification with the Hesder program's central idea is important, "otherwise it would be difficult for someone to identify with his students and with the world they live in" (Lichtenstein, first interview).[12]

As mentioned, the curriculum of the Hesder yeshivot examined here concentrates on in-depth Talmud study. The study of halakha is also important.

One of the goals of Talmud study is to give the students the skills necessary for independent study (for instance, Rabinovitch, first interview). Another educational goal is to convey to the students that even after their time in the yeshiva, the Torah should continue to be a part of their lives; the idea is that they should want to carry on studying Torah and be steeped in "love of the Torah" (*ahavat Torah*).

PREPARATION FOR MILITARY SERVICE

The Hesder yeshivot examined in depth in this study stressed that educational (as opposed to physical or psychological) preparation for military service is done shortly before conscription so as not to distract the students from their studies. Preparation includes lessons focusing on typical halakhically problematic situations (such as kashrut questions, Shabbat restrictions) encountered during service so that students will know how to cope when faced with these situations in reality. Discussions are also conducted on how one should behave during military service. For instance, in the Har Etzion yeshiva, such discussions deal with the question of how to relate to commanding officers, since "yeshiva students are usually stuck-up" and do not treat their junior commanding officers with due respect (Amital, first interview). In some yeshivot, military personnel meet with the students. Contrary to the Mekhinot, Hesder yeshivot are not involved in physical preparation for military service (such as building up physical stamina or teaching navigational skills).

Informally, preparation for service includes conversations with postservice students; these help the preservice students prepare themselves emotionally and mentally for service. Postservice students are expected to share their experiences not only concerning halakhic quandaries faced during service, but also about problematic social and personal situations they encountered during their time in uniform. Preservice students also learn about military service from their older study partner (*havruta boger*) and solicit advice from students who are veterans of the units they are entering. For instance, a student who was going to be stationed in the Artillery Corps tried to find out from postservice students in his yeshiva whether service in this unit is "really as bad as they say" (Mickey, first interview). The yeshiva heads assume that service will be a hardship for their students, both in terms of halakhic practice as well as culturally:

> After all, these young men have lived their whole lives in a kind of bubble, within a very supportive environment, with values shared by everyone. And suddenly they go out to places where things are not so simple. So we try to give

them ways [. . .] we try to give them the experience without the experience itself [which of course is impossible]. (Rabinovitch, first interview)

In spite of the formidable efforts to prepare the students, it is important to remember that this is "something they have in fact been preparing themselves for eighteen or nineteen years," as Rabbi Weitzman explains (first interview). For Hesder students, as for all Religious Zionist youngsters in general, military service is a rite of passage and shapes their masculine identity. If in Jewish society in nineteenth-century Eastern Europe entry into the yeshiva was the defining and shaping experience of manhood,[13] for this population in Israel the military experience is no less significant for male identity formation. Most of the students eagerly anticipate their military service even if they also have qualms about it. There is also a different, more private, test attached: during service their observance of mitzvot and practice of religion will require active commitment and choice, rather than being performed out of mere inertia. Many of these young men see military service as a crossroads where they will test their beliefs and practices and decide whether this is the road they choose to continue traveling in their lives.

DEMOGRAPHICS

Who, then, are the young men who choose to come to the Hesder yeshivot? From what sectors of the population do they originate? Do corresponding programs compete for the same students?

The data supplied by the Igud shows that the total number of Hesder students (in both active and unpaid service) between 1991 and 2003 has been steadily increasing (Association of Hesder Yeshivot 1991–2003). Comparisons with the number of students at the Mekhinot (Association of Mekhinot 1991–2004) indicate that the establishment of the Mekhinot has not significantly affected the number of students attending the yeshivot examined in this study. It is true that in the years when there was a relative rise in the number of Mekhina students (1991, 1997, 1998, 2002) a slight decrease in the number of yeshiva students can be detected. However, in the long term, the growth trend of the yeshivot continues, and the decreases were temporary fluctuations.[14]

Likewise, the Disengagement from the Gaza Strip does not seem to have affected participation in the Hesder program. In September 2005 (the beginning of the yeshiva academic year)—immediately after the Disengagement—there was a slight decrease in the number of students joining the program: from 1,267 in the previous year to 1,108 in 2005 (Association of Hesder Yeshivot 2003–2007).

The following year saw an increase, and 2007 saw 1,393 new students in the program. At present (2013), Hesder cohorts range from 1,200 to 1,400 new students a year. Igud spokesman Rabbi David Stav is of the opinion that the Disengagement is actually one of the causes of this increase in numbers: following the events of the Disengagement and the resulting painful sentiments in the Religious Zionist sector, youngsters from this sector prefer to serve less time in the military, and the Hesder program enables them to do so (Stav, first interview).[15]

It is difficult to gauge the potential student pool for each institution based on the statistics from the educational institutions that students attended before the yeshiva (submitted by Har Etzion, Petach Tikva, and Ma'alot). While in the past it was easier to discern patterns as to which high schools were potential recruiting pools for specific Hesder yeshivot (see Bar-Lev 1997), this has become much harder to determine in the twenty-first century.

Likewise, it is impossible to draw unequivocal conclusions about the students' socioeconomic backgrounds from the partial data supplied by the various yeshivot. The fact that most students come from the center of Israel and from the greater Jerusalem area might indicate a relatively high socioeconomic background, but no other data supplied supports such a supposition.

STUDENT EXPECTATIONS

As explained in the methodological appendix, in-depth interviews were the method used to ascertain students' expectations regarding the Hesder program. Unlike the interviewees in parallel programs, unless asked directly, Hesder students rarely referred to their reasons for selecting the program. Rather, they focused on the reasons for choosing to attend their specific yeshiva. For example, all the students at Har Etzion emphasized that the high level of studies at this yeshiva was the main reason for choosing it.

While the aspect of religious study was always their main concern, some students made their choice based on social considerations: most of their high school graduating class joined the Hesder program because "this is what's done" (Nerya, first interview), and Hesder was a natural continuation of their high school studies. A number of students stated that they had been impressed by the Hesder alumni they had observed. For example:

> I had a lot of friends who went to Hesder who were really wild when they were in high school, and in Hesder they changed completely; it was

amazing. And I thought: I want to be like that too! To be a better person. (Mickey, first interview)

Some students spoke of their desire to reinforce their religious identity before enlisting in the military; their studies would strengthen their commitment to observing mitzvot during military service. Others stated that they chose the Hesder program hoping that it would make their military service easier or because they wanted to enlist as part of a group, or hoped the yeshiva would help with military placement.

As mentioned above, the choice of a particular yeshiva was more important to the students than the choice to participate in the Hesder program itself, and most described their selection process in detail. Their explanations can be divided into a number of categories: the nature of studies, educational approach, and staff at a particular yeshiva; following in the footsteps of an acquaintance or brother; and physical or external features of the yeshiva. In the first category, a relatively large number of students mentioned that they liked the variety of subjects available at the yeshiva and considered it to have a "liberal educational approach." Some students were impressed by the rabbis, while others were impressed by the heads of the yeshiva (mostly by the heads of Har Etzion and Or Etzion).

In the second category, a substantial number of students followed in the footsteps of an older brother who had attended the same institution or had been influenced by an older educational figure (such as a homeroom teacher at their high school yeshiva or a youth movement counselor). Some students joined their yeshiva with friends from high school and came as part of a small group. Thus, most interviewees indicated that a social consideration was at work when they chose which yeshiva to attend. These considerations did not always supplement considerations from the previous category and only sometimes complemented them.

With respect to the ancillary features of the yeshiva, many students referred to the appearance of the yeshiva, physical surroundings, comfortable living conditions, and "a good atmosphere." This favorable impression was made during visits to the yeshiva while still in high school.

Most of the students interviewed at later stages of their service were of the opinion that high school pupils do not really have the means to make a proper decision as to which yeshiva to attend. In most cases—including their own—the choice was not made because of "some great or lofty" idea or ideal (Yaakov, first interview), but simply on the basis of "having a good feeling" about the yeshiva.

When asked about what they expected from their time of study at the yeshiva of their choice, most of the preservice students interviewed referred to expectations concerning the yeshiva's influence on their lives in the future. They felt that they would acquire skills that would help them to lead better lives as adults: "The yeshiva will build me up as a person who is able to go out and face life" (Eli, first interview). Students defined these skills differently. Some felt the experience would help them shape their worldview or form their identity. Others spoke of skills that would enable them to combine religious life with life in society at large: "how to deal with a secular world. With the outside world. To maintain a high level of spirituality. Not to decline into mediocrity [. . .] to keep a high spiritual level throughout your entire life" (Amir, first interview). Some students expected their time spent in the yeshiva to have a crucial influence on their future lives, including how they would build their families, educate their children, and choose a profession in life.

Additionally, preservice interviewees expected to enrich their knowledge of the Torah and to become proficient Torah scholars to some extent. Interestingly, when asked about general expectations, none of the Hesder interviewees referred directly to the issue of military service.

When asked specifically about their expectations concerning the way their time at the yeshiva would affect their military service, interviewees said that they expected to receive some sort of spiritual and/or halakhic preparation for their military service. Some thought that the yeshiva would prepare them for their encounter with a different sector of Israeli society:

> [Military service] is the first time that I personally [. . .] and religious people in general come into contact with secular people [. . .] when you leave high school, you feel that this is something you want to improve and enrich—in religion [. . .] especially before you go to the military, before you meet something else. (Ronen, first interview)

Some students also expected the yeshiva to strengthen their motivation to serve in the military by clarifying the importance of military service from a religious point of view, although others felt that preparation for serving in the military should not be separated from other aspects of attending a yeshiva. Studying in a yeshiva prepares one for life in general and thus also for military service. A person who studies for a significant period of time before enlisting has the opportunity to mature. He undergoes a process that by definition prepares him, among other things, for military service. Interestingly, despite their feelings regarding the importance of studying, none of the preservice students interviewed spoke of the option of lowering his medical profile with the aim of getting an easier noncombat posting.

The expectations of Hesder students, as illustrated through the interviews, are not confined to the present. Rather, they view the time they spend in the program (five years in total) as part of a lengthy process and expect to notice the effects of their time at that yeshiva in the future. Most of the interviewees' expectations regarding military service are to get past it and return to the yeshiva in order to complete their course of study. It does not appear that the interviewees have doubts as to their religious identities or are seeking answers to dilemmas and questions of faith. They hope that the yeshiva will help them to become bnei Torah (sing. ben Torah): mature religious individuals who wish to continue studying Torah as adults and to live their lives according to the Torah in the broader sense of the term.[16] This suggests that the role of the Hesder yeshiva in the context of military service is of lesser importance than its part in the larger context of education and its influence on one's life in general. It seems, in fact, that the students do not conceive of the yeshiva and their military service as one integral experience, but rather that their military service in many ways is an interruption (albeit an important one at times) of the more significant experience of yeshiva life.

MILITARY SERVICE IN THE HESDER PROGRAM

As mentioned above, half of the Hesder students stationed in the Infantry Corps still serve in separate homogenous units for their entire term of service (Stav, first interview). Conversely, after completing their training, students stationed in the Armored Corps are integrated into active heterogeneous units where they serve with other religious non-Hesder soldiers and secular soldiers. Soldiers serving in noncombat supporting units do not serve in separate homogenous units at any time. Allowing yeshiva students to serve in separate units during training and afterwards enables the IDF to incorporate religious soldiers' needs into the official timetable. The IDF can permit time for prayer, including instances when a longer time for prayer is necessary (such as on Rosh Hodesh—the beginning of a new month—Mondays and Thursdays, when a portion of the Torah is read, etc.). Considerations can be made for fast days that occur during training, supplying religious "equipment" essential to leading a religious way of life (such as providing a Torah scroll during field training), and the like.

Yeshiva students' units are comprised of students from several Hesder yeshivot and not of students from one single yeshiva. Students who participated in this study generally spoke of an easy and comfortable atmosphere among the students from the various yeshivot, but said that this was not always the case. Differences between the yeshivot and their respective outlooks were sometimes the cause of social tensions in yeshiva students' units, and the interviewees referred to the efforts necessary to overcome these tensions—efforts that were not always successful. For instance, two students from Har Etzion serving in the Givati Brigade served with students from the Moreshet Ya'akov yeshiva. As one of the interviewees put it:

> Moreshet [Ya'akov] students are of "the common people," so to speak. Most are Mizrahi and are less religious.[17] This, like, shattered the myth that you can take a religious unit as a symbol [and a role-model for the other units] [. . .] because they wouldn't get up to pray [in the morning] and they would mess up lots of things that we really wanted to convey to others [outside the unit]. (Noam, first interview)

Noam is speaking of a certain image the students of Har Etzion wished to project to the rest of their company: one of a devout, cohesive, and morally superior unit. Having students in the unit who didn't share this idea ruined their plans. However, by the end of their military service, friendships between the students from these two yeshivot were forged and were even maintained for some time after their joint service. One of the students who participated in the follow-up study a year later, who was also a student from Har Etzion, served in a different infantry unit with other students from Moreshet Ya'akov and reported similar difficulties (Sagi, second interview). Likewise, a student from the Petach Tikva yeshiva who served with students from the Hesder yeshivot in Haifa, Nahariya, Acre, Shdemot Mehola, and Ma'ale Adumim spoke of tension between the various groups arising from disagreements over general behavior and the interpretation of halakha (Elichai, second interview).

Generally speaking, students who served in the Armored Corps described more difficulties than did those in the infantry, mainly due to serving in heterogeneous units (units not exclusively made up of yeshiva students) during later stages of their service. Students who did not serve in combat posts also reported difficulties arising from being in secular surroundings—mainly feeling very lonely (Chaim, first interview).

Some postservice students expressed resentment about serving in separate homogenous units. Their opinion was that the yeshiva students cannot make any substantial contribution to the unit in which they serve, since their separate service ensures they don't get to know other soldiers in the company. One student remarked that it would be better if the yeshiva students were dispersed throughout the platoons. Since they are considered a strong and highly motivated group, posting them throughout the company would boost motivation and performance throughout the unit and benefit everyone (Yaakov, first interview). This demonstrates that even prior to then Major General Elazar Stern's decision to integrate yeshiva students into heterogeneous platoons, there were students in favor of such a move.

Another group, made up mainly of postservice students, commented on the fact that the differences between yeshiva students and other soldiers have both positive and negative effects on the formers' military service. First, Hesder students begin their service as a group, even when the platoon is made up of students from more than one yeshiva:

> Yeshiva guys, when they join the platoon, you get about forty guys. The "law of communicating religious guys" works like crazy.[18] Everyone gets to know everyone else in minutes [. . .]. [That first day] you see one platoon [in the company] where everyone is together, there are a lot of laughs, and it's great. And there are two platoons where no one knows anyone else. They are afraid of one another, they don't know the other guy—whether he is a thief, a cheat, a liar, or a friend you can trust. (Yaakov, first interview)

Social cohesion, belonging to the same general social group and the same program, gives the students a sense of self-confidence. They are not as apprehensive as other new recruits, who usually arrive alone and must get to know their new environment. One of the results of this confidence is that the soldiers are not afraid to confront the military system (Tziyon, first interview).

Another influential factor is age at conscription. The average age of a Hesder conscript is twenty. They are older than their commanders, and this influences their attitude toward their NCOs. Added to this is their critical attitude toward the military system: "Yeshiva students are used to thinking about everything they read and hear rather than performing automatically. Military discipline is built on the opposite principle," and this is a certain way to brew trouble (Noam, first interview). As noted, part of their preparation for military service at the yeshiva includes discussions with rabbis on the need to treat one's commanders with respect. However, as one of the students stated, it seems that this message is not really taken to heart (Yossi, first interview). Despite these difficulties, conversations with yeshiva students' commanders show that, on the whole, Hesder students are considered disciplined soldiers.

CONTACT BETWEEN THE HESDER YESHIVA AND STUDENTS IN THE MILITARY

During their service in the military, the yeshivot make an effort to keep in touch with their students. Some of the postservice students and students who participated in follow-up interviews reported that they did not have a strong relationship with their yeshiva while in the military, however. This group consisted mainly of soldiers who served in noncombat posts, and during interviews these students stated that to the extent there was any contact it was initiated by them not the yeshiva itself. Thus, it appears that it is more difficult for the yeshivot to maintain contact with students who do not serve in a group—meaning, in a yeshiva students' unit. Although students in noncombat positions may feel slighted by the relative lack of contact from the yeshivot, it seems to be mostly a matter of logistics: it isn't possible to visit individual soldiers, and since yeshivot do not usually phone students on a regular basis, the absence of visits is equated with no contact.

All the students participating in follow-up interviews and most of those interviewed postservice said that they themselves visited the yeshiva during their military service. Most could only visit on holidays or Shabbat when they were on leave. It seems that these visits constitute the main avenue through which students maintain their connection with their yeshiva.

The yeshivot, however, have additional instruments through which they may sustain their ties to their students in uniform. According to the interviewees, most of their contact with the yeshiva during their service occurred by mail: the yeshivot mailed various items such as pamphlets, packages, letters from the rabbis addressed to all the students on active duty, and personal letters from students at the yeshiva. In addition, representatives from the yeshiva visited the students serving in a yeshiva students' unit. Students serving in combat units reported that the yeshiva would send visitors two to four times during their service. As can be expected, students who served in smaller groups or in noncombat posts reported fewer visits and less concrete contact with the yeshiva. For instance, a student who served in the Infantry Corps said that since he enlisted with a very small group of students from his yeshiva—as opposed to enlisting with his entire class—there were no visits from his yeshiva faculty during his entire service (Meir, first interview).

In general, students who served in noncombat roles reported that the yeshiva "makes more of an effort" for students in combat units than for them. They tried to justify this by saying that service in the military was more difficult for combat soldiers from a religious point of view: "I think that we, those with low medical profiles, felt a bit like second-class citizens [. . .] it is obvious that we suffer less [and so] they make less of an effort for us" (Tziyon, first interview).

Most students reported almost no contact by phone with the yeshiva. There were a few who reported that some teachers called them on their own initiative to find out how they were. Others said that when they felt the need, they phoned a teacher with whom they felt they had a special connection. Understanding the need for closer contact, Rabbi Drukman (first interview) said that up until a few years ago there was a teacher whose job it was to keep in touch with the students who were on active duty, but that due to budgetary issues, this post was eliminated. Conversely, the Ma'ale Adumim yeshiva appointed a teacher to be in charge of keeping in touch with students on active duty. This post was created in 2005.

Contact by telephone with the yeshiva, as well as with others in the same class, has become easier in recent years due to the proliferation of cellular phones, making students more accessible than in the past. In addition, the fact that it is possible to leave messages (text or voice mail) means that contact can be maintained even if the student is unavailable due to training or battle.

In general, all the interviewees said that the contact with the yeshiva, even if not close, was meaningful for them: "It's very empowering, this connection [. . .], you feel that you are part of a group, that there is someone behind you [supporting you]" (Tzvi, first interview). Another significant relationship for the students was that with friends from their yeshiva class. All nineteen students who participated in the first year of the follow-up study reported contact with their classmates. Half of the interviewees emphasized that this contact was mainly with those they served with in the same IDF unit or with their close friends, but said that in general, being in touch with their *shi'ur* (class) is significant and a meaningful support mechanism. The fact that they come from a similar background, are going through similar experiences, and are mentally and emotionally "in the same place" (Elichai second interview) helps them cope with the difficulties they encounter in the military: "Most of what's tough in the military is psychological [. . .] yeshiva students who are with their friends don't have this [problem]" (Sagi, second interview).

Even students who claimed they were not in need of support remarked that it was still important for them to be in touch with their classmates. One student commented that when he met with his yeshiva friends, he had the feeling that "this was more than just meeting with the guys. I mean, . . . you feel that, in some way, you are meeting the yeshiva," and this was very important to him (Eli, second interview). During the second year of the follow-up study, only two students from the class of 2003 were still on active duty, while the rest of their classmates had already returned to their studies. Both felt that their yeshiva class still supported them. The contact among classmates was maintained mainly by telephone, although students reported that they also tried to meet whenever possible.

* * *

Clearly Hesder yeshivot maintain close contact with their students who serve in the yeshiva students' unit in the infantry. This is quite logical: it is easier to visit a large group of students at once, while it is much more difficult to visit students who are dispersed in various units or serve in small groups, such as those who serve in the Armored Corps. Additionally, students who serve in the Armored Corps benefit from the high status of combat soldiers, while students who serve in noncombat posts feel very lonely and unappreciated. Since both soldiers in the Armored Corps and students who are not in combat posts usually come across more halakhic problems than those who serve in the yeshiva students' unit, the yeshiva's attitude toward them is highly significant. This will be discussed in greater detail in Chapter 8 and in the third part of this book.

To conclude, Hesder yeshivot perceive themselves as educational frameworks that do much more than "prepare" students for military service. Their main aim is to raise bnei Torah and their curriculum, staff, and mind-set are all geared toward this end. However, military service is not ignored. While the amount of attention paid to it and the importance attached to service in the IDF varies from yeshiva to yeshiva, all uphold their agreement with the IDF and students expect their yeshivot to assist them as they go through their military service. One of the main reasons students choose to study before their service is the hope that they will not be alone while in uniform. They will be serving as part of a group, and their yeshiva will support them to a certain extent. Whether or not this actually happens will be explored in Chapter 8.

CHAPTER 5
THE SHILUV PROGRAM

The Shiluv program, established at the end of 1985, is a five-year program that affords young religious men the possibility of a full three-year term of military service while also enabling serious in-depth Torah study. In this respect, it serves as an alternative to the Hesder program. The program is run by the Religious Kibbutz Movement and, until 2009, was located on two kibbutzim: Ein Tzurim and Ma'ale Gilboa. In 2003, when both yeshivot were vibrant, one hundred students participated in the program—a very small number by any count. According to the agreement between the IDF and the Religious Kibbutz Movement when the program was established, it would consist of no more than 120 students per year. In fact, in all of its years of existence, its participants have never reached this number. By 2007 the number of students had dropped sharply, and in the academic year 2007–2008, there were barely enough students at Ein Tzurim to form a group for enlistment. The crisis affected the yeshiva as a whole and resulted in a number of structural changes, including the resignation of Rabbi Yoel Bin-Nun, the head of the yeshiva at the time this study was conducted. The following year, the Ein Tzurim branch of the program closed, leaving only the Ma'ale Gilboa branch.[1] The Shiluv program constitutes the smallest Torah studies program for men examined in the current study.

As part of the Shiluv program, students attend yeshiva for a year, after which they enlist individually (rather than as part of a group as in the Hesder program). After serving between eighteen and twenty-four months, the students return to the yeshiva to study for a year. Following this second period of study, they return to the IDF to complete a total of three years in uniform. After their discharge from the military, a few students return to the yeshiva for additional study time before beginning their academic studies or joining the work force. Thus, like the Hesder program, the course of the Shiluv program is five years long; however, the time dedicated to Torah study is not subtracted from the students' obligatory military service.

THE NATURE AND STRUCTURE OF THE SHILUV PROGRAM

Initially, the Shiluv program offered young men from the Religious Kibbutz Movement the option to study before enlisting, while still following the movement's official position opposing a shorter term of service, as enabled by the Hesder (Bigman 2005, 258–259; Bar-Lev 1997; Rosman-Stollman 2000).[2] Accordingly, the program was intended mainly for conscripts from a kibbutz background. In practice, most of the participants do not come from a Religious Kibbutz, but rather are from urban backgrounds.

The Shiluv program does not belong to the Igud, and is not officially affiliated with it in any way. When the program was established, the Shiluv yeshivot requested Igud recognition, but were refused due to ideological differences between the programs (Bigman, first interview; Bar-Lev 1997, 116). Still, they are connected to the Igud financially; government funding for the program is channeled through the Igud. Due to past tensions, Shiluv staff members feel they are being discriminated against monetarily by the Igud. They are not alone in these feelings. Heads of the women's study programs also believe the Igud does not allocate funds fairly and have resorted to legal action (see Chapter 7). Like the Hesder yeshivot and the Mekhinot, the Shiluv program is funded by tuition paid by the students' parents, governmental support, and donations. Acceptance to the program is not conditioned upon a student's financial ability to pay tuition. At Ma'ale Gilboa, for instance, a student who is unable to pay tuition can subsidize his attendance by carrying out various odd jobs at the yeshiva (Rosman-Stollman 2000, 272).

PROGRAM CHARACTERISTICS AND MILITARY SERVICE AS A SHILUV STUDENT

Unlike other programs for men examined here, the Shiluv is an offshoot of a preexisting institution: the Religious Kibbutz Movement's yeshiva. Founded in Ein Tzurim in 1977 as the Religious Kibbutz Movement's center for Torah studies, it continues to hold various classes and courses for all of its members. It was but natural to include the Shiluv as one of its programs. But unlike the Hesder program, where the young students—either pre- or postservice—are the focus of the program, in this case, the Shiluv students are not the only program at the yeshiva.

While studying at the yeshiva, students are encouraged to perform volunteer work in the community. Shiluv students study with study partners (*havruta*) from the kibbutz and serve as youth counselors at the local branch of the Bnei Akiva youth movement.

The program's daily study schedule is similar to the traditional yeshiva curriculum and therefore to the curricular structure at Hesder yeshivot. An examination of the Shiluv's actual curriculum, however, shows that the content of the classes departs from tradition (Rosman-Stollman 2000, 273–275). Classes include not only traditional study of the Talmud, but also critical study, Bible, and

Jewish philosophy, including contemporary and sometimes controversial thinkers. Unlike the Mekhinot (discussed in the following chapter), theological studies (*emuna*) are hardly addressed.

Shiluv students enlist as individuals and not as a group. Their military roles are determined according to their abilities; unlike the Hesder conscripts, they are not limited in their options. Pursuant to the agreement with the IDF, after approximately a year and a half of active service, Shiluv conscripts may return to their studies at the yeshiva for twelve months. Some prefer to postpone their return in order to complete a certain period of service. For instance, some prefer not to leave their companions during combat duty; others delay their return in order to arrive at the yeshiva at the beginning of a study period (*zman*). Arriving in the middle of a *zman* would mean that they would join classes that had begun during their absence, and thus they will have missed substantial portions of the material. There are also social reasons for postponing one's return to the yeshiva: some prefer to arrive at the yeshiva at the same time as the other members of their class and spend the year together.

Since the students in the Shiluv program enlist as individuals, they are in need of assistance when navigating the military's bureaucracy and when finalizing their postings. With this end in mind, the faculty includes a rabbi whose job is to assist the students in their dealings with the military. Any student who wishes to postpone his return to the yeshiva or return earlier than intended must coordinate it with the rabbi in charge.

From conversations with the students and follow-up interviews, it seems that, unlike the Hesder and the Mekhinot, the Shiluv program does not have a great deal of weight in its dealings with the IDF. While students in other programs felt that their institutions were able to influence the IDF regarding matters such as postings, medical profiles, and so on, Shiluv students felt that they were not being helped enough. For instance, shortly before their induction in August 2003, the students found out that they were to be posted in the HIRMAK units,[3] an unpopular posting. This posting aroused special indignation, since the IDF had ignored the students' preferences as stated in the official questionnaire given to them by the military itself. In addition, these postings would mean that they would serve together as a group rather than individually in various units—something they preferred.[4] The program personnel were entirely unaware of the IDF's intention and were apparently unable to act fast enough to change the posting.

However, a compromise was finally reached: it was stipulated that more than half of the Shiluv students to be stationed in the Infantry Corps would be posted to HIRMAK (which they did under duress). A smaller number were stationed in more prestigious infantry units. The students' conclusion from this affair was that the IDF viewed the Shiluv students as "pushovers" who could be stationed anywhere and whose preferences could be ignored. They also concluded that the program had no influence over the IDF. One result of these perceptions might be that students who desire stationing in more popular units will prefer the Mekhinot, which are seen as having more clout in the military system.

CURRICULUM AND FACULTY

The heads of the yeshivot at the time this study was conducted held slightly different views concerning the program's goals.[5] Rabbi Bigman made a clear distinction between the Religious Kibbutz Movement's goals and those of the Shiluv program. In his opinion, the yeshiva has three goals. The first is to educate its graduates to be working family men (*ba'ali-batim*) who are scholarly, God-fearing, and pluralistic in their outlook on life. The second is to be a place that creates a new kind of Torah scholar—one who would be able to "engage in a wider discourse with the secular and academic worlds . . ." The third is to be the nucleus of a rejuvenation of Torah studies—a place where one need not be afraid to address controversial issues (such as halakhic attitudes towards non-Jews), and where scholars readily tackle the challenges the modern world presents to Orthodox Judaism (Bigman, first interview).

Rabbi Bin-Nun, on the other hand, regarded the Shiluv program as a worldview in and of itself and saw it as encompassing the yeshiva in its entirety. Shiluv (literally, "integration") should be the lynch pin of all aspects of life, including all facets of Israeli society "without any concessions or special arrangements" (Bin-Nun, first interview).[6] In Bin-Nun's view, serving the community, involving overseas students in the yeshiva, and so on are all part of this ideal. Rabbi Bin-Nun was also of the opinion that Torah studies themselves should be influenced by the idea of the Shiluv: the studies should be viewed as a combination of Bible study, Rabbinic sources, and Jewish thought rather than focusing on one subject (such as Talmud).

In general the Shiluv program espouses a more open-minded approach concerning traditional modes of study. This approach is reflected in the program's libraries, which include works of a kind not usually found in such institutions, such as Talmudic research literature (Rosman-Stollman 2000, 275). Consequently, other yeshivot and Mekhinot, and especially rabbis from Mekaz Ha-Rav, do not take a favorable view of the methods and curriculum prevailing in the Religious Kibbutz Movement's yeshivot.

Unlike the leaders of the Hesder yeshivot, who did not refer to the issue of commitment to halakha when discussing their students and objectives, both Rabbi Bigman and Rabbi Bin-Nun conceived of this as a personal message that should be conveyed to their students. The fact that these rabbis were prepared to discuss the issue of commitment to halakha and the phenomenon of secularization openly is in stark contrast to most of the leaders of the other premilitary programs, who routinely shied away from this discussion. The reluctance to include the issue of commitment to halakha in their agenda comes across, at best, as an effort to conceal the issue, and, at worst, as an attempt to ignore it.

A clear message of commitment to halakha contradicts the common perception of the Religious Kibbutz Movement yeshivot as lax in their religious observance. This impression may be due to the fact that these yeshivot are generally seen in Religious Zionist society as being too liberal regarding religious issues. Another reason for this image might be that the Ma'ale Gilboa yeshiva is also considered politically leftist, while most of the Mekhinot have a reputation for being politically right-wing, a reputation shared with many Hesder yeshivot.

Also, the composition of the faculty is intended to maintain the more open-minded nature of the yeshivot in the Religious Kibbutz Movement. Rabbi Bigman emphasized his interest in a plurality of views among the faculty that would preserve the balance of opinions in the yeshiva. Faculty must be individuals of moral sensitivity who are receptive to many different views (Bigman, first interview). Rabbi Bin-Nun expressed the view that a member of the faculty does not necessarily have to agree with every opinion voiced in the yeshiva, but that he should be willing to "accept us as we are" (Bin-Nun, first interview). Unlike Rabbi Bin-Nun, Rabbi Bigman said that some kind of military service is a condition of employment.

PREPARATION FOR MILITARY SERVICE

As in other aspects, preparation for military service was handled differently in each of the yeshivot. Throughout the school year, students at Ein Tzurim could attend a class on halakhic issues during military service, although it is interesting to note that most of the interviewees did not attend it. In Ma'ale Gilboa, preparation for military service takes place at the end of the academic year and includes halakhic as well as psychological preparation (the latter consists of a lecture given by a psychologist), and a medical doctor's lecture aimed at raising the students' awareness of the possibility of injury during military service.[7] Rabbi Bigman stated that the goal of the yeshiva was to encourage the students "to identify with the Torah" during their first year at the yeshiva. This process would also prepare them for military service, so no real additional preparation would be needed.

Both yeshivot hosted talks by representatives of various military units and other pivotal military personnel. The talks enabled students to ask questions of officials and also afforded various units the opportunity to recruit students. Additionally, students had the chance to discuss problems that might arise during their service in the military with postservice students who visited the yeshiva or were still studying in it. Neither of the yeshivot engaged in any kind of physical preparation for service in the military (such as developing physical stamina or navigational skills).

As a result of this scant preparation, some students felt that they were unprepared physically for service (for instance, Michael, first interview); some, however, took this lack of preparation in a positive way. Unlike the students at other programs, most of the Shiluv students (although not all) did not state that they were eagerly looking forward to their service. They considered it to be an important event, albeit not necessarily something positive to look forward to. In the interviews, they indicated this was also the way their yeshiva viewed military service and that the lack of hands-on preparation for service was a direct result of this sentiment.

DEMOGRAPHICS

What sort of young man joins the Shiluv program? As described in previous studies, Shiluv students are mainly from the greater Jerusalem area and from the Religious Kibbutz Movement itself (Bar-Lev 1997, 7–123; Rosman-Stollman 2000, 276–277, 294). More recent data show that the number of students from religious kibbutzim and moshavim—for whom the program was originally created—has been declining since the end of the 1990s. A comparison with data from the Mekhinot shows that children of kibbutz and moshav members now prefer to attend the Mekhinot (Association of Mekhinot 1988–2007; Yeshivat Ha-Kibbutz Ha-Dati, Ein Tzurim 1986–2003).

Most of the Shiluv students interviewed in this study had deliberated between the two Religious Kibbutz Movement yeshivot. This indicates that both yeshivot drew on the same demographic pool, and it explains the difficulty of maintaining two yeshivot with a sufficient number of students in each. Half of the interviewees had also thought about attending a Hesder yeshiva, specifically the Hesder yeshiva in Otniel. However, their final decision was influenced by the importance they attached to serving a full military term of three years, and ultimately they preferred the Shiluv to the Hesder program. Some students had also looked into attending various Mekhinot. They chose the Shiluv mainly because they thought that Torah study at the Mekhinot was not serious enough and because of what they perceived to be intellectual inflexibility in the Mekhinot.

STUDENT EXPECTATIONS

In order to examine students' expectations, in-depth interviews were conducted with Shiluv students (see the methodological appendix). The reasons the students gave when asked about their choice of the Shiluv program can be divided into two main categories: value-based reasons (the importance they attached to Torah studies and the importance seen in service in the military), and social and practical reasons (such as the desire to raise one's medical profile, the need to follow social conventions, and so on).

The first subcategory of value-based reasons includes those related to Torah studies and to the Shiluv program's guiding ideology. Both graduates and students interviewed for this study chose the Shiluv program because they wanted to study Torah or to experience the unique style of instruction offered by the Religious Kibbutz Movement's yeshivot. Almost all the interviewees stated that the main reason they chose the Shiluv program was to be able to serve a full three years without it impinging on the quality of their Torah studies. As one of the graduates put it, "It is important to me to serve in the military for three years, so Hesder was not an option [. . .] the Mekhinot seem to me to be a bit . . . shoddy [*hafifnik*]." And so he chose the Shiluv (Shaul, first interview).

Another subcategory was the quality of the scholarship itself in the Religious Kibbutz Movement's yeshivot. Eight students spoke favorably of the plurality of opinions and the liberal atmosphere in the yeshiva:

As far as what you are allowed to say and what you are allowed to think are concerned; things you are allowed to argue about and discuss [. . .] there was a feeling, like: this is a place where things that don't come up elsewhere, come up here. (Ronny, first interview)

The academic freedom available within the yeshiva was also given as a reason for choosing the Shiluv program: the fact that students can choose their own curriculum was important to them.

When discussing the social and practical reasons for choosing the Shiluv program, students referred to the expectations of their social environment. Three of the interviewees said they felt that they were expected to study Torah for a year before enlisting; the question was only which program to choose. "This is what everybody does, and I was persuaded that it is important to study for a year before enlisting" (Chen, first interview). Some students chose their study venue based on friends or family (coming to a yeshiva in order to study with friends; choosing to study where a family member studied in the past and so on).

When asked about their expectations, most students referred to long-term results: they expected that the time spent at the yeshiva would enrich their proficiency in Torah studies and scholarship; that they would acquire tools for a lifelong ability to study Torah independently; that they would be guided in shaping their worldview and in creating their spiritual world. As one of the preservice students put it, "A worldview is something that is constantly being shaped, but I think that significant progress will be made this year" (Nadav, first interview).

Regarding their military service, half of the preservice students interviewed had no expectations at all. The others hoped that they would begin their service with a more mature outlook on life.

The viewpoints expressed indicate that Shiluv students have internalized the program's messages about the importance of preservice Torah study. The students' expectations centered mainly on the impact that the yeshiva and Torah studies have in the long run, while military service was perceived as an issue of secondary importance. This trend is similar to that seen among the Hesder students, but slightly different from the views held by the Mekhinot students, as will be discussed in the following chapter.

MILITARY SERVICE IN THE SHILUV PROGRAM

As mentioned above, Shiluv students do not enlist as a group, and before their service they submit an official questionnaire listing their preferred postings—like all other young men before conscription. Based on an agreement between the program and the IDF, a Shiluv student who is stationed in an elite unit must leave the Shiluv program and may not return to the yeshiva for a second study year. Upon acceptance to the elite unit, he is required to sign a form forfeiting his right to return to the yeshiva for a second study period after eighteen to twenty-four months of service (Rosman-Stollman 2000, 279). This stipulation, however, remains confined to theory. Military units sometimes forget to have Shiluv students sign the appropriate form in which they agree to leave the program, or are unaware of the need to do so. These units are then taken by surprise when the soldier's discharge orders come through. Follow-up interviews of the Shiluv students who took part in this study and interviews held with alumni show that students serving in elite units usually feel committed to their unit and do not take advantage of the option to return to the yeshiva, despite the bureaucratic lacuna.

While most students are ambivalent about leaving their comrades and returning to the yeshiva to study, some come to the yeshiva hoping that upon their return to active service they will receive a better military posting. Whether the return to the yeshiva was motivated by a desire to study or by more prosaic considerations, Rabbi Bigman estimated that around 70 percent of each class returns for unpaid leave (SHALAT) of varying lengths. The results of the follow-up stage of this study bears this out: of the students interviewed during and after their service (graduates and students), almost all returned to the yeshiva for some amount of time. It should be pointed out, however, that these students do not always exercise their right to return to the yeshiva for a full year. Many return for only a few months, sometimes because they are serving in an elite unit or taking part in the officer training course. This is still a significant achievement, since returning to the yeshiva lengthens the students' military service, and by choosing to study they are knowingly extending their service.[8]

Students are highly motivated and wish to serve in combat units whenever possible. All interviewees who were physically able named combat units as their chosen venue of service. As in the other programs surveyed, none of the students attempted to downgrade their medical profile in order to receive a desk job. Indeed, one student, whose medical profile exempted him from service, volunteered.

CONTACT BETWEEN THE SHILUV PROGRAM AND STUDENTS IN THE MILITARY

When asked about contact between the yeshiva and its students in uniform, Rabbi Bigman (first interview) remarked that "there is not enough." In spite of this, most of the students said that they had been in touch with the yeshiva during this time. After four years of the follow-up study, only two of the students who had served in combat units and had found it difficult to visit the yeshiva said that they had very little contact with the yeshiva. Others did not say that they had close contact, but noted that they were in touch with the yeshiva in one way or another.

It seems that most of the contact between the yeshiva and its students consists of students' visits. Even after three years of military service, interviewees in the follow-up study (including those who had officially left the program) said that they try to visit the yeshiva, especially on Shabbat when there is a class weekend. The frequency of the students' visits depended on their military postings and their desire to visit the yeshiva. Unlike other programs, quite a few students remarked that they had been in contact with the yeshiva via telephone. Both graduates and students in the follow-up study reported that every now and then someone from the yeshiva would call to find out how they were doing. One graduate said that during Operation Defensive Shield (2002) Rabbi Bigman knew where this student was serving and called to ask how he was. When relating this story, the manner in which the student expressed himself and his tone of voice gave the impression that this meant a great deal to him (Carmel, first interview).[9] Even though they did not admit this openly, it seems that the students were happy with the yeshiva's interest in them (for instance, Nir, third interview).

Despite the fact that the students were dispersed among quite a few units, the interviewees reported that the yeshiva made an effort to send representatives to the students' various military ceremonies. Unlike Hesder soldiers who served in noncombat posts, Shiluv students who were stationed in such posts did not seem to feel neglected. This might be because all the students serve as individuals and everyone is visited rarely, if at all.

All the students in the follow-up study reported that they were in touch with at least some of their classmates. This was true over the entire course of the follow-up study: contact with friends from the yeshiva was still reported during the fifth round of interviews. Students kept in touch mainly over the phone, but some also said that they made an effort to meet their friends. Such meetings took place during class reunion weekends, and some students would arrange to meet each other at central bus stations and spend time together at the station before returning home or to their bases (Nir, third interview).

An interesting trend came to light when the students were asked whether their classmates gave them any emotional support during their service in the military. Half of those interviewed during their first year of service said that they had not received any support. Some of those who felt that they had been supported didn't think that this was connected in any way to the time spent together in the yeshiva: "It was the same as with any other friend" (Idan, second interview). Others thought that the time spent together did affect their relationships with their classmates: "It's not the same as with friends from home, because [in this case], there is a depth [. . .] the depth of [the experience of] the yeshiva" (Nadav, second interview). Slightly surprisingly, in the second and third years of service all but one of the interviewees now felt that their class was a source of emotional support. Why did they change their minds? This might indicate that their connection to their friends became more important to them as their term of service progressed. Their concept of the nature of these friendships, however, reflects an opposite trend. While in the past the friendships hinged more on experiencing yeshiva together, this dimension dissipated as their military service progressed. Most of the follow-up students (second and third years in uniform) thought that their relationships with their yeshiva classmates were no different from those with other friends. Two students referred to another dimension of the relationships related to the yeshiva: "They [friends from the yeshiva] represent a different world, and conversations with them are about other things" (Nadav, third interview). Or as the second student put it, "It's a kind of relationship . . . it's hard to explain. When you study Torah, you can't study with someone you don't like" (Asaf, third interview).

It seems, therefore, that for the students, their relationships with their classmates are important, and that they usually becomes stronger as their time in uniform progresses. Their relationship with the yeshiva is not as close, but it is still important, explaining the fact that they visit the yeshiva in their spare time.

* * *

In conclusion, both the program and the students who join it view a full course of service as an important component, although they do not invest a substantial amount of time preparing for it. This is in stark contrast to both the Hesder and Mekhinot programs: in the former, military service is given less attention and time and in the latter it is given more. While the Shiluv program is closer to the Hesder program in that it sees military service more as a necessity and that Torah study in its more traditional sense is their true raison d'être, like the Mekhinot, the Shiluv program attaches importance to a full three-year course of service and does not feel Torah study justifies a shortened term in uniform. The Shiluv program is longer and demands its members shift back and forth between the civil and military spheres, and provides a broader religious education than its sister programs. This can be more difficult and even confusing for students, as will be demonstrated in Chapter 8.

CHAPTER 6
THE MEKHINOT: PRESERVICE PREPARATORY SEMINARIES

As of 2010, there are eighteen religious Mekhinot (Mekhina, sing.),[1] literally, "preparatories," where male Religious Zionist students study for a year and "prepare" for service in the IDF. These are attended by graduates of religious high schools and high school yeshivot. Students attend the Mekhina for a year and then enlist in the military for a full three-year term of service. As will be discussed below, the year, recognized as deferred service time by the IDF, may be extended by six months. The Eli Mekhina also offers the option of returning to the Mekhina for another year of study after military service. It also offers a program for alumni who wish to continue to study Torah while beginning their academic studies (see Bnei David site 2011).

It is commonly thought that the Mekhinot were established in order to make it possible for religious students to serve in the military while maintaining their religious identity: the Mekhinot prepare the students so that they will be able to withstand the pressures of a system that is not user-friendly for an observant person. Not all heads of Mekhinot accept this assumption—unlike some of the students, who expect a certain level of reinforcement and preparation, as indicated by the name of the program (preservice preparatory seminaries).

Founded in 1987 following the encouragement given by Major General (res.) Amram Mitzna, the first Mekhina, Bnei David, in the settlement of Eli (henceforth Eli), is headed by Rabbi Eli Sadan and Rabbi Yigal Levinstein. According to Rabbi Sadan (first interview), the program was established after Mitzna asked Rabbi Levinstein to return to serve in the military. Rabbi Levinstein had left the IDF in order to bolster his Torah studies and turn to a career in education; he was studying at the Mercaz Ha-Rav yeshiva at the time. Mitzna claimed that the Religious Zionist sector does not encourage its young men to take up command posts. This is to the detriment of the IDF, which loses potential officers. Instead of taking up command posts, Religious Zionist soldiers enlist, serve, are discharged, and then go on with their lives. They do not commit to a longer military career and therefore, in Mitzna's opinion, do not truly contribute to the greater good.

Levinstein approached Rabbi Sadan, with whom he had studied in the past, and the two agreed with Mitzna's observation: true, members of the Religious Zionist sector officially fulfill their duty by enlisting as required by law; however, they are not invested in the IDF "at a level at which they truly take responsibility and behave as true partners [in the military]" (Sadan, first interview). The solution they proposed was to have more Religious Zionist soldiers join the officers' corps and see a military career as possible and even desirable.

After much deliberation, Rabbis Levinstein and Sadan concluded that young men are not sufficiently prepared for life in Israeli society in general, and for service in the military in particular.

> This is a *mental*, spiritual, problem. [. . .] The [religious] educational system is preoccupied mainly with the question of the conduct of a religious person, but not with the construction of a spiritual world [. . .] [not] how to face secular and Western culture, intellectually and spiritually. [In order] to do this as an individual, you must have deep religious conviction and recognize the truth of your convictions. (speaker's emphasis, Sadan, first interview)

Both rabbis thought that this was what was lacking in the religious educational system, and that this gap meant that young adults were not confident about their ability to maintain their religious identity after taking up command posts. Therefore, they preferred to leave the military as soon as possible without the additional burden of a command post.

Their conclusion led the rabbis to establish a program that would give these young adults the tools to deal with military service and enable them to serve a full three years in the military, if not more.[2] Thus, although the heads of the program would not say so explicitly, the Mekhinot were indeed established with the aim of spiritually preparing young adults from Religious Zionist society for service in the IDF. In other words, this was the only program designed with the explicit objective of mediating between the two frameworks so that young men would be able to continue to serve in uniform without foregoing their social group's conflicting demands. While the Hesder and Shiluv programs see service as an avoidable constraint that must be addressed, the Mekhinot program sees it in the broader context of contributing to society and to Religious Zionism as well.

Sixty-seven students attended Eli during its first academic year (1987–1988). The number of students increased significantly over the coming years, indicating the demand for a program combining Torah study and military service in the Mekhina format. Bnei David set three goals, which would later become the blueprint for other Mekhinot. The first goal was to assist the students in constructing a spiritual world—an issue neglected by the religious educational system, in the opinion of the founders. The second was to support the students during their service in the IDF, both from a halakhic point of view (answering halakhic questions arising during military service) as well as by bolstering their morale. In other words, the student should feel he is prepared for the military experience when enlisting, and the Mekhina should continue to follow his progress from a practical halakhic perspective without neglecting the more basic need to boost the student's morale as necessary. This leads to the third goal: to encourage students to take responsibility and to want to participate fully in events and developments in the state as a whole and, particularly, in the IDF (Sadan, first interview).

Over the next fifteen years, more religious Mekhinot were established. As of 2012, there are fourteen such Mekhinot situated all over Israel. As explained in the methodological appendix, for the purpose of this study, the Mekhinot at Eli, Atzmona, Rosh Pina, and Yatir were examined in depth.

The administrative office in charge of the Mekhinot is the Security and Society Department (Ha-Agaf Ha-Bitchoni-Hevrati, formally Agaf Ha-Noar VeHa-NAHAL) in the Ministry of Defense. Among other roles, it has the authority to approve the establishment of new Mekhinot as well as the appointment of the heads of these Mekhinot (Duvdevani, first interview). Brigadier General Yehuda Duvdevani, who was appointed head of the department in 1996, was greatly impressed with the Mekhinot and asked their rabbis to assist in the establishment of parallel secular Mekhinot:

> I said to them, "Gentlemen, do you think that such a successful thing as you have now should be only for the religious sector? [. . .] What do you want our future leadership to look like? Only secular? Do you want to see only religious soldiers sitting at the General Command table? Or do you want there to be a balance, like the balance which exists in the People of Israel (Am Yisrael)?" They said, "[There should be] a balance." I said, "Okay. I want you to help me [. . .]," and on that same night it was decided that the number of Mekhinot should be increased and that secular Mekhinot should be established. (Duvdevani, first interview)

Following this decision, Duvdevani formed a committee, composed of himself and Rabbis Hager-Lau, Sadan, and Peretz,[3] to approve new Mekhinot. According to Duvdevani, they set rules as to who can be the head of a new Mekhina:

> He must be a military man, a person of principles, first of all in his Judaism—this is from a religious point of view, yes?—and he must be a rabbi, a man of status, he must be an *educator* [. . .] a spiritual father. He must be open-minded. He must know that he . . . he takes children whom he shapes for leadership [. . .] he must be a leadership figure! Of the first degree! If he is

not, he will not be able to take the pressure. (speaker's emphasis, Duvdevani, first interview)

It was also determined that the new Mekhinot would not be located in well-established areas, but rather where they could strengthen and contribute to a small community. A large number of religious Mekhinot are located in the West Bank, and this is some indication of their prevalent political outlook.

THE NATURE AND STRUCTURE OF THE MEKHINOT PROGRAM

Unlike the women's programs (see Chapter 7) and the Hesder and Shiluv programs, the Mekhinot are attended almost exclusively by preservice students, thus departing from the multigenerational format discussed earlier.[4] Consequently, students are more or less part of the same age group and all belong to the same study program. This is due to the fact that the Mekhinot did not develop out of existing organizations, as in the case of the Shiluv program, but were established as independent bodies. However, unlike in the Hesder program, students do not automatically return to the Mekhina after their military service. Students do not attend the Mekhina during or after their military service, unless they choose to visit. Therefore, there is very little interaction among the age groups.[5] In keeping with this aspect of the program, the Mekhinot's administration is aimed at serving the Mekhina students exclusively.[6]

The Mekhinot do not have regular contact with the Hesder's Igud. However, when issues concerning their students' military service call for intervention, it seems that the organizations cooperate with each other. For instance, when the question of integrating women in combat units was being discussed, the Mekhinot and the Hesder's Igud came together to coordinate their position and presented it jointly to the IDF (Sadan, first interview; Hager-Lau, first interview). Nevertheless, there is a certain tension between the Igud and the Mekhinot, although the heads of the Mekhinot refrain from speaking out against the Igud.

The Mekhinot have their own official umbrella organization similar to the Igud called the Association of Mekhinot (Igud Ha-Mekhinot). This organization is lead by Rabbi Moshe Hager-Lau, head of the Yatir Mekhina.

As Duvdevani commented, the location of the Mekhinot is of prime importance. When interviewed, both Rabbis Hager-Lau and Peretz spoke of the importance of the community in which the Mekhina is located and its contribution to the educational atmosphere at the Mekhina. Rabbi Hager-Lau explained that the relative geographical isolation of Yatir means that students are not tempted to leave the Mekhina to go out for fun, since there is nowhere for them to go. It is easier to sit down and study when one is physically far from centers of entertainment (Hager-Lau, first interview). Rabbi Peretz spoke of the example set by the inhabitants of Atzmona, where the Mekhina was situated at the time: "The guys come face to face with pure Torah [. . .] people who are willing to do everything for their ideals and observe every detail [of the halakha]. . . . There are no TVs in the settlement; no newspapers" (Peretz, first interview). Rabbi Peretz emphasized that the nature of the community and the fact that the members studied Torah and are knowledgeable about halakha "and [even though they are scholars] guess what? They have chosen to live in 'the world of actions' [*olam ha-ma'aseh*]" and are farmers. All of this presents an important example for the students (Peretz, first interview).[7]

Like the other programs examined here, the Mekhinot's funding comes from three sources: the students' parents, the state, and donations. The Ministry of Education transfers state funding to the Mekhinot. Accordingly, the Mekhinot may only expand by a maximum of 15 percent each year in order to allow the government to calculate funding properly.[8]

Things were not always so simple. During the 1990s, the state did not fund the Mekhinot at all (Hager-Lau, first interview). At other times, the state funding was meager: 150 NIS per student [approximately fifty USD] (Sadan, first interview). During this time, the religious Mekhinot's association with the secular ones exacerbated, to a certain degree, their financial predicament. When the secular Mekhinot were established, the religious ones agreed to share the state's funding, with the aim of bolstering the general concept of the Mekhinot. As Duvdevani put it:

> And what was the main point? The religious Mekhinot *relinquished* [part of their] funding to the secular Mekhinot. [. . .] [It is] the same cake, and it had to be shared with two new ones [the two secular Mekhinot that opened in 1996]!" (speaker's emphasis, Duvdevani, first interview)

In other words, the religious Mekhinot were willing to forgo much needed funds in order to ensure there would be secular and heterogeneous Mekhinot rather than refuse to share the budget and quash the possibility of a nonreligious section of the program. These facts contradict the usual perception of the Mekhinot as narrow-minded and religiously zealous.

At the beginning of the academic year 2007–2008, the Mekhinot's budget was reduced substantially to such a degree that there was a real danger the entire program might have to close down (Kashti and Shragai 2007; Shelach 2007). As a result, the government passed the Mekhinot Law (2008) to allow additional funding and ensure the Mekhinot would not disband due to monetary troubles.

CURRICULUM AND FACULTY

Preparing students for life in general—as opposed to preparing them exclusively for service in the military—was seen as the main goal of the program by all the Mekhina heads interviewed. The four rabbis commented that religious high school education tries to prepare students for their matriculation exams, without giving much thought to other aspects of life. Issues pertaining to faith or shaping the students' spiritual world are hardly raised. On the other hand, the religious education system generates "quite a bit of hatred for Talmud studies" (Davidovitch, first interview), and this influences young men when they choose not to study in a yeshiva where Talmud is the educational focus.

While there are variations between Mekhinot, the above facts indicate that the common main goal of the Mekhinot is

> to shape students to be religious individuals who are motivated by Torah and Torah-based idealism to act in Israeli reality. In the practical areas of Israeli life [. . .] military [service] is a jot—albeit a large one—in Israeli life. Actually, the idea is much greater than military service. The idea [of the Mekhina] is that for the rest of their lives [the students] will be proactive, not egotistical and self-centered. And everything they do will be motivated by a feeling of responsibility, of belonging to this people and to this land. (Peretz, first interview)

In other words, time in the Mekhina is spent trying to deepen the student's spiritual worldview and faith. It is through the prism of his studies that he will be able to find his place in Israeli society and contribute to it. None of the heads of the Mekhinot interviewed here referred to creating a Torah scholar as one of the program's goals. The Mekhinot stress actions stemming from studies rather than studies alone as a goal.

While most of Mekhinot curriculum focuses exclusively on religious studies, the Rosh Pina Mekhina has a slightly different curriculum, and this affects the Mekhina's funding. Aside from Torah studies, students study Arabic rigorously with the help of military instructors. Rabbi Davidovitch, the head of the Rosh Pina Mekhina, was a senior officer in the Intelligence Corps. This unit has ties with the Mekhina. Students found suitable and who pass an Arabic exam are stationed in Military Intelligence in a variety of postings.

The faculties in Mekhinot are made up of teachers who have a background in Torah studies as well as military experience. Both in Eli and Atzmona, the faculty is expected to have studied Torah and spent many years in yeshivot of high standing

(Sadan, first interview; Peretz, first interview). Rabbi Hager-Lau said that it was most important that a member of the faculty should be a teacher who also likes the students:

> It's really easy to become discouraged about this program. There is quite a gap between the yeshiva world and the world that young adults live in, and this is extremely discouraging. And every year you have to start anew because you get a new group [. . .] every time they put us through "boot camp" with new pranks and crazes of their generation. It's very hard to be a faculty member in a Mekhina. And so you really have to like teenagers and know how to talk to them and engage them. (Hager-Lau, first interview)

Rabbi Sadan also commented on the importance of a faculty member's charisma and put forward three criteria for hiring a teacher: he must have an extensive background in Torah studies and must have attended a high yeshiva for many years; he must have a spiritual outlook and be knowledgeable in the matters of faith that are a central part of the Mekhina's teachings; and he must be not only a teacher, but also a pedagogue. "Who is a pedagogue? A person who makes students admire him and want to follow him [. . .]. [I am looking for] charismatic Torah scholars" (Sadan, first interview).

Rabbi Peretz spoke of the importance of conveying a consistent message to the students:

> I most definitely am not a pluralist. And I also won't have pluralism [in our Mekhina]. I mean, I will not present seven different approaches [for the students] to choose from. I will try to make sure that my approach will be fair, clear, and open-minded enough, but we are loyal followers of Rabbi Kook's approach, and we do not hide this. We are not ashamed. [We are] *proud of it!* And we think this is an approach which includes *everything.* (speaker's emphasis, Peretz, first interview)

Rabbi Davidovitch, on the other hand, underlined the importance of having a heterogeneous faculty:

> We have on our faculty—I purposely hired them—a teacher who takes a more Kabbala-inspired and spiritual approach. We have a teacher who is more versed in the halakhic side of things [. . .] so this is where we have the heterogeneous aspect of the faculty. This is the beauty of it, and I believe in it [. . .]. It might be problematic from a pedagogic point

of view. It's easy to put someone into a kind of mold, then put it in the oven. Sometimes whatever is in there overflows, but sometimes that is what makes it beautiful. This is my belief. (Davidovitch, first interview)

Rabbi Davidovitch's approach is thus very different from that of Rabbi Peretz, as well as from those of the educators at Eli.

As well as teaching aptitude and personality, a teacher's past in the military is also a consideration when hiring faculty members, although the rabbis were not unequivocal when referring to this criterion. For instance, when Rabbi Davidovitch was asked about the military background of his faculty, he said: "Everyone served [in the military]." When asked what would happen if a person who had not served in the military applied for a job, he answered: "I don't think this would happen here" (Davidovitch, first interview). In other words, due to the nature of the program, it is inconceivable that someone who had not served in the military would want to be a member of the faculty. Rabbi Sadan pointed out that, in any case, very few people from the Religious Zionist sector do not serve in the military one way or another. He himself wants to see a positive attitude toward military service in a potential member of his staff (Sadan, first interview). In practice, there are many officers among the Mekhinot's staff. At the time this study was conducted, in Eli, for instance, three teachers were battalion commanders in the reserves (Sadan, first interview).

Physical education instructors are also part of the faculty of the Mekhinot. Students train in order to ensure they are physically fit in time to enlist. Particular effort is made to prepare them for the tryouts for the more elite units. Eli employs a navigation instructor as well. In the past, a social activities counselor was part of the staff at Yatir and dealt with social problems, met with the students once a week for a group discussion, and organized various social events as well as the duty roster (Hager-Lau, first interview). At Rosh Pina—as part of its unique curriculum—there are also two (female) Arabic teachers.

Unlike the other Mekhinot examined here, at Rosh Pina students have no extracurricular duties. At the other three Mekhinot, students are almost exclusively in charge of the day-to-day running of the Mekhina: they have kitchen duties, clean their rooms and the study hall, and perform guard duty. Eli employs a professional cook and a janitor who takes care of major maintenance problems; the students are in charge of everything else (Sadan, first interview). The idea is to foster the students' sense of personal responsibility. In all three Mekhinot, performance of these chores is strictly monitored—unlike actual study. Rabbi Hager-Lau, for instance, stated that this issue is nonnegotiable, and that a student "who doesn't want to [do this will] not [be] here" (first interview).

In general the Mekhinot curriculum emphasizes theology (*limudei emuna*), and Talmud studies are allocated less time. In Yatir, for instance, Talmud studies take up only three hours a day. The comparison to a Hesder yeshiva in this regard is marked. Talmud classes themselves differ, too, from traditional studies. Classes focus on issues that are not likely to have been studied by the students in their high school Talmud classes, such as topics related to agriculture and rain (Hager-Lau, first interview). Rosh Pina emphasizes the study of Jewish philosophy and Jewish thought (*mahshevet yisrael*), and the head of the yeshiva mainly instructs the students in the philosophical teachings of Professor Yeshayahu Leibovitch.[9] In Eli and Atzmona, the focus is on the teachings of Rabbi Kook, in line with the outlook of Mercaz Ha-Rav.

The *mekhina le-chaim* (lit., "preparation for life") program in Eli for postservice students focuses on values similar to those taught in the preservice program. Rabbi Sadan explained that after military service, "a sort of spiritual medical postcombat facility [TAGAD] is needed.[10] After battle, you need to repair things that require fixing [from a spiritual point of view]." The program also tries to help the students choose a profession and to find a direction in life that will "help society in general," meaning that one of the program goals is for students to be involved in social and political aspects of Israeli life, and the program helps them acquire the tools with which to do so. For instance, as part of its postservice agenda, the Mekhina runs a four-year program in which two alumni are awarded a stipend and a scholarship for law school; in return, they attend the *mekhina le-chaim*, combining law and Torah studies. These students also commit to working in the public sector rather than in "some private law firm and making money" (Sadan, first interview).

Various speakers are invited to address the students at Eli, Yatir, and Atzmona. Rabbi Hager-Lau and Rabbi Peretz said that the aim is to present the students with role models in the form of these guest lecturers, who are inspiring either due to personal aspects of their lives or to their military pasts. Military personnel are allowed to come and speak in an attempt to recruit students to their units. Rabbi Sadan noted that if a certain corps is having manpower difficulties and approaches the Mekhina, its representatives will be permitted to speak to the students and try to recruit them (Sadan, first interview).

PREPARATION FOR MILITARY SERVICE

Unlike the Hesder program, in which preparation for the military takes place shortly before enlistment, Mekhinot students begin preparation for service when they enter the program. Preparation is both mental and physical.

Aside from physical education and Torah study, the Mekhinot offer practical mental and spiritual preparation: discussions of halakhic and moral dilemmas that the students might encounter during their service. For instance, what should a religious soldier do when he does not have time to pray during the day? What should one do if his comrades pick oranges in someone else's orchard (Peretz, second interview)? In general, Rabbi Peretz emphasized the importance of moral and ethical behavior (*midot*) and viewed such instruction as part of preparation for service in the military.

The approach to military service is slightly different in Rosh Pina. First, the head of the Mekhina stressed that he himself sees the military as a necessity and this view differs from that of other Mekhina heads and apparently also from some of the students' views, all of whom see military service as a religious commandment.

Furthermore, Rabbi Davidovitch did not refer at all to preparing the students for service in the IDF. There is one physical education class a week, but no navigational skills classes, outdoor trips, etc. As in other Mekhinot examined in this study, there are theology classes (*limudei emuna*), but at the end of the interview, Rabbi Davidovitch noted:

> We try to equip [the students with] the skills [to deal with military service]. [. . .] [The students say,] "We want you to reinforce us [from a religious point of view]." So I say to the guys: "Listen, once we bought some computer chips called 'reinforcement' and when we installed them, they shorted out. So we sent them back to the factory, and since then we have been using another method. [. . .] Ask questions which will *maybe* be answered. You have to do 80 percent of the work [. . .]. We can't make promises. We will give 20 percent and you will make up the rest." (speaker's emphasis, Davidovitch, first interview)

The tone here is very different from that of Rabbi Peretz, for instance (cited above). While it seems that at Eli and Atzmona the rabbis are prepared to map out a clear path that the students need only follow, at Rosh Pina the approach is different. The students are expected to plan their own road with minimal guidance from the Mekhina faculty. This approach is more reminiscent of some of the Hesder yeshivot and of the Shiluv program rather than of the other Mekhinot examined here. Indeed, some of the students at Rosh Pina are not satisfied with this aspect of the Mekhina. They expected to receive a more concentrated dose of faith-related matters and to feel more spiritually prepared for military service.[11]

DEMOGRAPHICS

As demonstrated by the differences described above, each Mekhina tries to appeal to a slightly different demographic sector and has a particular pedagogical approach. While over the years Eli has become more yeshiva-like,[12] the atmosphere in most Mekhinot is entirely different. There are Mekhinot in which

> students are given more leeway to feel their "individual self" and get rid of the pressure they accumulated during their high school education and to be free of all other obligations [. . .]. So you find students with [long] hair, earrings, and all kinds of other things. This is a different educational approach which manages to do great things and change a person into something entirely different. (Davidovitch, first interview)

It seems that there is some truth to these observations. Some Mekhinot have rules that would be entirely superfluous in a Hesder yeshiva; for instance, girls cannot visit the Mekhina and students may not wear earrings or use drugs or alcohol.

Who, then, attends the Mekhinot program? Of the Mekhina students interviewed for this study, two did not deliberate at all before choosing their Mekhina program. A fair number of the students had thought about attending a Hesder yeshiva, but were put off either by the reduced military service or by the program itself and the nature of the studies there, which didn't suit them personally.

A look at the data from Atzmona illustrates that students originate from a wide variety of locations. The initial location of the Mekhina in the Gaza Strip did not appear to influence enrollment, and new students continued to apply in spite of the area's dangerous reputation. Even the March 2002 terrorist attack on the Mekhina—when five students were killed—did not influence attendance, and there was no decline in the number of applicants the following year. Likewise, the Mekhina's relocation to Yated—near the Egyptian border—after the Disengagement from Gaza (2005) has not affected the number of students at the Mekhina. During the academic year at the time of the Disengagement (2004–2005), 123 students studied at Atzmona. There was a slight increase in the numbers the following year (132 students) and a decrease in 2006–2007. However, 2007–2008 showed 129 students at the Mekhina, indicating no significant drop in attendance (Association of Mekhinot 1988–2007).

Yatir, on the other hand, attracts more students from the center of Israel, including the region of Samaria in the West Bank. There are fewer students from the north of the country. This may be due to the fact that the Mekhina is located relatively south, and students from the north would rather not go as far south as Yatir. It is interesting to note that in Yatir, as in Atzmona, there are many students from communal and agricultural communities—in contrast to the Shiluv program.

Another interesting point is that while the students at Atzmona originate from high schools considered elitist, hardly any of the students at Yatir come from similar institutions, such as Neve Shmuel. On the contrary, some Yatir students are graduates of the ORT vocational school network.[13] These data bear out comments by the head of the Mekhina on his lack of selectivity when accepting students to the program. The Mekhina usually accepts all applicants (Hager-Lau, first interview).

Another important point is that in spite of the Mekhinot's commitment to the advancement of Israeli society in general, at the present only one religious Mekhina is located in a development town (Kiryat Malakhi). This Mekhina is under the auspices of the Or Etzion Hesder yeshiva and attempts to reach local teenagers of Ethiopian origin (Eliav, first interview).

Based on an in-depth examination of the Mekhinot and conversations with the students, it appears that students come from a solid socioeconomic background. Surprisingly, there are very few students of Ethiopian origin or from the former Soviet Union,[14] despite the Mekhinot's self-proclaimed social aims. Unequivocal conclusions concerning the sector of the population from which the Mekhina students come cannot be drawn, however, due to the absence of systematic data. A greater degree of cooperation from the Mekhinot would yield more precise conclusions.

STUDENT EXPECTATIONS

As explained in the methodological appendix, the in-depth interviews conducted for this study yielded complex answers regarding the reasons students chose to attend the program in general, and a specific Mekhina in particular. One main category of answers was that the students saw study as an end in and of itself (*lishmah*). Most of the students who emphasized the importance of study itself and the fact that they wanted to attend an institution where the study of Torah would play a significant role were enrolled in Eli. In general, interviewees said that they wanted "a break for a year"; "a year to myself" during which they would be able to study. Eli students specifically expected to be able to improve their ability to study and to increase their knowledge. For instance, one Eli student recounted that he had expected to enrich his knowledge of the Talmud and to improve his ability to study, but in practice:

The whole year I did nothing but study like crazy. [I would be up] from 6:00 a.m., I didn't sleep a lot, and I took notes on everything. But in the end, what I *really* got was the idea of *love* for the Torah. [. . .] It's like that thirst when the rabbi speaks and you . . . your whole body listens to him. It's something really basic. [Something] that I *didn't* have. A kind of respect and love [. . .]. At least in retrospect, that's worth more than the other things [that I expected to get when I came here]. (speaker's emphasis, Yoni, first interview)

Thus the search for knowledge is intertwined with the desire to forge an identity and construct a way of life. Yoni felt that he might have gained knowledge, but the main thing he learned was love of the Torah, a value that has now become part of his religious identity. And, as in other programs, a subcategory of the students who chose the program out of a desire to study viewed the year at the Mekhina as an opportunity to explore faith-related issues and to shape their identity in general before entering the military.

But this implies something much deeper regarding the high school education of these young men. The wish to solidify their sense of themselves and their religious identity during their year at the Mekhina means that this was not achieved during their high school days and highlights a severe lacuna in the Israeli religious education system. Consequently, Mekhina students tended to view this year as an opportunity to forge a more solid foundation for their religious identity—and to consciously choose to observe mitzvot of their own free will. A student at Atzmona described it thus:

If you are going to follow a certain path your whole life, then *I* expect [. . .] to really feel that I am doing so after making it clear [. . .] that I understand that this is the path I am taking, because I examined it, and because I know that this is how it should be and that this is what I want. (speaker's emphasis, Evyatar, first interview)

Within the group of students who expressed a desire to enter the program in order to pursue "study as an end in and of itself," there were those who wished to "strengthen" their faith, to some degree or another. There were students who feared that if they entered the military immediately after graduating high school, they would not be able to maintain their religious identity. A year at the Mekhina, they felt, would help them to preserve their religious observance.

Like Hesder and Shiluv students, some of the Mekhina students spoke of more prosaic reasons for choosing to attend the program, and for choosing their

Mekhina in particular. Many students said that they simply liked the place: they were either taken by its physical beauty, or said that while visiting they liked the faculty or were impressed with the head of the Mekhina. Two students said that they just came to their Mekhina without much forethought.

The combination of Torah and Arabic studies was given as a specific reason for choosing Rosh Pina. One of the students commented, "I didn't want to study Torah the whole day. I wanted, like, to combine [it] with something else" (Uri, first interview). Another student admitted that in fact the opportunity to study Arabic was the sole reason he chose Rosh Pina, and that if he hadn't thought that it was important to study Arabic, he would have gone to a heterogeneous (secular and religious) Mekhina.

Another pedestrian reason was following (or not following) the example set by a friend or brother. A student who followed his brother explained:

> My older brother went to Eli, and I saw guys, his friends, and [. . .] I was
> very jealous of . . . I don't know what to call it. They had something that
> I really wanted to have. (Yoni, first interview)

Some alumni spoke of other reasons: choosing a Mekhina where studies were said to not require much effort, going to a Mekhina because in Religious Zionist society one was expected to do so, and so on.

Another category of answers focused on the hope of preparation for military service and serving according to the program's course of service. Students said that they wanted to serve a full three years, and this was an important factor in their decision to go to a Mekhina. In addition, many thought that the Mekhina would also prepare them for military service in more practical ways (developing physical stamina, or preparing them for concrete halakhic problems that might arise during their time in the military, as opposed to study that would increase their commitment to the halakha, etc.).

One of the results of studying at the Mekhina and preparing for service was increased motivation. As students better comprehended the importance of the military and of military service, they felt they acquired a broader perspective on the IDF, which encouraged them to serve: "If I know what I am doing and why, then this will give me more motivation for military service itself" (Uri, first interview). A number of students interviewed prior to enlistment thought that the Mekhina would help them get better military postings and it would accompany them throughout their time in uniform.[15]

On the other hand, there were students—mainly from Eli—who emphasized that such considerations related to military service were secondary: Torah study was aimed at helping them deal with service in the military, but the study itself remained their primary consideration.

MILITARY SERVICE AFTER STUDYING IN THE MEKHINA

Unlike students in the Hesder and the *midrashot* (which will be discussed in the following chapter), Mekhina students do not serve in separate units. During their year at the Mekhina, most of them spend time trying to secure a suitable military posting. While the IDF tends to place soldiers according to its own preferences, it does take the draftees' wishes into consideration. Additionally, exams and tryouts are held for the more prestigious posts such as reconnaissance units and special forces.

Most of the preservice interviewees had specific preferences: to serve in a certain corps, or a specific infantry brigade, or in a reconnaissance unit. Few had no preferences as to where to serve at the time of the interviews. Of the alumni and the students interviewed in the follow-up study (first and second years in uniform), most students served in various infantry units (six of whom served in elite units). During subsequent months of service, nine students and alumni joined the officers' corps and three others held noncommissioned officer posts. One officer signed on for long-term service in the standing forces, and another also planned to stay in the IDF for the next few years. In other words, most Mekhina students serve in combat positions and a fair number extend their service as officers.

Understandably, students who served in noncombat posts served in very heterogeneous units and alongside mostly secular soldiers. Students who were stationed in infantry units reported that they served with at least one other Mekhina student. Those who served in reconnaissance and elite units said that they had served with a relatively large number of Mekhina students as well as students from other programs—sometimes up to half of the unit was made up of such soldiers. For instance, one of the students who served in the Duvdevan unit served with another four Mekhina students as well as a number of Hesder students who had left their program (Nitai, second interview). Students assigned to regular infantry units reported serving with fewer Mekhina students and with fewer students from other preservice study programs in general.

Students who served alongside other religious soldiers usually said that they were happy about it and that it helped them throughout their service—even if only in regard to technical issues such as making up the minyan for prayer (Shachar, second interview). One of the interviewees elaborated:

If you have to fight, you don't fight your battles alone. And when you are [part of] a group, then you are treated with more consideration. [. . .] [When you are alone], then [everyone else] can eat at a nonkosher place and you have to manage somehow. But if out of twenty, ten are religious, then [we, as a group] can't go to an Arab restaurant. (Tzur, second interview)

Serving alongside religious soldiers is not intentional, however. Mekhinot do not encourage group enlistment, despite the difficulties this would alleviate. Rabbi Peretz said he prefers that no more than two students serve together in a unit because, although serving alone is difficult, if there are more than two soldiers together, they become a clique. This goes against the program's aim, which is to "encounter Am Yisrael and not ourselves" (Peretz, first interview). The follow-up study, however, indicates that in practice this is not the case, as described above. Contrary to Rabbi Peretz's preference, many of his students serve together with other religious soldiers.

CONTACT BETWEEN THE MEKHINOT AND STUDENTS IN THE MILITARY

Unlike students in the Shiluv and the *midrashot*, Mekhina students can be part of a large graduating class. Technically, it is difficult—if not impossible—for a Mekhina to maintain contact with a class of 110 or more students during their military service. Rabbi Sadan speculated that at any given time there are between 450 and 500 students from Eli in the military. The Mekhina designates a liaison in charge of maintaining contact with each graduating class while they are in uniform. This is usually a graduate of the program who studies at the *kollel*. The liaison is supposed to phone the students monthly in order to keep in touch (Sadan, first interview).[16]

Representatives of the Mekhinot do not visit the students during their service, unlike in the Hesder and the Shiluv programs. However, if invited, the Mekhinot's representatives attend the students' military ceremonies (Hager-Lau, first interview).

Barring visits and because phone calls are sporadic, contact with the Mekhinot takes place mainly through the distribution of newsletters. Students from Eli, Atzmona, and Yatir reported that they were sent items in the mail: a class newsletter and/or a circular, and booklets of texts that could be studied before the holidays (Yinon, second interview; Tzur, second interview). The Mekhina at Rosh Pina does not send its students any mail and does not maintain official contact with them. Interviews with the students give the impression that the contact between this Mekhina and its students is extremely weak.

Students can also actively maintain contact with their Mekhina, mostly through visits. There are usually two class weekends per year, and students make an effort to attend when their class is meeting. Students also try to visit when possible by coming for a free weekend or during the holidays (Shimon, second interview; Micha, second interview). Some students call their teachers on their own initiative. Closer relationships with the faculty can be seen in the smaller Mekhinot. For instance, a student from Yatir said that he also calls the secretary to find out how she is (Yinon, second interview).

In contrast, some students and alumni commented that they did not have ongoing contact with the Mekhina during their service (Benny, second interview; Yochai, first interview). They were not necessarily bothered by this, and some said that the degree of contact with the Mekhina was right for them (Nitai, second interview).

Even though contact with the Mekhina is not always close, it seems that many of the alumni and the students in the follow-up study maintain their relationships with the other members of their class. This trend continues once alumni are out of uniform. Five years after the beginning of this study, each of the sixteen students remaining in the follow-up study kept in touch with their classmates in some way or another, including students who got married during this time. During military service, these relationships were maintained mainly over the phone, but some of the students also spent time together when their military schedules permitted it.

All the students in the follow-up study reported that they missed the Mekhina after enlistment. They all missed their friends and the time they had spent together. Most students interviewed during the first year of the follow-up study said they missed the chance to be able to study. However, in the second year of the follow-up study, hardly any of the participants still missed studying. After three years of military service, only one student missed being able to study while most missed the Mekhina environment as well as their fellow students. This indicates that the most important component of the program for them was social rather than educational.

For many students, classmates served as a source of emotional support during their military service. More than half of the students interviewed in the first year of the follow-up study thought that their Mekhina friends offered support, to one degree or another. For instance, one of the students explained that:

> I can talk to them freely, let's say, more than I can with my other friends.
> Because they're in the [military] system, and it's enough that they know
> where I am [serving] and, like, they know the system. It's much easier to

talk to them. Another thing is [. . .] I have friends that I regularly turn to for advice. (Yaniv, second interview)

Interestingly, in the second year of the follow-up study, the number of students who felt that their classmates had been a source of emotional support during their service increased slightly from the previous year. Some interviewees felt that their classmates were a source of support, but that they themselves didn't need such assistance:

If I want support, I'm sure that I'll find it. I just . . . maybe it's because of my nature, I like being very, very independent, less reliant [on other people]. But I know that if, for some reason, I need support [. . .] I'm sure that I'll get it [from my friends]. (Benny, second interview)

In their third year of service, of the students interviewed for the follow-up study, more than half felt that their classmates gave them emotional support. The remaining interviewees felt that they were given more support by friends in their military unit, especially after having fought together in the Second Lebanon War (2006). As in previous years, there were also students who did not feel they needed support.

Making such declarations is completely logical. They are, after all, young men serving in the military, and it is no surprise that they are unwilling to admit the possible need for support and assistance. It is therefore impressive that most of the interviewees acknowledged the support of their classmates. This indicates the central role played by their friends—specifically their Mekhina friends.

Generally speaking, as in the case of the other programs, the nature of the contact between the Mekhina and the students depends, to a large degree, on the student. Some interviewees pointed out that any contact they had with the Mekhina was due to their own initiative.

Students recounted that when they came to visit or called, the members of the faculty were happy to see them and made them feel welcome. "They make you feel good" (Shimon, second interview). However, most Mekhinot do not keep close tabs on their students, and if the students wish for a closer relationship, they must take the initiative.

* * *

In conclusion, despite the fact that they resent this description, Mekhinot are indeed "preparatories" in many ways: for the most part, they prepare their members for military service both through their educational curriculum and their more practical aspects (physical fitness training, navigation skills classes, and inspirational guest lecturers). Students expect to be prepared for service in practical ways and religious study alone is not what they hope to find at their Mekhina. While Mekhinot state that they have a social responsibility to a broader community, in practice students come from a more clearly defined background than any of the comparable programs and are not diverse. During service itself, while students feel they gained much regarding Torah study and religious education, this is not the most important factor for them in the long run. The social factor impacted them more, according to the follow-up study. However, students do expect their Mekhina to help them during their time in uniform, as will be seen in Chapter 8.

CHAPTER 7
THE GAR'INIM PROGRAM:
JEWISH ORTHODOX WOMEN AND THE IDF

Most religious women do not serve in the IDF. Rather, they are given an exemption for religious reasons. However, about 25 percent of the graduates of religious women's high schools serve in the IDF. A small percentage does so within religious women's preservice study programs.

The Ma'ayan, Hadas, and Be'er programs are part of the Gar'inim service track founded by Lieutenant Colonel Rabbi Shimon Elmaliach. The program follows the pattern of the NAHAL nuclei (called *gar'inim*, sing. *gar'in*), which are made up of active service (SHARAP) and unpaid service (SHALAT).[1] The Hadas program, headed by Rabbi Ohad Tehar-Lev, is part of Midreshet Lindenbaum in Jerusalem. The Ma'ayan program is part of the women's *midrasha* in Ein Ha-Natziv;[2] a member of the Religious Kibbutz Movement. Rabbi Eli Kahan headed the program until his death in 2008, after which Rabbi Avia Rosen took over as head of the program. Today Rabbi Avia Rosen heads the *midrasha*.[3] Be'er is an offshoot of the pluralistic study program Bemidbar in Yeruham, and the youngest of the three programs. The present head of the program is Ms. Tami Biton.

RELIGIOUS ZIONIST WOMEN, TORAH STUDIES, AND MILITARY SERVICE

Much has been written about women and the military in general, and in particular about women and the IDF. However, this study is not concerned with the place of women in the IDF or the IDF's approach to gender equality or to the feminist movement. The present study focuses on women who wish to fulfill their civic duty and serve in the IDF, just as their secular counterparts must.

Although military service for women is regulated by law in Israel, religious women who want to serve must contend with the widespread interpretation of the Jewish Orthodox halakha opposing women's conscription and the Zionist Religious sector's generally negative attitude toward the issue. In this context, questions concerning the gender marginalization of women in the IDF are not as pertinent as in secular society. Religious women who enlist through the Gar'inim program are concerned with questions regarding their place as religious individuals in a secular society, not as women. They are searching for a way to serve in the IDF under conditions dictated by religious constraints.

Insofar as they are aware of these gender issues, this awareness develops as a result of their military service.[4]

For women from Religious Zionist society—as for their secular counterparts—military service is considered a rite of passage (Ben-Ari and Levy-Schreiber 2001, 109). As discussed above in the context of Religious Zionist young men, this rite of passage also has a more personal dimension: it is a test of religious observance. One way for women to deal with this challenge is to attend a *midrasha* for a year of preservice study.

Midrashot are the feminine equivalent of yeshivot. They offer a framework for high-quality Torah studies for women. The first *midrasha* was established in 1977 when Rabbi Chaim Brovender, in response to a request by four female students in America, founded the Bruria *midrasha*—which was to become the Lindenbaum *midrasha* in 1986—one of the Ohr Torah Stone institutions (Elor 1998).

In spite of the religious establishment's initial opposition, based on hostility toward women's study of Torah in general (and Talmud in particular), since the end of the twentieth century, women's *midrashot* have been largely accepted as part of a Religious Zionist woman's education (Ross 2004). An examination of current responsa on websites such as moreshet.co.il and kipa.co.il indicates that studying at a *midrasha* is now taken for granted: questions do not revolve around the actual idea of study but rather raise concerns regarding the amount of time a woman should dedicate to Torah study, which *midrasha* to attend, and so on. Changes are also reflected in questions concerning women's Talmud studies: if in the past there was a tendency to prohibit such studies absolutely, today one commonly finds that Talmud studies are given partial sanction, even among more conservative sectors in Religious Zionist society.[5]

The most interesting indications that women's Torah study is no longer considered radical are found in articles criticizing the Gar'inim service track. Most arguments against the program target the students' military service, while there are no arguments whatsoever against their study of Torah. The only criticism not directed against military service itself is that the time spent at the *midrasha* extends the period during which these women remain single.[6] Of course different rabbis support different study programs, and they are not all considered to be of equal worth and quality.

As of 2013, twenty-five *midrashot* are registered in the Midrashot Forum, the umbrella organization for such institutions. These are affiliated with various sectors within Religious Zionist society, and several different kinds are found all over Israel. Traditionally, the study of Torah is male territory, and the entrance of women into this domain has empowered them and invested them with cultural capital, thus threatening the status of male students. The heads of the *midrashot* do not accept this argument or see themselves as a threat to the rabbinic establishment, and they deny the accusation that they are motivated chiefly by a feminist impetus. Rachel Keren, a pivotal teacher at the women's *midrasha* at Ein Ha-Natziv, and at one time the head of it, stated:

> It is not the feminist motivation, the desire to equalize the status of women and men, which has motivated women to decide to dedicate time to Torah studies. The most difficult question that young women grapple with is their [identity as a] religious [person] and not their [identity as] religious women. (Keren 2001)

The students wish to shape their religious world independently. Like the Mekhina students, some wish to examine how committed they truly are to a religious way of life. In any case, they want to prove to themselves that if they remain observant, they do so out of choice rather than out of inertia. As part of a process of forming their identity before military service, their aim is to construct a religious world for themselves (Rosenberg 2000, 22). These women are motivated by their desire to be themselves rather than to be "like the men," and this is not necessarily a battle against discrimination. It is the act of studying itself that clarifies for them the distinction between themselves and men. This means that the result might be revolutionary, but the motivation is not (Keren 2004). This important point must be kept in mind when examining these women's choice to serve in the military within the Gar'in framework.

THE BEGINNING OF THE WOMEN'S GAR'INIM PROGRAM

As mentioned above, about 25 percent of female graduates of the Religious Zionist educational system enlist in the IDF. Most are not graduates of *ulpenot*,[7] but rather of comprehensive high schools, and a high percentage of these women enlist independently and individually rather than as part of a group (Lasloi and Rich 2001, 81). Only 1.4 percent of the graduates of the Religious Zionist educational system enlist through the *midrashot* program.

Until the mid-1990s, a Religious Zionist woman who wanted to serve in the military usually did so in one of three ways: as part of a religious NAHAL nucleus (*gar'in*); as a soldier-teacher in the program run by the Ministry of Education's Department of Torah Culture (Tarbut Toranit); or as an education NCO (*MASHAKit hora'ah*). A minority of religious women served in other posts.

Beginning in 2000, the option to enlist with assistance emerged. The Aluma project, whose first class completed the program in the summer of 2003, does not actively encourage young religious women to enlist but is willing to help those who have made up their minds to do so. Aluma runs a hotline for those interested in serving in the IDF. The project also holds informational meetings and seminars to inform young religious women of their options and service venues. The program encourages women to serve only in posts it considers to be suitable for young religious women (mainly instructor posts). However, there has also been an attempt to assist women who wish to serve in other posts (Porat and Una 2003). The Aluma project, like military service in the framework of the Department of Torah Culture (Tarbut Toranit), does not function as a preservice study program. Rather, it attempts to lend support to women who have decided to enlist despite their legal right to an exemption. Aluma's contact with its members is limited to the time they spend in uniform and focuses on each soldier individually, rather than offering a comprehensive framework. Although each class is also called a *gar'in*, the program does not in fact function as a *gar'in*, since the women contacted the project individually and serve as individuals. While the members meet once in a while, Aluma Gar'inim are not as cohesive or comprehensive as *midrashot* Gar'inim, and for this reason cannot be included in the current study.

Unlike the other programs discussed here, the Gar'inim program offers its students a halakhic "umbrella." *Midrashot* students are perceived as women who have given enlistment serious consideration, studied its various aspects, and enlisted after studying and deepening their Torah-based worldview. Enlisting in a Gar'in is taken as testimony to the fact that women who enlist are not "damaged" and are not part of a marginal religious phenomenon—rather, these students have taken a step that they consider to have religious meaning (Grizim 2004). In other words, the dialogue between a Gar'in student and Religious Zionist society focuses on her perception of Orthodox halakha and its ruling regarding women's conscription. A woman who studies and enlists in the framework of the Gar'in program essentially argues that she is serving in the IDF *because* she is religious rather than in spite of her religion.

This idea is a thorn in the side of many Religious Zionist rabbis. If, in the past, some young religious women would individually turn to rabbis to receive a halakhic dispensation in order to serve in the IDF, the Gar'inim program has now given a sweeping halakhic sanction of women's military service. Any member of a Gar'in can serve and has no need of convincing rabbis to allow her to do so. Each *midrasha*'s halakhic approach toward service in the IDF is different, but it is clear that they do not think that the halakha prohibits women from serving in the military.

Other arguments have been made against the program, all of which are halakhically based (Kahan 1998). But all its critics forget that religious women served in the IDF long before the creation of the program itself (Grizim 2004; Porat and Una 2003). Increasingly, young religious women ignore the perceived halakhic ban on women's military service, and their numbers are growing even outside the Gar'in program.[8]

While it has always been clear to Religious Zionist society that its male conscripts must be supported and assisted during their time in the military, the military service of young religious women has been entirely ignored; the Gar'in program is meant for these women. The self-declared aim of the program—as put forward both by the *midrashot* and by Rabbi Elmaliach, who is the liaison between the IDF and the *midrashot*—is to help these conscripts deepen their religious identity before enlisting and to support them during their military service (Tehar-Lev, first interview; Kahan, first interview; Elmaliach, first interview).

According to Rabbi Elmaliach, the goal in forming the *midrashot* was not to cause a revolution but to respond to reality. In his opinion, it became necessary to recognize the situation rather than ignore it. It was time to stop giving young religious women who chose to enlist the feeling that they are shunned by society (Elmaliach, first interview).

As mentioned above, three *midrashot* run premilitary service programs for young women from the Religious Zionist sector covering the entire period of military service. Unlike the programs run by other *midrashot*, Ma'ayan, Hadas, and Be'er are officially affiliated with the IDF, and their members enlist according to standing agreements with the military.

There are other *midrashot* that run preservice study programs. These, however, are not geared toward students in uniform. In *midrashot* such as Nov or Migdal Oz a young woman can study for a year before enlisting, but she will then enter the IDF individually rather than as part of a group—and the conditions of her service will be the same as for any other Israeli woman. The Gar'in program is unique in that it offers students support throughout their entire time in the military, and the program covers the length in service similar to that of the Hesder yeshivot.

It was a coincidence that brought about the creation of the Gar'inim program for religious women. In 1996, Lieutenant Colonel Rabbi Shimon Elmaliach, who was the rabbi of the NAHAL Brigade at the time, was at a meeting in which the merger of the Education Corps and the NAHAL was being discussed. At the meeting, the head of the Department of Education in the Education Corps deplored the fact that religious women who wished to serve as education NCOs would enlist only if the IDF committed itself to stationing them in this post.

Lacking such a commitment, they would not enlist and would instead serve in the National Service program. Since the post of education NCO is considered to be "suitable" for women from a religious standpoint, and since in general many religious women are given this posting by the IDF itself, Religious Zionist parents and teachers usually perceive this service venue to be less problematic and are more willing to accept it. Elmaliach suggested conscripting religious women in the form of a NAHAL nucleus, thus enabling the military to station them in prearranged posts, as is done in the case of other NAHAL nuclei (Elmaliach, first interview).

The existing NAHAL nuclei program is based on periods of active duty and unpaid service. The term of unpaid service is usually spent on a kibbutz or a new settlement. Since the 1980s, unpaid service can also be spent working in development towns or other socially challenged areas. Time spent in unpaid service is not included in the counting of military time served, so members of a Gar'in must make up this time—thereby extending their overall term in uniform. In the Gar'in program, unpaid service time is spent at a *midrasha*.

The pattern of the Gar'inim members' service in the military follows that of women's service in the NAHAL Gar'inim: twenty-three months of active service and approximately a year at the *midrasha*. A study term takes place before enlistment, but it is not counted as part of the program, and is partially calculated as unpaid service. For their active duty in the IDF, Gar'in members are earmarked for the Education Corps and serve as education NCOs, thereby solving the problem that caught Rabbi Elmaliach's attention and initiated the program.

During the program's first year (1997–1998), Gar'inim were formed in two *midrashot*: Lindenbaum (Bruria) in Jerusalem and the Religious Kibbutz Movement's *midrasha* at Ein Ha-Natziv.

According to Rabbi Elmaliach's description, all of the involved parties intended to create a framework that would allow women from Religious Zionist society to enlist in a manner that would accommodate their needs as observant women, while at the same time meeting the military's needs. Rabbi Elmaliach emphasized the cooperation of the IDF, the heads of religious high schools, and the *midrashot*, as well as others from the Religious Zionist sector who assisted him in the process of establishing the Gar'in program. At the same time, he did not conceal the fact that he encountered difficulties along the way and that the creation of these Gar'inim was not met with enthusiasm on the part of Religious Zionist rabbis. His attempt to secure the public blessing of a number of prominent rabbis for the program was unsuccessful (Elmaliach, first interview).

Over the years, a number of changes have been made to the program. For instance, in 2002 the members of the Hadas Gar'in at Bruria were given the opportunity to serve in the Intelligence Corps. The essential nature of the program remains the same, however, and most of the participants serve in the Education Corps.

A third Gar'in program was created in 2003. After a number of high school students expressed a desire to combine military service with Torah studies and communal service, Tami Biton from the Bemidbar *midrasha* in Yeruham and Leah Shakdiel opened the Be'er program. After hearing of this new initiative, Rabbi Elmaliach offered to include it in the existing Gar'inim service track (Elmaliach, first interview; Shakdiel, first interview). The Be'er program stood to gain from this offer since it would afford its students substantial organizational backing, and accepted his proposal. However, Biton and Shakdiel did not wish to force their students to serve as education NCOs, and therefore Be'er agreed to join the program on the condition that Be'er students be able to serve anywhere in the IDF. This clause is still in effect, and Be'er enables its participants to serve in any post in the IDF as well as in the National Service program (Biton, second interview).

THE NATURE AND STRUCTURE OF THE GAR'INIM PROGRAM

Like the Shiluv program, each *midrasha* was founded as an independent entity. It was only later that they developed a framework combining military service and Torah studies. The women's programs are funded by sources similar to those of the men's programs. The students' families pay tuition, but their financial ability does not impinge upon a student's eligibility to attend the *midrasha*. Scholarships and discounts may be offered. Some of the *midrashot*'s funding comes from governmental sources, like that of the Hesder yeshivot.

A substantial part of the *midrashot* funding is made up of donations. Because the Lindenbaum *midrasha* is part of the Ohr Torah Stone network, it has a solid economic foundation. Ein Ha-Natziv is also part of a larger organization—the Religious Kibbutz Movement—which oversees its budget, as well as those of its yeshivot. Unlike the older *midrashot*, Be'er experienced many financial difficulties in its first two years, both because of its precarious status as a new organization and because it was not eligible for governmental funding (due to several technical and bureaucratic problems). At the end of its second year, Be'er was recognized as a *midrasha* eligible for governmental funding, and its financial status seems to have improved (Biton, second interview).

The women's programs encounter some difficulties in regard to government funding. Like the Shiluv program, government funding for the women's programs is channeled via the Hesder program's Igud, and it seems that the Igud does not entirely approve of these programs. Various interviewees hinted that the Igud tries to manipulate the budget in such a way that the Hesder would be given more funding than the other programs—so much so that the *midrashot* have battled the Igud in court after the latter's refusal to allocate them their share of funding (Ohr Torah Stone vs. the Minister of Religion, Supreme Court case 6318/99). A compromise was reached, but the Lindenbaum *midrasha* has reserved the right to reappeal if the need should arise (Tehar-Lev, first interview).

Each of the *midrashot* has a slightly different schedule, but in all of them, twenty-three months are spent in active service—following the service plan of women serving in NAHAL Gar'inim. The first stage of the Gar'inim program is a period of study (as in the yeshivot). Students study for approximately four months prior to official enlistment. This period is not counted by the IDF as part of the program but rather is the young women's own free time. They enlist after Passover (usually April) and then take part in a three-month long education NCOs' training course, after which they are stationed on one of the Education Corps' three bases: Havat Ha-Shomer, MECHVA Alon, or Kiryat Moriah in Jerusalem. The IDF may not station Gar'in members at any of its other bases.

After completing their training, Ma'ayan participants serve for another ten months and then return to the Ein Ha-Natziv *midrasha* for a study term. This is followed by an active service term, and then another study period at the *midrasha*. This schedule is very similar to that of the Shiluv program.

Hadas participants serve for thirteen consecutive months after completing the training course, followed by a study term at the *midrasha*. They then return to complete their active service, after which they are discharged from the military with no official obligation to return to study. However, some choose to go back to study at the *midrasha* for a few months before continuing on to academic studies or other civilian plans. Hadas participants who serve in the Intelligence Corps, rather than as education NCOs, serve for twenty-three consecutive months after enlistment and then return to the *midrasha* for a study term (Elmaliach, first interview). Similar to the Education NCO service track, *midrasha* students serving in the Intelligence Corps do so at one designated base in the center of Israel, and the IDF may not station them anywhere else.

After enlisting in January, Be'er participants continue to study for another term of unpaid service. Their active service is made up of one continuous period, followed by a return to the *midrasha* for a final study term (Elmaliach, first interview).

As mentioned above, the military may station Gar'inim members only on previously agreed-upon bases, unless alternative arrangements are coordinated with the *midrasha*. Likewise, the military is obliged to discharge the participants so that they may return to their *midrasha* for unpaid service. Approximately twice a month, a representative from the *midrasha* comes to visit the students on base. The IDF must allow these meetings to take place and excuse students from their duties so that they may participate. Similarly, when the *midrasha* holds special weekends and reunions on Shabbat, the members of the relevant Gar'in are supposed to be allowed to attend.

Officially, joining the officers' corps negates this agreement, and the student leaves the Gar'in program. The IDF is no longer obligated to station her with the other members of her Gar'in, to make it possible for her to attend her Gar'in's various meetings, or allow her to leave for unpaid service with her Gar'in. However, officers are sometimes able to attend their Gar'in's reunion on Shabbat at the *midrasha*, and in the past there have been special meetings held for the officers (such as the case of the Hadas class of 2003, described below).

CURRICULUM AND FACULTY

All three *midrashot* see themselves as a framework whose aim is, as Rabbi Kahan put it, "to raise women to love Torah and be God-fearing" (*ahavat Tora ve-yirat shamayim*) (Kahan, first interview). The heads of Ma'ayan and Hadas also spoke of their wish to shape students who have a sense of obligation to observe mitzvot and to be better religious individuals (*ovdot ha-shem*). Thus the programs focus on Torah studies, and consequently the faculties all have a strong grounding in the subject.

Unlike the men's programs, the *midrashot*'s faculties also include women— most of whom hold academic degrees. At the time of its establishment, Be'er was the only program that was run exclusively by women, with Tami Biton as the general administrator and Leah Shakdiel as the head of the academic program (Rosh Beit Ha-Midrash).

The heads of the programs said that they do not consider military service to be a necessary requirement for the faculty. However, Biton commented that she would not like her faculty to be made up entirely of teachers who had not served in the IDF. In general, the heads of the programs were interested in hiring teachers who had a sense of commitment to the state of Israel, the Torah, and mitzvot, and wanted teachers who would not only instruct the students but would also be able to offer an overall educational experience. Like their counterparts at the Religious Kibbutz Movement yeshivot, all the heads of the women's programs stated that they wanted a heterogeneous faculty. For instance, Rabbi Kahan said that he did not want too many of his teachers to have a Hassidic orientation, and he would make sure to have part of his faculty balance this out (Kahan, first interview).

The *midrashot*'s curriculum varies from one program to another. All the students interviewed for this study pointed out how the heterogeneous views of their teachers were reflected in the classes. As a student at Hadas put it:

> They don't tell us, "This is the way!" We study *everything*! [. . .] It is important for them [the teachers] that we should always know that they don't have personal access to the truth. They say, "There is no one truth." They do say, "Such-and-such would be preferable," and all that, but at the same time, they tell us there is not one truth. (speaker's emphasis, Sharon, first interview)

As mentioned above, Ein Ha-Natziv and the Lindenbaum *midrasha* follow a traditional study model and include independent study. Classes cover a variety of subjects, from halakha and proficiency in halakhic literature to the teachings of Rabbi Kook and Hassidism. Rabbi Tehar-Lev stressed the importance of Talmud study, including developing the tools needed for independent study. He saw great importance in instilling in his students a love of learning, specifically a love of studying Talmud.

Conversely, Ein Ha-Natziv stresses the need to tailor a study agenda for each student. Although Talmud study features in the schedule, it is not the focus of the program. Rabbi Kahan was careful to reiterate his wish to see all the students as individuals with unique characteristics: "Each worships God in her own way." However, the value he was most interested in impressing upon his students was commitment to halakha. Halakhic questions and deliberations are of utmost importance, but in the end halakha must be observed in and of itself (Kahan, first interview).

Be'er's focus is more intricate. During their time at Be'er, students both study and work with the community in Yeruham. Unlike in other *midrashot*, Gar'in members live in a commune and support themselves through various educational and welfare-related jobs such as extracurricular teaching and community documentation. Each member must supply a certain amount of money to the commune every month, although not all their jobs are paying ones. The commune may instruct a member to take a paying job over a volunteer one in order to pay its bills. Rent for the two apartments members reside in and a hot lunch are provided by the *midrasha*, but the Gar'in must pay for the rest of its expenses such as utility bills, municipal taxes, and running its own kitchen for the remaining meals. This is a unique feature of the Be'er program and illustrates the diverse goals it has: Gar'in members are not only studying Torah, but also experiencing life as adults and as productive members of society.

Since holding a job is pivotal, students work and volunteer in the mornings and study in the afternoons and evenings. Accordingly, tuition amounts to approximately half of that paid in parallel programs.

Biton sees *midrashot* in general as institutions that foster internal development. It is a year "in which you are investing in yourself. You study, you are stocking up energy [for the future], gaining tools, fortifying your way of life out of choice, studying Torah *lishma*." But a year of social contribution (in addition to study) adds a completely different dimension: "Much more external work, toward society. The exact opposite of concentrating on yourself." And this combination makes Be'er a demanding program (Biton, first interview).

In some aspects Be'er's curriculum is similar to that of Ma'ayan and Hadas. Studies commence after lunch and include traditional subjects such as Talmud. The curriculum also includes less traditional topics. For example, once a month, on a Friday, students study a *midrashic* text and interpret it in small groups through art, creative writing, and so on (Biton, first interview).

Despite the differences between the *midrashot*, all students felt that their classes introduce them to a variety of topics and none of the faculty ever imposes a single mode of behavior on them. The students said that the faculty naturally stresses the importance of observing halakha and mitzvot, but within the halakhic framework there is no dictation of a sole path one must follow. In this respect the *midrashot* differ sharply from most Mekhinot, which stress a single educational message and are closer to the Shiluv program and some of the Hesder yeshivot.

PREPARATION FOR MILITARY SERVICE

Both heads of Hadas and Ma'ayan felt the programs' main role was to support the students throughout their time in uniform. This "accompaniment" (*livui*) begins before conscription and can be seen in the preparation for service.

The Hadas program tries to prepare its members practically for service. Students undergo official preparation including psychological guidance (lectures by psychologists); halakhic-spiritual preparation including discussion of potential dilemmas concerning modesty (*tzniut*), human dignity, and other issues that may arise when serving with secular soldiers; and practical-halakhic preparation including discussion of possible dilemmas such as observing Shabbat on base. Students are instructed during their entire time at the *midrasha*; however, three months before conscription these classes become more intense.

Rabbi Tehar-Lev feels it is imperative for students to enter the IDF with the capability to address potentially complicated situations and with the tools to solve such problems independently throughout their service. These situations may involve technical (halakhic) issues, or they may have to do with more fundamental questions concerning their lifestyle, commitment to halakha, faith, and so on.

Conversely, members of Ma'ayan receive less structured preparation for service. Although here, too, the faculty discusses questions concerning values, principles, and halakhic issues, the program holds that Torah study is the best preparation for military service. A young woman who has studied seriously all year will be prepared for service. This idea is also accepted in Be'er, and Biton believes daily life in the Gar'in to be the best preparation for service.

DEMOGRAPHICS

What sort of young woman joins the Gar'in program? The larger *midrashot* (Ein Ha-Natziv and Lindenbaum) share the same pool of potential students and compete over them, although in general all three programs target a very similar audience.

Overall, the program is quite small. Between eighty to one hundred students join the Gar'in program every year. Similar to the Shiluv program, the greater Jerusalem area (including Ma'ale Adumim and the Etzion Bloc) is overrepresented in all three *midrashot*. Religious kibbutzim and moshavim are represented in every class, but their percentages are relatively low. There are very few members from urban southern Israel. Additionally, very few women from settlements in Samaria (and Gaza before 2005) join the program, although Judean settlements are represented. In the earlier Hadas classes there were quite a few students from Ra'anana, in central Israel, and in the past six or seven years there has been some rise in the number of women from Mitzpeh Hosha'aya in the Galilee.

Most of Be'er's students come from Jerusalem and the surrounding area. Additionally, a substantial percentage of Be'er students come from religious kibbutzim. Interestingly, although it is located in southern Israel, none of the students originate from urban communities in the region but rather from kibbutzim in the area.

The only solid assertion to be made from the partial data available concerns the origin of the students. Most students come from the greater Jerusalem area (see also Grizim 2004). The Religious Zionist community in Jerusalem is usually perceived as being different from those in central and southern Israel.

This impression is bolstered by informal conversations with students. For example, they pointed out that in Religious Zionist communities in the greater Tel Aviv area it is less acceptable for women to wear pants (rather than skirts or dresses); they conform to a stricter dress code in terms of modesty, and in general these communities are less liberal than those in Jerusalem. This has implications regarding the sanctioning of military service for women. Furthermore, both Gush Etzion (the Etzion Bloc) and the city of Ra'anana have large Anglo-Saxon Olim (immigrant) communities, and it is possible that their parents' origins influence the ability of these women to enlist. Since their parents did not grow up in Israeli Religious Zionist communities where military service was seen as problematic, the parents do not feel that their daughters' service in the IDF presents a religious dilemma.

Due to its location, Be'er can potentially recruit students from the south of the country. These women are notably absent from the Gar'in program in general and both Tami Biton and Rabbi Elmaliach spoke of their wish to encourage women from the region to join. However, Be'er has been unsuccessful in its attempts to do so, partly due to the opposition of local high schools to the program and their reluctance to allow Gar'in representatives to visit their campuses and introduce the program (Biton, second interview).

In an interview with the *Haaretz* daily (Sheleg 2004b), Rabbi Tehar-Lev noted a change in Religious Zionist attitudes in general and in the rabbinical establishment in particular toward women's military service. He detected a growing acceptance of women's military service even outside the Jerusalem area. It is possible that the coming years will signal a demographic shift in the Gar'in program, with more women from central and southern Israel joining it.

CONTACT BETWEEN THE MIDRASHA AND STUDENTS IN THE MILITARY

The *midrashot* stay in closer contact with their students than the parallel programs for men. As noted above, a member of the faculty visits students on military bases approximately once every two weeks. While Hesder rabbis visit their students sporadically, visits to members of the Gar'in program are mandated by the agreement between the *midrashot* and the IDF.

Alumnae and students in the follow-up study spoke of how important these meetings were to them: They were "like a breath of fresh air," and they looked forward to the opportunity to see their teachers, especially during difficult periods in their service. Some were happy to be able to meet the faculty and speak with them. Some looked forward to the opportunity to study and have an intellectual discussion (Tamar, first interview; Limor, first interview).

Meetings consist of more than a Torah class. They also include an open discussion, food, and opportunities for the teachers to talk to the young women and see how they are coping. The Be'er program also realizes this and organizes meetings. However, since Be'er members are not concentrated on designated bases like members of Ma'ayan and Hadas, it is harder to visit them. In addition to the visits, all of the *midrashot* keep in touch with their students by mailing them newsletters and bulletins, similar to the programs for men. Facebook also plays a part in maintaining contact, although most students have limited Internet time while in uniform.

Besides printed material, students receive occasional phone calls from faculty members, especially during the more intense parts of their service. The number of phone calls and degree of personal contact with the *midrasha* varied according to the personality of each individual student, just as was seen with the male students. Some Gar'in members had frequent contact with members of the faculty, while others only received bulletins and letters and attended meetings on base. However, all the students agreed that when they came to visit, the *midrasha* was always most welcoming.

As mentioned, Hadas and Ma'ayan students return to their *midrasha* to study for set periods of time during their military service. It is important to note that most students felt their second period of study was even more meaningful than the initial year of study before conscription. Some felt this was because they were more serious about their studies. Since this study period occurs as part of unpaid service, only Gar'in members who truly wish to study return to the *midrasha*, and this has a decisive impact on the level of the classes (for example, Ma'ayan, first interview).

Other students felt that since their military jobs were so draining, their second phase of study was mentally and spiritually important for them (Avital, second interview). Like some Shiluv students, a small number of Gar'in members hoped that upon their return to the IDF they would receive a better posting than before.

However, during the follow-up study, it became apparent that it was not the *midrasha* that played the most important role in supporting the students during their service in the IDF. Almost all of the interviewees noted—without prompting—their close contact with other members of their Gar'in. Even students who had very little contact with their *midrasha* maintained their connections with their classmates. They visited and phoned each other even when they served on different bases or within different units on the same base. The contact was both social ("they are my friends and I love them") and emotional, serving as a source of support. Gar'in members who noted the supportive function of the Gar'in itself saw it as an even more substantial source of encouragement than the faculty or the *midrasha*. For example:

> I'm really happy I'm in the Gar'in. [. . .] It helps to know that in this world of the army, where you work with different people every three months, there is something stable: the Gar'in. It really helps. It's the best thing in the world to have them. (Noga, second interview)

During the third round of interviews for the present study, students emphasized this aspect again, especially those who had become officers. Entering their second year of military service, they felt the Gar'in—or at least parts of it—was important to them and that their friends were a substantial source of support. At this point in their service, not all maintained close contact with every single member of their original class, but they stressed that the friendships they did maintain were significant. Interestingly, after their discharge, half of the students who traveled abroad did so with at least one member of their Gar'in.

When examining the interviews over the entire period of this study, it seems that despite the mail and meetings organized by the *midrashot*, the main form of contact with the *midrasha* is not something tangible or concrete. Rather it is the feeling of belonging that is pivotal. Most interviewees raised the point that they felt the *midrasha* cared for them and would be willing to come to their aid if they only asked. This feeling of belonging, even when they are removed from the *midrasha* physically, affords the students a feeling of security. They have a "safety net" while in uniform, even if they do not choose to use it.

STUDENT EXPECTATIONS

As a result of the semistructured interviews used in this study, when asked to explain their motives for joining the program and their expectations, Gar'in members supplied complex answers. Every interviewee recounted a number of reasons for coming to her *midrasha* and joining the Gar'in. Of these, we can discern a number of categories and subcategories of motives and expectations.

The most prevalent reason for joining the program was the wish for a year of *lishma* study. All the students expected to enrich their knowledge of Torah.

Like Mekhinot and some Shiluv students, most students felt that upon their completion of high school, their Torah education was still sorely lacking, and they expected to deepen their knowledge during a year of study at a *midrasha*. Some students felt it important to acquire tools for future independent study and thought this was something they would be able to do in the program (Dafna, first interview; Basmat, first interview).

A subcategory of the students who wished to pursue in-depth Torah study saw the year at the *midrasha* as an opportunity to shape their lives and identities—both generally and as Jews. Like students of the Mekhinot and Shiluv, Gar'in members spoke of their hope to shape their worldview during the year so that their observance of halakha would be a matter of choice rather than a product of their upbringing (Orit, first interview; Maya, first interview). Furthermore, some students hoped to form a general worldview and understand their identity—not just their identity as Orthodox Jews—during their time in the Gar'in program (for example: Nava, first interview; Dafna, first interview). In this regard, the *midrasha* is seen as a "break" that allows the young women to examine their lives and ask fundamental questions about their values, identity, and so on. Students used the phrase "time for myself," and claimed that after this period of introspection they would be better prepared mentally for military life (Einat, first interview).

The second main category of motives and expectations alluded to the role of the *midrasha* during the students' military service. Of the alumnae and preservice students interviewed, approximately half noted the fear of being alone in the IDF as a motive for joining the program. It was important to these students to have someone to turn to outside the military system should they encounter difficulties during their time in uniform: "To not feel you are lost within a [greater] framework" (Nava, first interview).

Some students hoped they could turn to the *midrasha* with halakhic dilemmas and questions and thought it could protect them from the "secular atmosphere" they would encounter in the IDF. They also hoped the *midrasha* would help them battle possible religious erosion during their service (Avital, first interview; Hagit, first interview; Einat, first interview). A few interviewees expected the program to prepare them for service mentally and halakhically in more practical ways. In other words, they would not just talk about the dilemmas, but would learn specific strategies for handling situations and difficulties.

Be'er students added a category of expectations not addressed by members of the other Gar'inim. Due to the community service aspect of their program, Be'er members did not use terms such as "time for myself," but spoke about the importance of integrating study with practical actions. Some of them stressed that they were learning things beyond Torah study, such as how to live in a commune, and that this was significant to them (Noa, first interview).

Besides these reasons, there were students who joined the program due to more "technical" incentives: a small number failed the initial preservice testing phase needed to serve as an education NCO and wanted a second attempt afforded by the program; and a number of students were afraid to enlist alone and wanted to make sure they joined the IDF with friends. However, these students were a minority and most of those who joined for technical reasons stressed that once they were part of the program they were glad they chose it. Some of these interviewees noted that the technical reasons were minor compared to the wish to study.

The alumnae emphasized how important it was to them that the *midrasha* maintained contact with them (visits, Gar'in weekends) and saw this as part of the *midrasha*'s responsibility toward them (Tamar, first interview; Limor, first interview). The feeling that the *midrasha* did not forget about them during their service was important to them.

However, alumnae stressed that during their service, they felt there was a clear distinction between the IDF and the *midrasha,* and that the *midrasha* did not interfere in military matters. The meetings, in their opinion, could not be considered meddling: "It's different in the army: you're a soldier, they are here [the *midrasha*]" (Nili, first interview). The meetings allow respite from the military routine but do not change it.

Interviewees noted that, all in all, the program had met their expectations, but that there had been disappointments as well. Some interviewees wished the *midrasha* had been more involved in their service and had kept better tabs on what they were going through emotionally and professionally. Similar feelings were voiced by students of Hesder, Shiluv, and Mekhinot. However, Gar'in members understood that it was beyond the ability of their *midrasha* to be in close personal contact with each and every student. Others were disappointed with various aspects of the curriculum and their actual studies (such as Limor, first interview; Tamar, first interview).

The alumnae believed the *midrasha* continued to feel a form of responsibility toward them even after their discharge from the IDF and that, if needed, it would help them in any way it could. Once a *midrasha* student, always a *midrasha* student. As one of them put it:

> The *midrasha* will stay with me in many ways [. . .] I see how the *midrasha* relates to girls who used to study here. If they come to visit. Or if

something happens, God forbid, then Rabbi Eli [Kahan] goes [to help].
And even though it wasn't someone who studied here for a million years.
I think it's something that continues. (Limor, first interview)

Interestingly, students who married a year or two after being released from the
IDF invited their rabbis to the wedding and made sure they played a part during
the service.[9] This most certainly indicates both the level of contact on the part of
the students as well as a high level of commitment on the part of the rabbis.

* * *

In conclusion, Gar'in members joined the program for both ideological-
educational reasons (mainly the wish to enhance their Torah education and their
commitment to an observant way of life) as well as more technical reasons (usually
the fear of serving alone and without the backing of a strong framework able to
counter the military system). Most Gar'in members are from the greater Jerusalem
area, religious agricultural communities, and cities and towns where there is a
relatively noticeable Anglo-Saxon immigrant community. Members of the Gar'in
served as a meaningful support group for each other during service—at times even
more so than the *midrasha* itself—as will be illustrated in the following chapter.

CHAPTER 8
MEDIATION IN PRACTICE

As shown in the previous chapters, students expect their study program to offer a certain amount of support and "accompaniment" (*livui*) during their service in the IDF. Students join study programs both in order to achieve fundamental and educational aims, as well as hoping their study program will come through for them should they encounter serious problems while in uniform. While the study programs view military service differently, have various curriculums, and differ in their ideologies, all realize that their students anticipate support during their time in the IDF and that they are expected to mediate between their students and the superstructures to which they belong. To this end, study programs for both women and men stay in touch with their participants throughout their time in the military. Such a relationship with the students also brings about a certain degree of involvement in the military on the part of the study programs.

This chapter will use three case studies to examine problems encountered by the programs' students during their military service on a general as opposed to a personal level, and will examine the ways in which students choose to address the dilemmas they face. These include the initiative of Major General Stern (the head of the IDF Manpower Division at the time and now a member of Knesset) to disband the Hesder units and disperse those soldiers among various IDF units; coed military service; and ideologically motivated refusals to comply with orders.

As a rule, when the study programs for men interfere in the military sphere, they usually do so on the general level; it is only rarely that the rabbis become involved in the problems of one specific individual. Even then, their intervention will most likely take place through an official channel rather than through direct contact between a rabbi and a military commander. A prime example of an issue in which the rabbis are involved is that of coed service in the Infantry Corps, which they oppose.[1]

Another good example of a subject seen as meriting rabbinical intervention is the issue of disobeying orders to evacuate settlements in Judea, Samaria, and the Gaza Strip. This topic became more heated in the context of the Disengagement from the Gaza Strip in the summer of 2005, when the settlements in the Strip, as well as some in northern Samaria, were evacuated. Most of the Mekhinot are located in the West Bank; this is no coincidence and is a clear reflection of the political views held by these institutions. Many of the Hesder yeshivot are also located in these regions. On the other hand, the Religious Kibbutz Movement yeshivot have long served as representatives of the left wing of Religious Zionist society—from both a religious and political point of view. The *midrashot* that run the Gar'inim program are not clearly identified with any specific political camp.

Another general issue that has served as a source of disagreement between the IDF and, in this case, the Hesder program is the initiative of Major General Stern (who served as the head of the IDF Manpower Division during 2004–2008) to change the structure of the yeshiva students' units. His aim was to station groups of no more than twelve yeshiva students in "regular" heterogenic units (Tadmor 2005; Stern 2007). This would, on one hand, fulfill the requirement for a prayer quorum (*minyan*), and on the other hand, enable the yeshiva students to be a more organic part of the unit. March 2005 saw the first attempt to implement this program and station such groups of twelve yeshiva students in "regular" units. After much deliberation, as of 2010, Mador BENISH informs the Hesder yeshivot of the quota of students who must serve according to the Stern Initiative, and the Igud decides which yeshivot will send their students to "regular" units and which will send theirs to homogenous units. After the 2013 elections, a new initiative stands to lengthen Hesder service by one month, and is seen as a continuation of the Stern Initiative. We will now survey each of the cases mentioned above and discuss how the study programs attempted to mediate in each case.

COED SERVICE: HA-SHILUV HA-RA'UI[2]

In 1998, around the same time that the nomination of a new chief rabbi for the IDF was being discussed, the issues of coed service and the expansion of women's roles in the military gave rise to intense debate in the yeshivot and Mekhinot. It should be noted that these were by no means new issues. By this time, female physical education (PE) instructors, as well as female instructors in the Armored and Infantry Corps, had been serving in the IDF and training soldiers for years. However, various solutions had been devised to deal with the problems brought about by the presence of female soldiers in these units (an explanation of the halakhic issues involved appears in Chapter 3), and, in any case, the existing situation was in no way as problematic as coed service in combat units would turn out to be.

According to the press, Rabbi Eyal Krim—the head of the Ateret Yerushalayim Mekhina at the time—was behind a letter that called upon the heads of the yeshivot and Mekhinot to refuse to send their students to serve in the IDF due to grave problems related to modesty and observance of the Sabbath (Sheleg 1999). Some attempts were made to address these problems, but it seems that the implementation of the suggested solutions left much to be desired, and the tension between the study programs and the IDF remained.[3]

This situation was exacerbated in 2001 due to the integration of female soldiers in field units, where there is a great deal of physical contact between the soldiers (male and female)—as opposed to coed service in noncombat units. At the end of February 2001, a meeting of what was known as the Shiluv Ha-Ra'ui forum (a forum intended to develop the "proper integration") took place. The forum was convened under the auspices of the Manpower Division, and a number of leading rabbis, as well as representatives from IDF military training bases, took part. During the meeting, the participants addressed various halakhic issues arising from the presence of women in combat units, especially in the naval officers' course. At the end of the meeting, a decision was made to form a steering committee to deal with these concerns.[4]

It seems, however, that the situation did not improve much, and tensions came to a head in the summer of the same year, when Hesder and Mekhinot students submitted a petition to the chief of staff protesting the coed service instituted in field units. A month later, apparently following an emergency meeting of the Hesder and Mekhinot rabbis, Major General Yiftach Ron-Tal (at the time the commander of the Ground Forces—Mifkedet Zro'a Ha-Yabasha, or MAZI) was given the task of solving this crisis. The chief of staff at the time, Shaul Mofaz, then convened a committee, headed by Ron-Tal, to address the problem and come up with possible solutions.

In June 2002, the committee published its conclusions and guidelines under the title of *Ha-Shiluv Ha-Ra'ui*. One important conclusion was that in every coed unit, there would also be an exclusively male company in which religious soldiers could request to serve.

In practice, more and more voices were heard arguing that the recommendations of the Ron-Tal commission were not being properly implemented and that students found themselves having to deal with numerous modesty-related issues. At the end of 2004, Rabbi Aviner, for instance, wrote that in light of the situation, it was possible that:

> We should suggest to our military that religious soldiers be allowed to be stationed in all-male combat units, as in the past [. . .], but if this is not possible, the Mekhinot should be transformed into Hesder yeshivot [. . .] although this is a great pity that [these soldiers] will not serve in the military for a long period, with all its concurrent merits and qualities, but a short and pure service is preferable. (Aviner 2004)

In a similar fashion, Rabbi Sugarman—who takes a favorable view of military service—said that:

> This area [of modesty] has become more problematic than that of kashrut [. . .] if we do not participate [and enlist in the IDF], then you will say [that] we are draft dodgers. We want to do our part, but [the decision makers must] let us! (Sugarman, first interview)

The issue of modesty thus presents the rabbis with a true test of the religious soldiers' ability to serve in the military. As they see it, there can be no compromises in this regard: a religious soldier cannot serve in a unit where a female shooting instructor comes into close physical contact with trainees while instructing them on a shooting range, for example. For a religious soldier to be in such a situation goes against his basic education and worldview.

Major General Yair Naveh, the head of the Home Front Command during this time, himself an observant Jew, took a different view. In an interview in the weekly right-wing, religious newspaper *Besheva*, he argued that coed service does not pose a significant obstacle to religious soldiers' service in the military. In Naveh's opinion, the situation prevailing in the IDF is good and the religious soldiers' needs in regard to modesty are met with the greatest consideration (Edelman 2004).

The experiences of the students interviewed for this study indicate few serious problems related to coed service. Of the Mekhinot and Shiluv students who served in the Infantry Corps and the Armored Corps (both graduates and students in the follow-up study), few reported having had serious modesty problems. These students did not consider other contact with female soldiers problematic halakhically. They usually had no problem with female instructors and viewed classes taught by women as the same as those taught by men. Still, all interviewees from the Mekhinot and Shiluv programs reported having encountered vulgar language, as well as what they considered to be improper attitudes toward women. These phenomena are problematic from a *tzniut* point of view and at times shocked the students.

Hesder soldiers who served in yeshiva students' units came across problems that Shiluv and Mekhinot students did not necessarily view as serious, yet they troubled the Hesder interviewees. For instance, the presence of female PE instructors, even when modestly attired, or of female instructors in the Armored Corps who did not come into physical contact with the soldiers during training sessions were a source of discomfort for the Hesder students but not always for students from other programs.[5]

In 2004, a committee was formed with the aim of examining the implementation of the Ron-Tal commission's recommendations; Rabbi Yilon Farhi (Lieutenant Colonel, res.), a teacher at the Eli Mekhina, was appointed as chairman. The committee found that the *Shiluv Ha-Ra'ui* was only partially implemented (*Haaretz* November 21, 2004).

The reasons for this partial implementation are probably multifarious. On one hand, it is in the IDF's interest to station women in combat units and to extend the range of postings available to them. This interest is supported by women's organizations putting pressure on the IDF, as well as by voices inside the military itself in favor of equality. The challenge posed by appeals to the Supreme Court, filed by young, preservice women and female soldiers who wish to serve in posts open exclusively to males, is a real one that has come up in the past (see, for instance, the case of Alice Miller). There is a clear attempt to allow women to serve anywhere, when possible. However, the IDF is well known for its tendency to improvise and solve problems without in-depth planning and without proper attention paid to consequences. For example, an interviewee recounted a situation where a dormitory that was part of the soldiers' housing units on his base happened to become available as part of the unit was on leave. The administration on base saw this as a convenient opportunity to use that dormitory for female soldiers who happened to require housing at that time. It did not occur to the military administrators that there would be anything wrong with such an action, and they were completely unaware of the discomfort it caused religious soldiers (Dor, second interview). In other words, disregard for the "proper integration" guidelines sometimes stems from the wish to integrate women in the military and sometimes from sheer obliviousness. Therefore, it would seem that the guidelines of the *Shiluv Ha-Ra'ui* were not sufficiently internalized, and that there is only a limited awareness of religious soldiers' sensitivities.

In light of the present circumstances, the threat implicitly made by the Mekhinot and the Hesder yeshivot is that if the current situation persists, their students will prefer to serve in the NAHAL Haredi Battalion, where women are banned from the base entirely and such blunders do not occur. Similarly, there have been cases in which a Mekhina has initiated private meetings with IDF representatives to discuss potential consequences of certain IDF practices. For instance, the Eli Mekhina made it clear to the navy that in the absence of a commitment on the corps' part to a course of service that would include only male soldiers, its students will not enlist in the navy; the navy subsequently consented to this request (Gross 2002). However, this kind of solution is merely ad hoc and does not address the root of the matter.

The Farhi report brought about the formation of a new commission to examine the problems it had uncovered. Rabbi Avi Rontzki, then rabbi of Itamar (later the chief military rabbi) and the author of a responsa collection for soldiers, was appointed to lead the commission. This group—dubbed "the Modesty Guard" by the press—toured various bases throughout the country, solving specific problems and recommending the construction of separate housing units on a number of training bases. In addition, it also published instructions concerning joint (male and female) guard duty, training sessions led by female instructors, and the like. The nrg.co.il site (part of the *Ma'ariv* daily newspaper), which reported on the commission's activities, quoted anonymous officers who were opposed to the new regulations:

> The rabbis are behaving like a labor union and forcing their views on the IDF [. . .] they are taking advantage of the fact that the religious combat soldiers comprise a large part of the combat corps in order to bend the IDF to their will. (Rappaport 2005)

A few years later, in 2008, three soldiers from the Har Brakha Hesder yeshiva disobeyed an order to participate in a course led by female instructors. This was a professional course in which the female instructors presented and lectured, but did not come into physical contact with the soldiers. The students were subsequently court-martialed for disobeying orders (E. Melamed 2008). The incident caused an uproar in the media and gave rise to a heated debate within Religious Zionist society. Various arguments against the student-soldiers were heard within Religious Zionist society: How would these soldiers react when taught by female rather than male lecturers at university? How would they conduct themselves after their military service if they refuse to hear women explaining anything? Likewise, they had the option of presenting their position to their commanding officers rather than immediately disobeying orders (see, for instance, Shelach 2007). Rabbis, including Rabbi Rontzki, then chief military rabbi, denounced these soldiers' behavior, arguing that disobeying orders was unjustified (E. Melamed 2008). Rabbi Rontzki pointed out that since the guidelines of the "proper integration" had been respected—the female instructors were in uniform as opposed to civilian clothes that might be inappropriate, and their participation consisted only of lectures—he felt there was no justification at all to disobey orders. Rontzki's position was supported by other rabbis, and the Igud did not support the Har Brakha students' position.

On the other hand, the head of the Har Brakha yeshiva, Rabbi Eliezer Melamed, supported his students, arguing first that the "proper integration" was a compromise to begin with, and second that instruction in this course went against the guidelines of the "proper integration," which dictate that female soldiers should not instruct soldiers in the field, even if they are in uniform and do not come into physical contact with the soldiers (E. Melamed 2008).

That this case attracted active and intense interest for a few months indicates both its importance to the larger debate and the profound problem it revealed: soldiers from the Religious Zionist sector of society, especially those from Hesder yeshivot, attach growing importance to modesty issues as defined by halakha, and are accordingly willing to disobey orders that touch upon these issues. On the other hand, this affair served to emphasize the fact that modesty-related issues do not usually lead to soldiers disobeying orders and most definitely do not typically make daily or even monthly headlines.

The findings of the Ron-Tal commission and the Farhi report demonstrate how the rabbis of the Mekhinot and the Hesder yeshivot are very much involved in the IDF's general functioning. On the other hand, the wide publicity given to the case and the way it was conducted are a reflection of the fact that such blatant interference does not happen routinely. The rabbis chose to confront the military and force it to formulate a policy that would suit their students' needs in relation to an issue that they consider essential and crucial. In this case, the rabbis feel that they are trying to protect their students—and that students ask for such protection. The modus operandi of the rabbis of the Mekhinot and Hesder yeshivot is usually to address specific halakhic problems and deal with them professionally with the IDF, rather than creating public controversy over every problem they encounter (Sheleg 1999). In this sense, the debate following the case of the Har Brakha yeshiva students in 2008 is an exception which shows that issues rarely come to a head in this fashion.[6] Accordingly, the conduct that led to the formation of the Ron-Tal commission and the Farhi report is exceptional. The heads of the study programs prefer to avoid creating such situations, but when they feel there is no other choice, they are willing to resort to public measures.

Major General Ron-Tal himself recognized the fact that this part of the population has special needs:

> In fact, the religious soldier carries a system of beliefs with him, values and codes of conduct which dictate permissible and forbidden behavior, namely, mitzvot—more so than the secular soldier. And he has great difficulties. At times, military society is *less attuned* to these needs than it should be. (speaker's emphasis, Ron-Tal, first interview)

Ron-Tal considered the rabbis' interference in the matter of coed service legitimate. As a proponent of the idea of a people's army, Ron-Tal argued that an effort should be made to allow each and every person to serve in the military:

> I could have said: "Then let them [whoever is against coed service] not enlist! [. . .] [But] I established a service venue which allows *each and every* religious soldier *not* to follow this course [of coed service]! While still enabling him to choose *every* possible military posting. This is the wisdom of the *Shiluv Ha-Ra'ui*. But at the basis of this is the idea of the people's army. Not a practical idea, but rather something very principled and general. (speaker's emphasis, Ron-Tal, first interview)

Thus, in order to allow the implementation of the idea of a people's army, Major General Ron-Tal was willing to accept the rabbis' interference. Such acceptance on the part of the military system allows the rabbis a certain degree of supervision over the military and forces it to be more attentive to the religious soldiers' needs. While Ron-Tal was also of the opinion that the rabbis should refrain from any meddling that might impinge upon the military's ability to function, he thought that in practice, rabbis know the rules of play and do not go too far.

There is no doubt that as far as the rabbis of the Hesder yeshivot and Mekhinot are concerned, the issue of coed service is the most sensitive issue in their relations with the military system. Since the issue of modesty and coed service touches upon profound halakhic issues, there is a greater incentive on the part of the rabbis to act. It is true that there are differences of opinion among the rabbis, and not every head of a Mekhina or yeshiva thinks that lectures given by female instructors in uniform are problematic halakhically. But in general there is a consensus that coed service brings in its wake halakhic problems that must be addressed. Until a comprehensive solution is found, it is to be expected that this subject will continue to surface. The research for this study indicates that, should a crisis in the relations between these two sides come about, it will probably be caused by issues related to modesty.[7]

DISOBEYING ORDERS FOR IDEOLOGICAL REASONS

Another problem concerning religious soldiers that has made headlines in recent years is that of disobeying orders to evacuate settlements, especially during the Disengagement from the Gaza Strip.[8] This issue began to attract public attention in 2003 following the evacuation of illegal outposts, in particular that of Havat

Gilad in late 2002. The forces that evacuated this outpost in Samaria included religious soldiers, and the preparations for the operations entailed a desecration of the Sabbath. Moreover, apparently a number of officers knowingly lied to the religious troops, claiming that the IDF's then chief rabbi, Brigadier General Yisrael Weiss, had authorized the forbidden actions on Shabbat, thereby compelling the soldiers to desecrate the Sabbath while thinking that their actions were permitted. These events brought about a serious crisis between the IDF and the minister of defense and the Igud.[9]

Even before the localized event of the evacuation of Havat Gilad, halakhic opinions for and against refusing orders to evacuate outposts appeared in the Religious Zionist press and elsewhere. In October 2004, the debate intensified following a halakhic ruling by former chief rabbis Mordechai Eliyahu and Avraham Shapira supporting the refusal to obey orders. In contrast, a halakhic ruling against disobeying orders was given by Rabbi Shlomo Aviner, the rabbi of Beit El and the head of the Ateret Cohanim yeshiva, who is considered a popular source of spiritual authority.[10] Even after the Disengagement, the two camps continued to hotly debate the issue in the press and through the dissemination of pamphlets discussing related halakhic and civil aspects.[11]

Rabbis of the Religious Kibbutz Movement responded to this issue by signing a petition against disobeying orders (Yom Pkuda site 2004). Likewise, in an interview in *Haaretz*, Rabbi Bin-Nun voiced fierce opposition to any refusal to obey orders (Shavit 2005). In taking this stand, the Religious Kibbutz yeshivot's views were in line with the general position of the Religious Kibbutz Movement.

The state of affairs in the Hesder yeshivot was less homogenous, with eight yeshiva heads publicly in favor of disobeying orders and four publicly against it; these views appeared in various public petitions.[12] Some rabbis presented an alternative to disobedience and directed their students to not ignore their orders outright, but rather to explain to their commanders that they are unable to comply with such a command.[13] In various individual interviews and opinions published in the press, Rabbis Cherlow, Amital, and Lichtenstein voiced unequivocal opinions against a refusal to comply with orders (Reichner 2004; Wolman 2004; Cherlow 2004, 2004b). Rabbi Drukman expressed his views on the matter during a lecture in the yeshiva after the evacuation of Havat Gilad, saying that one should make an effort not to be in the forefront of the evacuating forces (termed "grey refusal" or "grey disobedience"), but that when left with no other option, one should not disobey orders.[14] The other rabbis interviewed in this study did not express their views in public.[15]

During an interview conducted for this study, Rabbi Kostiner, the head of the Mitzpe Ramon Hesder yeshiva, raised the issue of the refusal to comply with orders without being asked about this topic. He predicted that no yeshiva or Mekhina student would disobey an order to evacuate settlements. In his opinion, if religious soldiers had not refused orders that desecrated the Sabbath during the evacuation of Havat Gilad—a basic halakhic commandment—they would definitely not disobey orders to evacuate settlements—a debatable halakhic issue (Kostiner, first interview).

A number of meetings related to the issue of disobeying orders also took place at the Har Etzion yeshiva before and after the Disengagement. Various speakers took part in these sessions—from rabbis at the yeshiva to public figures, such as Professors Avi Ravitzki and Ruth Gavizon, and parliamentarian Dan Meridor— all of whom voiced their opinions on coming events. After the Disengagement, a student who served as an officer in the military and voluntarily took part in the evacuation joined the debate. The yeshiva students were exposed to various facets of the issue, and the expression of different sentiments was considered legitimate. The contents of these meetings were collected and published after the Disengagement and are a reflection of contemporary public opinion at the yeshiva, as well as a revelation of the spectrum of opinion within the yeshiva itself (Barth and Barth 2007). This book is unique, since it was published by a commercial publisher and offered for sale in bookstores throughout Israel, rather than being available only to the yeshiva students, indicating its relevancy to a wider audience. However, the book and the public stand taken by some of the Hesder rabbis highlight the fact that most of the heads of Hesder yeshivot did not express their opinions publicly.

The heads of the Mekhinot were publicly opposed to disobeying orders. In February 2005, the Eli Mekhina published a pamphlet titled *Our Loyalty to Torah and the Military: A Discussion by Rabbi Eli Sadan Regarding Orders to Evacuate Jewish Settlements.* This pamphlet was sent to all students who were on active military duty. In it, Rabbi Sadan voiced firm opposition to disobeying orders:

> *Refusal to comply with orders is not a good thing,* and encouraging collective disobedience can definitely undermine the foundations of the military and the country. Thus, first of all, our basic position is that *we are against disobedience and against encouraging disobedience*; we are also against airing threats in the media that we will disobey orders. (emphases in the original, Sadan 2005, 16)

In the pamphlet, Rabbi Sadan recounted a meeting of all the heads of the Mekhinot—religious, mixed, and secular—at which the issue was discussed. At the end of this meeting, the Mekhina heads published a joint declaration against disobeying orders (for the text of this declaration: Sadan 2005, 53–54). However, heads of the religious Mekhinot continued to have misgivings about the situation, and Rabbi Hager-Lau from Yatir expressed himself vehemently, arguing that every effort should be made to avoid involving regular forces in the evacuation of settlements (Rotenberg 2005).

During interviews conducted for this study, the students at Atzmona raised the issue of disobeying orders on their own initiative as early as 2003, as did one student from Ma'ale Adumim and one from Yeruham. The student from Ma'ale Adumim related that "the prevailing spirit at the yeshiva is in favor of disobeying orders," but said that officially, none of the rabbis discussed this issue with the students; neither had the head of the yeshiva come out in favor of disobeying orders (Nerya, first interview). The student from Yeruham was of the opinion that part of his commitment to the military is not to disobey his orders: "In a certain sense, there is an obligation to behave the way the military wants you to, even in cases where this does not really match your worldview" (Daniel, first interview).

In Midreshet Lindenbaum an interesting situation emerged in which Rabbi Tehar-Lev, the head of the program, was unequivocally opposed to disobeying orders, but one of the most influential rabbis at the *midrasha*, Rabbi Shuki Reich, was understood (by the students) to be in favor of disobedience. Both these rabbis presented their views in a meeting at the *midrasha* held for the students who were about to take part in the Disengagement (Orit, fourth interview; Yael, third interview). In contrast, the students at Ma'ayan and Be'er said that they had not heard the heads of their programs express their views on the refusal to comply with orders explicitly, but that they understood that they were against this (for instance, Miriam, third interview).

When interviewed during active duty, but before the Disengagement took place, most of the students in the follow-up study (male and female) said that they would not explicitly refuse to obey orders. Of the Hesder students in the follow-up study, most said that they would not disobey orders, but more than half said they would engage in "grey disobedience": "You can carry out the evacuation of settlements like you carry out routine menial jobs [*avodot RASAR*] on the base" (Ronen, second interview), meaning that you may look busy or like you are doing your job, but in fact you are not doing anything at all. "If I am manning a roadblock to stop people who are against the evacuation from getting there [to the site of the evacuation], I will look to my right and the settler will go past on my left" (Avishai, second interview).

Of the Mekhina students participating in the follow-up study, less than half said that they would not disobey orders. Several stated that they would not do so outright but would employ "grey disobedience," and a few were unsure about how they would behave when called upon to evacuate a settlement. Of the Shiluv students in the follow-up study, almost all said that they would not disobey orders. All the female students in the follow-up study said that they would not disobey orders, but three of them said that this question was irrelevant, since they would not be called upon to participate in the evacuation of settlements. Perhaps surprisingly, of all the interviewees, only two students (one from Ma'ale Adumim and one from Yatir) said that if they had no choice, they would go to jail rather than actively evacuate settlements. One female student who lived on a settlement said that although she would not disobey orders, she would request not to participate and expected that her commanders would consent to this, out of consideration for where she lives. Again, these positions were voiced at a time when the possibility of an evacuation seemed real, but before the Disengagement of 2005 was carried out.

When asked about the messages concerning disobeying orders emanating from their various institutions, almost all the Mekhina students said that their institutions were against this. A few thought that their Mekhina called upon its students not to disobey orders, but also to refrain from evacuating settlements; encouraging "grey disobedience." It seems, therefore, that in spite of the fact that some of the Mekhina heads are disciples of rabbis who were in favor of disobeying orders,[16] they themselves conveyed disapproval of this.

At the same time, a rumor that the heads of the Ateret Cohanim and Ma'ale Efraim Mekhinot were encouraging their students to disobey orders made the rounds in the press (Harel 2004). This seemed strange, since the former Mekhina is affiliated with the Ateret Cohanim yeshiva, headed by Rabbi Aviner, who opposed disobedience very vocally. Apparently, Rabbi Ze'ev Sharon, the head of the Ma'ale Efraim Mekhina, who was also opposed to disobedience, personally requested that Ehud Barak (the minister of defense) find out who was responsible for spreading this rumor (Rotenberg 2005b).

This state of affairs is especially interesting when one takes into account that the Atzmona Mekhina itself was evacuated during the Disengagement in the summer of 2005. The students and faculty of the Mekhina left it peacefully, after the students and the soldiers who had come to evacuate them even danced together. Later, some of the students were critical of this, arguing that even if active resistance was not to be sanctioned, there should not have been dancing before leaving the Mekhina. The Mekhina ultimately moved to Yated, a small community on the Egyptian border in southern Israel, and a large part of the faculty did not return to teach after the Disengagement. It seems that their departure was due to disagreements over the manner in which the Mekhina was evacuated.

Interviews conducted with students two years after the evacuation indicate that the move to Yated was a watershed. Even students who supported Rabbi Peretz's conduct during the Disengagement said that they no longer feel a sense of belonging and do not visit the Mekhina often (for instance, Shachar, fifth interview). The evacuation of the Atzmona Mekhina is a clear demonstration of the Mekhinot's attitude toward compliance with orders to evacuate settlements, even though they paid a price for it.

When asked about messages conveyed in the yeshivot in relation to disobeying orders to evacuate settlements, students at Har Etzion, Or Etzion, Yerucham, and Petach Tikva had the impression that their yeshivot were opposed to regular forces disobeying orders. A student from Petach Tikva recounted a conversation where Rabbi Cherlow stated to students that a student who disobeys orders "should find himself another yeshiva" (Tomer, second interview). Students at Har Etzion said that they had read an interview with Rabbi Lichtenstein in one of the weekend papers (referring to Wolman 2004), and that they inferred Rabbi Lichtenstein was firmly opposed to disobeying orders. In an interview with the *Haaretz* daily, students from Ma'ale Adumim said that they would disobey orders to evacuate settlements (Shragai 2004). However, students in the follow-up study said that the yeshiva had not expressed any official opinion on the matter. The position of Rabbi Rabinovitch—the head of the yeshiva—in favor of disobeying orders was clear to them, but Rabbi Haim Sabato and Rabbi Yitzchak Shilat (influential rabbis in the yeshiva) were known to be against this.[17] Students at the Golan yeshiva were less certain about the yeshiva's message on this matter, but it seemed to them that the yeshiva, while opposed to disobeying orders, did encourage "grey disobedience."

Shiluv students all said that they would not disobey orders.[18] A student at Ma'ale Gilboa said that it was his understanding that the yeshiva's position was based on events that took place during 2003. As mentioned in Chapter 5, during the August 2003 induction, many of the Shiluv students were forced to enlist in HIRMAK units and were upset about it. They threatened to strike and not leave the IDF induction center until their demands for stationing were met:

> So the yeshiva said that whoever disobeyed orders and would not leave the IDF induction center (BAKUM), the yeshiva would not help them. The yeshiva is against disobeying orders—period. (Nadav, third interview)

In other words, the Religious Kibbutz Movement's position on the general issue of disobeying orders was clear to its students, even without this being discussed explicitly. It would not allow its students to disobey orders, even when these were deemed unfair, as demonstrated by the events of 2003. This case was perceived as being the same.

In practice, the students from the men's study programs who were part of the IDF's regular forces—as opposed to reserves or career military personnel—were not positioned in the front line of the evacuating forces, and thus they were not forced to even consider disobeying orders. Students enrolled in officers' training courses—cadets who were designated as part of the evacuating force—were excluded from the front lines and were stationed in administrative or rear echelon posts in order to ensure they were not faced with problematic situations; these placements were usually made on their commanders' initiative and not due to general IDF policy. The few students from the study programs who were involved in the actual evacuation did so voluntarily. Thus, cases of disobeying orders on the part of soldiers in the front line of the evacuation did not involve soldiers from the study programs. In contrast, there were occurrences of "ordinary" religious soldiers who disobeyed orders during the actual evacuation, such as the case of Avi Bieber, who refused orders while being filmed by a TV crew.

Cases of disobedience involving students from the preservice study programs did occur, but farther away from the evacuation and never on the front lines. It seems that these cases were more an attempt to take a political and ideological stand. The most well-known case was that of Hesder soldiers from the Lavi Brigade who were stationed at a road block and refused to prevent people who were not inhabitants of Gush Katif in the Gaza Strip from entering the area; this was not related to the evacuation per se, but rather to the IDF's efforts to seal off the area and avoid dealing with larger numbers of civilians than absolutely necessary. These soldiers were court-martialed, and their unit was disbanded (Greenberg and Weiss 2005).

Of the study programs examined here, it was the women's Gar'inim program that bore the brunt of the activity on the front line of the evacuation; this was unforeseen and had not been discussed or planned for ahead of time. Due to the need to use female personnel and the relative accessibility of the Education Corps (in comparison to other units), officers and NCOs from this corps were called upon to participate on the very front line of evacuation, bodily removing civilians from their homes.

The testimony of the interviewees shows that *midrasha* students who took part in the evacuation did not refuse orders. Some tried to avoid being on the front line by means of requesting medical exemptions, while others were able to secure postings in rear positions; there were no cases of outright refusal to obey orders during the Disengagement itself. However, approximately a month before the Disengagement, two students from Hadas refused an order to go to Kfar Maimon during the anti-Disengagement demonstration there in July 2007 and were court-martialed. They later recanted, apologized in writing, and during the Disengagement itself were stationed at the Re'im base in the south.

While Be'er members did not participate in the evacuation, four female interviewees from the Ma'ayan and Hadas Gar'inim did.[19] The female students who participated on the front line of the evacuation said that they received much support from their programs and their teachers; this support took the form of frequent phone calls and even visits. One student was angry at Rabbi Reich, who came out in favor of disobeying orders, and thought that this was irresponsible behavior. She was hurt and unsure of her feelings about him in light of her experiences: "I asked him many halakha-related questions during my military service [before the Disengagement], and I am deliberating about what I should say to him next time we speak" (Yael, third interview).

A few of the male students who participated in the follow-up study were involved in the Disengagement in 2005 in some way, although they did not physically evacuate people from their homes. At the time, these students were either attending an officers' training course or were already serving as officers in noncombat roles. Another student, from Eli, was given a month's leave from an officer's training course due to the fact that he lived in one of the evacuated settlements. This student was present at the evacuation—as an evacuee—and after some deliberation, returned to the officers' training course after the events. At a later stage, he put in a request—which was granted—to be discharged from the military before completing his full term of service.[20]

In the case of male soldiers who took part in the evacuation—although not in the front line—support was not as obvious as it was with the female students. A student from the Petach Tikva yeshiva said that no one from the yeshiva called or asked after him, even though he thought they knew that he was taking part in an officer's course at the time and thus was involved in the Disengagement. A student from Ein Tzurim also said that the yeshiva did not contact him, but "they might have sent a letter [which] I didn't read" (Tal, fourth interview). And indeed, the last circular of the *zman* opened with a letter from the heads of the yeshiva that was aimed at supporting the students (Krechmer-Raziel 2005). Ma'ale Gilboa students also received a letter from the head of the yeshiva written to offer them support. "And if I had still been deliberating [about taking part in the evacuation], this letter did away with that" (Idan, third interview).

Students from Eli reportedly had more contact with their institution. An interviewee spoke of two meetings in a synagogue in Givat Shmuel that were held before and after the Disengagement for Eli graduates who were on active duty. Rabbi Sadan spoke at the first meeting, and Rabbi Levinstein at the second. It appears that the aim of the meetings was to support the students, especially after the event. It was the student's understanding that during the meeting that took place before the Disengagement, Rabbi Sadan directed the students not to disobey orders, but also not to actually evacuate people from their homes. The Eli student reported that during the Disengagement, the rabbi in charge of keeping in touch with his class called to check in with him. This student also called the rabbi again later due to difficulties he had experienced during the evacuation: "Sometimes you need someone to tell you something you already know yourself. To remind you" (Micha, fourth interview).

In general, all of the students who took part in the evacuation said that their main sources of support were their families, and, to various degrees, their friends from their study programs. When asked about their fellow soldiers, most explained that they were not a significant source of support "since they did not understand what I was going through" because of their different backgrounds.

In the wake of the social trauma caused by the Disengagement, a decline in enrollment in the preservice study programs was expected. This decline was predicted as a response to a combination of things: the violent dispersion of an anti-evacuation demonstration in the outpost of Amona in February 2006; the moderate messages conveyed by the study programs; and the aggrieved sentiments prevailing among Religious Zionist society in the wake of both the Disengagement itself and the violence in Amona. Furthermore, it was expected that not only would participation in the study programs decline, but that motivation to serve in the IDF would decrease (Harel 2007; Ettinger 2006). It seemed that the Mekhinot would be most affected and that their prospective students would prefer to serve in the NAHAL Haredi Battalion. It was also expected that female students would not participate in the Gar'inim programs due to the active role played by these students in the evacuation. However, in practice, there has been no long-term decline in the numbers of students enrolling in the Gar'inim program (Tehar-Lev second interview), and the Mekhinot have actually maintained a moderate increase in their numbers (Association of Mekhinot 2007). The Hesder Igud reports that more students are joining the program due to a decline in the motivation to actively serve in uniform following the Disengagement. This is indeed reflected in the numbers: 5,300 participants were in the program at the end of 2007 compared with 4,000 at the end of 2003 (Deutsch, first interview; Stav, first interview).

However, it is impossible to draw unequivocal conclusions regarding the impact of the Disengagement on registration in the preservice study programs due to a certain vagueness in the data. The increase in numbers may be a result of natural growth, could be driven by ideological and political changes, and perhaps might even be related to recent tendencies toward becoming more religiously stringent (*hithazkut*). That said, it can also safely be noted that there has not been a decline in the participation of Religious Zionist youth in the IDF nor in the numbers of students in the study programs, thus proving the aforementioned predictions wrong.

What of the ability of the study programs to mediate between their students and the superstructures during the events surrounding the summer of 2005? A comparison of the reactions of the heads of the Hesder and Mekhina programs to the issue of coed service reveals some interesting points. It appears that on issues perceived as inherently halakhic and ideological, these rabbis do not hesitate to try to impose their views on the IDF, both in public and indirectly. The students are well aware of this.

As far as the Disengagement was concerned, however, most of the study programs kept a low profile, contrary to prevalent public expectations. There was no concerted, official effort on the part of the heads of the programs to impose their will on the military like the one initiated with respect to the integration of women into the IDF—a much more halakhically problematic issue, as far as the programs' heads are concerned. Likewise, most of the students did not understand their programs to be in favor of an outright refusal to disobey orders, and they acted accordingly. Even according to the data released by the Yehudi Lo Megaresh Yehudi (A Jew does not expel a [fellow] Jew) organization—which spearheaded the main pro-disobedience campaign, and thus it would be in their interest to inflate the numbers of disobedient soldiers—fewer than seventy soldiers in the regular forces refused to take part in the evacuation. It is unclear how many of these were enrolled in the study programs. It is equally unclear what part these soldiers were called upon to play in the evacuation—namely, whether they were in the front line or elsewhere (Yehudi Lo Megaresh Yehudi site 2005).

The crucial point in regard to the Disengagement was the yeshivot's basic position on the issue of ceding land considered part of the Land of Israel and therefore possessing halakhic importance. Yeshivot that did not view the evacuation of settlements as halakhically prohibited did not direct their students to disobey orders—even though this was a sensitive and painful subject. According to these yeshivot, the issue at hand was a military one rather than a halakhic one. Yeshivot that perceived the evacuation of settlements as halakhically prohibited found themselves embroiled in a dilemma. Rabbis who thought that withdrawing from parts of the Land of Israel was unambiguously forbidden by the halakha could not sanction obeying orders under the existing circumstances. As long as their own students were not called upon to serve on the front line of the evacuation, however, these rabbis did not have to direct their students to disobey orders outright.

In this respect, the situation was very different from the reality brought about by the integration of female soldiers in combat units. As already pointed out, even if the specifics of halakhically prohibited and permitted behavior are not agreed upon, it is obvious that the formation of coed units is halakhically problematic.

Even so, the study programs' rabbis were not obtrusive in their interference in the military's conduct when it came to refusing to obey orders for ideological reasons. As noted above, the clearest example of this is the peaceful evacuation of the Atzmona Mekhina from the Gaza Strip. It seems that the prevailing strategy was to not take a clear stand on the matter—certainly not publicly. Agreements with the IDF regarding their students were reached quietly. This message of noninterference made its way to the students as well. Although there were cases in which soldiers disobeyed orders, these were few and far between, and participating students were not on the front line of the evacuation, but rather served in various posts in the rear—such as manning roadblocks aimed at keeping settlers out of the area and pitching tents for the evacuating forces. It is highly possible that there were also cases of "grey disobedience," but by their very nature, these are hard to examine and verify.

Given their role as mediators, it seemed logical to assume that the study programs would continue in this role during the Disengagement as well. Were they able to fulfill this function? Did they continue to protect their members from conflicting demands? Were they able to mediate between the greedy institutions themselves?

In order to evaluate how successful mediation actually was, we must examine its effects on the students themselves: Were they confused? Did they feel torn between their commitments, with no support system to help them maneuver within a difficult situation? As the students are the reason for the entire framework, if they do not feel supported, there is no justification for its existence.

Officially, during the period before the Disengagement, the IDF did not appreciate the delicate situation in which the heads of the study programs found themselves. The loudest voices within Religious Zionism demanded that the programs support disobedience unequivocally.[21] The chief of staff threatened to abolish the homogeneous Hesder units. Senior officers wondered why the rabbis wouldn't make a decisive stand against disobedience. There was no sense of dialogue even when the chief of staff met with some of the heads of the Hesder yeshivot. Public suspicion toward the study programs escalated as well. The Israeli media asked repeatedly why the Mekhinot rabbis did not denounce disobedient soldiers, while strangely ignoring the booklet published by Eli, for example (Sadan 2005). This climate forced the individuals to choose sides and to do so publicly.

The study programs did not respond in the same fashion, as described above. When a *beit midrash* (house of study) took a clear stand on the issue, it gave its students a reference point and to a large extent helped them formulate their own opinions. Even students who did not agree with their *beit midrash*'s stand felt able to express an opinion when a clear attitude was stated. Policy was not dictated to students, but an unambiguous position was pivotal in allowing students to form their own perception of the dilemma.

While it could be assumed that when the *beit midrash* did not present a clear position it would be easier for individuals to come to independent conclusions, in practice, the opposite occurred. It was apparent from the interviews that being able to discuss the issue at hand was important and helped the students. Students of programs that did not voice a clear stand were confused and bewildered.

Some proof of this point can be found in the behavior of the heads of two important Torah institutions that were evacuated during the Disengagement: Rabbi Rafi Peretz of the Atzmona Mekhina and Rabbi Shmuel Tal of the Torat Ha-Haim yeshiva.[22] Both rabbis were evacuated peacefully and in an organized fashion with their students, despite their known right-wing political views. This had a great effect on their students. The evacuation of the Mekhina and yeshiva could have turned violent, perhaps even more so than the evacuation of the synagogues at Kfar Darom and Neve Dekalim.[23] However, the example these rabbis set prevented conflict and certainly protected their students from public criticism.

When assessing mediation during the Disengagement, it seems that it succeeded only partially: While students did not disobey orders, the majority were upset by the situation they found themselves in and felt pressured by their conflicting loyalties. Some were able to sort their feelings out using their study programs, while others did not feel they were able to do so. The entire concept of mediation, supposedly, is to prevent the creation of such feelings and to shield soldiers from the conflicting demands of the greedy institutions to which they belong. Since in general the study programs were unable to do so completely and unequivocally, their mediation was not completely successful. However, they did not fail entirely.

The partial failure was caused by a number of factors. First, public opinion played an important part in pressuring students to conform to the minority position of disobedience. This was especially true of students who lived in settlements at the time. A good example of these pressures are the stories students told of friends and neighbors who approached them during Shabbat prayers and of uncomfortable situations they found themselves in during furlough at home during the period before the Disengagement. The "orange" campaign conducted before August 2005—which included the distribution of orange streamers and stickers at central bus stations while soldiers were boarding buses to their base or home, and active attempts to convince soldiers to sign petitions stating they would disobey orders to evacuate civilians—was another component of this pressure. Both the explicit public opinion and vigorous campaigning were nonexistent in the case of mixed gender service. It is possible that with regard to the Disengagement, some of the study programs found it very difficult to withstand the public pressure voiced in this form and preferred to avoid making a public stand against it. At the same time, they also feared the wrath of the military system and so avoided siding with the very vocal public sentiment. It is also possible that the public character of the opposition to the Disengagement made dialogue through the mediating frameworks impossible, thereby thwarting any likelihood of reaching an agreement quietly.

Second, the situation proved to be one that left very little maneuvering room. The IDF could not exempt all Religious Zionist soldiers from participation in the Disengagement. Allowing them to avoid physically evacuating civilians from their homes was not stated as official IDF policy, but in practice it was possible. On the other hand, the voices supporting soldiers who planned to carry out their orders were feeble. In other words, dialogue was an improbable possibility to begin with, since there were no real options for compromise.

Third, the military mission itself and the human aspect raised the stakes, and tension was already high. The dilemma of following orders was not limited to Religious Zionist soldiers, but included all soldiers who opposed the Disengagement ideologically or halakhically.

Additionally, the IDF seemed unable to form a consistent policy when dealing with disobedient soldiers. In certain units, disobeying orders resulted in court-martialing and sometimes relocation to another unit. In other units, offenders were merely restationed within their unit and not reprimanded further.

Moreover, the greedy structures themselves seemed unable to maintain a working relationship through the mediating structures. Even before the Disengagement itself took place, the IDF no longer trusted the study programs (as the chief of staff stated in the press), especially the Hesder yeshivot. This elevated IDF suspicions of the study programs and of Religious Zionism in general. There were no confidence-building measures, and therefore the actions of each *beit midrash* didn't have the chance to be viewed in a positive light and were interpreted negatively. Loss of trust rendered the mediating structures irrelevant. However, individual officers were open to listening to their religious soldiers in general and study program students in particular.

In practice, the IDF was aware of the delicate situation students found themselves in and usually did not force them to choose between their loyalties. A student who did not want to actively participate in the evacuation but also did not wish to disobey direct orders was accommodated. At the same time, even rabbis who publicly supported the disobedience of soldiers ordered to actively evacuate civilians from their homes did not instruct students serving on the perimeter of the evacuating force—such as those who were ordered to guard checkpoints—to disobey their orders.

This modus operandi may change, however, as a new means of disobeying orders has recently surfaced. It seems that one Hesder yeshiva, Har Brakha, has decided to break the rules of play. During their swearing-in ceremony in October of 2009, a group of Hesder students displayed a sign protesting the ongoing evacuation of the deserted Homesh settlement and saying they would not participate in subsequent evacuations if called upon.[24] Such a public display of political opinions in the IDF was unprecedented. The following month, another group of students protested similarly. Rabbi Eliezer Melamed, the head of the Har Brakha Hesder yeshiva, supported the students who participated in this action, as did Rabbi Elyakim Levanon of the Elon Moreh Hesder yeshiva.

The IDF disciplined the soldiers for taking a public political stand when in uniform; a punishable offense in the IDF. The defense minister, Ehud Barak, threatened to annul the agreement between the IDF and the two Hesder yeshivot who supported these actions if the heads of the yeshivot did not recant.

According to the state attorney's response to the Supreme Court (Supreme Court of Israel, Case 2/10), IDF representatives met with the Igud after the second incident and explained that it views these incidents in the most serious terms and asked the Igud formally to deal with this sort of insubordinate behavior immediately. The heads of the Igud met with Rabbis Melamed and Levanon; Rabbi Melamed refused to change his position on the matter and to categorically denounce insubordination. Consequently, the IDF recommended to the Defense Ministry that the agreement with Har Brakha be annulled and that it no longer be recognized as a Hesder yeshiva: if it cannot recognize military rules of conduct, it cannot expect to receive preferential treatment, and its students will not be able to serve a shortened term of service. Should the students at the yeshiva wish to remain within the Hesder framework, they would be allowed to move to another yeshiva and continue the program.

In order to allow Rabbi Melamed a chance to explain his position, the deputy defense minister met with him on December 13, 2009. As a result, Rabbi Melamed promised to issue a public denouncement of the political stance taken by his students and to state a clear position against insubordination, but he refused to elaborate. The defense minister invited the rabbi to meet with him personally, but Rabbi Melamed refused (Supreme Court of Israel, Case 2/10: 9–10).

In light of Rabbi Melamed's behavior, his support of disobedience, and his refusal to discuss his position with the minister, his yeshiva was removed from the list of approved Hesder yeshivot, and his students no longer qualified for a Hesder course of service as of December 13, 2009.

Surprisingly perhaps, the Igud sided with the IDF in this matter. Rabbi Melamed was not offered support, as he himself admitted and students at the yeshiva pointed out.[25] Moreover, the Igud tried to pressure him to modify his behavior so as to smooth over differences and solve the crisis. Clearly the Igud, as well as the majority of Hesder rabbis, felt Rabbi Melamed had crossed a line and that such behavior could not be supported (Tesler 2010). The case of Rabbi Melamed indicates that the preservice programs do not necessarily "belong" to one of the superstructures, but rather attempt to achieve a working relationship with both in order to help their students. In addition, it also shows that the heads of the programs are capable of impressing norms of acceptable behavior upon their students. Even if Rabbi Melamed's claim that he never encouraged his students to display the offending signs is true, the fact is that students of other yeshivot and Mekhinot did not do so and did not end up being court-martialed for disobedience. It was Rabbi Melamed's students who were sent to military prison during both of these incidents and incidents involving coed service, as discussed in the previous section.

DISBANDING HESDER UNITS

At the end of 2005, the head of the IDF Manpower Division (AKA), Major General Elazar Stern, announced his intention to disband the Hesder units—thus no longer offering the Hesder soldiers the option of serving in homogenous units (Rappaport 2005b). He justified this step by explaining that he was "opposed to sectarian or ideological frameworks—these harm the [idea of a] people's military and our ability to become familiar with each other. I want them to get to know each other" (*Yediot Aharonot* online January 25, 2005). In order to allow soldiers to maintain their religious rights, Major General Stern assured that there would be at least ten Hesder soldiers in each platoon, ensuring the possibility of forming a quorum for prayer (*minyan*). The timing of Stern's announcement was criticized in the media; some thought that it was due to the issue of the Disengagement and disobeying orders and a desire on the part of the military to threaten the Hesder yeshivot rabbis, as well as to prevent situations in which entire platoons would refuse to comply with orders.

The yeshiva heads were opposed to this change. Their main argument against disbanding the Hesder units was the problem of modesty-related issues in the IDF, which presented their soldiers with considerable difficulties. Some of the yeshiva heads, such as Rabbi Tzafanya Drori, hinted that following the disbanding of the Hesder units, many students would join the NAHAL Haredi Battalion (Harel and Shragai 2005). Major General Ron-Tal implied that he was also opposed to this step, particularly due to its timing (Rappaport 2005c).

In May 2007, the head of the IDF Manpower Division published a leaflet aimed at the Hesder soldiers (Stern 2007), in which an attempt was made to explain the position of the IDF and the head of the Manpower Division concerning the changes in the Hesder soldiers' military service. This was done without the mediation of the rabbis and the Hesder's Igud; the letter was mailed directly to the students. This could be construed as being done in the hope that by addressing the soldiers openly without the help of mediators, the IDF would have greater success in explaining its position and the necessity of changing the current system. In other words, this was a way to deal with the possibility that the Hesder yeshivot would distort the message and its tone. The leaflet put a great deal of emphasis on the fact that serving in heterogeneous units would fulfill the IDF's ideal of a "melting pot" (*kur hitukh*) and bring about greater familiarity between various sectors of Israeli society. Another issue addressed in the leaflet was the idea of "sharing the burden." The new Hesder course of service would enable the soldiers to shoulder a more equal share of mandatory service in the military. This proves that the head of the IDF's Manpower Division thought that such principles were important to the Hesder students.

The students themselves were aware of the Stern Initiative, as it was called, and responded to it. Two responses to the initiative to disband the Hesder units were published in the Har Etzion yeshiva's circular at the time the idea surfaced in 2005. One response argued that during basic and advanced training, it would be better if the Hesder soldiers were to serve in homogenous units. After these stages were completed, dispersing the soldiers among other units might even be a good thing; this was already done in the Armored Corps (Bar Kokhva 2005).

The second response sided with the view that the idea to disband the Hesder units was politically motivated: "The decision to disband the Hesder units derives solely from discrimination against the yeshiva students, since there are other groups who serve together in the military and no one says anything about this" (Gvaryahu 2005). Gvaryahu was aggrieved by the fact that there were no attempts to disband the NAHAL, the NAHAL Haredi Battalions, or the other special units; only Hesder units were singled out for dissolution.

During the March 2005 induction of Hesder students, the military ran a pilot program for this new course of service. Major General Stern addressed the Hesder soldiers at the induction base (BAKUM), and, according to the interviewees, tried to persuade them to take part in the program. It appears that he did not treat the students' rabbis with respect when speaking about them; this caused quite a bit of antagonism toward him (Avishai, second interview). Ultimately, students from the Har Etzion, Ha-Kotel, Safed, and Otniel yeshivot were stationed in the mixed units.

A student from the Or Etzion yeshiva recounted that when the students found out that they were slated to be part of the program, some of them met with the head of their yeshiva, Rabbi Drukman. They told him that they were afraid of being drafted into heterogeneous units and were apprehensive that everything they had learned at the yeshiva would be lost. In response, Rabbi Drukman held a severe meeting with all the yeshiva students and emphasized that the students should be guided by the common good rather than their own personal considerations, and that they should enlist in heterogeneous units "for the people of Israel" (Eli, second interview). As of the end of 2012, the Igud manages the stationing of students in heterogeneous units. Approximately half of Hesder conscripts continue to serve in homogenous Hesder units, while the other half serve according to the new course of service. Hesder rabbis have not come out openly against the change of service venues, but nor have they supported it in public.

From a military point of view, it is interesting to note that a Shiluv student who served in a heterogeneous unit related that this integration was a source of conflict among the soldiers. Since the squad (kita) included both yeshiva students and other religious soldiers, about half the squad would be engaged in prayer, while the other half went on with various necessary activities (such as preparing the morning roll call and inspection). This "extra" work was perceived by the secular soldiers as discrimination. The student said that stationing fewer Hesder soldiers in each squad (between three to four, rather than five to six) would have had a positive effect.

Not all the Hesder students in the follow-up study were strongly opposed to being integrated into heterogeneous units. Of the interviewees in the follow-up study, about a third thought that this was basically a good idea; it should be examined and the logistical problems arising from it solved so that the students' needs would be met, and at the same time, the units' ability to function would not be impaired.

When asked about the disbanding of the Hesder units, not all interviewees from the Shiluv and Mekhinot were in favor of Major General Stern's new policy. Although it might have been expected that these students—who serve a full three years in the military—would support a more fair division of the burden of military service, some did not express any strong opinions on the matter. A few were even against this new policy. According to one of them, the head of the IDF Manpower Division has:

> Some cheek. Yes! What does he care? [...] I think that this is what was going through his head: I was alone [as a religious soldier in the military][26]— [so] everybody can manage! [...] People want to do their service this way [in Hesder]; why are you telling them not to? (Nadav 2005)

Nadav felt that since the NAHAL Bnei Meshakim, the Druze soldiers, and the Bedouin soldiers serve together, the head of the Manpower Division had no right to force the Hesder students to disband and serve in heterogeneous units. On the other hand, this student wondered why Major General Stern ignored the issue of the Hesder soldiers' shortened course of duty, which did create discrimination.

A few students from the Shiluv and Mekhinot thought that this was a "political decision." Similarly, in an interview with him after Stern's announcement, Rabbi Bigman did not condemn this move, but remarked that things could have been done in a less forceful way (Friedman 2005). He too hinted that it was a pity that the issue of the length of the Hesder students' military service had not been addressed in Stern's new initiative. And, indeed, at the end of 2007, the IDF requested the Hesder students' active duty be extended to two years; the Igud rejected this request (Ozeri, first interview). However, in practice, in 2010 the new Shiluvim program has lengthened the service of a number of Hesder students (Nir 2010). While the students participating in Shiluvim do not originate from prestigious yeshivot, it is nevertheless a substantial shift in the Igud's position. As mentioned before, new legislation in Israel lengthening Hesder service by an additional month is being negotiated as of the summer of 2013.

Even before Stern's initiative, during interviews held for this study with junior officers, the question of whether it would be better for yeshiva students to serve in heterogeneous units arose. Some of the officers were actually in favor of homogeneous units; for instance, a deputy company commander in the NAHAL brigade said that as far as the daily timetable is concerned,

I know I have one problematic platoon, and then I can make arrangements. I have one portable Holy Ark, so when we go out to the field, it goes with them [the religious platoon]. If I had three quorums (*minyanim*) in three platoons, it would be harder to get organized. (Lieutenant Barak, first interview)

Furthermore, Lieutenant Barak explained that he sends all the canned meat with more stringent kashrut directly to this platoon, and so on. "If they were dispersed among the units, I would be in trouble" logistically (Lieutenant Barak, first interview).

On the other hand, commanding officers at the company and battalion levels said that the main problem with the Hesder platoons has to do with their shortened course of duty. The military considers a company with a Hesder platoon to be a full company with all soldiers accounted for, although this is not the case. A third of the soldiers return to their yeshiva after a certain period, and this affects the company's combat capabilities (Captain Noam, first interview). Thus, it appears that the junior officers who come into direct contact with the Hesder soldiers are against dispersing the Hesder platoons. They prefer that any changes involve the length of their active duty rather than the structure of the units.

* * *

Based on these three issues of coed service, insubordination, and the dispersal of Hesder units, we can draw conclusions regarding the ability and motivation of the study programs to intervene in the military sphere. Even if the impression is that the Mekhinot and the Hesder yeshivot do not follow each and every one of their students on an individual level, from the cases described these study programs seem willing to influence the military on a general level—in an obvious and even aggressive manner. If these programs perceive that a problematic situation has come about for all of their students, they will demand that the military adapt itself to meet their students' needs.

Why is the IDF willing to accept this? First, such active interference does not happen on a regular basis. Interviews held with high-ranking officers included in this study reflect that the military understands the rabbis' motives when they become actively involved. While these officers do not always agree with the rabbis' actions, they do not see them as illegitimate.

Second, the large number of students from the Mekhinot and the Hesder yeshivot drafted into the IDF every year has an effect on the military's attitude toward these programs. In Eli and Atzmona alone, during any given year, there are more students than in the Shiluv and the *midrashot* put together. The Hesder yeshivot's influence is also related to the number of students sent to the military. The Hesder program supplies a large and consistent number of students who serve almost exclusively in combat roles, and this appears to affect the IDF's relationship with the Hesder program. In a given year, between 1,200 and 1,300 Hesder students are drafted; another 2,000 are at the yeshivot and, theoretically, can be mobilized and returned to active duty quickly—as indeed happened during Operation Defensive Shield in April 2002 and during the Second Lebanon War in the summer of 2006.

Another factor that influences the relationship between the rabbis and the IDF is the fact that many of the Mekhinot rabbis are still high-ranking officers in the reserves. Thus, they have an understanding of the IDF system. Additionally, the Mekhinot rabbis cooperate with the Hesder Igud on these issues. It is difficult to determine which of these factors has the greater influence, but the end result is clear: if they feel it is necessary, the Hesder and Mekhinot rabbis are able to impose their views on the military.

The situation is more complicated in the case of the Religious Kibbutz Movement yeshivot. On one hand, it seems that the military authorities do not accord the Shiluv the same status as the Hesder and Mekhinot programs. This is reflected, for instance, in the IDF's attempt to unilaterally determine the postings of the Shiluv soldiers drafted in the August 2003 intake (as described in Chapter 5). On the other hand, the yeshivot nevertheless managed to reach a compromise that enabled some of their students to choose their postings. Clearly, the small number of Shiluv students means that it has less value, as far as the IDF is concerned. Few officers are familiar with the program or even know that it exists. Having said that, the fact that the Shiluv soldiers are—according to their officers—of high quality and serve a full three years may have a counter-effect. In any case, from among the male study programs examined here, the Shiluv is the weakest in its relations with the IDF.

The IDF's attitude toward the female soldiers drafted through the Gar'inim program is extremely cautious, in spite of their relatively small numbers. The regulations governing these soldiers' military service are very clear—even more so than in the case of the parallel male programs. It appears that strict observation of these regulations prevents problems at the general level.

CHAPTER 9
PROBLEMS FOR INDIVIDUAL RELIGIOUS SOLDIERS DURING MILITARY SERVICE

While most students did not anticipate the problems described in Chapter 8, all were preoccupied to various extents with more personal and specific problems before being drafted. It is important to note that while one might assume young Israelis embarking on their military service might be concerned with political issues (such as having to deal with police work in the Territories or other aspects of the Palestinian-Israeli conflict), Religious Zionist soldiers are far more concerned with the problems we have been reviewing in the past chapters—religious observance, Torah study, and their ability to maneuver within a system that is very different from what they are used to culturally. Accordingly, before conscription, many hoped that their study programs and the time they spent studying would assist them when confronted with dilemmas.

The personal problems encountered by the students from the Mekhinot, Shiluv, Hesder, and Gar'inim programs can be divided into general problems and specific halakhic problems. The former category includes being given an undesirable posting, deferring one's service or changing one's posting due to medical problems, and the physical or mental inability to fulfill the job's requirements. Another problem was related to tensions within the yeshiva students' platoon concerning various issues of conduct (as described above). Students also encountered more profound difficulties: serious physical injury followed by forced recuperation at home; death of a friend or a subordinate; and participation in combat, with all the dilemmas and challenges this includes.

Mekhina and Gar'in graduates tended to underestimate their problems and to view them within the wider context of military service in general. For instance, a graduate from Eli said:

> Look, yes [there are problems]. [. . .] Three years—there are problems.
> [. . .] Like in any other part of life [. . .]. But if I compare it to the best
> moments [during military service], I think that there is no comparison.
> I came across many more good things than problems in the military.
> (Matan, first interview)

Despite this, there were some graduates who admitted that they had definitely experienced problems. As one graduate from Atzmona put it plainly, "It's no fun being religious in the military" (Yochai, first interview). Hesder graduates were usually less nostalgic and tended to describe more problems than the Mekhinot students did. Most of them took a matter-of-fact view of their military service: I was there, there were problems, I dealt with them, that's it. This, at least, was the tone during interviews and informal conversations. In this chapter we will briefly survey the religious and halakhic problems students encountered during their service, and then focus on the strategies they employed in order to solve both general personal problems as well as personal halakhic ones.

Personal halakhic and religiously natured difficulties can be categorized as follows: purely halakhic problems, such as a military kitchen that is not kosher; a feeling that one's religious observance has eroded; and the sense that the military environment is not truly compatible with one's religious way of life. We will now outline each of these categories, and then describe the strategies for coping with them.

HALAKHIC PROBLEMS DURING MILITARY SERVICE

When recounting halakhic problems, students spoke mainly of dilemmas related to the way the military system functions. In general, Hesder students encountered fewer technical halakhic problems when they served in homogenous units:

A soldier in a yeshiva students' platoon has *no* problems *at all* [. . .]. In principle, there should not be any problems. The army is *very, very* [strict]. It goes so far that guys who care about observing *halak* meat will be able to get it anywhere,[1] even in the field; even the canned meat will be *halak*. (speaker's emphasis, Liron, first interview)

However, students who served in the Armored Corps and in noncombat posts did come across serious halakhic problems; these were soldiers who were not stationed in yeshiva students' units.

In contrast, female students from the *midrashot* encountered problems that arose mainly from their military roles as commanders—especially as female commanders in charge of male soldiers. These include ensuring that a soldier shaves properly when he can do so only by using a razor that is forbidden by halakha; turning off lights on Shabbat for soldiers in detention—which also requires the female soldier to enter male housing units, something that is clearly problematic from a modesty point of view. Others pointed out social difficulties, some of which were also a problem for students in the male study programs. What should one do about a discotheque party at the end of a training course or a day at a water park where attendance is mandatory—even though this goes against the prohibition on coed swimming? How should one approach the awkwardness that arises when a secular soldier's family arrives at a base on Shabbat and offers food that cannot be consumed, since it was brought to the base on the Sabbath?

Although halakhic problems arose time and again during their military service and the students spoke of this often, when asked upon completing their service whether the IDF was able to deal with such problems and with religious soldiers, almost all the interviewees gave a positive answer and they almost always used the same words: "In general, yes." However, most qualified their responses by saying that one's ability to observe mitzvot while in uniform depends largely on one's own personality and posting. A soldier who demands his or her rights will find religious requirements met.

A common halakhic problem for soldiers serving outside a homogenous unit was kashrut. More than half of the Mekhinot and Shiluv students in the follow-up study encountered kashrut-related problems, especially when serving in outposts or during combat duty, or when serving in elite units. When assigned guard duty in outposts, soldiers usually live in rented apartments or prefab units without a regular kitchen staff and have no way of identifying who has previously cooked there and what they prepared.

In the case of the Hesder and Gar'in members, less than half came across kashrut problems. Those who encountered problems found they arose during outpost duty or on small bases where Hesder soldiers from the Armored Corps served. Usually, under regular circumstances, the Gar'in and Hesder students said that there was a very high standard of kashrut: "More than at home" (Nerya, second interview).

Follow-up interviews indicated that in some cases, when encountering problems, Hesder students approached the unit's rabbi and asked him to take care of kashrut issues in the kitchen. In other cases, the students told each other of the problem, but did not take any official action. For example, an interviewee described a situation where the cook added water to a certain dish on the Sabbath; a halakhically forbidden act. The soldiers in the yeshiva students' platoon told each other about this and did not eat from the specific dish, but "this was only on the individual level" (Daniel, second interview). While occasionally the students called their yeshiva to discuss halakhic problems, they tended to deal with these by themselves.

In general, Hesder students were more likely to turn to military rabbis for help than the Mekhina students. It seems that all Mekhina and Shiluv students who came across kashrut problems tried to address them themselves, while explaining their position to their commanders. Gar'in members usually had no need to turn to military rabbis for kashrut problems, since they encountered such dilemmas in purely social contexts.

Besides kashrut dilemmas, another problem commonly encountered by the students was that of modesty (*tzniut*). As expected, all of the male students who served in the Intelligence Corps and in other noncombat posts alongside female soldiers came across modesty-related problems at a higher rate. However, combat soldiers, too, spoke of such problems. As well as those described above, students from all the programs spoke awkwardly of immodest posters in the housing units, vulgar language, and rude behavior around female soldiers—all conduct that is extremely unacceptable in their social group and which they found very disturbing. A less serious problem reported was the presence of a female welfare NCO or company clerk in the soldiers' tents in the evenings (Noach, second interview).

EROSION IN THE OBSERVANCE OF MITZVOT

A decline in the observation of mitzvot was a central problem for most of the interviewees. At the same time, the longer the students served in the military, the less they felt this to be a problem, and there were even students who felt that their degree of observance had increased during their service. During the interviews held while still in their first year of service, students reported the highest level of concern in this regard. In subsequent interviews, they were less apprehensive.

Compared to the large number of students who felt their level of observance eroded during their first year of service, there were a few who felt a stronger commitment to mitzvot. This situation was reversed during the second year of service: few students from all the programs felt that their level of observance had declined further since the first follow-up interview. On the other hand, half of the Shiluv students on active duty, a third of the Mekhinot students, and almost a third of the Gar'inim members reported an increase in their level of observance. (During this year, the Hesder students who participated in the study were either at their yeshiva before going on to an officers' training course, or had already completed their active duty.)

The reason for this feeling of a heightened observance of mitzvot is unclear. One female student thought that the fact that she was an officer enabled her to plan her day better. Another female student felt that the reason she was stricter in her observance in specific religious obligations was due to the fact that she was unable to concentrate while praying, but "in the small stuff [such as blessings recited before eating], it helps a lot to remember who you are and what is important to you" (Maya, third interview). It is possible that the fact that most of them had completed their training phase—and in their final stationing had greater freedom with regard to their personal conduct—contributed to their ability to observe mitzvot.

Two of the interviewees experienced profound religious crises—one Hesder student who left the program in order to take part in officer training and one Mekhina student. During his second year of service, the Hesder student began to question his religious identity. The Mekhina student experienced a crisis after the Disengagement from the Gaza Strip; he felt a loss of faith and experienced a decline in his religious observance. In the last interview held with him, in 2007, the Hesder student chose not to define his religious identity and said he observed only some mitzvot (Shabbat, kashrut). When asked about his observance in the future, he replied that he did not know, and that he was continuously exploring the path he wished to follow. The Mekhina student, on the other hand, was more certain. In an interview in 2007, he explained that he still wears a *kipa*, but he does not observe mitzvot. He expressed regret that he had attended a Mekhina and said that, in retrospect, he should have gone to a Hesder yeshiva or into the Shiluv program.

When asked whether they knew if any of their classmates were no longer religious, all the Hesder students gave a negative answer. Some of the female *midrasha* students said that they knew of one or two classmates who were no longer religious. Most of the Shiluv and Mekhinot students said that some of their classmates were no longer religious or were unsure of their religious identity. However, they could not give numbers and only offered estimates. While clearly loss of religious identity does take place during military service, the present study could not establish the extent of this phenomenon.

FEELINGS TOWARD THE MILITARY ENVIRONMENT

Most of the interviewees—male and female—said that they were happy with their service in the military and that, in general, their fellow soldiers treated them with consideration as far as their religious needs were concerned. There were, however, events that emphasized the differences between them and the other soldiers. The participants were not surprised by these events, but this elicited a response that was absent in the answers they gave before being drafted. For instance, one student said that "it's strange to suddenly see them talking on the phone on the Sabbath [. . .] like, they are used to it and all that" (Noach, second interview). It seems that before starting their military service, the interviewees did not estimate correctly how much living alongside their secular counterparts would put them in awkward situations—even when these did not clearly harm their own observance. In general, the Hesder students found it more difficult to deal with the secular atmosphere in the IDF in comparison with the Mekhina and Gar'in members, in spite of the fact that most of them served in units made up of yeshiva students.

As mentioned above, one issue that shocked and astonished students was the attitude toward women and the language used in the IDF. Quite a few students said that they found it hard to deal with vulgar speech and conversations about their fellow soldiers' sex lives. A Mekhina student who did not serve with other religious soldiers said that he was aware that such language had an effect on him:

> There are things that you hear, and say, "I can't believe that they speak and behave this way." Slowly, this has an effect, no matter what. You try as much as you can [not to be influenced, but it doesn't work]. (Yaniv, second interview)

Another Mekhina student expressed some shock at seeing the way his fellow soldiers reacted to female soldiers on their base:

> They *really* went looking for them [the girls]. *Really*! Like: "Wow, look at her! Look at her!" Completely out of proportion. And I don't know if this was exaggerated because we are, like, in the military and don't . . . don't see girls at all. I have no idea why this was. But I was really unpleasantly surprised. (speaker's emphasis, Shachar, second interview)

These negative feelings concerning language and the attitude toward women did not dissipate during the second year of service. It should be stressed that these are not sheltered young adults who had no connection at all to secular society. Many of them belonged to coed youth movements and were quite familiar with Hollywood and television before being drafted. Their reactions are an indication of the substantial differences between the lifestyle of a young Religious Zionist adult and that of his secular counterpart.

In spite of the differences, friendships were made between the study programs' students and their comrades. In postservice follow-up interviews, all of the Mekhina, Shiluv, and *midrashot* students had made secular friends. Most of them had visited these friends' homes and hosted these friends in their own homes; this happened very rarely in the case of the Hesder students.

A year after leaving the military, most of the interviewees were still in touch with their friends from the military—secular and religious—through telephone conversations and e-mail. Some of the friendships were very close. Students traveled abroad with their secular friends, including all that this entails.[2] One of the Gar'in members asked a secular friend with whom she served to spend her wedding day with her.[3]

In contrast, Hesder students did not maintain contact with their secular friends. Even those who served in the Armored Corps—and thus in heterogeneous units— did not stay in close contact with their secular friends after being discharged. Two years after leaving the IDF, at the time of their last interview, they had practically lost touch with their secular friends from the military.

This underscores the fact that students who served continuously in heterogeneous units were able to form friendships that were not merely ephemeral. And this brings up another consideration: if Hesder students who served in the Armored Corps were unable to maintain friendships with their secular counterparts, it appears that stationing Hesder students in heterogeneous units will not necessarily achieve the social cohesion sought by the IDF Manpower Division.

STRATEGIES IN PROBLEM SOLVING

From the outline drawn here, clearly students encounter personal difficulties aside from the general ones described in Chapter 8. As illustrated in the previous chapter, study programs usually address general issues. Is this the case with more personal dilemmas, or must students employ other strategies of problem solving in order to cope with the problems described in the pervious pages?

When encountering professional problems such as an undesirable posting or trouble with a commanding officer, students do not usually seek assistance from their respective programs during military service. The study program serves mainly as an empowering support system and as a safety net to be used only when all else fails.

This attitude is in keeping with the general message conveyed by the heads of the Mekhinot to their students. The Mekhina heads interviewed in this study ruled out any chance of them involving themselves in the question of a student's posting. Rabbi Peretz emphasized:

I don't interfere with anything in the military, unless there is an obvious injustice [committed] [. . .] no pulling strings (*protektziyot)* or anything like

that. You have to manage on your own, and whatever you're worth—
that's what you get to work with. (Peretz, second interview)

Unlike the Mekhina heads, the heads of the Hesder yeshivot were more
willing to help their students deal with difficulties in the military, although this
willingness depended on the yeshiva in question. For instance, Rabbi Kostiner said
that if a student had a serious problem—a mental or psychological problem, for
instance—he would not hesitate to approach the Igud in order to "cut through red
tape" and deal with the problem as quickly as possible (Kostiner, first interview).
Rabbi Lichtenstein said that the yeshiva would become involved only in the case
of a halakhic problem; he noted that even in such cases, the students were not
always in the right and that the yeshiva is aware of this. Rabbi Cherlow admitted
that in most cases, the yeshiva is unaware of the students' problems, since they
themselves do not usually approach the yeshiva for help. Despite the rabbis'
position, unofficially, it is common knowledge that the Igud can be approached
and asked to intervene in military postings. During the interviews, however, no
students admitted actually doing this.

Two clear exceptions to this policy of nonintervention are the Golan and the
Or Etzion yeshivot; these two yeshivot are prepared to involve themselves not only
in cases of halakhic or psychological problems, but also in cases of unmistakably
professional difficulties. Thus, Rabbi Sugarman said that if a student was expelled
from an officer's training course on grounds the yeshiva perceived as unjust, the
yeshiva would intervene and pressure the IDF to reinstate the student.[4]

In practice, Hesder rabbis do intervene in the military sphere. One of the
Golan yeshiva graduates said that the yeshiva students' platoon in which he
served was not let out for the weekend for technical reasons, and they turned to
their yeshiva for help: "We knew that the yeshiva would jump right in. They [the
military] can't play around with us for no reason" (Liron, first interview). This
was not the only case students described, and one can only imagine a platoon
commander's reaction at his authority being so clearly sidestepped.

Shiluv rabbis will also sometimes become involved in professional issues. For
instance, Rabbi Bigman said that if a student is having a hard time psychologically,
the yeshiva will try to help him receive a transfer to another posting, and, if
necessary, will even appeal to the Kibbutz Movement's Security Committee for
help.[5] The yeshiva will also help a student return to it for a second study period
(SHALAT) (Bigman, first interview).

Students from Ma'ayan and Rabbi Kahan himself said that the express
position of the Ein Ha-Natziv *midrasha* was not to interfere at all during the

students' military service. Rabbi Kahan's view was that this was part of the process of learning and growing up that the students must go through. He also said that it was unfair for the *midrasha* to interfere on its students' behalf, and it is not proper for Gar'in members to be given this kind of preferential treatment. Since most soldiers have no authority outside the IDF to appeal to, the study program should only take action when there is absolutely no other option.

That said, the *midrasha* will intervene in the case of a halakhic problem. If a student were to find herself in a severe personal crisis, the *midrasha* would take action provided it was a matter of psychological well-being, but it would have to be an exceptionally difficult situation to justify such interference. Rabbi Kahan remarked that this is one of the differences between Ein Ha-Natziv and the Lindenbaum *midrasha*, and that the heads of the Hadas program are more willing to get involved on their students' behalf (Kahan, first interview).

Rabbi Tehar-Lev stated that he does not get involved with professional problems, such as a student who is unhappy with her posting. However, his *midrasha* will intervene in the case of personal problems. In his opinion, being in the military is harder for young religious women than it is for young secular women. The encounter between an *ulpena* graduate and the secular military system can sometimes cause genuine culture shock.[6] Thus, in his opinion, these young women are justified in their need for greater assistance and support than secular women (Tehar-Lev, first interview).

This is also the case at Be'er: the faculty tries to help students deal with both halakhic and general problems that arise during military service. Biton emphasized that the *midrasha* does not have much influence due to the fact that it is a new institution. But it recognizes its responsibility to its students: "It's not 'you spent a year with us' and that's it [. . .] we take responsibility for them" (Biton, first interview).

When presented with halakhic problems, at times, Hesder students enlisted the help of their yeshivot. Almost all the interviewees called their yeshivot during their military service to ask about halakhic issues, such as Shabbat dilemmas. Some Hesder students asked for advice on a more frequent basis. However, many Hesder students said that they prefer to find solutions themselves and not to call the yeshiva "for every little thing." There were students who said that they sometimes inquired about halakhic issues retroactively in order to find out whether they had done the right thing and how to behave in the future.[7]

In addition to questions addressed to rabbis verbally, halakhic questions about military service are also posted on the Internet, on sites such as Kipa and Moreshet. Other questions appear in the responsa sections of various weekend circulars. However, the questions that appear on the Internet and in the circulars are usually of a general nature and do not require an immediate response. For instance, questions about reserve duty submitted ahead of time are more common than questions submitted by soldiers on regular duty. The impression is that soldiers who are in need of a quick response would rather call one of their rabbis or a soldiers' hotline if possible (S. Cohen 2006).

During their first year of service, when asked about approaching the Military Rabbinate when needing halakhic assistance, most of the students (male and female) said that they approach military rabbis only in regard to technical issues (such as maintaining kashrut in IDF kitchens). When they are in need of halakhic advice they usually require a quick response, and when the IDF rabbis are asked, "until they [the military rabbis] give you an answer and all that . . . ," it's already too late (Yaakov, first interview). Some of the Hesder students in the follow-up study said that they had asked the advice of military rabbis regarding issues pertaining to life on the base where they were stationed, such as kashrut and *eruv*. A student from the Petach Tikva yeshiva said that they were taught at the yeshiva that "each place has its local [halakhic] authority" and that in the military, the halakhic authority is the military rabbi, and he is the one to be consulted; accordingly, this is what he did (Tomer, third interview). In general, it seems that out of the students in all the programs, the Hesder students tended to approach the Military Rabbinate for help, while the Shiluv and Mekhinot students were more inclined to manage by themselves.

As far as practical problems related to halakhic issues (such as kashrut and Shabbat) are concerned, the female students' behavior was very similar to that of the male students. The female students would approach the *midrasha* only in exceptional cases, and they did not tend to post questions on websites like Moreshet and Kipa. The *midrasha* sites also do not include responsa concerning specific conduct when in the military.

When faced with dilemmas they felt unable to deal with, the female students tended to turn to their rabbis at the *midrashot*. Questions of this kind usually involved issues of personal conduct and ethical behavior in situations posed by service in the military, rather than technical issues related to observing mitzvot in the military. For instance, should one cover for a comrade who behaved improperly during a training course?

Since the appointment of Rabbi Yisrael Weiss as chief military rabbi, and even more so during the terms served by Rabbis Rontzki and Peretz, the standing of the Military Rabbinate has been improving. Both the yeshivot and Mekhinot rabbis, as well as the students, accord the Military Rabbinate greater respect and cooperate with it more than they did in the past.

Another noteworthy point is the fact that sometimes a Mekhina student called a rabbi from a Mekhina other than his own for halakhic advice. Such cases happened either because the student was pressed for time and used a phone number he had handy at the moment, or because of the situation he was in at the time. For instance, a student in the follow-up study said that he served with students from Eli, Atzmona, and the Shiluv. Due to the personal dynamics that developed among this group of soldiers, they preferred to act as a group in all halakhic dilemmas and only consulted the Atzmona rabbis (Shachar, second interview). A deputy company commander, and also a graduate of Eli who was the commander of a yeshiva students' platoon, preferred to call Rabbi Eyal Krim, who was not his rabbi but ran a halakhic hotline for soldiers. According to this officer, he was given Rabbi Krim's hotline number at a military event and favored consulting it rather than Rabbi Sadan of Eli, since the latter "does not really deal with the practical aspect" of halakhic rulings, while the former has the reputation of a rabbi who is familiar with the way things work in the military (Lieutenant Barak, first interview). According to an article in *Haaretz* (Harel 2000), Rabbi Krim tends to consult with high-ranking commanders in the field before handing down a complicated halakhic ruling—though usually his experience and military background allow him to give a ruling on the spot.[8]

Shiluv students, too, called their yeshiva for advice, usually to ask about unusual halakhic dilemmas they were unable to solve on their own. The students stated that they preferred to solve halakhic questions independently. Shiluv students generally consulted their yeshiva regarding matters of principle. For instance, a student asked for advice regarding the principle of observing Shabbat in the military: In problematic situations, should he be concerned only with his own observance of the Sabbath and make every effort to not desecrate the day? Or should he try to make sure that his entire unit does not violate Shabbat? Students preferred to ask such questions face-to-face when they visited the yeshiva—or when rabbis visited the bases—rather than over the phone.

Similarly, Hesder students called their teachers for general advice regarding difficult situations, rather than asking about specific halakhic issues. For instance, a graduate of Har Etzion said that during Operation Defensive Shield (2002), he was forced to violate the Sabbath even though he thought that the circumstances did not justify it. He called his teacher simply to discuss his feelings rather than the halakhic implications. He recounted that he found this conversation very beneficial. Other students reported similar situations.

In other words, students tend to use their study programs to receive moral support for halakhic issues rather than to ask for a concrete halakhic response.

Study programs and their staff serve as a psychological tool that students use in order to cope with complex halakhic dilemmas or with extra-halakhic aspects of a halakhic dilemma. Purely halakhic difficulties are either addressed independently, through a military rabbi, or with the help of a civilian rabbi or hotline deemed suitably equipped to solve the problem. Consequently, the study programs are not prominently involved in the military routines of their students. While the previous chapter showed that study programs are not afraid to influence military conduct in issues they deem matters of principle, students usually do not enlist their help in personal matters. Is this impression correct? Do commanding officers of student-soldiers indeed agree that the study programs do not meddle in routine military matters? How does the IDF itself feel about the study programs and their involvement in the IDF's sphere of influence? These questions will be explored in the following chapter.

CHAPTER 10
SENIOR AND JUNIOR OFFICERS' VIEWS
ON THE STUDY PROGRAMS

As described in the previous chapter, Shiluv, Mekhinot, and Gar'in students do not commonly turn to their institutions for assistance concerning halakhic problems, unlike Hesder students, who consult their yeshivot more often about such issues. Though when they do, it is usually concerning matters that involve additional dimensions, not exclusively halakhic, and students are more interested in receiving moral support than a concrete halakhic responsum in these cases. As noted, when it came to professional problems, students in the follow-up study and graduates of the various institutions reported only a few cases in which they turned to their programs for help. Such reports would mean that study programs do not meddle in the military system regularly, but rather only in extreme cases, as described in Chapter 8.

This chapter explores the relationship from the point of view of the military system in question. Does the IDF feel that the study programs and their rabbis usually "mind their own business" and only interfere in extreme situations, or is it only the students and study programs who perceive the situation this way? In reality, do IDF officers and commanders view it in an entirely different light? Since the dominant perspective in Israeli public opinion is that rabbis and study programs regularly interfere and meddle in the day-to-day running of the military system, this topic is pertinent.

Contrary to conventional views in Israel, the impression given by the students is supported by interviews with junior military personnel. Most of the Infantry Corps and Armored Corps officers (ranking from platoon commander to company commander) who were commanders of the Mekhinot, Shiluv, and Hesder students interviewed here could not recall a situation in which a rabbi had interfered on a student's behalf, and they also had not heard of such a case being reported by their fellow commanders. Most of the junior officers rejected any possibility of direct contact between them and the programs' rabbis.

There were, however, a very small number of cases of outright interference by Hesder rabbis in military matters, including rabbis who directly contacted officers regarding students with psychological problems and a rabbi who tried to prevent a student's dismissal from a training course considered more prestigious (Lieutenant Didi, first interview). It seems, therefore, that the rabbis—in particular Hesder rabbis—will meddle in the military sphere, although cases of blatant interference are relatively few and far between.

The attitudes of senior officers are slightly more complex. Brigadier General Avi Zamir, head of the Manpower Planning Division of the IDF at the time of the study, claimed that while he is aware of the fact that the Mekhinot prefer that their students be stationed in the field units, they do not interfere at all in matters of military postings (Zamir, first interview). Zamir added that Mekhinot and Shiluv students make an effort to be accepted to elite units and, "all in all, this demographic group competes for slots in the best units and posts in the IDF." From his tone, one may gather that he approves of this (Zamir, first interview). He confirmed that rabbis from all the study programs do not interfere in their students' postings.

On the other hand, the commander of Ground Forces (MAZI) at the time of this study, Major General Yiftach Ron-Tal, pointed out the involvement of Hesder and Mekhinot rabbis:[1]

They don't interfere, they are involved. And as long as they are involved, this is a good thing [. . .] because their involvement is of the kind that usually is aimed *to preserve* this course of service and *to nurture* it [. . .]. Look, their involvement, or their protests, regarding the "proper integration" (*Ha-Shiluv Ha-Ra'ui*) of the women, was correct. Nothing can be done about this. I agree with every word they said. But [. . .] they could not *interfere in the way* in which we decided to act. [. . .] This is the distinction I make between the right kind of involvement, positive involvement, and negative interference. It's the same with parents. Forget this [topic] for a moment. Let's assume [that we are talking about] a father and a mother and not a rabbi. We don't want a father and a mother interfering in our business. But their contact with the commanders can be very important! They can direct our attention to things that we did not know about! But in the end they have *to accept* our decisions. This is positive involvement rather than negative interference. (speaker's emphasis, Ron-Tal, first interview)

The rabbis do not attempt to interfere in the specifics, such as postings. However, when it comes to matters of principle, such as coed service, they do get involved—as they themselves admit and as illustrated in Chapter 8. The impression one gets from conversations with representatives of the military is that the IDF does not regard this as overstepping on the part of the rabbis, and that such involvement is perceived by the military system as appropriate and kept within proper limits.

In contrast to this feeling, individuals within the IDF posited that the *midrashot* are involved in routine military matters, although, as noted, the degree of involvement differs from one *midrasha* to another. Some commanders in the Education Corps were of the opinion that the *midrashot* interfere quite blatantly in any matter on the students' behalf, especially when it comes to placements and participating in officers' training courses.

When interviewed regarding the meddling of the study program in IDF matters, junior officers (platoon and company commanders, both male and female) spoke mainly of *midrashot* rabbis and of Lieutenant Colonel Rabbi Elmaliach interfering in the stationing of Gar'in members within the Education Corps. A notable example was that mentioned by the commander of the Training and Command Course (Hadrakha uPikud) at the time of this study. Lieutenant Yehudit complained that rabbis are blatantly involved in the placements of their students—a fact that invalidates the course's staff's opinions when determining stationing (Lieutenant Yehudit, first interview). She recounted that she had not been told ahead of time that Gar'in members may be stationed only on certain bases, and that she understood it was possible to station these soldiers on any base as long there would be two female religious soldiers serving there. When the Gar'in students found out that they were not being stationed according to the policy that was in place, they notified Rabbi Elmaliach, who approached the officer directly and also spoke to the training base's commander. This resulted in changing the entire placement plan of the course and upsetting the staff. However, Lieutenant Yehudit admitted that the new placements did not harm the Education Corps and that most of the Gar'in students were ultimately stationed in suitable positions. She saw the matter as one of principle, and what upset her was the unashamed interference of rabbis in professional military matters (Lieutenant Yehudit, first interview).

Rabbis Elmaliach and Tehar-Lev did not conceal the fact that at times the *midrasha* or Rabbi Elmaliach interfere on behalf of a student in decisions regarding placements. This is done in order to preserve the agreement between the program and the IDF and also to assure parents that the *midrasha* does not go back on its word. When it promises that students will receive a certain course of service, this is exactly what will happen.

For instance, in the past there was a case of a student who requested to be posted to the Bedouin reconnaissance unit, which contradicted the arrangement with the IDF. Rabbi Elmaliach and her *midrasha* prevented her from being stationed in this unit. From this, and in particular from the report of the commander of the Training and Command Course, the *midrashot*, Rabbi Elmaliach, and the IDF all take great pains to abide by their agreements and to station the Gar'in members in preapproved posts. The personal opinions of both the students and their direct commanders are not taken into consideration at all. Decisions are guided by a wide perspective of the rules, and are not made to suit a specific student or commander; the working assumption is that if the general framework of the agreement were to be damaged, this would cast a shadow on the entire program's course of service. The *midrasha* feels an obligation toward parents and toward Religious Zionism as a social group. It cannot allow students and officers to change the guidelines decided upon by the program and the IDF. To do so would invalidate the program and chip away at its integrity. Young women enlisting through a *midrasha* would no longer be able to claim they were doing so in a more sheltered and religiously "safe" environment.

The higher-ranking IDF officers are, in comparison with the lower and intermediate ranks, more accepting of the rabbis' interference on behalf of their female students. Captain David, a senior instructor at the Havat Ha-Shomer base, said that it is naïve to think that only the Gar'inim members use personal connections to solve placement problems. Every soldier who is unhappy with his or her posting can use personal connections, and the *midrasha* students are no different (Captain David, first interview). Captain David claimed that he had approached Lieutenant Colonel Rabbi Elmaliach for help in the past when he wanted to send a student under his command to an officers' course but encountered problems, hoping to utilize the more senior officer's connections. This officer perceived the rabbis as another element that could help the Gar'in students—much like concerned parents:

> [The rabbi] doesn't tell me how to run the base. He asks questions and expects answers and that is okay. It's like a mother who phones. It's like parents being involved. It's annoying, but it's built-in [the system]. That's the way it is. (Captain David, first interview)

He emphasized that, in any case, the rabbis do not overstep, and that he felt the degree to which they are involved is acceptable.

The chief education officer at the time the main body of elite interviews was conducted (2002–2003) was Elazar Stern, and most of the Gar'inim soldiers served under his command. Stern also thought that the degree of interference on the part of the *midrashot* rabbis (as well as that of the yeshivot and Mekhinot rabbis) was appropriate: "They get involved out of a bit of concern for their soldiers.

I think this is rather legitimate [. . .] I don't feel that they cross [the line]" (Stern, first interview). Both Stern and Captain David gave the impression that the IDF cooperates with the study programs on issues concerning the Gar'inim's students, and the military is aware that the welfare of their students is the *midrashot*'s first priority—not the good of the IDF.

Junior officers, as well as some of the Gar'in members during and after their military service, spoke of the problematic aspects of the structure of the Gar'in itself. For instance, the scheduled meetings of the students with their rabbis on base (see Chapter 7) cause part of the staff to vanish all at once.[2] This creates an awkward situation in which the remainder of the staff has to work extra hard because of the Gar'in members' absence. On the one hand, attendance at these meetings is mandatory for the Gar'in soldiers and absence is a punishable military offense. On the other hand, their absence from their military posts causes much grumbling among their comrades.

It should be noted that what is perceived as special privileges given to the Gar'in members is sometimes a result of the military's insistence on keeping the letter of its agreement with the Gar'in program, even at times against the will of the students themselves. For instance, one of the interviewees reported a case in which the Gar'in students requested to skip their meeting with the rabbi in order to avoid the negative impact on the course they were instructing at the time. Most of the staff in this course was made up of Gar'in members, and there was no way to arrange for substitutes for them all. Their commanders refused to authorize their absence (Sarit, first interview).

On the other hand, despite the rules, at times Gar'in members are not released from their duties to attend meetings, due to their commanding officers' decisions. Thus, even if at the more senior levels the terms of the agreement are strictly observed, this is not necessarily the case at the junior levels of command.

It appears that the military tries to honor its agreement with the Gar'inim program. As a system, the IDF realizes that this is the only way to make sure that all sides will keep the agreement. Lieutenant Colonel Rabbi Elmaliach also gave the impression that both he and the *midrashot* are strict about observing all the terms agreed upon with the military. This commitment is based on the idea that a breach of minor obligations will lead to compromises on the more essential points. Violations of the agreement with the military might create an impression that the Gar'inim do not lend their students sufficient support, and this in turn could result in a decline in the program's numbers—something the IDF does not wish.

In general, from interviews with senior officers, clearly the IDF wants the manpower supplied by the study programs. It sees these students as highly motivated and recognizes that the study programs boost this motivation to serve and to be stationed in combat positions. Major General Ron-Tal explained that, as he understands it, the importance of military service is conveyed to the students in no uncertain terms:

> A statement like, "Our contribution to society is more important—on the most fundamental level—than that of the society to us." This equation— most young people *in the world* do not agree with this! *States* do not agree with it anymore. *The laws.* All the basic laws. All the constitutions in the world today! All these place the individual above, let's say at the *very top* [of the list of priorities], and [the good of] society is below that [. . .] and the military is an organization that nullifies individual liberties. [. . .] And these guys [from preservice study programs], during their study, are doing something that flies in the face of all of this! They are being taught how important the military is. That contributing [to society] is important. This [studying and being guided towards military service] doesn't happen in the case of other soldiers who enlist. (speaker's emphasis, Ron-Tal, first interview)

In other words, because Western society values the individual, most conscripts think first and foremost of their own private good. According to Ron-Tal, students of preservice programs, by contrast, think of the general good first and therefore place the good of the military system above their own personal wants. Moreover, Ron-Tal thought that, in general, the IDF reaps the benefits when a soldier is conscripted after studying, and that is particularly true in the case of Mekhina students:

> These guys' perception of the importance of their contribution to Israeli society through military service—not just any service but combat service—is one that in fact results in them making substantial concessions in order to reach command posts, to continue their military service, to view the military as a way of life. [. . .] So there are two things that are combined here [when they study before serving]. On one hand, strengthening their faith, but in the end, this contributes to a more beneficial military service. (Ron-Tal, first interview)

Thus, according to Ron-Tal, by the very virtue of their faith, these individuals are *more* loyal to the IDF than other soldiers are. This would explain why he views study program favorably.

The senior officers interviewed for this study—Zamir, Ron-Tal, and Stern—all spoke with great enthusiasm about the Mekhinot, and, to some extent, also about the Shiluv soldiers. According to Brigadier General Zamir:

> We are dealing here with a significant and high-quality segment of the population. They are highly motivated to be stationed in combat units and reach command posts in the IDF. To volunteer for the voluntary [special and reconnaissance] units. And we make every effort to offer assignments suitable for their high capabilities and considerable wishes. (Zamir, first interview)

Zamir's statement here indicates that the Manpower Division in the IDF is ready to grant the Mekhinot's requests concerning posting their students in the field and in elite units.

The three senior officers interviewed said that one of the considerations in cooperating with the study programs is related to the importance of maintaining the IDF's identity as a people's army. As Zamir put it:

> We are dealing with a high-quality demographic group, with a certain lifestyle, and we, as a system, have to make an effort to integrate them in the best way possible, by virtue of the concept of the people's army. And this demographic sector has the option of not enlisting. They can go the way of *torato umanuto*.[3] And some of them [can choose this option]. A large part. And here the IDF [. . .] makes every effort to enable their lifestyle. (Zamir, first interview)

When asked specifically about the Shiluv—which has no more than 120 students a year and is thus a small program numerically—Zamir compared it to Hesder, saying:

> And Hesder has one hundred thousand [students]! That's a lot! [. . .] What's the difference between the two?! But it doesn't require many more resources needed [to run the Shiluv program] than those [necessary] to enlist the MAKAM [soldiers who complete their high school diplomas during their military service]. (Zamir, first interview)

Thus, Zamir contended that the numbers of students in each program are not the main motive for cooperation, as far as the IDF is concerned. The concept of a people's army is a far more important incentive for the military system when dealing with the various study programs. Zamir interpreted this to mean that the IDF should try to meet the Shiluv students' needs just as it makes an effort to meet the needs of soldiers from disadvantaged backgrounds. According to him, the military's desire to assist in the enlistment of soldiers from Religious Zionist society is enhanced by that fact that these students have the option to not enlist at all, similar to the ultra-Orthodox sector.[4]

The military interviewees addressed Gar'in students separately. Like the Shiluv program, the Gar'in program calls for some effort on the part of the military system. Officers from the middle and higher ranks said that the program is important for the same reason that it is important to draft young adults from Religious Zionist society in general: maintaining the military's identity as a people's army.

> I think that it [the Gar'inim and the option to enlist as a Gar'in] strengthens the connection with the religious population [. . .] this is proved by the fact that there are some who feel more comfortable going to a Gar'in. I think that there are parents who have more peace of mind when their daughter goes to a Gar'in. [. . .] And I understand them! [. . .] The military has its own kind of ethos, which is not the ethos of many other places, and it is also not the ethos of the religious sector. (Captain David, first interview)

Captain David is thus of the opinion that it is important to offer an option where religious women and their families will feel more comfortable and protected. The chief education officer also surmised that there are students who would not enlist if they did not have the option of the Gar'inim program (Stern, first interview).

On the other hand, the IDF is also motivated by a more practical reason when accepting the Gar'in program and its needs and demands. Captain David thought that the program increases the number of female soldiers from the Religious Zionist sector, and these are automatically stationed in the Education Corps. In the absence of the Gar'in program, these women would chose the option of National Service rather than enlist in the military:

> I need them to enlist. [. . .] Not because of social and ideological reasons [but], bottom line, this is a bottomless resource. I mean, for me, someone has signed a standing order [to send me] girls of the highest quality [. . .]. There is a battle for this quality [manpower for the Education Corps]. *I*

have a standing order! No one can take these girls from me! This means that when I want to motivate a company commander to improve his cooperation with the Gar'inim or to be cautious or pay attention to areas in which they must be more sensitive [this is the argument I can use]. These are unusually high-quality girls. [. . .] Now, I have others like them; not from a Gar'in and not religious! But if I can reserve such girls [for my unit] . . . this is purely in my interest. (speaker's emphasis, Captain David, first interview)

The chief education officer at the time also remarked on the quality of the manpower as a reason to cooperate with the Gar'inim, explaining that utilizing the idea of a Gar'in, "I can supply some kind of framework for serving together [. . .]. So I get [soldiers who are] as good as those in the pilots' training course"[5] (Stern, first interview). Stern was also aware of the fact that the nature of their posting in the military was important to Gar'in members:

Look, it can't be helped, there is no equality in the military! There are no equal opportunities! And don't let anyone tell you any stories [to the contrary]. Even if we declare that we are open to anything and that a girl can serve anywhere—go to the Golani Battalion, and you won't find one female combat soldier there, and neither in the Paratroopers Battalion or in the NAHAL! [. . .] What can I tell the girls?! I can't challenge them in this way [by serving in combat units]. (Stern, first interview)

They can, however, be given the challenge of serving as NCOs in the Education Corps; they are high-quality soldiers, and this is why the Education Corps wants them. Lieutenant Colonel Rabbi Elmaliach (first interview) agreed that the IDF is motivated mainly by the need for high-quality manpower, as well as the desire to continue to be a people's army, and that is why the IDF is willing to make substantial concessions toward the Gar'in soldiers.

* * *

To conclude, in general, the more senior an officer, the more sympathetic they were toward the study programs and their staff and the more understanding they were toward possible interference in the military sphere. More junior officers who encountered meddling, especially those in contact with Gar'in members, were unforgiving and unhappy with these incidents, even when they were rare. Gar'in commanding officers were more likely to encounter meddling than commanding officers of Hesder students, and commanders of Shiluv and Mekhinot students saw the least involvement of rabbis of all the junior officers interviewed. This, naturally, would explain the feelings of Gar'in commanding officers toward the *midrashot*.

Additionally, the fact that senior officers did not feel that rabbis unduly interfered in the military sphere indicates that they understand the dynamics of the relationship between the civilian and military spheres in this context. They feel that it does not inhibit their actions, needs, or wishes to an unacceptable extent. It is a price they feel is not too high, and they sense it is a fair exchange for the volume and quality of manpower they gain in return. Moreover, it allows them to continue to benefit from the appearance of accommodation: the IDF accommodates this sector of Israeli society and is therefore still a people's army. In their opinion, the military sphere gains more than it loses from the current arrangement, and in any case, its losses are not too severe.

CHAPTER 11
MEDIATION AS COMMUNICATION:
THE PROGRAMS' ROLE IN CONVEYING MESSAGES
BETWEEN STUDENTS AND SUPERSTRUCTURES

After understanding the extent to which the study programs are involved in the military sphere, the extent to which they attempt to mediate in general and more personal issues, and how students use their study programs when solving religious problems while in uniform, we can now turn to discussing another dimension of mediation. Students hope to convey certain messages using their study programs, both to their social group and to the IDF. The superstructures, too, try to use the study programs as communication venues when discussing larger social issues—as well as the treatment of the student-soldiers in question. This chapter will discuss this facet of mediation.

In addition, the study programs are independent entities with interests of their own: they wish to survive as institutions; they have ideological agendas, economic considerations, and educational goals. These create messages that they themselves generate and communicate to their students, to the IDF, and to Religious Zionist society—rather than merely channel. These messages will also be described in this chapter.

MESSAGES COMMUNICATED BY STUDENTS
THROUGH THE STUDY PROGRAMS

The students in all preservice study programs expect their programs to convey messages for them both to the IDF and to the Religious Zionist sector. These messages are slightly different from one program to another. Hesder students try to convey to their social group that they are in the process of becoming bnei Torah. Serving in the military will not damage their Torah scholarship or their identities as young adults who are loyal to an observant way of life. At the same time, they are fulfilling their duty to serve in the military—a duty that is not only a civic one, but also a religious one.

Some of the Hesder students who were interviewed before their military service stated that they planned to leave the program after their first year and serve a full three-year term of service. These students deliberated the morality of serving for a shorter time in order to study Torah: "You want to study Torah.

Okay. Learn [. . .] but this doesn't have to come at the expense [of full military service]" (Tomer, first interview).

This dilemma is, of course, unique to Hesder students. It might be neutralized in the case of students who then serve in heterogeneous units as a result of the Stern Initiative (as opposed to homogenous yeshiva students' units). Although service in these units is still shorter than the usual three-year term other male conscripts serve, serving alongside soldiers from other sectors of Israeli society may send out the message that Hesder students are willing to go above and beyond in order to fulfill their duty to serve. A student who serves in a heterogeneous unit presents himself as someone who is ready to make certain concessions on matters that are important to him for the greater good of the society in which he lives.

On the other hand, serving shoulder-to-shoulder with soldiers who spend three full years in uniform might enhance a Hesder student's feelings of guilt, since he will return to the yeshiva to study while his comrades stay on in the military. This experience might even cause some Hesder students to extend their time in the military. Examining these issues in depth will only be possible in a number of years, once several more Hesder classes serve in heterogeneous units. However, a recent, nonacademic survey indicates that as much as 40 percent of Hesder students regret their shortened term of service and feel that lengthening it would be appropriate (Ekstein 2013).

As part of the attempt to deal with the moral difficulty inherent in a shortened period of military service, Hesder students try to convey another message to Israeli society. Both Hesder students and rabbis spoke of the important role of the Hesder students in the reserve forces. For instance, Rabbi Kostiner claimed that reserve duty is the most important justification for shortening Hesder students' service in the regular forces. According to him, the time one spends in the regular forces is not a true indication of one's contribution; this is better proven by the amount of reserve duty a citizen does throughout his life. In his opinion, Hesder students do more reserve duty than average (Kostiner, first interview).[1]

Unlike the messages conveyed by Hesder students, Mekhina students wish to convey to their social group that they are interested in studying and deepening their commitment to halakha. They intend to enlist after sufficient spiritual preparation. They wish to conduct themselves as "people of faith who live in reality" (to quote various students and Mekhina rabbis), taking part in all practical aspects of life. Living in reality is perceived as an integral part of their identity as observant Orthodox Jews. Attending a Mekhina does not mean that they are less committed to their religious observance or to scholarship. Rather, they are motivated by ideology and deep personal convictions.

Gar'in students wish to convey to Religious Zionist society that they have given the idea of serving in the IDF a good deal of consideration. They engage in study, enrich their religious world, and build their identity as observant women. Serving in the military is not an indication of lessened spiritual, religious, or moral commitment—quite the opposite.

The strict observance of the terms of the agreement between the IDF and the *midrashot* helps transmit another message: the Gar'in program "protects" its members, and they are not exposed to the military system in the same way that non-Gar'in female soldiers are. Even if this is not entirely true in practice—as noted above—this sentiment is prevalent and reinforces the message that the Gar'in program is "safer" and thus worthy. A "serious" young religious woman can serve in the military in the Gar'in program without worrying about compromising her identity and values. Since the Religious Zionist social group is still very much a traditional society, such reassurance is important.

Shiluv students are trying to send a message not only to Religious Zionist society, but also to Israeli society in general: quality Torah scholarship does not have to come at the expense of protecting Israel's security. The level of their scholarship equals that of the Hesder students, and thus one can be a true Torah scholar while serving a full term of service. During interviews, some of the Shiluv students spoke out against Hesder students (whose shortened military service they felt was unjustified) as well as against Mekhinot students (whose level of scholarship they felt was flawed because they do not study as much independently). In this sense, although they constitute a minority among the study program students, Shiluv students tried to explain that their program is the only one that enables one to be a good citizen without giving up significant Torah scholarship.[2]

Aside from messages students wish to convey to their social group, they also wish to send an important message to Israeli society in general: they are part of Israeli society and of the State of Israel. Additionally, Hesder students add the caveat that although they want to serve and be part of Israeli society, due to the requirements of maintaining a religious way of life, they cannot serve in "regular" units or for a full three years. That said, they gladly share the burden of military service in order to contribute to the state and society within their limitations and will continue to contribute to society their entire lives. In contrast, Mekhinot and Shiluv students try to convey the message that they are willing to go to great lengths in order to contribute rather than isolating themselves in the world of the Torah. As the Mekhinot students put it: they are people of faith prepared to live in a world of actions, and therefore they serve in the IDF with all that this entails. Gar'in students also wish to convey to Israeli society that living an observant lifestyle does not come at the expense of their commitment to the state or their desire to fulfill their civic duty.

These messages are especially important in light of the ongoing crisis in Religious Zionist society following the Disengagement in the summer of 2005, and particularly after the evacuation of Amona (February 2006). Military service has become an important way to distinguish between young adults who feel committed to the country and wish to engage in a dialogue with society and those who feel alienated from the state and its values and feel that their values and the principles they hold dear are being persecuted and delegitimized by Israeli society.

Just as they convey messages to their social group, the students also attempt to be heard by the IDF. Students from all study programs try to convey a message of loyalty and excellence: They will be good soldiers and will invest effort in their military service. However, if their values are not protected, they will not be able to do so. The IDF must meet their needs or it will lose these soldiers. If, however, an effort is made to take their needs into consideration, they will be the best and most loyal soldiers possible.

Military service as a religious obligation is another message the students wish to convey, adding a dimension of loyalty to their service. Students—mainly, but not exclusively—from the Mekhinot pointed out that service in the military is part of their religious faith. For instance, a student at the Rosh Pina Mekhina explained that military service is a mitzva, just as the wearing of phylacteries is (Eran, first interview). As a student at Eli put it:

> It's true that the state wants me to serve in the military, but I don't do it because I am *forced* to. I do it [. . .] because my Torah, the same Torah that I'm studying now in the *beit midrash*, wants me to serve in the military. This is not something external [to me and my beliefs], and the state is, like, forcing me to enlist. (speaker's emphasis, Yoni, first interview)

These sentiments are reinforced by Rabbi Sadan. He explained that military service is "not only a civic duty but also a religious, moral, and Torah-ordained duty. The entire process of gaining independence in a sovereign state. It is a privilege and a mitzva to be part of this" (Sadan, first interview). Following Ba'al Ha-Turim,[3] who said that "the garments of priesthood are like the garments of war" (Ba'al Ha-Turim, Leviticus 6:3), Rabbi Sadan explained that

> just as a *cohen* [priest in the Temple in Jerusalem] carries out his holy tasks for the people of Israel, for the common good, thus a soldier takes off his individual garments and puts on a uniform. (Sadan, first interview)

Sadan views this as a religious and moral duty of the highest degree. Indeed, it seems that the Mekhinot students internalize this message, and, as noted, would like the IDF to understand it, too.

While it is not always clear if the message of military service as a religious obligation comes from the students themselves, or rather this is something that they picked up in the Mekhina, a comparison with students in the other programs seems to illustrate that the Mekhina is not the sole factor that contributes to the formation of this idea: students from the other programs also commented on the halakhic dimension of their military service.

However, Shiluv students, specifically, barely framed military service in religious terms. They preferred to see it as the performance of a civic duty and only therefore a religious obligation. In other words, it is only because three years of military service are required by law by the state that this becomes a religious requirement. Sharing in this burden is a civic duty, and therefore fulfilling it is a mitzva. Military service in and of itself is not a positive element nor is it religiously required.

Most Gar'in members tended to view military service as a mission carried out for the greater good; this influenced their choice of posting:

> I understood that this post [of education NCO] allows one-on-one influence and that seemed more real to me than teaching soldiers how to drive a tank. (Maya, first interview)

Since military service in and of itself is important, one should choose a post that will allow the greatest contribution possible.

Likewise, Hesder students spoke of military service as a part of their religious loyalty and of enlistment as an important contribution to the people of Israel and the state: "I go [to the military] based on this feeling. That I am actually going [there] for the entire nation" (Ira, first interview).

There were, however, differences between Hesder yeshivot as far as perceiving military service as a mitzva is concerned. Students from Yerucham and Petach Tikva used the word "mission" (*shlihut*) when speaking of military service. Students from the Ma'ale Adumim Hesder yeshiva, just like Mekhina students, said that the yeshiva's position is that when in the IDF, a student should do what the military requires, and not necessarily what one wants or prefers to do.

In contrast, students from Har Etzion said that the yeshiva sees military service as a necessity rather than a positive thing in and of itself: "That going to the military is like going to the bathroom: you go in, do what you have to, flush, and like, leave it all behind you" (Barkai, first interview; cf. Lichtenstein 2002, 15).

When recounting the yeshiva's position, none of the preservice students from Har Etzion endorsed it. These interviewees, like students in the other programs, tended to view military service in a positive light. They did, however, fully understand the yeshiva's message, in particular that of Rabbi Lichtenstein, that the military is an important necessity, but under no circumstances a positive thing.

Thus the view of military service as a religious obligation is one the students wish to convey both to their social group as well as to the IDF and Israeli society. It explains why they undertook to study and serve within the framework of their choice.

Likewise, Gar'in members want to convey another general message that is aimed more specifically at the IDF. The students expect that due to the fact that they enlist as a group—rather than as individuals—the IDF should understand that they are to be treated differently. It cannot treat them high-handedly, since the *midrasha* will protect them. Their observance of mitzvot is not of marginal or little importance. As one of the students put it in a follow-up interview:

> A girl who goes to a *midrasha*—she is also often more religious to begin with—because she wants to study. I can't say that this is true of everyone, but girls who are less religious will arrive in the army as "more or less" religious, these are girls who will not go to a *midrasha* [. . .]. They come from a religious family and observe religion, but [. . .] this is not a burning issue for them. (Hagit, second interview)

It seems that these students' commanders understand this message well. As Captain David said:

> Most of the religious girls who used to come to the Hava [Havat Ha-Shomer base]—I am talking about four or five years ago—would take a break from their religiosity. [. . .] You wouldn't guess from appearances that she is [religious] [. . .] and this is something that I think the Gar'inim did. In time, they supplied a framework that you can belong to and stay religious. (speaker's emphasis, Captain David, first interview)

In other words, the message sent by the students via the *midrashot* concerning an observant lifestyle and the boundaries set by the halakha is understood by the IDF.

Naturally, in the context of ideas conveyed between Religious Zionism and the students, Gar'in members cannot help but be involved in the halakhic debate concerning women's conscription, as described earlier. The *midrashot* lend women's military service halakhic and social legitimization. As one of the Ma'ayan students noted, a reason for going to the *midrasha* was: "To know that I am not [. . .] serving in the military and feeling like a *criminal* [. . .] the Gar'in means this is not a compromise with halakha" (speaker's emphasis, Ya'ara, first interview). Meaning that since she was serving as part of a Gar'in, she was not going against halakha.

To conclude, students use their study programs not only to help them prepare for military service and to cope with problems during their time in uniform, but also to help them communicate messages they deem crucial both to their social group and to the IDF, explaining themselves and their motives for their chosen venue of study and service. They use their study programs to indicate how they wish to be perceived and treated, and as a social statement.

MESSAGES COMMUNICATED TO STUDENTS
THROUGH THE STUDY PROGRAMS

The students are not the only ones who use the study programs as a venue for communication. Both the IDF and Religious Zionism use the programs to communicate messages to the student-soldiers. Interviews held with students from all the programs show that the main messages conveyed by the programs can be divided into three categories, with each program stressing a slightly different emphasis: study and the observance of mitzvot; proper conduct as citizens and members of Am Yisrael; and messages relating to military service. Some Mekhina students said that the last category was not a separate one, but rather subsumed within the first two. Hesder and Shiluv students, similarly, discerned few messages pertaining exclusively to military service. However, for the purpose of an analysis of the relationship between the students and these two greedy institutions, we will maintain the distinction between these three categories.

As noted above, all Mekhina heads interviewed here raised the issue of strengthening their students' religious identity. The idea implicit here is that the Mekhinot's aim is to reinforce the students' commitment to halakha and the observance of mitzvot. The heads of the Shiluv program were clear that commitment to halakha was a key message they wished to communicate to their students. However, Rabbis Bin-Nun and Bigman emphasized the importance of the quality of the scholarship in the program: the program is not committed only to the halakha, but also to "serious" study.

In a similar fashion, according to the heads of the Hesder yeshivot, the aim of their program is to nurture their students as Torah scholars. They hardly mentioned the issue of reinforcing their students' religious identity and commitment to halakha. The heads of the Hesder yeshivot focused on issues of scholarship: their aim is to give their students the skills to enable their future studies; emphasis is on study of the Talmud. Rabbi Lichtenstein, who explained the difference between the Mekhinot and the Hesder programs, referred to this directly:

> The very name "Mekhina" [preparatory seminary] indicates the nature of the program. Its aim is to preserve the student's ties to the legacy of the Jewish people [*kodshei moreshet yisrael*] and his identity as a believer and observant Jew. [. . .] One should not be satisfied only with maintaining what already exists, as far as ties to the Torah and a sentiment of God-fearing acquired by a young adult by the time he is nineteen. [. . .] And this is where the difference in structure and concept [between Hesder and the Mekhinot] lies. While in the Mekhinot the religious study chapter is usually seen—and at times realized—as preparation for military service, and is carried out under its shadow, in Hesder yeshivot, even the military chapter is perceived as a part of a larger religious process, within which [. . .] the student-soldier is planted. (Lichtenstein 2002, 14–15)

In other words, the struggle against secularization is important, as is strengthening the students' commitment to mitzvot, but Hesder yeshivot do not dedicate themselves to these issues. Their aim is to cultivate Torah scholars; reinforcing the students' observance of mitzvot and nurturing their religiosity are by-products of this aim. This message seems to be one sent by Religious Zionism as well as the yeshiva itself, as an independent entity.

The heads of the *midrashot* also referred to stressing commitment to halakha and mitzvot as part of the program's aims, to different degrees. Rabbi Kahan spoke of commitment to halakha as an important aim; he would like to see the students "[being able] to live well with their religious identity" (Kahan, first interview). Biton spoke of the integration of a social and religious message—the social aspect should "derive also from a religious view, a very halakhic one, of interpersonal relations" (Biton, first interview). It is interesting to note that, unlike the heads of the Hesder yeshivot, the heads of the *midrashot* did not evade a discussion of secularization and sheltering their students from the domination of the military system. Such aims are deemed important and taken seriously by the *midrashot*. This might be related to the fact that the *midrashot* students are female, although this was not specifically stated in the interviews.

The message sent to the student-soldiers in this context is primarily the importance of maintaining a religiously observant, orthodox, way of life. While each program may frame this message differently (stressing commitment to halakha, stressing the importance of Torah scholarship, and so on), the core message is one that originates from Religious Zionist society and its fears when faced with the conscription of its young men and women, as described in Part I.

This raises the question of the degree to which the students are aware of these messages. The preservice Mekhinot students interviewed here identified a message of commitment to halakha and mitzvot, and hardly mentioned the issue of scholarship as a significant message.[4] When asked about the Mekhina's main message, approximately half of all preservice Mekhina students perceived the importance of continuing to observe mitzvot as the Mekhina's main message, both during and after military service. Contrary to the feelings of most Mekhinot heads,[5] this message does indeed come across in the various Mekhinot.

It seems that the Gar'in students are also well aware of the message regarding the importance of observing mitzvot. They pointed out that their programs would like them to be observant women in the future, and that "religion will really be a part of our lives [. . .] that this will be a part of everything we do" (Miriam, first interview). Similarly, they felt that their program would like them to engage in Torah studies and some kind of public service (education, leadership roles, or social engagement) during their postservice lives.

Messages relating to general conduct as citizens and part of the Jewish collective (*banim le-am yisrael*) were most dominant among the ideas communicated by the Mekhinot. Many students cited some variation on the saying "to be people of faith in a practical world"—bringing their religious identity to bear upon everything they do, and participating fully in all spheres of social activity.

Hesder students made almost no reference to Torah studies and proper conduct as distinct issues. They mainly identified messages regarding the importance of scholarship itself, and the ties between Torah study and everyday life. For example, students at Har Etzion, Yerucham, and Petach Tikva spoke of the importance of being a part of society in general and not letting the study of Torah come between a person and real life:

> To hear a baby crying outside the walls of the yeshiva. This means [. . .] not to get sucked into studying and staying inside the yeshiva, to be a righteous person to oneself and forget the world around you. Quite the opposite: [one must] make a [social] contribution. (Ronen, first interview)[6]

Students at Ma'ale Adumim and Yerucham spoke of the importance of making a practical contribution to daily life—in the form of volunteering, for instance.

Study is not the be-all and end-all: "One still has (kitchen) duty once a month; one still has to teach here at the Kol Ya'akov [elementary] school two hours a week. One still has to be a decent human being" (Yoel, first interview).

From the interviews with the students, it becomes apparent that the Hesder program focuses on messages related to Torah scholarship and its impact on the students' everyday lives. These ideas are two sides of the same coin. In their opinion, being a Torah scholar is unequivocally tied to their commitment to Am Yisrael. One value leads to the other.

Several Shiluv students pointed out that their yeshiva is interested in cultivating Torah scholars and religious leadership, and they also noted a message of commitment to halakha: "To be open while still being committed. Committed to halakha" (Tal, first interview). About half of the preservice Shiluv interviewees identified a message of social involvement and the need to contribute to the common good. A similar number of students said that their yeshiva emphasized the importance of studying and spoke of the importance of independent study, inquiry, and seeking answers. This is true even when a question has no answer, and sometimes "one has to live with the questions" (Yoav, first interview). Other students spoke of messages of pluralism, the importance of personal moral conduct, and social involvement. It seems that out of all the programs discussed here, the messages identified by the Shiluv students were the most varied. These messages are specific Shiluv messages, and while they may be indicative of the wishes of the students' parents, they do not necessarily represent messages conveyed by Religious Zionism in general.

Do the messages communicated by the programs influence the students? It seems that these messages are very influential during the students' first year of study. Most of the Mekhina students in the follow-up study spoke of a change in their attitude to mitzvot during their time at the Mekhina—a change that had a practical influence on their observance of mitzvot. Gar'in students likewise observed this change in themselves—as opposed to Hesder students, who indicated that there was very little variation in their practical observance. Approximately half of the Shiluv students also felt a transformation.

About half of the Mekhina students who were interviewed reported a change in their general attitude toward mitzvot: some of their actions that had previously been carried out merely technically now acquired an emotional dimension; obligations they fulfilled in high school in order to avoid punishment were now done of free will. For instance, one student noted: "My whole attitude to Torah and mitzvot has changed. It has changed from [feeling like] 'the yoke of mitzvot [ol mitzvot]' to, shall we say, 'the pleasure of the yoke of mitzvot [no'am ol mitzvot]'"

(Yoni, first interview). In other words, the obligations were now ones he followed gladly and without a feeling of oppression, as in the past.

Half of the preservice Mekhina interviewees said that they felt a real change in their practical observance, and they were now stricter about what they called the "small stuff": blessings, ritual hand washing, prayer in general (and in a *minyan* in particular), wearing tzitzit, conduct toward their friends and parents, etc. As noted, students spoke of a certain deterioration of observance during their military service; they indicated that this was most tangible regarding prayer. Thus, the influence of messages conveyed by the program during the first year of study eroded during their military service.

Gar'in students also reported that their attitude to mitzvot changed during the first period of time spent at the *midrasha*. Most indicated a heightened awareness of the importance of observing mitzvot. Almost half of the Gar'in interviewees, like the Mekhina students, said that they were more strict about the "small things," such as prayer and blessings.

More than half of the preservice Hesder students felt that their attitude toward mitzvot changed since they began attending their yeshiva. However, this change was related mainly to their attitude to the mitzvot themselves—their meaning and significance—rather than to the way they fulfilled them: "The desire to observe mitzvot; the desire to understand their content" (Elichai, first interview). Many Hesder students were aware of a change, again, "in the small things." Some said that they were more strict regarding prayer. A few said they were stricter about blessings; stricter about issues relating to conduct with the opposite sex in general, as well as observing religious boundaries set between sexes (such as the concept of *yihud*, forbidding a man and a women to be alone together if they are not married to each other). They also paid more attention to desirable character traits (*midot*), the importance of study, and making sure not to waste the time they could spend studying. The changes Hesder students undergo when studying at their yeshiva are less dramatic than those experienced by Mekhina students, and the process they undergo is of a more internal nature:

> The spiritual tension as a whole has, bottom line [. . .] gone one step up. At the end of the day, in my daily life, I am searching [. . .] for God and religion and the way it affects you. (Ronen, first interview)

Half of the preservice Shiluv students felt a change in their attitude to mitzvot. Several interviewees said they changed their concept of the mitzvot and now had a better *kavana* when fulfilling them.[7] Like Mekhinot students, Shiluv students also spoke of a practical change: they were stricter about blessings, ritual hand washing, and prayer in a *minyan*.

It seems, therefore, that the messages regarding religious observance and moral conduct, originating both from Religious Zionism and the study programs themselves, are understood by the students and internalized, at least during their first year of study. The practical implications erode to various extents during their military service, but all students understand what is being asked of them, even if they do not implement this request in their daily lives in the long run.

As far as messages related specifically to military service are concerned, most of the students from the male study programs felt that they were unequivocally expected to serve in combat posts—provided they met the necessary physical requirements. Eli students deliberated whether their Mekhina preferred for them to serve in a reconnaissance unit or in a "regular" combat post in one of the infantry battalions. Most of the students at the Atzmona Mekhina felt they were encouraged to serve in the "regular" battalions; those of the Givati Brigade in particular. It seems, therefore, that the message encouraging service in the field units is indeed one communicated by the Mekhinot to their students—as reported by Brigadier General Zamir and Major General Ron-Tal when interviewed.

Officially the Mekhinot do not encourage their students to enlist in any specific unit. Rabbi Peretz recounted that the Mekhinot's only real intention is to encourage their students to have a "meaningful service in the IDF" and to serve in a combat unit if they are able. However, both Rabbi Peretz and Rabbi Hager-Lau said that they encourage their students to serve in "regular" battalions rather than in reconnaissance units. Rabbi Sadan claimed that Eli is a yeshiva and that "our engagement with [issues related to] the military is on the margins [of our activity]." As far as he was concerned, it makes no difference which infantry unit a student ends up in. At the same time, he stated that about 40 to 45 percent of the students end up in elite units (Sadan, first interview). It seems that the student who observed that the "Mekhina would not be disappointed if I serve in the YACHTIYOT [reconnaissance battalion units]" was correct regarding the entire program. Students accepted to elite units are perceived as a success and enhance a Mekhina's reputation.

Most of the Shiluv students interviewed did not feel they were being steered toward a specific military posting. Those who did think the yeshiva was sending them a message felt that it was to encourage them to make the greatest contribution possible wherever the military chose to station them. One student felt that there was a message that the students should enlist in the so-called Project to Improve the Battalions (such as the Golani Project and the Givati Project); funneling quality manpower to battalions that are considered less attractive. In an interview,

Rabbi Bigman indeed pointed out that the yeshiva cooperates with the military on this issue.

Another student said that the yeshiva encourages students with low medical profiles to serve in the Education Corps, and "this seems to me to be, like, a very fine thing" (Nadav, first interview). Shiluv rabbis spoke mainly of encouraging their students to return to the yeshiva for a second period of study.

As far as the military service of the Gar'inim students is concerned, students are explicitly encouraged to serve as instructors in the Education Corps. Both Rabbi Kahan and Rabbi Tehar-Lev emphasized the ideological aspect of serving in these posts; this is a "post of loving-kindness." Instructor posts are considered "female" posts, and are also thus perceived by society at large (Sasson-Levy 2001, 282). Biton said that even if the *midrasha* doesn't oppose service in other posts and allows its students to serve in unusual roles, it strongly encourages them to serve in educational posts (Biton, second interview). It is therefore not surprising that Be'er students felt their program tended to envision them as instructors in the Education Corps, since:

> There are a lot of religious [girls who serve in this capacity], and it's really convenient. [. . .] It makes maintaining your religion easy. [. . .] It is also a very important job. (Hagit, first interview)

From a gender studies perspective, limiting service to posts defined as "loving-kindness" roles can be seen as an attempt to keep Gar'in members in "female" roles and keep them from "male" spheres of combat—perhaps also with the aim of making their service more acceptable in Religious Zionist society. However, since halakhic considerations still play a role, it is important to note that part of an instructor's activity includes serving as a commander of other (mostly male) soldiers and teaching them. From a halakhic point of view, this can be problematic, if not completely unacceptable. Thus, the picture is not as clear as it might seem: serving as an instructor, while seen usually as a gendered role in the IDF in general, can be viewed as breaking into "male" roles in the context of religious society.[8]

Interviews illustrated that all pre- and postservice *midrasha* students, as well as those in military service itself, were highly motivated to serve in instructor posts. They believed in the importance of such service and of the contribution they were making to Israeli society, and were thus interested in serving in this capacity (for instance, Sarit, first interview; Tamar, first interview).

Contrary to Mekhina, Shiluv, and Gar'in interviewees, Hesder students spoke at length of their yeshivot's attitude toward serving as officers. In order to join the officers' corps, Hesder students must obtain permission from the head of their yeshiva, since this step essentially requires them to leave the Hesder program. In noting a yeshiva's attitude toward joining the officers' training course, it is possible to glean insights into its view of military service in general. For example, the Golan yeshiva students underscored the yeshiva's positive view of serving as officers: "In principle, as far as I know, the yeshiva encourages [a situation in which] about 20 percent of the guys in each class take part [in the officers' training course]" (Liron, first interview). Students at the Yerucham Hesder yeshiva felt that their yeshiva encourages them to serve as officers, to a certain degree, and communicates to the students the message that "it would be terrible if no one would serve as an officer, [but] on the other hand—not too many students should do so" (Shmuel, first interview). Rabbi Blumenzweig said that it is important for the students to understand the significance and ramifications of serving as an officer, but that this is ultimately the student's decision (Blumenzweig, first interview).

On the other hand, as to be expected, students at Har Etzion spoke of their yeshiva's negative attitude toward service as an officer:

> [Students] usually ask Rabbi Lichtenstein [for permission], and the answer is usually no. Not a comprehensive "no," but [. . .] something like "I think it's better if you return to the yeshiva. It's more important now." (Chagai, first interview)

Students at Ma'ale Adumim did not perceive any defined message concerning service as an officer. Rabbi Rabinovitch said that the Ma'ale Adumim yeshiva encourages service in command capacities, "but we do not encourage this at the expense of deepening Torah scholarship." Thus, a student who chooses to participate in an officers' training course commits in writing to complete his time at the yeshiva after his military service (Rabinovitch, first interview).

A yeshiva's attitude to service as an officer has a direct influence on the way the yeshiva treats students who are officer cadets. Since 2004, the Yerucham yeshiva holds a course aimed specifically at students who are about to serve as officers. Students who have completed a course for squad commanders return to the yeshiva for eight months before continuing their officers' training. During this time they focus on issues related to leadership and halakhic and moral dilemmas they might encounter in their capacity as commanding officers. In 2005 the course focused on potential practical halakhic problems that a religious officer might come across. For instance, an officer might have to give a soldier access to a car when he knows that this soldier will use it on the Sabbath. In addition, participants in the course addressed ways to deal with various general situations in the military and leadership-related questions (Daniel, third interview). While the course at Yerucham is an unofficial one, a similar course is well established at the Golan yeshiva. Students designated for the officers' corps return to the yeshiva for four months before their course begins (Sugarman, first interview). During this time they complete the study of an entire tractate of the Babylonian Talmud and study individually with rabbis at the yeshiva (Sheinwald, first interview).

The positive attitude toward volunteering for command posts may be due in part to the fact that relatively many of the Golan yeshiva's alumni are officers. Rabbi Eliezer Sheinwald—a teacher at the yeshiva when interviewed, and the head of the Shesder program in Modi'in today—claimed that the presence of role models who are both respected Torah scholars and officers influences the students' views on military service in general, and serving in command posts in particular (Sheinwald, first interview). In comparison to the other yeshivot examined here, the Golan yeshiva's attitude to military service and service in command posts was the most positive.

A program's attitude toward joining the officers' corps is indicative of its attitude toward military service in general. Encouraging students to become officers means they will serve for a longer period of time. For Hesder, Shiluv, and Gar'in members, it means leaving the program; a sacrifice on the part of the study programs as well as the students. When the head of a program encourages students to become officers, he or she is essentially saying that such a step is justified and good in moral and religious terms. Therefore, encouraging service as an officer highlights the positive way in which a program views military service and the importance attached to doing one's military job well even at the expense of Torah study, and vice versa.

In addition to attitudes toward service and service venues, Hesder rabbis also spoke of general messages concerning personal conduct while in uniform. Most of the rabbis spoke of the importance of the students conducting themselves as bnei Torah, and as such—as Rabbi Rabinovitch put it—"not to give in to the risks posed by military service to one's moral conduct"; not to "supplement equipment [lehashlim tziyud]";[9] not to use profanity or lie; to treat one's fellow soldiers with respect; and so on (Rabinovitch, first interview).

As well as messages concerning the time dedicated to studies and time served in the military, all of the interviewees perceived long-term messages conveyed by their programs. When talking about the way of life promoted by their yeshiva, half of the Shiluv students interviewed said that the yeshiva would like to see them live lives committed to halakha, have families, and set aside time for independent

Torah study. Some of the Shiluv students felt that their yeshiva would like them to pursue some kind of academic education. A number thought that the yeshiva would prefer them to engage in a profession that made some sort of contribution to society at large (such as social work or teaching). There were also a few students who thought that the yeshiva would like them to be active in their communities (teaching Torah to others on a regular basis, for instance). These are all messages both their social group and their study program are glad to have the students internalize.

When asked, most of the Hesder interviewees thought that their yeshiva would like them to integrate life in society at large with a life guided by the Torah. Students from Or Etzion, Yerucham, and Har Etzion felt that the yeshiva would prefer its graduates to choose professions related to education. Students from Yerucham specifically felt that, in general, the yeshiva would prefer them to choose professions that make a contribution to society and have a dimension of loving-kindness (*hesed*). All this suggests that Hesder students are aware of the general messages conveyed by their program.

When referring to their life in the future as envisioned by their Mekhina, about a quarter of the Mekhina students interviewed thought that their program would prefer them to have careers in the military. Students from Eli said that the Mekhina would like them to return to study in Mekhina's postservice study program. All of the interviewees agreed that the Mekhina was not trying to make them into Torah scholars, but rather, as one student from Atzmona put it:

> The aim is to produce men of faith who will be active in the real world. Doctors, lawyers [. . .] but [also men] who act based on principles of Judaism. Of sanctity. [. . .] That there should be some connection with your spiritual world. That you should not sever the material world from the spiritual world. (Benny, first interview)

When referring to his motives in supporting Mekhinot in general, Yehuda Duvdevani spoke of the Mekhina students' long-term contribution to the state:

> We do not nurture them [the students] only for the military. The student is now being educated [to be] . . . a civilian who can lead [. . .] in every [professional] area he might choose. The basic education that he gets in the Mekhina, which complements that given to him by his parents, his youth movement, will enable him to be a leader in possession of Zionist principles we favor. Do we succeed in all of this? Not everything can be a success! (Duvdevani, first interview)

However, in spite of Duvdevani's caveat, it seems that the students understand this message, and they understand what the Mekhina expects of them. When speaking of this, while they emphasized the issue of Jewish values, it is still clear that they understand these values are inevitably linked to Zionist values. Commitment to the state and the Jewish people are values that, to the Mekhina students, are clear and self-evident.

On the topics of the importance of Torah study and observance, military service, and general life choices, the study programs both channel messages from Religious Zionism as well as deliver their own messages. While Religious Zionism would like to see its members in prestigious military positions and reaping the social benefits offered by these positions, it prefers they avoid long-term military careers because it is a difficult way of life for a religious family (see S. Cohen 2008). Therefore it is not encouraged categorically. To be an officer can be acceptable, but most young Religious Zionist men and women are expected to understand that the military is not a preferred way of life for "nice observant boys/girls." They should do their best during their time in uniform, but then return to civilian life and move on to build a family and a career. This view is transmitted to the students by all the study programs, excluding the Mekhinot, which do encourage a military career, as discussed earlier. To be fair, this is no secret. Students who join the program, as well as their parents, realize Mekhinot encourage students to join the officers' corps and are aware of the ideological stand these study programs take in regard to long-term military service.

At the same time, students want to do their best during their military service and see it as important, whether only from the point of view of fulfilling a civic duty or also from a religious point of view. They understand the importance of joining the officers' corps and are not afraid to do so when able. In most cases their study programs encourage and support them in this decision. In other words, the study programs also convey messages from the IDF about the importance of service and, more importantly as far as the IDF is concerned, of service where the IDF needs them most (in the Battalion Projects or as an education NCO, for example). As illustrated in the previous chapter, the messages Ron-Tal would like to see are communicated.

TENSIONS BETWEEN THE PROGRAMS

As mentioned at the beginning of this chapter, study programs are not only mediating structures, but also independent entities with their own agendas. These influence their relationship with each other and, at times, with the IDF, and can lead to tension between programs. Conflicts are mainly ideological, but are also influenced to a certain extent by mundane issues such as perceived competition over the same pool of potential students. Since tensions affect cooperation between the programs as well as their relationship with the IDF, the more important of these issues merit mention in the following pages.

At the beginning of the 1990s, as the Mekhinot program began to gather speed, it was not gladly accepted by the more senior institutions and figures in Religious Zionist society. At first, one source of controversy arose due to competition over the same demographic group. A familiar argument against the Mekhinot is that they "steal" students from the Hesder: instead of going to the Hesder program, students who have the ability to be serious Torah scholars choose to attend a Mekhina for a year.

In an interview, Yehuda Duvdevani, one of the pivotal figures in establishing secular Mekhinot and the head of the Youth and NAHAL Department in the Education Ministry at the time, related how then head of the Igud Rabbi Brun approached him personally to complain about the Mekhinot during their first years:

> [Brun said:] Yehuda! You are taking the kids from me and passing them over to the Mekhinot! [. . .] I said to him: Rabbi, this is [actually] good! We have kids who drop out [of Religious Zionism, becoming secular]! Twenty-five percent drop out of the yeshivot! Let's support them in a way which I think [is good]! The support of an entire year with values and all that, and let's send them [to the military] like tigers! (Duvdevani, first interview)

Rabbi Lichtenstein, who is both the head of the Har Etzion Hesder yeshiva and a member of the committee that approves new Hesder yeshivot, was also opposed to the creation of the Mekhinot. In his opinion, they would reduce the number of students attending the Hesder program:

> The moment a young man is faced with two options which were very different—either to study Torah or to serve in the military (which in the eyes of many, whether this is justified or not [. . .], to go to the military without studying at a yeshiva is halfway to becoming secular)—when these were the options, then one turned right and one turned left. Then something was put in the middle. Naturally, this attracts some of those who would have gone straight to the military and some of those who definitely would have gone to Hesder. Part of the argument among the Hesder yeshivot about the Mekhinot is about the proportions: if

the situation is one in which 80 percent would have otherwise gone to the yeshivot and 20 percent to the military, or vice versa. (Lichtenstein, first interview)

Rabbi Lichtenstein claimed that originally, the Mekhinot, in order to win the approval of Religious Zionist rabbis, used the argument concerning secularization in the military:

> When they established the Mekhinot, they [the heads of the program] spoke differently. And I am not sure if they were being entirely decent about this. They sold Rabbi Avraham Shapira [the head of Merkaz Ha-Rav yeshiva and previously the chief rabbi] [the idea] of the Mekhinot and said to him: "We will not take anyone who otherwise would have gone to a yeshiva. There are those who otherwise would only go to the military, and we will save souls," and he bought this [what can I say?], but of course, the reality is different. (Lichtenstein, first interview)

Thus, according to Rabbi Lichtenstein, the heads of the Mekhinot first claimed that their intention was only to give religious "support" to young adults who would have enlisted immediately after finishing high school and would not have considered religious study otherwise. Going to a Mekhina was supposed to help such young observant adults to withstand the pressures of an environment that presented them with many challenges. They would not be given a yeshiva education, but in any case the Mekhinot were not attempting to attract those who would have attended a Hesder yeshiva; the aim was to "save" them from secularization. However, in practice, according to Rabbi Lichtenstein, the Mekhinot are not limited to such young men and also attract high school graduates who could have chosen the Hesder program in the pre-Mekhinot era. Thus, at least some of the more well-established Hesder yeshivot feel that the Mekhinot are chipping away at their pool of potential students.[10]

These sentiments are actually echoed in a way by the heads of the Mekhinot. As they claim to be concerned first and foremost with the role of Religious Zionism in the military, rather than reinforcing the ability of these young adults to withstand the pressures of secularization in the military, clearly they hope to attract the best and the brightest. In other words, they do indeed wish to target good students and not just "save souls."

When asked about the accusation of "stealing" students, Rabbi Sadan was indignant and claimed that Hesder yeshivot find it hard to deal with the fact that not every "serious" teenager wants to attend a Hesder yeshiva. According to him, it is not true that "serious guys go to Hesder and the Mekhina students are not as good [. . .] the Mekhinot are not a place for someone to 'fix' his *kipa*. I don't accept this [view]. This is part of the idea that religious [youth] go to study Torah and secular [youth] go to the military," and that whoever goes to the military becomes secular (Sadan, first interview). Sadan stressed that Mekhinot are a place where young adults who have a different understanding of the world can study. It is interesting to note that Rabbi Kostiner, a graduate of Merkaz Ha-Rav himself, was among the most outspoken rabbis against the Mekhinot, based on the idea that young adults whose religious identities are more fragile attend the Mekhinot. In his opinion, in order to preserve the religious identities of such youngsters, it is far better that they enlist through the Hesder program, since the Mekhinot are unable to fulfill such a task (Kostiner, first interview).

It seems that, in fact, the tension between the Mekhinot, the Igud, and the Hesder yeshivot is not only a question of students choosing to attend one program or another, but also an ideological disagreement: What is the right way to study Torah? What is the right attitude to take toward the military? Is the military a necessary evil, and thus military service is to be treated merely as a civic duty, or is it an ideal to be followed ex-ante, one which has a sacred dimension? Rabbi Sadan described a student who is a senior officer in the Givati Brigade and physically stops terrorists from reaching their targets: "Is this not a great mitzva?! Is this not holy work?! Is his not a great and important contribution [even though he does not spend all his time studying]?!" (Sadan, first interview).

While the Mekhinot employ ideological arguments, the Hesder yeshivot prefer to focus on arguments concerning "stealing" students. Out of the nine Hesder rabbis interviewed here, only Rabbi Sugarman addressed the issue of the Mekhinot in ideological terms. When referring to the argument that Hesder soldiers isolate themselves in their units, he said that after advanced training, the students are dispersed among the combat companies anyway. However, he explained that the problems the Mekhinot students encounter—mainly modesty-related—prove that Hesder students cannot enlist as individuals; the atmosphere in the military makes this impossible (Sugarman, first interview).

On the other hand, Rabbi Sugarman pointed out that there is a major difference between the Hesder and Mekhinot programs regarding halakhic rulings in the military. He cited as an example the methodology of halakhic rulings found in the book *Ke-Hitzim Be-Yad Gibor* by Rabbi Avi Ronztki (chief military rabbi until 2010); he found the rulings concerning Shabbat especially problematic. Rabbi Sugarman was also critical of rulings made by Rabbi Krim (head of the Halakha Branch in the Military Rabbinate since 2008), to whom many Mekhina students turn for halakhic advice, judging these rulings to be lenient: "We know him. [. . .] This style [of problematic rulings] is typical of a group of officers who came out of Merkaz Ha-Rav" (Sugarman, first interview). Even if the claim that the rulings by Rabbi Krim and other Mekhina rabbis are overly lenient cannot be backed up by actual halakhic arguments, the fact that Rabbi Sugarman addresses these issues in ideological terms serves to emphasize the other Hesder rabbis' silence in this regard.

Hesder and Mekhina rabbis rarely voice opinions regarding the Shiluv program. During interviews, the heads of the Hesder and Mekhinot programs focused on each other, ignoring the Religious Kibbutz Movement's yeshivot. This deafening silence is interesting and may be due to ideological reasons. For example, in a rare reference to the Shiluv, Rabbi Cherlow wrote in a responsa on the Moreshet website:

> If indeed the Shiluv yeshivot prove that they can attain the same achievements in Torah and in their influence on Israeli society that the Hesder yeshivot have attained [. . .]—this will be a challenge for the yeshivot and all of them will have to become Shiluv yeshivot. However, I know no other way than that of the Hesder to achieve an optimal accomplishment of both of these things. (Cherlow 2002b)

On one hand, the absence of any reference by Hesder and Mekhinot rabbis to the Shiluv program may reflect the formers' disdain for the level of Torah scholarship in the Religious Kibbutz Movement yeshivot. Yet, the small number of Shiluv participants mitigates the professional insult inherent in this lack of reference, and the instability of the Shiluv program has made the issue marginal.

It is, on the other hand, possible that the tension also has a political aspect. As mentioned before, the yeshivot of the Religious Kibbutz Movement have the reputation of being bastions of left-wing politics, as opposed to the Hesder yeshivot and the Mekhinot, which are usually known to hold right-wing views. This perception of the Religious Kibbutz Movement is enhanced by the fact that Rabbi Gilad from the Ma'ale Gilboa yeshiva was a member of the left-wing Meimad political party and served as a Meimad MK. Likewise, that Rabbi Bin-Nun served as the head of the Ein Tzurim yeshiva after the ideological change he underwent following the assassination of Yitzhak Rabin further reinforces this point. While in the past he was one of the most outspoken members of Gush Emunim, following the Rabin assassination, Bin-Nun crossed party lines and became a vocal supporter of the peace process.

However, despite political differences, the root of the tension between the Hesder and Mekhinot programs and the Shiluv program concerning the course of military service itself is deeper: If one can study Torah at a comprehensive and profound level—or at least at a level comparable to that provided by the Hesder yeshivot—how can shortened military service be justified? On the other hand, if it is possible to both study extensively and serve a full three-year term, what is the justification for studying Torah for only one year, as in the Mekhinot? The Mekhina at Eli seems to be addressing such issues by becoming more like a Shiluv yeshiva. The Post-Army Beit Midrash for advanced Torah study reflects an understanding that one year of study is insufficient.[11] Likewise, the establishment of a Hesder yeshiva in Modi'in (Shesder), where the students serve a longer term of military service, undermines the basic concept of the Mekhinot and other Hesder yeshivot. Nevertheless, as noted earlier the relative failure of the Shiluv program effectively neutralizes the debate. Having said that, as long as the Shiluv program exists—even if it has few participants—it presents a challenge to the larger programs and necessitates a response.

Another aspect of the disagreement between the programs is related to secular studies students undertake independently during service. During their last year at the yeshiva (fifth year), when considered still conscripted to unpaid service (SHALAT), many Hesder students take distance-learning classes unrelated to their yeshiva studies. These classes include courses at the Open University and those that prepare students for the psychometric exam: steps toward being accepted at a university. The yeshivot do not approve of such studies, and students try to conceal their activities.[12] At the same time, some non-yeshiva studies take place openly at some Hesder yeshivot. Fifth-year students at most Hesder yeshivot study for a bachelor of education at a teachers' training college affiliated with the yeshiva. Most yeshivot encourage such studies, hoping to promote an education-affiliated career among their students.[13]

All of these issues indicate that the men's study programs perceive each other as possible competition. The competition is not only over governmental funding, as described previously, but also over potential students. Surprisingly, the ideological debate is not vociferous, and the various programs often cooperate with each other, especially when dealing with the IDF. As described in Chapter 8, both the Hesder and Mekhinot programs cooperated when approaching the IDF regarding issues of coed service. The tendency of the Hesder yeshivot and the Mekhinot to ignore the Shiluv only serves to highlight the degree of cooperation between the two programs: while they both view the Shiluv as a problematic program, they prefer to frame it as of little importance.

* * *

To conclude, this chapter illustrates that students are able to alert the superstructures to their needs, wishes, and demands. At the same time, students are aware of messages the IDF and Religious Zionism would like to convey. Thus the study programs seem to both empower students by allowing them to communicate with the superstructures, as seen in this chapter, as well as assist them in drastic situations, as seen earlier in Part II.

There are, however, a number of questions worth exploring in this context: How successful are these structures in mediation? While Chapter 8 indicates that they are apparently not able to succeed in their mediation all of the time or for all of their members, are there general conclusions we can consider regarding their mediation? Furthermore, can anything be learned from this case in the broader context of civil-military relations in Israel? Are there implications for civil-military relations in general? These questions will be the subject of Part III.

PART III

SUMMARIES AND CONCLUSIONS

CHAPTER 12
STUDY PROGRAMS AS MEDIATING STRUCTURES

In light of Part II, it seems safe to conclude that the preservice study programs are indeed mediating institutions. They stand between the individuals and the superstructures, allow the individuals to continue to conform to their personal values, and even project those values onto the superstructures.

Part II also demonstrates how their capacity for mediation is even greater when dealing with students who serve in homogeneous Hesder units and the Gar'in program. In the context of homogeneous—or semihomogeneous—service, students continue to preserve their lifestyle while in uniform. The *midrashot* and yeshivot are largely able to regulate the pressures military life exerts on the students' lives by causing the IDF to conscript them as "Gar'in members" or "Hesder students."

Consequently, the study programs serve as mediating structures in the sense that they allow young men and women who belong to them to contend with the military system using familiar values and beliefs that are transferred to the military jobs to which they are assigned. The students see their military service as the realization of personal, religious, and national values. This boosts their motivation and encourages them to become better soldiers. The religious dimension added to their service—a dimension that varies in its importance between the programs—strengthens this all the more. Additionally, as Part II elucidates, the ability of the programs to actively shield students in cases where they have been wronged (or perceive themselves as having been wronged) by the military system empowers the students and allows them to better manage military reality.

However, previous examples discussed in Part II show that there is a difference in this capacity for mediation between the programs, as the students themselves noted. When asked during the first year of the follow-up study whether their preservice studies helped them manage problems that arose during their service as religious soldiers, almost all Hesder students answered affirmatively. Likewise, most Gar'in members felt their studies helped them "get through" their time in uniform. However, fewer Shiluv and Mekhinot students felt this way. Only about half of the interviewees of the latter two programs thought preservice study helped them cope with the problems they encountered as religious soldiers in the IDF.[1]

Students from all programs who felt their year of preservice study helped them deal with military life noted two main components: mental and attitudinal preparation ("I knew what I was getting into and therefore was more prepared";

"I was more mature than I was right after finishing high school"; "studying put service in a context conducive to coping"), and halakhic faith-based preparation ("I had more halakhic knowledge and knew how to manage halakhic dilemmas"; "I knew where I stood religiously and knew which lines I would not cross"). Mekhinot students who appreciated the preparatory effect their preconscription studies had on them also spoke of practical preparation for the IDF and of the fact that their knowledge of navigation and physical fitness helped them with the professional aspects of their service. Hesder students thought their conscription as a group was very helpful when dealing with the military system. Gar'in members tended to see the preparation they received as focusing more on identity (specifically religious identity) and maturity, and less on practical halakhic preparation.

As discussed in Part II, most of the students expected their study program to "accompany" them and stay in touch during their military service. Even when they did not expect the program to actually offer active assistance, they did expect it to serve as a safety net if a seemingly unsolvable situation arose.

Homogeneous service allowed better support of Hesder students by their yeshivot. It is easier to coordinate visits when the students serve in one unit. Additionally, their conscription and service are experienced with mutually supportive acquaintances rather than strangers. This is a marked difference from most other soldiers in the IDF, who are conscripted alone.

Service as part of a group was key to an easier adjustment for *midrashot* students, too. Even though students forged strong friendships outside their Gar'in after their initial period of training, entrance to the IDF as part of a familiar group was important. Similarly, Mekhinot students who served in elite units with friends admitted to feeling more support than those who served alone.

Interestingly, serving with other religious soldiers—even those who were not students of the same age group or the same study program—was considered an empowering factor. Despite the tension that arises between students of different programs, as described earlier, generally students felt positively about serving together. In other words, study programs do not only offer support to their own students, but unintentionally support students from parallel programs.[2]

Another facet of military service influenced by study programs is the ability to form friendships with nonreligious soldiers. While most Hesder students— especially those who served in homogeneous units—did not make lasting connections with nonreligious soldiers, members of other programs spoke of meaningful friendships with secular members of their units. Almost all Shiluv, Mekhinot, and Gar'in interviewees had hosted secular friends in their homes and/ or were guests at nonreligious friends' homes. Hesder students rarely followed suit.[3] Accordingly, after returning to civilian life, Hesder students did not maintain contact with nonreligious friends, while students of parallel programs usually did. Moreover, these students and their nonreligious friends continued to spend time together after discharge, including—in some cases—traveling abroad together, as described in Part II.

Aside from preparation before and accompaniment during service, students expected their study programs to be a place where they could return both physically, when on furlough or for class weekends, and also metaphorically, allowing them to feel as if they were at their study program even when on base or when studying alone. It was important for students to be able to return mentally to their year of study during difficult times in their military service, and they raised the subject during follow-up interviews.

The study programs indeed stand between the individual students and the two superstructures discussed here: Religious Zionism and the IDF. First, study programs allow students to project an image of religious "seriousness," conscious observance of mitzvot and halakha, to their social group. In the case of Gar'in members, students stress their commitment to a religious, halakhic, way of life, and to being loyal citizens. Their commitment to halakha will not change due to their military service, since their studies have prepared them for their time in the IDF and, if needed, their *midrasha* will protect them.[4] They are enlisting halakhically well prepared, and their social group should distinguish between them and young women who are conscripted in other ways and are thus in "halakhic danger."

Another message students wish to convey to Religious Zionism is embedded in their choice of a specific program, yeshiva, Mekhina, or *midrasha*. For example, when choosing Eli, a student is projecting an image of serious study, rather than one of someone who just wants "a year for myself." These are "serious" people who will continue to contribute to the society in which they live due to their year of study at the Mekhina. The fact that Eli students stressed that they chose to come to Eli because they were impressed by alumni corroborates this. Analogous examples can be cited for each of the programs described here.

There are also messages students wish to convey to the IDF itself, and their year of study does this as well—as illustrated in Part II. The military system recognizes that students of preservice programs are conscripted after absorbing ideas and ideals that are desirable in a soldier. The IDF must pay a price for this positive disposition, but it is willing to pay it: it accepts that study programs will ensure the IDF stands by its obligations and that students will not be required to transgress any halakhic obligation without just cause. In this way the study programs empower their students with regard to the military system. It seems that

Rabbi Elmaliach (first interview) was correct in his observation that ideally every soldier should enlist as part of a group that is able to protect their interests in the face of an arbitrary and insensitive military system in which it is especially difficult for women soldiers to cope.

The military's obligation to uphold Gar'in members' rights specifically is so well established that the students themselves, as well as junior officers, are at times upset about the IDF's policy regarding them. Students sometimes viewed this as the overprotectiveness of their *midrashot*, and at times it seems they would prefer dealing directly with the IDF as Shiluv and Mekhinot students do. On the other hand, the military system, specifically the higher echelons, seems to understand the *midrashot*'s behavior and does not try to change the rules of the game in its own favor. Both the IDF and the *midrashot* understand that if they do not meticulously observe the structure of the program, it will lose whatever legitimacy it has in the eyes of Religious Zionism. This means that the program allows very little flexibility, and the students cannot always communicate directly with the IDF without the mediation of their *midrashot* as long as they are considered part of the program. If the Gar'in program is perceived as a structure that protects its members and affords them a venue of service that is not as exposed to the secular and mixed gender aspects of military life, Religious Zionism may be willing to accept women's service in the IDF as part of a Gar'in. Similar to the process spearheaded by the Hesder program, the women's social group may see the *midrashot* as trustworthy enough and not view their students as acting against the wishes of the rabbis. However, in order to build up its reputation, the Gar'in program must continue to keep strict tabs on its members and to establish itself as a protective program.

This aspect indicates that of all of the programs examined here, it is the *midrashot* that fashion the more integral boundaries between the military and the social group they represent: *midrasha* students will forever be students, even when they are in uniform.

Despite all they do for their students, at times the study programs do not empower them. The preservice study programs for men are tailored first and foremost for combat soldiers. This is especially true in the Hesder and Mekhinot programs, where there is little attention paid to the problems a noncombat soldier will encounter. This is rather surprising given the extensive attention these programs pay to the issue of mixed gender service. The students who require the most preparation for serving with women are those who will serve at desk jobs, where men and women fill the same posts and work in the same offices. Many noncombat students felt that they were not prepared properly for this aspect of their service (Weinberger and Beitner 2007, 9). Additionally, noncombat students come into contact with many sectors of Israeli society that students who are assigned combat positions do not encounter during their service, including people who view service as a waste of time, those who come from problematic backgrounds, and those who have never met a religious person before. For example, a Mekhina student who served in a noncombat post recounted how the soldiers he served with could not comprehend why he would have preferred combat service, since this was something they tried to avoid (Micha, second interview).

In the Mekhinot's case, this attitude toward combat service might be influenced by the fact that most of the heads of the program served in combat posts and are not as familiar with noncombat positions. In the case of the Hesder yeshivot, this apparent preference for combat service manifests in the fact that only combat students receive visits, which certainly magnifies the loneliness felt by noncombat soldiers.

During follow-up interviews, students in noncombat posts felt less protected by their study programs and more alone within the military system. Their noncombat service does not affect the messages they try to send to Religious Zionism, but they feel inferior to combat soldiers to a certain extent.[5]

Aside from their function as mediating structures, each of these organizations actively formulates its own independent messages for its students, as demonstrated in the previous chapters. While students understand the messages conveyed by the superstructures through their study programs, each *beit midrash* has its own attitude toward the IDF, and students internalize this message, too. Gar'in members understood the role of education NCO to be a worthy one and befitting a religious woman. Shiluv students were well aware of the yeshiva's thoughts on military service not being a value in and of itself, while Mekhinot students tended to attribute positive connotations to military service. Hesder students felt their yeshivot were generally willing to intervene on their behalf.

As shown by Eliezer Don Yehiya, the study period at a yeshiva is one of intense socialization—specifically regarding values and lifestyle, including attitudes toward the state and its society (Don Yehiya 1998, 443). This is also true for Mekhinot and *midrashot* students. The messages conveyed by the study programs include loyalty to the programs themselves, but this does not contradict the messages sympathetic to the superstructures. In this sense, the Disengagement of 2005 tested the ability of the study programs to maneuver between the sometimes-conflicting messages transmitted through them by both Religious Zionism and the IDF.

It is important to note that although they serve as mediators, the study programs consider the best interests of their students, the IDF, and Religious

Zionism. But they also have their own interests in mind: their wish to continue to exist, to attract a "good" student body, to enjoy the support of generous donors, and so on. These interests become clearer when examining the policy of each program regarding students who wish to join the officers' corps and the attempt to enable students to return for a second study period (in the Shiluv program).

Students noted that their study program felt an obligation both toward them as individuals and toward the IDF; they tried to represent both the interests of the Religious Zionist sector and the People of Israel (Am Yisrael). However, they were aware of the specific, more "selfish" interests of each program.

Turning from the conclusions we can draw based on Part II and moving on to more general observations, two points should be stressed. First, as indicated by officers interviewed as well as some of the students, preservice study programs do not have to take place in a yeshiva or similar Torah setting in order to function as mediating structures that protect individuals. The military system views graduates of nonreligious Mekhinot as possessing traits similar to the graduates of the religious programs: maturity; motivation; internalization of values; and commitment to the IDF, the state, and its citizens. Although this is not the focal point of the present study, it is worth noting the similar way in which the IDF sees all preservice study programs.

Second, the study programs refute the convention in Israel that young people are educated (both generally and religiously) during high school. If this were the case, and students felt their education was complete at graduation, there would be no need to continue to study after graduation and before service. The difference between a yeshiva high school and a Hesder yeshiva or a high yeshiva (*yeshiva gvoha*) should be the equivalent of the difference between high school and university: in high school, students set the foundations upon which their higher education can be built. However, graduates who feel they need more time to study in order to consolidate their identities (religious or otherwise) obviously do not feel "educated" enough upon graduation. If preservice study is devoted to filling in gaps a student notes in his or her education, this is indicative of a serious flaw in the educational system. Furthermore, since students of preservice study programs usually come from better high school institutions—as noted in Part II—and yet they still feel unprepared for life, the Israeli educational system can be criticized even at its more successful end.

In this regard, the study programs serve not only as mediators, but also as "fixers" for areas where the educational system has failed. Naturally, one can argue this idea as being a chicken-and-egg problem: Did preservice study programs enable the educational system (particularly the religious branch) to concentrate on the material in the matriculation exams and neglect more general issues, since it knows students will be continuing their education after graduation? Or perhaps it is indeed this neglect that caused the preservice programs to flourish? Whatever the case may be, clearly the study programs do not compete with the Israeli educational system, but rather attempt to respond to a social demand. The existence of nonreligious Mekhinot reinforces this observation.

After noting specific conclusions and observations, and in light of the mediating functions we now see that the study programs fulfill, a number of more general conclusions can be drawn regarding civil-military relations in Israel. These include the uses of mediation and multidimensional mediation, as well as the limits of mediation.

USES OF MEDIATION

After close examination of the Israeli model, it is clear that employing a mediating structure allows for the regulation of pressures and demands on religious soldiers under certain circumstances, but not always and never completely. Moreover, each of the study programs is largely autonomous. As expounded upon in detail in Part II, each *beit midrash* has its own educational-ideological agenda, and this influences its ability and willingness to regulate demands and protect its individuals. In turn, this affects its ability to mediate successfully.

However, the fact that mediation is partial, intermittent, and variable is not necessarily a negative thing. The existence of different, flexible models allows each individual to choose the mode of mediation he or she prefers. An individual seeking more comprehensive mediation can choose a mediating structure with more integral boundaries (see Chapter 1) that allows the superstructures (the IDF and Religious Zionism as a social group) minimal interference within its sphere of influence and vice versa. In the Israeli case, the *midrashot* and Hesder yeshivot that send students to homogeneous infantry units are the two programs that maintain the most distinct separation between their students and the military system. As discussed in Part II, parallel programs do not establish boundaries that are as clear or as defined as those of these two programs.

Furthermore, at times the *midrashot* and the Hesder yeshivot also attempt to take a more conservative stand regarding issues within Religious Zionism itself and do not limit their actions to the military sphere. In other words, boundaries are set between the mediating structure and both Religious Zionism and the IDF, with no necessary preference for either one of the greedy structures in question. The students are their chief priority, and the study programs attempt to protect them not only from the "greediness" of the IDF, but also from the equally greedy demands made by Religious Zionism.

This model contrasts with that of the Mekhinot and Shiluv programs, where boundaries are less defined. When addressing their unique core issues (there is no consistent agreement between these programs regarding which issues are core) both the *midrashot* and the Hesder yeshivot define their boundaries clearly and protect them. However, issues that are deemed less fundamental are not given the same attention. When faced with lesser problems while dealing with the military or Religious Zionism, students must, for the most part, fend for themselves and use independent judgment.

At the same time, a member of any program may choose to communicate directly with the larger greedy structure to which he or she belongs. As seen previously, it is clear that students of the Mekhinot and Shiluv programs prefer direct contact with the IDF during active duty. Hesder and *midrasha* students who join the officers' corps must deal directly with the military system. However, since their commanding officers are always aware of their affiliation,[6] students may still utilize the potential mediation option afforded by their study programs should they feel the need. This potential has a strong influence on ongoing military relationships. The *possibility* of mediation proves more important than its actual use.

From interviews with senior IDF officers it is apparent that the IDF accepts these various avenues of extramilitary communication. It does not view them as undue interference on the part of the programs or as a breach of military discipline on the part of the soldier-students.

MULTIDIMENSIONAL MEDIATION

The mediation of the study programs examined in this book is not one-dimensional, between a given individual and a superstructure. Chapter 1 showed that communication does not only take place through the mediating structure. The mediating structure is but one element—albeit the main element at times—in a system of communication constructed between individuals and the greedy institutions they belong to, as seen in Figure 2 on the next page.

Although in many instances individuals converse with both the IDF and Religious Zionism through their study programs, this does not mean they don't communicate directly as well, without mediation and help. The form of communication chosen depends on the circumstances and the personality of the individual. As seen throughout this study, students and officers speak to each other freely with no rabbi present. Students also register complaints, write letters, and submit forms directly to the military system without mediation. This is direct communication between the individuals and the IDF without the input of an intermediary.

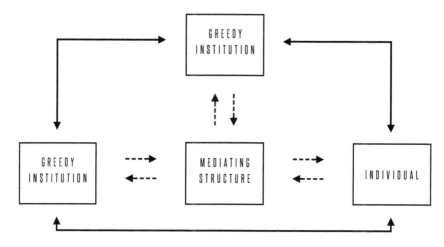

FIGURE 2   • *Solid arrows—direct relations*
         • *Broken arrows—mediated relations*

At other times, students prefer to communicate with the superstructures almost exclusively through the study program. It is also possible that the same individual will choose direct communication at a given time and indirect for other stages of service, or a combination of the strategies. For example, joining a study program is a way of ensuring that much of the communication with the IDF before active service will only be conducted through a mediator: the study program. However, once in uniform, some students will decide to have very little contact with their study programs, preferring direct communication with the military sphere.

Other structures not analyzed in depth in this study are involved in the mediation process, such as the students' families and Israeli society at large. Families use the study programs to send certain messages to their children (the family's wish to see its son or daughter continuing a religiously orthodox way of life, for example), and the students themselves are aware of this and respond in kind (i.e., studying before service proves they are taking a responsible step before entering the IDF). Israeli society uses the study programs as agents of socialization. Students see the programs as a way of proving to Israeli society that they are loyal citizens despite the fact they need special provisions, at least before their military service.

These dynamics also have a political aspect. This is particularly true with the Hesder program, which enjoys political support—especially from Religious

Zionist parties past and present (Ha-Ichud Ha-Leumi-MAFDAL, Ha-Bayit Ha-Yehudi)—in the Knesset. Conversely, the Mekhinot have less political clout, and the Shiluv and Gar'in programs have no real political power. So, although developments in the political sphere certainly influence the study programs, they do not affect each of the programs equally. The scope of the present study did not allow for an in-depth description of all of these variables.

As stated above, mediation in the case of the study programs is certainly not one-dimensional. They mediate not only between the students and the larger structures of the IDF and Religious Zionism, but also between the superstructures themselves.

As discussed earlier in this book, Religious Zionism is interested in influencing the IDF. It would like to see the IDF maintain its identity as a Jewish force, adhering to Jewish halakha, keeping all dietary, Sabbath, and modesty restrictions, and embodying specific moral standards. In addition, certain segments of Religious Zionism expect the IDF to implement the political position they hold concerning the Palestinian Authority, to foster the settlement project in the West Bank, and so on.

At the same time, Religious Zionism as a social group wishes to obtain sociocultural legitimacy for the people and institutions it comprises through the military service of its members. By serving in the IDF, members of Religious Zionism are seen by Israeli society as loyal and contributing citizens. Military service still offers social dividends in Israel, and members of Religious Zionism who serve reflect favorably on their social group (Levy 2007). These are sociopolitical aspirations as well as religious ones. They are conveyed to the IDF through a broad range of communication venues: the political sphere, media, responsa, speeches and teachings of influential public figures, halakhic rulings, and, of course, through mediating institutions such as the study programs.

While messages conveyed through these other communication venues have the potential to sound threatening at times, communication through a mediating structure allows for better dialogue between the parties. A meeting between the heads of Hesder yeshivot (representing their students and, consequently, a certain segment of Religious Zionism) and the head of the Manpower Division of the IDF, where the rabbis broach needs and demands for change, is inherently different from those same rabbis voicing their demands in the press. Deliberations held through a mediating structure are more focused and disciplined. Negotiations are practical, and the actual needs and interests of the students (such as requests for military stationing and specific considerations for modesty) are discussed together with the interests of the programs themselves (timetables for induction and discharge, visitation possibilities, etc.) as well as the considerations of Religious Zionism as a social and political group. (The most prominent recent example of this type of negotiation was with respect to conduct pertaining to the Disengagement plan of 2005.) These demands are modified and moderated by the needs and interests of the IDF and the Manpower Division, which are likewise presented. Naturally, negotiations are influenced by communications held through parallel channels: the media, political actors, and personal relationships. However, the action itself takes place within the mediating structure. Focusing discussions within it allows both sides to reach solutions for localized problems and avoids the accumulation of larger issues, thereby regulating tension between the greedy structures. It also prevents issues from being discussed publicly, where the context may lead to a shouting match rather than productive negotiations.

The above highlights an additional point made in previous chapters: the military system also seeks to influence Religious Zionism and does so in a variety of ways—the mediating structures are just one. As discussed earlier, senior IDF officers, both in public statements and in interviews conducted for this study, spoke of their expectations regarding the Religious Zionist sector: more involvement in the IDF itself (service in infantry units and not only in elite units); enrollment in the officers' corps; and greater numbers of religious women in the IDF, to mention but a few issues illustrated in Part II. The fact that the IDF voices these demands—some specifically to the Mekhinot—strengthens the hypothesis that this is a conscious attempt to influence Religious Zionism and its members through mediating structures and not the students alone.

Additionally, as it understands that messages conveyed through the Mekhinot and their counterparts reach individuals more quickly and clearly than by other means, this channel of communication is reinforced by the IDF. However, when the IDF feels the need, it is willing to approach students directly. The aforementioned personal letter written by the past chief of the Manpower Division, Major General Elazar Stern, and mailed directly to Hesder students when he felt the Hesder yeshivot were distorting his message, is a case in point (E. Stern 2007).

In other words, mediation done through the study programs is definitely bilateral (to and from the military system and to and from Religious Zionism). It is also multidimensional (between the systems themselves, and between each of the systems and the individuals in question, and vice versa). But it is not the only channel of communication, and students and systems communicate through other channels and directly.

Nor is the role played by the study programs themselves one-dimensional. The rabbis and heads of the programs execute a range of functions, as described in earlier chapters. They serve as halakhic decision makers for their students, but frequently do so for other members of Religious Zionism as well. While they are expected to support and accompany their students before and during the students' military service, this role doesn't change or cancel out their role as congregational or community rabbis. In theory, at least, both roles remain equal.

Another role played by the study programs is more fluid and changes from one program to another: attempts to intervene in the spheres of the IDF and Religious Zionism and to influence both systems in a larger sense vary according to personal and institutional ideologies and interests. In this context, each rabbi represents his own personal agenda and the agenda of his specific *beit midrash*. This was demonstrated quite clearly during the debate regarding disobeying orders to evacuate settlements, which culminated in 2005. When a rabbi voicing opinions in favor of or against disobeying orders is the head of a study program (as opposed to being a "regular" rabbi), his position is seen as representing the view of his *beit midrash* and even the larger framework of the study program he belongs to, even if he does not mean for this to happen. For example, the head of the Ramat Gan yeshiva, who advocated the disobeying of orders during the events of 2005, was not seen as voicing his own private opinion, but as representing the official position of his yeshiva and, to a certain extent, representing the official position of the entire Hesder program.[7] Even if the rabbi himself claims he is only representing his own views, and although the Association of Hesder Yeshivot (the Igud) allows heads of yeshivot certain autonomy, it is impossible to disregard the fact that many listen to him and take his teachings seriously specifically because of his role as head of a study program. The individual members of his yeshiva and community also regard his opinion as the opinion of the yeshiva.

Following this framing of the study programs not only as mediating structures, but also as independent actors, we can look at their own interests and goals. These are not always connected to the objectives of the structures they mediate between. The study programs would like to see a certain reality prevail both in Religious Zionism and in the IDF. An IDF where soldiers and officers behave according to the norms of Torah and halakha—specifically the "proper integration" doctrine regarding gender integration in combat units—and a Religious Zionism where all act as a ben Torah in the workaday world and not only in the spiritual one are both things the study programs would like to see. At the same time, each *beit midrash* has its own specific ideological and educational agendas. These individual "flavors" were discussed at various points in Part II.

Some study programs do not regard these interests as only aspirations or ideals. They attempt to bring about changes that further their ideology: volunteer programs initiated by yeshivot; educational programs or classes that encourage students to think in a certain manner or to join a specific type of profession in the future; and voicing a clear social agenda. All these, together with other forms of action, are intended to steer students toward a certain path in life.

While some programs try catalyzing concrete social change, others are less active or are even inactive concerning a proclaimed ideological bent. These facts, and many others adduced in this study, illustrate again and again that the mediation carried out by the study programs has many levels and dimensions and that while the model of the relationship given in Figure 2 represents the general situation, it oversimplifies reality.

Furthermore, the Israeli case demonstrates that the presence of a mediating structure is not always a positive thing. First, students of study programs are viewed as having conflicting loyalties. The mediators themselves and the rabbis who head them are perceived as a threat to the entire system whenever it seems there is a conflict of interest between the IDF and Religious Zionism. Second, it cannot be denied that the mediating structures sometimes detract from certain elements within each of the greedy institutions to which they relate. Rabbis give halakhic decisions that threaten the authority of both the Military Rabbinate and other Religious Zionist rabbis. This has been the case for quite some time, but it became very clear during the Disengagement in 2005 when most study program rabbis refused to call upon their students to disregard their orders—much to the chagrin of other rabbis within the Religious Zionist sector. However, despite these drawbacks, it seems that all parties in the Israeli case are willing to pay a certain price and keep the present form of the relationship.

The key to understanding the existence of mediation between the military and the religious systems seems to be the willingness of the parties to maintain some form of communication in order to secure reciprocal gains. Without the possibility of tangible benefits, it is highly unlikely either side would be motivated enough to make concessions for the sole purpose of keeping the option of communication viable. Seeing tangible results and reaping real benefits encourages both sides of the equation to continue the relationship despite its flaws. It is by no means an altruistic venture.

Before moving on to examining the precise contribution made by the study programs to the individual students and the greedy structures, an additional point must be addressed. There are those who claim that the study programs actually create the problems they then attempt to solve. Were it not for the study programs, according to this argument, young people from the Religious Zionist sector would be less aware of the problems military service poses to their religious identity, and they would serve with their secular counterparts with no qualms. It is the act of studying in these academies that turns these young men and women into more religiously aware individuals and encourages religious extremism.[8] For example, many students begin to observe dietary commandments in a stricter manner than their parents do, or they pay closer attention to the separation of sexes than before. Had they not joined a study program, the level of observance they upheld at home would not have caused friction with the military system—at least not to the extent it has. In the reality of the yeshiva world in twenty-first-century Israel—goes the argument—yeshivot and Mekhinot fuel a process of religious extremism that has negative implications for the relationship between Religious Zionism and both the IDF and Israeli society at large. If it were possible to turn time back to the days before study programs existed, all religious problems within the IDF would be less severe.

Moreover, this process is a vicious circle: Students grow up, marry, have children, and ensure that their children enroll in study programs. These children, in turn, hold more extremist views, and so the process continues.

This is a significant argument, but it fails to recognize history and past experiences. Young religious men and women served in prestate paramilitary organizations such as the Hagana and later in the fledgling IDF. Their course of service as religious individuals in a secular environment was never easy. While the attention given to these problems has grown over the years, the problems themselves have always existed. The Hesder program came into being in response to problems encountered by religious soldiers. It was a solution pushed from below, not enforced from above. It is true that we are witnessing a process of religious "strengthening" in the ranks of Religious Zionism in general and among the students of these programs in particular. However, this is not a trend led by the study programs. It is a general tendency seen today in the religious sector in Israel that feels threatened by the ultra-Orthodox (Haredi) camp on the one hand and the secular world on the other. Not wishing to be seen as "nice" religious individuals who will agree to anything requested by the secular world, and attempting to show they are no less observant than the Haredi world, many young people adopt stricter interpretations of commandments and observances. This is especially true in the category of modesty and relations between the sexes. The study programs are part of this trend, but they are responding to it rather than initiating it.

THE CONTRIBUTION OF MEDIATING STRUCTURES IN THE ISRAELI CASE

Students and their commanding officers in the IDF noted repeatedly that being conscripted as part of a study program was helpful to them as individuals. The main elements of support were the studying itself, conscription after an intensive non-high school curriculum, and the support and accompaniment (potential and real) of their study program during service.

The Israeli case indicates that the individuals benefit from the mediating structures. Other young Israelis of the same age who are conscripted alone immediately following high school usually enter the rigorous military system confused and lonely. In comparison, members of the study programs are less helpless, better prepared, and more aware of their abilities. They are more empowered and able to stand up for themselves, even though in certain ways their military service will be more difficult due to their halakhic constraints. In this respect, students of the programs discussed here are similar to graduates of mixed and secular Mekhinot.

On the other hand, it is difficult to discern whether this advantage is truly due to the study programs or rather that these young people are more confident because of their age. If all Israelis were to be conscripted at the age of nineteen or twenty, perhaps they too would be more mature and able to cope better with the military framework. Although it is not possible to answer this question, it still would not address the aspect of accompaniment (*livui*) available to students during their military service. Therefore, even if maturity serves as an advantage, it is not the only variable coming into play. Being able to turn to their program during their service is a source of empowerment for students and is therefore an advantage of conscription through a study program.

For the study programs themselves, the benefits are obvious: their own survival depends on the mediating function they fulfill. On the other hand, they must actively maneuver between all the elements in question in a way that will best assist their students, which is no easy feat. The main role of the study programs is to protect their students from both socioreligious and military pressures and to ensure they are not torn between their sometimes-conflicting loyalties.

Do the mediating structures benefit the greedy superstructures? When examining the Israeli case, it appears that the mediating structures allow each of the superstructures to meddle in the other's sphere of influence.

The relationship between the various actors can be viewed in two ways. First, it seems that the relationship is one of mutual coercion. The Religious Zionist system wants to force the IDF to conform to its wishes through the mediating structures using the overt and covert threat of banning conscription halakhically in its present form, and therefore depriving the IDF of choice human resources. The IDF can and has threatened Religious Zionism with disbanding the special conscription programs that allow preferential service conditions. From this perspective, which views mediation as problematic, the mediators "belong" to one side of the equation and serve as its "agents" in the sphere of the other. In other words, the mediators are not impartial. They pick sides and serve that side's interests. Seeing the situation thus means that the mediating structures "belong" to Religious Zionism, act in its interests, and therefore are a tolerated nuisance for the IDF. The military system is willing to stand the study programs and accept certain terms in order to obtain quality manpower that it wants and appreciates and that it fears it would not acquire otherwise. Officially, the IDF uses the terminology of "a people's army" in order to justify its concessions in this regard. In practice, most of the young people in question would join the IDF regardless, though it is unclear whether or not the IDF is aware of this fact.

It is also possible to see the entire relationship in a different light. The mediating structures allow Religious Zionism to live up to its ideals and the IDF to attract young Religious Zionists. In other words, it is a win-win situation and not a zero-sum game. This is a more positive perspective and indicates that the relationship discussed here can be interpreted in many ways, depending on the eye of the beholder.

Although the study programs seem to "belong" to Religious Zionism, in practice, the situation is far more intricate. As soon as the boundaries between the IDF and Religious Zionism have been opened, even partially, it is no longer possible to guarantee that the military system will not attempt to influence the Religious Zionist sector. The IDF, too, is able to communicate messages to this social group and its members through the study programs. Messages regarding disobeying orders, becoming an officer, motivation, viewing military service as a civil obligation—all these are transmitted by the military system to Religious Zionist members via the study programs. When Rabbi Brun explained to Hesder students that once they choose to go to a junior command course they should understand that they have chosen to go to an officers' course and cannot back out, he was voicing a military concern—not a Religious Zionist ideal. This means that the benefits for the IDF are not just highly motivated, quality manpower with fewer social and disciplinary difficulties. The IDF is also able to use the study programs to project its values.

Additionally, as the case of Rabbi Melamed and his yeshiva at Har Brakha demonstrated, the study programs do not automatically side with what is perceived as "their" side of the equation. As shown in Chapter 8, the Igud and heads of Hesder yeshivot sided with the IDF and attempted to pressure Rabbi Melamed to accept a compromise. They did not accept his view of the situation, but rather supported the position of the IDF and the minister of defense.

Above all, mediating structures are a sign of good will between the two competing greedy structures. Showing readiness for dialogue presents both sides in a positive light, as long as neither tries to break the status quo.

THE LIMITS OF MEDIATION: WHEN MEDIATING STRUCTURES FAIL

Despite all the supporting evidence, mediation is not a magical cure. It is not always able to regulate pressures. In the Israeli case, the limits of mediation are apparent when discussing the issue of disobeying orders during the Disengagement of 2005.

As described at length in Chapter 8, in 2005—specifically during the summer of that year—a vocal group within Religious Zionism called upon soldiers to refuse to cooperate with their orders to evacuate settlements in the Gaza Strip. This demand was directed especially at religious soldiers, specifically students of Hesder yeshivot and the Mekhinot. Various petitions in favor of disobeying orders, as well as the general mood of the public, certainly made the study programs and their students feel pressured to choose a definite position and support disobedience.

In hindsight, it seems that during the period of time before the Disengagement, a part of the Religious Zionist sector tried to break out of the consociational structure and force its minority opinion on the majority in Israel.[9] This would have destabilized the status quo in Israeli society. Without the option of mediation, students of study programs would have found themselves in a very precarious position.

As discussed earlier, the issue of disobedience during the Disengagement serves as an excellent test case for the mediating abilities of the study programs. It was an extreme case where the individuals were torn between their role in one greedy structure (the IDF) and the messages they received as members of another greedy structure (Religious Zionism).

As described previously, some of the programs actively supported their students (especially Gar'in members) who participated in the actual evacuation. Rabbis and teachers phoned students during their training for the assignment, during the Disengagement itself, and afterwards. Some of the students received letters from their *beit midrash*. The specific preparation the *midrashot* arranged for their students and the meetings held after the Disengagement was over attempted to help the students cope better with the difficult situation they were in. The parallel programs for male soldiers did not offer this kind of assistance, and in general it is clear that the female students received far more support than the male students. This may be due to the fact that education NCOs and officers (predominantly female) found themselves at the forefront of the evacuation, while most of the male students were stationed farther away from actual contact with civilians, and they were not responsible for evacuating them from their homes physically—as illustrated by the discussion of the events in Chapter 8.

Clearly the case of the Disengagement delineates the limits of mediation empirically. There was no collective policy for all study programs, pressure on the students was not regulated, and many students found themselves in the exact situation they feared at conscription—being torn between the greedy structures they belonged to, with no support system to turn to. On the other hand, there were students who were supported and assisted by their *beit midrash*. Furthermore, even those students who did not need to participate in the evacuation but were required by their social group to "take sides" needed their study programs to help them regulate pressures. As seen in Chapter 8, when the *beit midrash* presented a clear position, students were better able to formulate their own opinion and act accordingly—even if they did not agree with that position. In any case, when their program stated a position, it deflected social pressure from the individual students. In other words, mediation hinged to a large extent on the personality of the head of each program, the personality of the student in question, and the specific situation at hand during the Disengagement.

Yet another test case for the limits of mediation is the integration of women in combat units in the IDF. As demonstrated in Part II, Religious Zionism saw— and continues to see—this as a unilateral step that completely violates the status quo. In return, it threatened to transfer the preservice study program students to the NAHAL Haredi program (meaning they would no longer be dispersed throughout all units of the IDF). It organized demonstrations and sanctioned petitions. However, unlike during the Disengagement, better use was made of the mediating structures. Rabbis and officers held joint discussions and formed committees, and in the end an agreement was reached. It is by no means a perfect agreement; many problems remain, as described in Chapter 8, but the avenues of communication have stayed open and active despite the tension. As of the end of 2011, the *Shiluv Ha-Ra'ui* (the "proper integration") is upheld in most cases and indicates that both sides are making an effort to solve their differences.

It is unclear what will happen if the IDF decides to implement the Segev Committee's report (2007), which calls for further integration of women in combat units. Rabbi David Stav, the Igud's spokesperson, noted that the Igud plans on opposing any attempt to implement the report (Stav, first interview), and the IDF is certainly aware of this.

Thus, to conclude, the study programs attempt to mediate between their students and the superstructures to which they belong. They are not always successful in doing this completely and fully at all times, but are able to assist most of their students most of the time. This is an important accomplishment when considering just how powerful the IDF is in Israeli society and how civilian structures are usually unable to influence it or cause it to accommodate them. The fact that so few instances can be pointed out where mediation was not successful indicates that usually the relationship between all parties is a working one that benefits the various players, and that critical situations are few and far between.

CHAPTER 13
COMPARISONS AND CONCLUSIONS

As a large portion of this book dealt with the Israeli case, its main conclusions also focus on Israel. Still, the findings here have ramifications beyond the Israeli model and expand the theoretical framework constructed by Berger and Neuhaus (see Chapter 1). After investigating the conclusions for the Israeli case, we can observe the implications for the general sphere of civil-military relations, especially the place of mediating structures in this relationship. I will also offer a number of questions this book raises to stimulate further research.

In the Israeli case, it has been shown that the use of mediating structures usually helps individuals serving in the military who are caught between two greedy structures to regulate pressures and cope better with relevant dilemmas. The more the mediating structure regulates interaction between individuals and the greedy structures (as in the case of the Hesder program), the less direct contact its members will have with the superstructures, and vice versa. Therefore, members of mediating structures do well to choose which specific mediator they prefer, since this will influence their interaction with the superstructures. As described in earlier chapters, members of the Mekhinot and Shiluv programs have more direct contact with the IDF than members of the Hesder or the Gar'in programs.

Even within each mediating structure, to a certain extent individuals can choose how much mediation they wish to utilize. Some students prefer to keep in close contact with their program and to "lean" on it more. Others prefer less contact and more independence during their time in uniform. However, the most important component of the mediating structures is the possibility of mediation or intervention. The individuals feel empowered in their relationship with the superstructures—especially the military system—by the idea that, should they need to, they will be able to enlist the support of their study program. Although they do not usually employ this mechanism—as we saw in Part II (and Chapter 10 especially)—its potential is important to the students, as demonstrated throughout this study.

Mediating structures do not always work, and even when they do, they are not always able to assist all of their members all of the time. During the discussion of three pivotal cases where mediation was greatly needed (disobeyment of orders, especially during the Disengagement of 2005, the "proper integration," and the Stern Initiative), it seems that mediation worked in general. Even though most of the public was greatly surprised that students of the study programs did not disobey orders en masse during the Disengagement, those who followed the actions of the study programs were not. Despite obvious problems, the study programs were able to regulate pressures and avoid such a situation. They continue to do so when the issue of refusing orders surfaces from time to time.

Why do mediating structures generally work well in the Israeli case? It seems that the key to keeping up a working relationship between all the actors involved is the premise that they want to cooperate. The IDF, Religious Zionism as a social group, the various study programs, and the individuals involved all think cooperation benefits them and do not see the other actors as enemies, but as legitimate players who are competitors at times. They recognize each other's legitimacy. Therefore, even when competing for the same resources, a compromise can be reached. It is these basic assumptions that allow for all the parties involved to have a generally civil working relationship, at least most of the time. This point becomes especially crucial when considering the possible implications of the Disengagement of 2005 and the even more recent Har Brakha affair. The previous discussion of these events suggests that when elements who are not interested in cooperation—or who are unwilling to recognize the legitimacy of one or all of the other players—appear to influence the interaction between the superstructures and the mediators, the other players try to ignore them or to push them away from the situation so that they do not ruin the carefully constructed "game" of cooperation.

While this point is extremely pivotal and explains why the Israeli case is so unique and generally works, it is not the only important factor to consider. The fact that boundaries between the civil and military spheres in Israel are fragmented also helps to maintain a working relationship between the parties. It allows for the mediating structures to maneuver and move back and forth between these spheres, physically as well as metaphorically, as demonstrated throughout Part II. This, together with the differences in conscription, explains why even though in the American and Indian armed forces there is a general tendency to accept the legitimacy of religious systems, adoption of the Israeli model of mediating structures is impossible.

The Israeli case is distinctive in many ways. However, it is still able to make a contribution to the study of civil-military relations theoretically and generally. It also raises questions for further research.

THEORETICAL IMPLICATIONS

Based on the Israeli case, we can draw at least one general theoretical conclusion. As demonstrated in Chapter 1, Berger and Neuhaus set forth a very general sketch of the mediating institution. They saw modern society as pitting "vast, anonymous, and potentially oppressive megastructures against the vulnerable personal worlds of individuals" (Berger and Neuhaus 1996, 145). Any structures that stand between the superstructures and the fragile world of the individual and mediate between them can be seen as mediating ones, according to Berger and Neuhaus. The idea of mediation through structures was one Berger and Neuhaus arrived at following their thoughts on the importance of limiting governmental power in issues of the welfare state. They saw the mediating structure as a mechanism supplying services to citizens instead of the state, following American neoconservative views.

Furthermore, Berger and Neuhaus highlighted the fact that many individuals must maneuver between their personal lives and the demands of superstructures, with varying degrees of success. Those who utilize mediating structures are more successful. This is due to the fact that "such institutions have a private face, giving private life a measure of stability, and they have a public face, transferring meaning and value to the megastructures" (ibid., 159). Both faces allow the individual to belong to numerous systems, and therefore an individual who is able to utilize mediating structures is better equipped to cope with modern society.

The Israeli case indicates that this model can be used not only for American society, but that it is relevant for other societies as well and can be applied outside the concept of the welfare state. It is a tool with wider implications than its creators realized at the time. It is certainly relevant when discussing civil-military relations. In comparing the Israeli case to other military systems, it is obvious that it is possible for individuals to cope with their situation without mediation, or with very minor mediating structures. Likewise, one might have a tooth pulled without anesthesia, but more pain will certainly be involved.

On the other hand, mediating structures cannot be used without regard to social context. There are societies where mediating structures won't be able to negotiate between greedy structures or manage most instances of conflicting demands. When they are able to mediate successfully, however, all parties gain from the presence of these structures. In this sense, the present study broadens the existing model and shows its growing relevance in the twenty-first century. It also indicates that this field is still largely unexplored and that many questions remain unanswered. For example:

What social and cultural conditions are conducive to mediating structures? Which social and cultural circumstances allow construction of mediating structures and which will resist or even prohibit such frameworks? Are socially cohesive societies less or more likely to employ such mechanisms? Is religious tolerance important to the founding of these structures or is its role marginal or even unimportant?

When would mediating structures supply a possible and even desirable solution? Under what circumstances is such a framework a welcome addition to regulating civil-military relations? Are there circumstances under which it is better to bar mediating structures from entering the civil-military equation?

Can mediating structures damage individuals using them? Previous scholarship has posited that the military cannot bridge social problems or "educate" civil society. Additional academic research has illustrated that selective conscription can exacerbate social schisms. Following these lines of reasoning, can mediating structures be equally unhelpful in that they heighten differences rather than encourage assimilation? Worse, can these mechanisms be detrimental to the individuals using them? Can the potential greediness of mediating structures overpower the initial premise of their establishment and turn them into sources of discord?

How successful are such structures over time? The Israeli case that uses mediating structures widely is only sixty-five years old. What will the coming decades show?

IMPLICATIONS FOR GENERAL CIVIL-MILITARY RELATIONS

When Luckham described civil-military relations, he stressed the importance of the relative strength of both sides of the equation, as demonstrated in Chapter 2. The Israeli case proves that this also affects the ability to create mediating structures. The relative strength of civil society vis-à-vis the military system will determine the nature of the mediating structure.

In order to demonstrate this point, a reiteration of the comparison in Chapter 2 of various military forces is in order. As illustrated before, the Iranian case demonstrates a model where the military system is completely subservient to the religious one. According to Luckham's typology (1971), it seems that in Iran the civil-military boundaries are permeable,[1] and the civil system is stronger than the military one. In this case, there is no need for mediation from the point of view of the religious system. Religious norms will be upheld within the military sphere, but military autonomy is severely restricted—and this means that military abilities are also limited. The military is closely monitored by Ideological-Political Directorate and might—justifiably—feel it cannot function properly as a military force. This causes disgruntlement within the officers' corps, as discussed in Chapter 2. Furthermore, religious interference in the military affects maneuvers, causes the military to reorganize its training program, and in general may cause it to be less prepared for combat.

The Iranian case of a distinctly religious military force has certain characteristics in common with the general worldview of students from some of the study programs discussed in the Israeli case, particularly the Mekhinot students, who lend a religious aura to military service. A soldier who treats his military duties seriously is seen as performing a religious duty. However, there are also marked differences between the Iranian and the Israeli cases. In the Iranian case, the religious system is unwilling to cooperate with the military system, or even to allow for a pretense of such cooperation. The Ideological-Political Directorate can be seen as mediating to a certain extent, but it mainly spies on the military system and attempts to control and oversee it. These are elements that do not exist in the Israeli case, as described throughout the study.

While students may see their military duties as part of a religious framework and speak of a desire for a "more Jewish military," they, and the heads of their programs, wish to continue a cooperative relationship with the IDF. There is no aspiration to take over the military system, and the heads of the Mekhinot balk at the thought of seeing only religious officers at the General Staff table. The fact that the religious Mekhinot have tied themselves ideologically and economically to the nonreligious and mixed Mekhinot proves this point.

Comparing the Israeli case to the American, Indian, and Turkish cases reveals a more complex picture. In these three cases, the boundaries between the civil and military spheres are well defined. When conscription exists (Israel, the U.S. before 1973, and Turkey), the military system comprehends that it is uprooting its members from their natural environment and must therefore supply all their needs, including their religious needs. When boundaries between the civil and military systems are integral, the military system cannot look to civilian structures for assistance in satisfying these needs. As a result, it is impossible to create strong mediating structures in these cases. The fragmented boundaries in the Israeli case, however, allow for strong mediating structures that can supplement the military's attempts to satisfy religious needs of soldiers.

In cases where the military is volunteer-based (the U.S. post-1973, India, and the officers' corps in Turkey), and civil-military boundaries are integral, the military system is justified in disregarding the religious needs of soldiers should it choose to do so. The military system may demand its members conform to its rules, even when this means transgressing religious obligations and commandments (such as blood transfusions for Jehovah's Witnesses, and the discharge of NCOs and officers in the Turkish military who are suspected of Islamist tendencies).

Mediating structures could help in defusing the situation and assist individuals when navigating the military framework. Still, the military system is clearly the only one authorized to set ground rules. Should it allow a religious soldier to practice his or her faith, it does so in the spirit of goodwill and not because it is obligated to do so. A religious individual need not enter the military system in a volunteer-based force. To do so indicates the individual's understanding that he or she will have to make certain religious concessions.

If the individual in question belongs to a religious minority, his or her situation will be even more difficult. The military system understands that it may be better for it to accommodate religious individuals, but it is under no obligation to do so—especially not actively. Integral boundaries facilitate such behavior on the part of the military system, since there can be no unsupervised interaction between soldiers and civilians in such a case, and religious civilian structures can't meddle in the military sphere at will.

Clearly the presence of strong mediating structures hinges on at least two factors: the nature of civil-military boundaries (as illustrated by Luckham), and whether the military in question is volunteer or conscription-based. Are there additional factors to be considered?

The Indian case considers the cultural and religio-cultural needs of minorities an important factor in their service, despite the fact that its civil-military boundaries are also integral (S. Rosen 1996). The possibility of growing facial hair for Muslims and Sikhs, incorporating turbans into the official uniform, and matching battle cries to regiment culture are elements that indicate a general tendency for accommodation in the Indian military. This is not done for altruistic reasons, but in order to achieve a balance between the diverse minorities and the heterogeneous nature of the Indian armed forces. The various social pressures, both from within the military itself and from Indian society, cause the military system to become more flexible. The civil system, in this case, seems more powerful than the military one.

It is impossible to ignore the American case when seen in this context. While in this case the civil system is also strong, its religious sector is unable to influence the military similar to its counterparts in India due to the separation of church and state. Nonetheless, although barred from the military sphere, the civilian religious system in the United States continues to try to assist believers in uniform. Various religious groups utilize the tools at their disposal, even if these are very weak mediating structures or structures that "belong" to the military system, such as the chaplaincy. Both the military and the religious systems want to ensure that chaplains function in the ranks and support believers. When the military system recognizes a Buddhist chaplain, for example, it is able to portray itself as liberal and open and enhances its image in the eyes of parts of the civilian population. The religious system receives an opportunity to support believers. Everyone wins.

Despite this, there are too few incidents where the superstructures—and even chaplains—protest regarding the difficulties believers encounter when in uniform, such as when Jews or Muslims are unable to keep their dietary laws or celebrate holidays, or when evangelists pressure nonevangelists. Individual soldiers must be aware of their rights, they must find a relevant chaplain or lay leader, and they must request appropriate accommodations. Soldiers who are unaware of their rights and are unequipped psychologically to demand them will not receive them. There is no organized general institution that alerts them to their situation or is able to mediate effectively between them and the military system. The U.S. military's attitude toward religious soldiers is not only a product of it being a volunteer force, but also a product of the integral boundaries between it and civil society. Even when it was a conscription-based military, the U.S. military did not allow civilian mediating structures of any form. It is therefore possible to deduce that the combination of integral boundaries and the historical role of chaplains in the U.S. military shaped the attitude toward religious soldiers. The transition into a volunteer force only reinforced this trend.

There is even less attention paid to the individual's religious rights in the Turkish case. The military accepts religious elements that are considered cultural (such as holidays and abstaining from pork), but looks askance at elements deemed overtly religious (prayer five times a day, and fasting that forces the believer to rest). Under no circumstances can religious observance be at the expense of one's military role.

The presence of alumni of religious state-sponsored high schools in a conscription-based military could serve as a good basis for a comparison of the Israeli and Turkish cases. In both cases, not only is it inevitable that believers will be found in the ranks and that these soldiers are not always willing to be more lenient in their religious observances in order to accommodate the military system, but the religions in question are law-based and therefore very greedy in their demands.

While Religious Zionism has been successful in creating mediating structures between itself and the military system in order to manage conflicting demands, in Turkey the military system is too suspicious of religious structures in general (and Islamist tendencies in particular) to allow any sort of mediation. As discussed in the previous chapter, the Israeli case demonstrates the importance of a willingness to maintain a working relationship between the parties in order for mediating structures to exist. This feeling is absent in the Turkish case, where the military system is too suspicious of the religious one and wary of any sort of accommodation.

The nature of the boundaries between the civil and military spheres in Turkey and the fact that the majority religion is an orthoprax law-based one may also be detrimental to the creation of mediating structures. As these boundaries are integral, the religious system is unable to intervene in the military system and has no way of introducing mediation of any sort. The fact that the military system is powerful and able to withstand civilian pressures no doubt reinforces this. An in-depth comparison of the Turkish and Israeli cases is long overdue.

In light of these observations—and aside from the nature of the military force (volunteer or conscription-based) and the boundaries between the civil and military spheres—we must also consider a number of other factors to discern when mediating structures are possible. The historical and social contexts must be examined, as well as the nature of the religion in question—orthoprax law-based or otherwise—and the relative power of the civilian and military systems. Considered together, these factors are able to predict when mediating structures can be created and what their relative strength will be.

UNDERSTANDING CIVIL-MILITARY RELATIONS IN ISRAEL

To conclude this study, it is worth noting the implication for civil-military relations in Israel. Since mediating structures exist in the Israeli case, and these are relatively powerful and well-established structures that are usually able to regulate pressures and mediate between all the various actors, this would indicate that civil society in Israel is relatively strong compared to the military system. As the Turkish case shows, when the military system is strong, it is able to veto the presence of powerful mediating structures and prevent their creation altogether—even in a conscription-based force.

This point is even more interesting when considering the prevailing view in Israeli scholarship: that the IDF is more far more powerful than civil structures in Israel (Kimmerling 1994; Levy 2003; Sheffer et. al 2008). However, rather than indicating that there is a militarization of Israeli society through these mechanisms, the mediating structures demonstrate a "civilization" of the IDF using civilian frameworks.[2] The IDF is willing to accommodate the study programs, allows civilian interference in the military sphere to a certain extent, and in general accepts civilian sanctioning of its treatment of its soldiers. From this perspective, the study programs illustrate a case where the religious system, which is a part of civil society, is able to influence the military system and is a formidable power willing to force the military system to conform to certain standards.

This conclusion is surprising in light of Israeli scholarship in the field of civil-military relations. Most scholars see the preservice study programs as agents of militarization in Israeli society, encouraging military norms and ideals and their place in civil society. However, the present study shows quite clearly that reality is far more complex. While the study programs are sympathetic to some of the IDF's needs and demands and are favorably predisposed toward it at times, they are not afraid to negotiate with the IDF and ensure that it accommodates their students in the way they feel it should. In most cases, they are capable of setting limits and making sure the military system upholds its side of agreements. While they are not always successful in shielding their students from the arbitrary nature of the military system, they can hardly be seen as active agents of militarization. In a society that is usually termed "a society of civilians" rather than a "civil society," this is no small feat.

METHODOLOGICAL APPENDIX

This study departs from a social studies perspective and utilizes mostly qualitative scholarship in its evaluations. Given that interviews make up a large part of the primary source material, an explanation of the methodology is in order. In order to understand the role mediating structures play and how successful they are, it was essential to speak to the people who formulate their policy, use their services, and those who are affected by them: heads of the programs themselves, senior and junior IDF officers, and—of course—students and program graduates.

As it was not possible to interview all heads of all the study programs examined here, a number of institutions were chosen, as explained below. These were: Har Etzion, Or Etzion, Mitzpe Ramon, Petach Tikva, Ma'ale Adumim, Ma'alot, Ha-Golan, and Yerucham—all Hesder yeshivot; Eli, Yatir, Rosh Pina, and Atzmona as representative of the Mekhinot; the Shiluv yeshivot at Ein Tzurim and Ma'ale Gilboa; the *midrashot* at Ein Ha-Natziv, Midreshet Lindenbaum in Jerusalem, and Be'er at Yerucham. Interviews were also held with students and graduates of these institutions, as described in detail below.

Interviews and conversations were conducted between December 2001 and September 2010. Interviews with personages (heads of programs, senior officers, etc.) were conducted in order to corroborate existing written information (either by the same persons or about them), or media coverage about the programs and the people who play parts in them. In some instances, interviews uncovered new information other sources failed to supply. This usually happened because of the nature of the interviews, which were conducted differently from a news interview, and the vantage point the interviewees were asked to assume. Since I was not attempting to trap them or to pose difficult questions, but rather to understand interviewee's motives, the framing of the interview as a learning experience influenced the entire conversation. In addition, the interviews focused on the mediating aspect of the situation, which is usually not dealt with or researched in the media or traditional written sources on the subject.

Furthermore, interviews were important in order to understand how the representatives of Religious Zionism and the IDF understood and experienced mediating mechanisms, how far they were willing to go in order to accommodate the other actors in the situation at hand, and when they expected the other side to accommodate them.

Accordingly, the interviews with pivotal individuals helped corroborate information and fostered a deeper understanding of the opinions of rabbis, officers, and other key people involved in the creation and growth of the study programs; but these interviews did not serve as the sole sources for the programs, and they were used mainly as supportive evidence (McCracken 1988, 29–30).

Interviews with students served as more important sources. Since the students themselves are the main judges of the mediation process and do not usually speak or write publicly, interviews were the only way to gauge their thoughts and experiences. This was also true for junior IDF officers, who are usually not permitted to voice their opinions on this topic while in uniform. Both the students and the junior officers are the groups most affected by mediating structures and witness first hand how these frameworks function.

Additionally, the interviews tried to determine what motivated students to join preservice study programs, and how they utilized these programs when dealing with their social group, Religious Zionism, and the IDF. The interviews explored several questions: Were students aware of the benefits of mediation before conscription? Did the possibility of mediation occur to them before conscription? Did it affect their choice of a certain program over the others, and so on? Interviews are usually conducted in order to allow an understanding of how interviewees view themselves and their world, and therefore these sources are primarily personal statements that can only represent each individual, not the group as a whole. However, when viewing the interviews together and comparing them, it is possible to arrive at more general conclusions, as explained below.

This study used two forms of semistructured interviews conducted between the end of 2002 and 2010. The first form consisted of one-time semistructured interviews conducted with heads of study programs, junior and senior officers in the IDF, influential individuals who helped create the programs in question or are involved in the running of these programs today, as well as alumni of the various programs. When warranted, a second conversation was held. Almost all of these interviews were taped, after the purpose of the interviews was explained and permission to record was given by the interviewees. All interviewees understood the tapes would be used for my research. When requested, I turned off the recording, and this part of the interview was considered off the record. A number of interviewees did not consent to the taping of their interviews and this request was respected.

The second form consisted of a number of rounds of semistructured interviews with two pools of students. The first pool was initially interviewed during the 2002–2003 school year. The second pool was first interviewed during the 2003–2004 school year. Both pools were interviewed during their study period before actual conscription. Students who agreed to take part in the follow-up study were then interviewed once a year during each of the following years of service and until after their discharge from the IDF. The initial interviews were conducted in person, while most of the follow-up interviews were conducted over the phone, due to the fact that once in uniform, it was difficult for interviewees to find time to meet me in person.

During our first conversation, each interviewee received an explanation as to the purpose of the interview, its scope, and my hope they would agree to be interviewed once a year until being discharged from the military. They were not asked to commit ahead of time to continuing to participate in the project. I then produced a tape recorder and asked for permission to record the interview. Almost all students agreed to this. When permission was given, the recording device was placed in plain sight for the duration of the interview. At the end of the interview, I asked for a contact number in order to conduct follow-up interviews in the future. All students, program graduates, and junior officers were promised complete confidentiality and understood the interviews would be used in my research and subsequent publication, with the condition of anonymity.

For phone interviews, after the initial explanation of the project, I asked interviewees for permission to tape our conversation. Some asked for an explanation as to how this could be done over the phone. Almost all interviewees agreed to the recording of our conversation. All junior officers interviewed by phone granted the same permission.

During the first year of the study (2002–2003), thirty-five students were interviewed: eight Hesder students, ten Mekhinot students, six Shiluv students, and eleven Gar'in members. Of these, thirty-four participated in the follow-up interview the following year (2003–2004), thirty-three during 2004–2005, thirty-two in 2005–2006, and twenty-six in the final research year for this pool (2006–2007).

The second pool of students, interviewed first in 2003–2004, consisted of thirty students: eleven Hesder students, nine Mekhinot students, four Shiluv students, and six Gar'in members. Of these, twenty-eight participated in the interviews the following year, 2004–2005,[1] twenty-eight in 2005–2006, and nineteen in 2006–2007. The steady drop in numbers can be explained by the fact that not all interviewees were willing to be interviewed every year and some lost interest and dropped out of the study. Others were unable to find time even for a telephone interview or changed their phone numbers and I was unable to reconnect with them. A number of students left to travel abroad upon their return to civilian life and were unreachable.

Semistructured interviews allow for a better understating of the interviewees' world due to the possibility of complex answers, rather than the yes/no and rated questions used in surveys (Leech 2002, 665–668). The interview has a set objective and the questions are constructed ahead of time, but the structure of the interview must allow flexibility and not force interviewees to conform to the interviewer's conceptions or hypotheses. Complex answers, the surfacing of issues the interviewer is unaware of, and the semistructured conversation of the interview produce information that one cannot glean from surveys, and this more easily allows for the proof or disproof of hypotheses. The structure of the questions, the manner in which they were asked, and the general process of the interviews were all modeled according the relevant literature (such as Kidder and Judd 1986; Leech 2002; Wengraf 2001; Wolvier 2002).

Interviews conducted with the heads of the study programs and senior officers can be described as elite interviews. I interviewed twenty heads of study programs,[2] four senior officers who had a direct connection to the study programs,[3] and a number of individuals who influenced the programs.[4] In addition I spoke to and corresponded with military sources in India and Turkey.

These interviews served a different purpose than the interviews with students and were treated somewhat differently. Usually, interviews conducted with politicians or public figures are classified as elite interviews and, as noted by the relevant literature, it usually difficult to approach the interviewees (Goldstein 2002, 669–972). At least one secretary and possibly other "gatekeepers" protect elite interviewees. Circumstances can also influence the ability to approach such interviewees. For example, IDF officers cannot be interviewed without permission from the IDF spokesperson; permission that is not usually granted easily. Naturally, the difficulty in interviewing senior officers affects research, and it affected the sample used in this study as well. The official IDF position concerning mediating structures presented here is based in part on the responses of the interviewees, and since military bureaucracy limited my sample, the picture depicted here is problematic. However, as noted by Goldstein (ibid.), such problems are inescapable when using elite interviews. While I did attempt to interview senior and middle-ranking officers outside of the accepted channels, I was not always successful, and in the end the sample presented here was determined to a large extent by personal connections and the limited cooperation of the IDF spokesperson's office.

Interviews with the heads of the study programs are also considered elite interviews. In order to allow for a representative sample, I was careful in choosing interviewees and this is by no means a random sample. I purposely interviewed rabbis from many sectors and ideologies. As the interview with Rabbi Tzvi Kostiner proved, it was not always easy to win the cooperation of heads of programs who originated from the Har Ha-Mor school of thought. Even once the interview with Rabbi Kostiner was set up, it did not proceed in a similar fashion to other interviews. Rabbi Kostiner did not answer questions, but managed the interview himself, refusing to allow me to tape our conversation and breaking it off abruptly at a certain point. He questioned my ability to understand the subject at hand and this affected his general attitude toward the interview. Representing yet another ideological sector, Rabbi Eyal Krim, a graduate of the Ateret Cohanim yeshiva and the head of a Mekhina and today an influential figure in the Military Rabbinate, refused to speak to me at all. Rabbi Eli Sadan of the Eli Mekhina agreed only to a phone interview and refused to meet in person. As Goldstein asserts, when using elite interviews and part of the sample refuses to cooperate, one can learn much from the refusals and not just from the interviews themselves. In other words, here, as in the case of the uncooperative IDF spokesperson, reality dictated the sample more than the research itself could.

It was relatively simple to interview all the heads of the Shiluv and Gar'in programs since there were only two yeshivot participating in the Shiluv program and only three women's *midrashot* that take part in the Gar'in program. On the other hand, it was impossible to interview all the heads of the Mekhinot and Hesder yeshivot, due to their numbers. The rabbis I did interview from the Hesder program (the heads of the Or Etzion, Ha-Golan, Har Etzion, Mitzpe Ramon, Yerucham, Ma'ale Adumim, Ma'alot, and Petach Tikva yeshivot) represent both the older and more established yeshivot with a great deal of influence, as well as newer and less known institutions and those with unique agendas. I chose yeshivot from both sides of the Green Line, from diverse ideological and political backgrounds, yeshivot from northern, southern, and central Israel, as well as from the greater Jerusalem area, whose heads studied in institutions ranging from Merkaz Ha-Rav to yeshivot outside of Israel. Even this sample was unable to cover the entire range of ideas and views present in the Hesder school of thought. However, I believe the main trends are represented.

The heads of Mekhinot selected for the sample were chosen mainly according to the size of their program. The sample includes four Mekhinot. The number of students enrolled in these four amounts to almost half of the entire age cohort participating in all the Mekhinot combined during each year of the study: in 2003, 366 students studied in Eli, Atzmona, Yatir, and Rosh Pina of the 777 students enrolled in the entire program; in 2004, of the 698 Mekhinot students that year, 321 students studied in the four sampled. This trend continues: in 2007, of 804 Mekhinot students, 315 were enrolled in the sample Mekhinot.

A number of individuals were interviewed again for various reasons. For example, after the Disengagement, it was important to speak to Rabbis Kahan and Tehar-Lev again since their students participated in the events.

As mentioned above, one-time interviews were also held with program graduates and junior officers (ranking up to and including company commanders), though these were by no means elite interviews. All in all, forty-one graduates were interviewed: fifteen Hesder alumni (including one still on active duty); twelve Shiluv graduates (including three on active duty); six Mekhina alumni and eight Gar'in graduates (including two on active duty). Of these interviewees, three Mekhina graduates, two Shiluv alumni, and three Hesder graduates are no longer observant. The sample does not include Be'er graduates since the program was too young to have any at the time the study was conducted.

Twenty-four junior offices were interviewed: four officers from the Education Corps, five Armored Corps officers, and fifteen infantry officers (seven platoon or company commanders in regular infantry units, seven platoon or company commanders serving in special operations or reconnaissance units, and one platoon commander stationed in the officers' training school).

Junior officers were interviewed in order to gauge the military attitude "in the field" and how officers who are in direct contact with study program members feel about these arrangements. Graduates were interviewed in order to hear how they saw things after completing the program and to get a wider perspective of it. Naturally, "memory adds details," as one graduate interviewed noted. But since I thought it was important to understand the connection (or lack thereof) alumni felt to their study programs, its place in their lives as they grew up, their attitude toward their fellow graduates, their opinion of the program, and so on, these interviews were important and informative. As Helman notes (1993, 25–48), this is how these young people comprehend their experience, and it is exactly this hindsight that was important in graduate interviews.

And finally, in order to retain the style in which thoughts were expressed, direct quotes from interviews are verbatim, with corrections made for clarity only. Names of junior officers, graduates, and students were changed, as well as some identifying details, in order to protect their privacy. Senior officers, rabbis, and individuals interviewed in lieu of an official posting are quoted using their full names and affiliations at the time of the interview.

Aside from the interviews, data concerning numbers of students, places of residence, and, in some cases, the previous study institutions of the students were supplied by some of the study programs. Most study programs do not usually keep a database for all students. When such a database is maintained, at times it is updated so that the current place of residence marked for each student indicates where he or she lives at present and not where he or she lived at the time of joining the program. When relevant information was shared with me, I was able to make better observations. The Igud, as well as the Mekhinot's parallel association, supplied me with general data concerning numbers of conscripts from their programs.

Military unit types are noted when it is important to be aware of the number of soldiers in question. When numbers were not relevant, the word "unit" was used interchangeably with whatever unit type was in question (such as "platoon," "company"). Unit was also used to indicate *tzevet*—a small group of soldiers who train and work together, usually up to twenty.

The terms "system," "framework," "structure," were used interchangeably for stylistic reasons. They all describe a broader and more fluid social construct than an institution.

A note on transliteration is also in order. Transliteration of the Hebrew follows the standard rules of the Academy of the Hebrew Language (2008) as stated in the guidelines on their website, http://hebrew-academy.huji.ac.il/hahlatot/TheTranscription/Documents/ATAR1.pdf, with a few minor exceptions. For instance, study program names and names of individuals are spelled according to their own accepted spelling in English (i.e., Elichai rather than Elihai; Atzmona rather than Atsmona).

Finally, student-soldiers are usually termed as students throughout this study. Since this is the way their programs and the IDF view them and refer to them throughout their years in uniform, it was only fitting to use this term when relating to them in these pages.

GLOSSARY

Am Yisrael. Lit., "the People of Israel." Usually used to speak of the Jewish collective, not necessarily limited to Israeli Jews. This term is sometimes used to imply the Jewish People as an entity with a shared heritage, history, and values, despite the fact the individuals may not agree on what exactly these mean.

bedi'avad. Halakhic behavior that is acceptable ex post facto, but not the preferred course of action. The opposite of *lekhathila*.

beit midrash. Lit., "house of study." A study hall for religious studies. Sometimes referring to the essence and school of thought in a certain yeshiva.

ben Torah (**bnei Torah**, pl.). An individual whose life is centered on the Torah and derives from it. A mature religious individual who wishes to continue studying Torah as an adult and to live life according to Torah in the broader sense of the term.

company. A military unit comprised of approximately three platoons.

eruv. The Shabbat perimeter inside which one is allowed to carry items on the Sabbath.

Grey refusal or grey disobedience (*sarvanut afora*). To avoid outright refusal of orders, but to not be involved directly in carrying them out. For example, asking to be transferred to guard duty or kitchen duty in order to avoid evacuating a settlement, or avoiding contact with the people being evacuating and rather moving their possessions or packing up their homes after the people themselves have gone.

halakha. Jewish religious law. The combined body of oral and written tradition on the proper conduct of a Jewish way of life.

havruta. A study partner for religious studies. Also, a method of religious study: independent study of a religious text or topic with a study partner.

lekhathila. Preferred halakhic behavior ex ante, from the onset. In a case when all things are equal, the best course of action sanctioned by halakha. The opposite of *bedi'avad*.

lishma. Lit., "for its own name." To do something for its own end and not as a means to another end. For example, studying in order to obtain knowledge rather than in order to receive credit or a grade.

livui. Lit., "accompaniment." In the context of this book, to keep tabs on students while in service and ensure their physical and mental wellbeing while in uniform.

Mador BENISH. Acronym for Mador Bnei Yeshivot, the Department of Yeshiva Students in the IDF. The military liaison and bureaucratic office in charge of religious students who defer their military service in order to study Torah. The office acts as a liaison together with the Igud in dealing with the bureaucratic matters pertaining mainly to Hesder students.

mamlakhtiyut. A term that refers to a particular school of thought within Religious Zionism. The *mamlakhti* attitude recognizes the mandate of the state to rule and make decisions and in general stresses the sovereignty of the state. Rabbi A. Y. H. Kook and his school of thought are usually cited as the founders of this attitude.

midrasha (*midrashot*, pl.). A religious seminary where women study Torah.

mitzva (mitzvot, pl.). A religious obligation.

Mizrahi. Lit., "eastern." Jews descended from the Jewish Diaspora in Middle Eastern and North African countries.

NAHAL. An acronym standing for No'ar Halutzi Lohem (Pioneering and Fighting Youth). A service venue originally aimed at the children of farming communities in Israel as well as an infantry battalion.

National Service (**Sherut Leumi**). Rather than serving in the military, the option of volunteer service within the civilian community, out of uniform, is a possibility for certain groups within Israeli society. These include religious women, Arabs who have Israeli citizenship, and Israelis who are physically unfit for service but wish to volunteer.

platoon. A military unit comprised of approximately thirty soldiers.

SHALAT. An acronym standing for Sherut Lelo Tashlum (lit., "nonpaid service"). A defined period of time during in which a person is still officially considered a soldier, but does not wear a uniform, receive a military salary, or spend time on a military base. Rather, soldiers on SHALAT are engaged in various semiservice activities, such as bolstering a young kibbutz or volunteering in a development town (NAHAL soldiers), or attending a yeshiva (Hesder soldiers).

SHARAP. An acronym standing for Sherut Pa'il (lit., "active service"). A period of time during which a student is, for all intents and purposes, a regular enlisted soldier, with all that this entails.

Ha-Shiluv Ha-Ra'ui. Lit., "the proper integration." The name of the IDF program aimed at ensuring religious soldiers are not forced to have contact with the opposite sex in halakhically compromising situations, while also making sure women can serve anywhere in the IDF.

torato umanuto. Lit., "Torah is his vocation." The arrangement according to which a religious man can affirm he is a full-time Torah scholar and therefore exempted from service.

tzniut. Modesty in the broadest sense. Not only in matters of unrevealing dress, but in all matters concerning behavior and relations with the opposite sex.

yeshiva (yeshivot, pl.). A religious seminary where men study Torah.

yeshiva gvoha. Lit., "high yeshiva." A yeshiva where students devote themselves exclusively to study without necessarily ever leaving and/or enlisting. These are usually attended by older students.

zman. Lit., "time." In this context, it refers to a term of study in the traditional yeshiva schedule. There are three such terms: *zman Elul* (the month of Elul term, which runs during the month before the High Holydays); *zman horef* (winter term, beginning after the High Holydays until the beginning of the month of Nissan, usually corresponding roughly with April); *zman kayitz* (summer term, beginning with the month of Iyar [usually May] and ending on the Ninth of Av [Tisha'a BeAv]). While the names and general scheduling of the terms are the same, the exact dates of the beginning and end of each term may vary from one yeshiva to another.

NOTES

Introduction

1. Two recent publications include Amos Harel's best-selling book, *Teda Kol Em Ivriya*, on the social changes in the infantry, and Reuven Gal and Tamir Libel's volume on the religionization of the IDF, which was reviewed and discussed prominently in the media.

2. Some discussion of religio-ethnic, non-Jewish minorities can be found in Chapter 4.

3. Since throughout their service these individuals are usually viewed through the prism of their preconscription study period, this book will refer to them as student-soldiers.

Chapter 1

1. Segal 1986; S. Cohen 1997.

2. Berger and Neuhaus gave a very preliminary outline for mediating structures. Others have attempted to deepen our understanding of the term within more defined fields, mostly in matters pertaining to the welfare state (for example, Novak 1980).

3. Not including individuals who consecrate themselves to their religious beliefs in some way, such as monks and nuns of various sorts living within temples and monasteries.

4. In such a case, it could be termed a "total institution," as coined by Goffman (1961), and discussed earlier.

5. As described above, some religions are greedier than others, and it is important to note that not all religions allow the bearing of arms. This book only considers religions with provisions for military service.

6. For a discussion of religious sects and sectors and the need to differentiate visually between believers and outsiders, see Baumgarten 1997, 5–11.

7. Again, we are only considering religions that accept the idea that violence is permitted under certain circumstances. Even when a religion such as mainstream Islam, Judaism, or Christianity allows the use of violence under certain circumstances, it does not tolerate the behavior described here.

Chapter 2

1. Such as Islam based upon shari'a and Judaism based upon halakha.

2. In order to avoid confusing orthodox religions of this nature with orthodox and ultra-orthodox denominations within religions (such as those discussed later in Judaism), the terms "orthoprax" and "orthodox" will only be used together with the terms "law-based" and "non-law-based."

3. As in some other conscription-based forces, it is possible for conscripts to volunteer for certain posts. For example, in the Israeli military, a conscript can volunteer to serve in the paratroopers. However, this does not make the conscript a volunteer. It usually does include an extension of service or other special requirements. Soldiers might agree to accept less

favorable terms of service due to their wish to serve in a more prestigious unit or because of their belief that this venue of service will benefit them in some other way.

4. For the role played by the Soviet commissars, their relations with the military's commanders, the problems raised by their definition as both military and ideological actors, the political education of the enlisted soldiers, etc., see Colton 1979, 58–68, 70–74. The parallels on this point between the Red Army and the Iranian army are noticeable and are worthy of further study. Grounds for such a comparative study have been laid by Katzman in his book about the Revolutionary Guards, see Katzman 1993; Bruno and Bajoria 2007.

5. While Turkey is not defined as an Islamic state, most of its citizens are Muslims, and when the Turkish military must contend with religious soldiers, they are predominantly Muslim.

6. Such interference was one of the reasons for the coup in 1960 (Jenkins 2001, 26–27).

7. Service may be deferred for higher education. Students who study abroad for extended periods of time may pay a fine and are exempted.

8. For example, while it is possible to see citizens smoking or even eating during the Ramadan fast in cities, it is a rare occurrence in rural Turkey.

9. Kerman, an ex-Turkish soldier, private correspondence. The full blessing is "Tanrımız Hamdolsun, Milletimiz Var Olsun, Afiyet Olsun" (Blessed is our Lord, long live our country, and bon appétit). I am grateful to Özgül Erdemli for the translation of the Turkish.

10. For example: UK Border Agency, Home Office, *Operational Guidance Note: Turkey*, (2013): 21, http://www.refworld.org/pdfid/519257234.pdf.

11. Third Section, "Partial Decision as to the Admissibility of Application no. 45824/99" by Ziya Çelikates and Others against Turkey (October 3, 2002), accessed February 2013, http://www.echr.coe.int/; Third Section, "Final Decision as to the Admissibility of Application no. 45824/99" by Sedat Şen and Others against Turkey (July 8, 2003), accessed February 2013, http://www.echr.coe.int/.

12. Despite EU demands that the MGK relinquish its power, in practice it still functions and continues to monitor officers' behavior. See "Constitution lies at heart of military supremacy in Turkey," *Yeni Şafak* (January 24, 2010), accessed February 2013, http://yenisafak.com.tr/English/?i=237505&t=24.01.2010.

13. Since the number of chaplains per military base is limited, sometimes a soldier of a denomination or religion not represented by clergy on base will volunteer to serve as a lay leader for his or her fellow believers. This role is fulfilled in addition to the soldier's official military duties.

14. This article was the result of a Supreme Court petition by an American Jewish officer regarding his right to wear a skullcap in the U.S. Air Force. See Goldman vs. Weinberger, Supreme Court Case 475 U.S. 503 (1986), accessed June 2009, http://caselaw.lp.findlaw.com/scripts/getcase.pl?court=us&vol=475&invol=503.

15. See, for example, "Isle Muslims in Military Service Keep Faithful to Their Religion," American Muslim Armed Forces and Veteran Affairs Council site (October 2001), accessed June 2003, http://www.amafandvac.org.cf. "Serving Allah and America: Muslims in the

military strive to reconcile religion," AMAF and VAC site (November 12, 2002), accessed June 2009, http://www.amafandvac.org.

16. See an official U.S. military document on medical treatment for Jehovah's Witnesses (July 2002), accessed June 2009, http://www.watchtowerinformationservice.org.

17. The British military model—as opposed to the German one—is based on the idea that troops are more motivated by personal social ties that precede their military training. Therefore, it is best to recruit soldiers together with their social group and rely on their civilian social obligations when building troop cohesiveness. Officers for these troops, similarly, will come from the upper social strata of the same region. As the soldiers are already used to seeing these individuals as authoritative figures, they will also accept them as leaders on the battlefield.

18. When asked specifically if the Indian military employs the services of chaplains of some sort, the Indian military attaché in Israel responded: "No. There are only volunteers or civilians. No official duties are assigned for this purpose" (Indian military attaché, pers. comm., June 20, 2005).

19. Official Indian military document, *Additional Directorate General Recruiting and Publicity* (Chapter 31, n.d.), accessed February 2013, http://indianarmy.nic.in/rtg.doc.

20. See photos in Singh 1987, 5, 10.

Chapter 3

1. See, for instance, Goren 1994–1996, vol. 1–3; Yisraeli 2001; Yisraeli 1992. Regarding the process that Religious Zionism underwent from thinking of the state in terms of a theocracy to this approach, see A. Cohen, 1998.

2. The *mamlakhti* attitude recognizes the mandate of the state to rule and make decisions and in general stresses its sovereignty. Rabbi A. Y. H. Kook and his school of thought are usually cited as the founders of this attitude.

3. Part of this approach, usually represented by the school of thought of Rabbi Kook and his religious seminary (yeshiva) Merkaz Ha-Rav, views the state as a holy creation, the "dawning of redemption" (*athalta d'geula*). Thus the IDF, as a representative of the state, enjoys a similar aura and is accorded a special status by large parts of Religious Zionist society.

4. While it is possible to include the Military Rabbinate in the category of mediating structures, as will be discussed later, Religious Zionism did not create the Military Rabbinate and it is an internal IDF structure.

5. While it is possible to justify the offensive aspect of military service by applying the Nahmanidian view that the commandment to conquer the Land of Israel—making sure it is in Jewish hands—is ongoing, this view was not generally used to justify conscription. Rather, it was and is invoked when discussing the evacuation of settlements and cession of lands for peace-making purposes, and the Maimodian position was used more prevalently to justify conscription, especially that of religious scholars.

6. Tensions between religious and secular Israelis are not new and have been discussed widely in scholarly and popular writings. See, for example, Horowitz and Lissak 1990; Sheleg 2000.

7. Practically, a nonreligious member of the crew can change places with the religious member and open the hatch. However, this situation will produce additional halakhic difficulties for the religious soldier due to the fact that he "assisted" in a transgression, and whatever the case, the social damage is already done. For further elaboration on this subject: Min Ha-Har 1973, 110–113; Rubin 1998, 132.

8. Such situations are commonplace during military service. In practice, different soldiers respond to these situations in different ways (consulting with a military rabbi or a civilian rabbi, or ruling on one's own based on halakhic knowledge), depending on the circumstances at hand.

9. See, for instance, the discussion concerning this issue in the officer training course and Rabbi Eliezer Melamed's monitoring of the situation: Melamed, *Besheva*, July 8, 2004: 50; Melamed, *Besheva*, July 29, 2004: 42.

10. For a comprehensive bibliography of the relevant responsa, see Binyamin and Cohen 2000. For a survey of the more historical responsa, see Achituv 2002; S. Cohen 2006.

11. For a detailed history of the formation of the yeshivot, see Breuer 2004.

12. It should be noted that in the Religious Zionist sector, the ideal of Torah studies coalesced in a more gradual fashion in comparison with ultra-Orthodox society. In addition, this principle was adopted in a different fashion. In keeping with the Religious Zionist approach, which favors a combination of "Torah and Labor" (Tora ve-Avoda), Religious Zionist parents accept the idea that their sons should study Torah and encourage it after graduation from high school, but they undoubtedly prefer their sons become doctors or engineers rather than yeshiva rabbis. Study devoid of distraction is therefore an important principle, but one that should be followed during a limited time in one's life. After this, one should turn to more practical endeavours. Nevertheless, it is important to note that setting aside time each day for religious study in one's adult life is considered desirable and encouraged in all Religious Zionist communities.

13. See Rabbi Herzog, chief rabbi at the time of the founding of the State of Israel, cited in Y. Cohen 1994, 75.

14. For an extensive explanation of the historical and ideological background of this topic, see S. Cohen 1997.

15. One can draw a parallel between the case of a young religious conscript and that of an exceptional athlete or musician who wishes to continue their professional training despite mandatory conscription. For athletes and musicians, service in the military would harm their training and progress and thus also damage their professional future. As in the case of religious conscripts, the IDF provides a solution in the form of special programs: Sportai Mitztayen (Outstanding Athletes) and Musikai Mitztayen (Outstanding Musicians). A conscript in such a case is afforded certain allowances so that service does not interfere with the development of his or her special talent. However, this is where the similarities end. First, it is one thing to desperately want or feel an intense need to follow a certain course of action; it is an entirely different matter when one believes that one's actions are prescribed by a higher power. In the former case, a person is always acting on his own

volition. In the case of the latter, it is possible that a young religious man does not always intensely desire to study Torah, but he believes that a religious commandment obligates him to do so. Second, in the case of the Religious Zionist soldier, there are a number of mediating structures that assist the relations between both sides. An athlete or a musician does not have recourse to such structures. Furthermore, one cannot compare the numbers of those who make use of the religious frameworks and those who make use of the Sportai Mitztayen and Musikai Mitztayen, which are substantially fewer.

16. The following halakhic deliberations and discussions were compiled from responsa and other sources, especially the following: Cherlow, internal publications and Internet responsa; S. Cohen 1997; Y. Cohen 1994; Drori 2001; Karnei Shomron Yeshiva website 2005; Lichtenstein 2002; Shaviv 1994; Shilat 1988.

17. The subject of *kiddush ha-shem*—the sanctifying of God's name and the opposite of *hilul ha-shem*—has been framed differently in various historical periods. In the past, such as during the Middle Ages, when Jews were forced to convert or die, the term was understood to mean that those who were willing to die rather than forsake their religion were practicing *kiddush ha-shem*. In more modern contexts, *kiddush ha-shem* has been framed as anything that glorifies God's name—such as achieving a military victory.

18. Hesder literally means "arrangement." However, since the program's establishment and the important role it has played in social-military relations in Israel, the term has acquired independent status as the name of a group of religious seminaries (yeshivot) where one follows a prescribed course of military service together with study.

19. For examples (out of many), see responsa by Rabbi Yuval Cherlow, December 2004, accessed June 2009, http:www.moreshet.co.il/shut/print.asp?id=41635; http:www. moreshet.co.il/shut/print.asp?id=1988.

20. Such as Rabbi Kostiner of the Hesder yeshiva in Mitztpeh Ramon, see Kostiner, November 2004, accessed June 2009, http://www.kipa.co.il/ask/print.asp?id=17395. The founder of the Hesder program, Rabbi Goldwicht, also saw it as a compromise: see Shagar 2004, 107–108; Cherlow 2003, 151, note 1.

21. This privilege is not extended to young secular women who are unwilling to falsely present themselves as observant Jews. See Galili 2004. See also the Supreme Court ruling 2383/04, Laura Milo vs. the Minister of Defence, where the plaintiff requested an exemption on the grounds of conscientious objection. The ruling referred directly to the fact that women have the right to an exemption for reasons of religion and conscience (paragraphs 7–8). The appeal was rejected.

22. Serving in the National Service program was also approved by Rabbi Zvi Yehuda Kook, one of the most influential rabbis of the Religious Zionist sector, who was opposed to female conscription. See his responsa, published posthumously: Kook 1982, 387.

23. While this published source is somewhat dated, IDF officers from the Manpower Division have confirmed, off the record, that these percentages are still correct. As it is impossible to obtain current published sources from the IDF, this information must suffice.

24. For a survey of this, see Y. Cohen 1993, 7–8. For later opinions, see Sheleg 2002.

25. As Rabbi Shlomo Aviner puts it, "Two years of service in the National Service program is not recommended, nor is it recommended to serve for one year and spend one year in a *midrasha* [a women's religious seminary] since this raises the age of marriage. Rather, it is recommended to serve one year in the National Service program and at the same time engage in religious study (*limudei kodesh*), or to do so while studying [for a degree]. This too should not be set in stone [. . .] but this is the general direction." Ateret Cohanim site, accessed June 2009, http://www.ateret.org.il/hebrew/library.php?id=767. Rabbi Cherlow also gave his opinion in this matter: "I would prefer that girls serve two years in the [National Service program], but how can these women have time to serve, marry, acquire a degree, study at a *midrasha*, etc., during this time in their lives? Therefore, to begin with, women should serve two years in the National Service program, but a woman should not be criticized if she serves for one year only, on condition that she understands that she owes the public (*klal Yisrael*) a debt she will have to repay through her future conduct in life." Rabbi Yuval Cherlow, "Service in the Military by Religious Zionists," Moreshet (2002), accessed June 2009, http:www.moreshet.co.il/shut/shut2.asp?id=4817

26. For such concerns see, for instance, Tzviran 2005.

27. To be fair, one should point out that the military and secular society are not one and the same. Many times soldiers allow themselves to behave in ways they would never dream of behaving in civilian life.

28. There is reason to suppose that conscripts from other sectors also feel a similar shock when they enlist. Here we are concerned only with the reaction of conscripts from Religious Zionist society.

29. SHALAT (acronym): lit., "nonpaid service." A defined period of time during which a person is still officially considered a soldier, but does not wear a uniform or spend time on a military base. Rather, soldiers on SHALAT are engaged in various semiservice activities, such as bolstering a young kibbutz or volunteering in a development town (NAHAL soldiers), or attending a yeshiva (Hesder soldiers).

30. As mentioned above, one of the responsibilities of the Military Rabbinate is to address the needs of non-Jewish soldiers, although there are no non-Jewish chaplains in the IDF. Despite the fact that there are no places of worship for non-Jewish soldiers, these soldiers are entitled to time to pray and are excused from many aspects of operational duty during religious holidays. For example, Muslim soldiers who fast during Ramadan are exempt from physical activity, and mealtimes are adapted to fit in with the timing of the fast (IDF spokesperson's office 2005).

31. For a comprehensive illustration of the changing role of the Military Rabbinate, see Kampinsky 2007.

32. This tendency is well known and is an ongoing source of innumerable discussions regarding the existence of the Military Rabbinate alongside rabbis from the Mekhinot and the Hesder yeshivot. See, for example, Y. Rosen 2003.

33. Despite the fact the current chief military rabbi, Rafi Peretz (2010–), was himself the head of the Atzmona Mekhina.

Chapter 4

1. SHARAP (acronym): lit., "active service." This is used to denote a period during which a student is, for all intents and purposes, a regular enlisted soldier with all that this entails.

2. This program differs from one yeshiva to another. Some yeshiva students enlist for a year and a half and then return to the yeshiva and study for the remaining three and a half years (thus participating in the program for a total of five years). Students at other yeshivot enlist for only a year and four months, return to the yeshiva to study, and in the following year serve two more months in the military—thus completing a year and a half of active service and five years of the program. This pattern was set to correspond with the traditional yeshiva school year. Following the 2013 elections, it seems that Hesder students will serve at least one additional month in uniform.

3. The end of 2010 saw a shift in the program. In November 2010 a subprogram of Hesder was launched named Shiluvim. The program allows students to study for one year, serve a full two years in uniform, and return to their yeshiva for a final year of study. Thus, the program comprises four years instead of the traditional five, while enabling students to serve longer in the IDF proper. As the program is still new, it is not included in depth in this study. See Nir 2010.

4. During the transition to a new head of the Igud in 2008, an additional position was established to field students' complaints and address them when needed so that the head of the Igud would not need to focus on the personal problems of various students.

5. See, for instance, a student's question concerning tuition addressed to Rabbi Cherlow, the head of the Petach Tikva yeshiva: "Our financial situation at home is not easy, and I would like to ask for a discount." Rabbi Cherlow responded: "Financial issues will not bar a student from attending a yeshiva." Tzohar site, accessed January 18, 2005, http://www.kipa.co.il/tzohar/ask_show.asp?id=53639.

6. The Mechanized Infantry Corps, also known as Gdudei Ha'tish'im, is not considered by the students to be a "good" service venue, and is seen as less prestigious than serving in regular infantry units.

7. Rabbi Brun denied any connection between the placement of yeshiva students and the desire to prevent a disproportionate concentration of casualties in case of war (Brun, first interview).

8. Interviewees recounted attempts to falsify a higher medical profile in Hesder yeshivot in order to be given a higher combat placement; for example, Yoel, second interview.

9. A typical platoon comprises approximately thirty soldiers.

10. The Mitzpe Ramon yeshiva is slightly exceptional in this regard. The head of the yeshiva, Rabbi Tzvi Kostiner, distinguishes between the yeshiva itself and the Hesder program. Although the yeshiva is considered a Hesder yeshiva, according to its head, he is "hitchhiking with the Hesder program," and in practice, the yeshiva is run in a completely different way. The head of the yeshiva advises the students when to enlist, according to the progress they make in their studies and irrespective of the accepted Hesder timetable.

When asked about the aim of the Hesder, he said that the "Hesder has no real direction"; each yeshiva has its own ideology and level of religiosity, and there is no one educational policy that must be followed (Kostiner, first interview). It is thus difficult to include him in the same group as the other heads of the Hesder yeshivot. For a current description of the curricula at the Hesder yeshivot and the changes necessary to enable students to pursue their studies in the long run, see Goodman 2002, 151–169.

11. Lit., "the People of Israel." Usually used to speak of the collective, not limited to Israeli Jews. This term is sometimes used to imply the Jewish people as an entity with a shared heritage, history, and values—despite the fact the individuals may not agree about what exactly these mean.

12. It should be noted that Rabbi Lichtenstein did not serve in the military since he immigrated to Israel as an adult and past the age of conscription.

13. Both entering a yeshiva and military service are in many ways compatible with various rites of passage in other societies. See Grimes 2000, 100–107.

14. In 2010 approximately 1,700 students were enrolled in the Hesder program (Hager-Lau, second interview). Additional military sources confirmed this observation, off the record.

15. Rabbi Stav stated that the increase in the number of students in the Hesder program is at the expense of the Mekhinot; however, this is not supported by data regarding participation in the religious preservice preparatory seminaries (Association of Mekhinot 1988–2007). Rabbi Hager-Lau, head of the Association of Mekhinot, claims the number of Mekhinot students increases by 15 percent every year (Hager-Lau, second interview).

16. The definition of a "ben Torah" in the circular published by the Har Etzion yeshiva reads, "All the decisions made by a ben Torah are centered on the Torah and derive from it; he feels that God presides over all his actions; his speech is pure and fine; his conduct is honest and respectful towards others; he and his wife dress modestly, and he dedicates part of his time to Torah study." See *Daf Kesher* no. 666, A, 1998, http://www.etzion.org.il/dk/1to899/666daf.htm. For another definition of a ben Torah, see Selengut 1994, 237.

17. Mizrahi refers to Jews descended from the Jewish Diaspora in Middle Eastern and North African countries.

18. This is a slang term based on the concept of communicating vessels from physics similar to the idea of six degrees of separation. The term illustrates the (not necessarily true) idea that any two individuals belonging to the Religious Zionist social group have at least one friend or relative in common. Consequently, everyone knows everyone else.

Chapter 5

1. For a discussion of the reasons the program at Ein Tzurim closed, see Rosner 2008.

2. Officially, this position regarding the Hesder still exists today, and the Religious Kibbutz Movement expects its youth to serve for a full three years.

3. Acronym for the Mechanized Infantry Corps.

4. Although one might think Shiluv students would prefer to serve with their friends, in practice the students interviewed wanted "a little space." Serving with a friend or two would be fine, but they were not interested in serving with their entire class, Hesder-style.

5. Rabbi Yoel Bin-Nun, a controversial figure in Religious Zionist society, headed the Ein Tzurim yeshiva that has since closed. Rabbi David Bigman still heads the yeshiva at Ma'ale Gilboa.

6. In a published interview Rabbi Bigman expressed his agreement with this view (Friedman 2005).

7. Due to their high motivation, students tend to ignore the first signs of physical injuries such as stress fractures. They fear such injuries will cause them to fail military courses and prefer to ignore the pain. The yeshiva is aware of this tendency and attempts to alert students to the dangers this course of action poses to their health in the future.

8. That is, a Shiluv student who spent a year in the yeshiva, was on active duty for eighteen months, returned to study at the yeshiva, and then completed the mandatory three years of service would be discharged after spending five years in the Shiluv program. This is the same length as the Hesder program, but it includes twenty more months of active service. In comparison, a Mekhina student or a Shiluv student who did not return for a second year of study would be discharged after spending only four years in their respective programs.

9. During the interview with Rabbi Bigman, he recounted how at the time he suddenly realized that many of the yeshiva students were involved in combat and that he should call them. "But this was *pshita* [simple]!" and he was sorry he hadn't thought of it earlier (Bigman, first interview). His tone seemed to imply that he regretted that the yeshiva did not take the initiative more often due to the day-to-day work load, and that he felt they should invest more effort in students on active service.

Chapter 6

1. There are also approximately nineteen secular or mixed (religious and secular students) Mekhinot. The oldest nonreligious Mekhina was established in 1997 in Nili. No little attention has been given to the Mekhinot in the press, but as of yet, they have not been the subject of comprehensive academic research. See, for instance, Becker 1998; Sheleg 2003; Ministry of Education and Culture and Ministry of Defense 2002.

2. For another description of the establishment of Eli, see Gross 2002, 38–40.

3. Rabbi Rafi Peretz, at the time the head of the Atzmona Mekhina and as of 2010 the chief military rabbi.

4. This does not apply to Eli. As mentioned above, Eli has a program for postservice students, but this is an exception, and as of 2013, no other Mekhinot offer a postservice program.

5. The only interaction between different age cohorts takes place between first- and second-year students, since there are students who remain in the Mekhina for an additional period of study (from September until March of their second year).

6. The Rosh Pina Mekhina is an exception to this rule, since the head of the Mekhina is also the head of the regional religious council, and the council's secretary doubles as the Mekhina's secretary.

7. At the time of this study, Gush Katif—including Atzmona—had not yet been evacuated; this refers to the settlement as it was at the time.

8. For exact figures, see the Knesset report on the Mekhinot, 2008, accessed June 2011, http://www.knesset.gov.il/mmm/data/pdf/m02076.pdf; for the proposed amendment to the Mekhinot Law 2010, see: www.knesset.gov.il/privatelaw/data/18/2354.rtf.

9. Yeshayahu Leibovitch's teachings are not viewed favorably, to put it mildly, in the yeshiva world. For instance, his books may not be brought into the study halls of many Mekhinot, and would not be found in Hesder yeshivot either.

10. Acronym for Battalion Collection Station (Tahnat Isuf Gdudit), a facility to which injured soldiers from an entire battalion are brought during battle before being sorted according to medical status.

11. Informal conversation with Rosh Pina students, March 2003.

12. Eli's official name is Yeshiva Preparatory Seminary for the IDF, and it is sometimes also known as the "Bnei David yeshiva" (Sadan 2001).

13. Yatir (Beit Yatir) Mekhina student lists, 2000–2004. In general, from the interviews conducted, Yatir students appear less eloquent than those at Rosh Pina and Atzmona.

14. Based on my visits to Yatir and Rosh Pina.

15. This expectation was voiced mainly by students at Rosh Pina, but was expressed by students at other Mekhinot as well.

16. According to students, such contact does take place, but not always as frequently (Matan, first interview; Yoni, second interview).

Chapter 7

1. NAHAL nuclei are a cohesive group of young people who enlist together. Throughout their service they live and work together. This is the course of service on which the Gar'in program is modeled.

2. *Midrasha* (pl. *midrashot*), is the feminine equivalent of a yeshiva.

3. Rabbi Kahan headed the program during the time this study was conducted and therefore is quoted here. Since his outlook is still very influential at the *midrasha*, his ideas are still relevant when examining the program.

4. See discussion of the third session in Gal 2010.

5. See, for instance, the responsum of Rabbi Shmuel Eliyahu, son of the late Chief Rabbi Mordechai Eliyahu, to a direct question about women's Gmara studies on the Moriya site, accessed June 2009, http://www.moriya.org.il/shut/indexid.asp?id=4087. See also Rabbi Ya'acov Ariel's opinion in Cohen and Rich 2000, 7. Chana Kehat, a leading Religious Zionist feminist, explains that the younger generation takes the principle of a woman's right to study Talmud for granted, while the religious leadership is not yet ready to accept such values. This is, however, changing as this younger

generation matures, and the establishment is learning to accept the new reality (Kehat 2001, 355–364).

6. Recent years have seen an increase in the phenomenon of Religious Zionist single women. Some rabbis maintain that the *midrashot* contribute to this phenomenon since they raise the age of marriage even further. See Kahan 1998, 8–9; Bartov 2004, 28–30.

7. *Ulpena* (pl. *ulpenot*) is a girls-only religious high school within the Religious Zionist educational system under more strict rabbinical supervision than other religious girls' high schools in the system. Rather than a principal, a rabbi heads the institution.

8. See, for example, the rising number of calls to the Aluma hotline in Gal 2010, 29; Sela 2012, 3.

9. Usually, in such cases, both bride and groom had studied in a yeshiva, *midrasha*, or *mekhina* in the past. In most cases, the groom's rabbi officiated while the bride's rabbi played another pivotal part in the ceremony, such as reading the *ktuba* (marriage contract).

Chapter 8

1. The issue of mixed service is seen as a matter of concern mostly by Hesder and Mekhinot rabbis. Shiluv rabbis did not involve themselves in this matter.

2. Lit., "the proper integration." A program aimed at integrating more women in combat positions in the IDF while avoiding issues of *tzniut* that would prevent religious soldiers from serving in these units.

3. See, for instance, a report from a meeting between the staff at Training Base (BAHAD) 16, the IDF's Search and Rescue training center, and the heads of the Sha'alabim Hesder yeshiva and the command rabbi: *The Committee for Awareness [of the Needs] of the Yeshiva Student, Discussion No. 1—Summary,* June 11, 2000, IDF Archive 177/896/03. Other reports dealt with measures such as separate housing for men and women, reiteration of proper dress codes and modesty, etc. However, in a letter attached to the file, the representative of the Sha'alabim yeshiva, Rabbi Yehezkel Ya'akobson, states, "However, the basic problem has not been solved. [. . .] In the existing circumstances, yeshiva students cannot serve in the Search and Rescue unit. The military must decide whether it prefers the service of female soldiers or that of the Hesder soldiers." Yehezkel Ya'akobson, Summary of Meetings between the Ben Yeshiva Committee and Instruction Base 16, n.d., IDF Archive, 177/896/03. I am grateful to Roni Kampinsky for sharing these sources with me.

4. See Office of Human Resources, Minutes of the Meeting for the Proper Integration, March 4, 2001, IDF Archive 177/896/03. The rabbis cited in the minutes were the chief military rabbi, Rabbi Brun, and Rabbis Sadan, Sheinwald, and Levinstein. The minutes are not verbatim, but the general tone is not one of convivial agreement.

5. Interestingly, none of the Hesder students spoke of what would become a glaring problem in the following years: women singing publicly.

6. Additionally, the following year, Har Brakha became the instigator of yet another vocal controversy concerning the Hesder yeshivot and the IDF, as explained in the following

section. It seems that Rabbi Melamed has become fond of picking fights with the IDF but that the rest of the members of the Igud refuse to play along.

7. This observation is supported by an interview with Rabbi Cherlow and Rabbi Gilad held at the end of April 2005. Rabbi Cherlow voiced a position that Israeli society finds difficult to understand. In his opinion, the breaking point between Religious Zionism and the State of Israel is the disassociation from the most basic halakhic views: "We give our attention to the Disengagement and the like and not to the correct issues. The line, as least as far as I am concerned, is drawn at the point where the state decides that it no longer wants to be a Jewish State" ("Whoever is for the Lord, come to me," *NRG*, April 28, 2004, http://www.nrg.co.il). In other words, for Rabbi Cherlow, obeying orders is not a point of contention. As long as the state upholds its identity as Jewish, problems can be solved. If the state is no longer interested in upholding its Jewish identity, as a halakhic figure, he cannot sanction it. Thus, that the State of Israel is distancing itself from its Jewish identity is more essential than the withdrawal from Judea, Samaria, and Gaza. On the other hand, there are leading rabbis within Religious Zionist society who would not consider even this to be a serious issue. Rabbi Drukman and Rabbi Aviner were quoted in *Haaretz* as representing the view that even when problems come to light, even when the government desecrates the Sabbath, the state will always have a sacred dimension (Shragai 2004).

8. The issue of refusing to comply with evacuation orders has been on the public agenda in the past, with the evacuation of the Sinai Peninsula following the peace agreement with Egypt, the evacuations following the Oslo Accords, and particularly the evacuations in the summer of 2005. For the halakhic discussions concerning the evacuation of the Sinai and Yamit, see, for instance, Ariel 1983; Naor 2001. For the discussion after the Oslo Accords, see articles mainly in the *HaTzofe* daily throughout July 1995 and the publications found in Weinberger and Cohen 1999, 5–12. Due to the nature of events, discussions on this matter during the Disengagement from the Gaza Strip reached an intensity matched only by that which surfaced during the evacuation of the Sinai.

9. See, for instance, "Rabbi Cherlow to the Minister of Defense: You have created a rift in the military," *Arutz Sheva* online edition, October 21, 2002; Harel 2002.

10. Aviner 2002b; Aviner 2005. Rabbi Aviner's opinion was construed as an attack on Rabbi Shapira's ruling. In response to this perception, Aviner published an "important clarification" and explained that he respects Rabbi Shapira, but did not change his opinion: "Expressing an opinion does not constitute an offence against the Honorable Scholar [Rabbi Shapira]. This is the way of Torah" (Aviner 2005b). It should be noted that even during the evacuation of Yamit, Rabbi Aviner opposed any kind of refusal to comply with orders or any display of civil violence (see Don Yechiya 1998). In spite of the personal price he has had to pay for these views, Rabbi Aviner continued to debate these issues in his discussions of the weekly Torah portion in *Be-Ahava uBe-Emuna*.

11. See, for instance, a pamphlet by the head of the *kollel* in Kfar Darom, Rabbi Shaul Bar-Ilan, which points out the various offences a soldier would commit when evacuating a settlement: Bar-Ilan 2005. This pamphlet also includes recommendations from Rabbi Eliezer

Rabinovitch and Rabbi Avraham Shapira. In the weekly *Besheva*, Rabbi Eliezer Melamed attempted to clarify the issue from another point of view, arguing that refusing to comply with orders is a hallmark of good citizenship and serves to strengthen the foundations of the democratic state: Melamed 2005; 2005b. On the eve of Israel's fifty-eighth Independence Day in 2006, the year after the Disengagement, a series of pamphlets aimed at reinforcing a positive attitude toward the state was published. See, for instance, Drukman 2006.

12. Those in favor of disobeying orders were Dov Lior and Eliezer Volman (Kiryat Arba), Nachum Rabinovitch (Ma'ale Adumim), Michael Brom (Shiloh), Elhanan Bin-Nun (Beit Orot), Eliezer Melamed (Har Brakha), Elyakim Levanon (Alon Moreh), and Yehoshua Shapira (Ramat Gan). Those against were Yehuda Amital and Aharon Lichtenstein (Har Etzion), Yuval Cherlow (Petach Tikva), and David Asulin (Netivot). It should be noted that any opposition among Hesder rabbis and rabbis from the Religious Kibbutz Movement to disobeying orders does not constitute support for the Disengagement. See, for instance, "Rabbi Lichtenstein clarifies: I did not voice support of the Disengagement," *NRG*, February 28, 2005, accessed April 2005, http://nrg.co.il.

13. For instance, Rabbi Elyakim Levanon, head of the Alon Moreh Hesder yeshiva, directed his students to cry: "Given an order to evacuate? Start crying," *Ynet*, April 20, 2004, accessed April 2005, http://www.ynet.co.il.

14. Rabbi Drukman, "A lesson about the desecration of the Sabbath during the evacuation of Havat Gilad," accessed February 2013, http://shiurim.moreshet.co.il/web/shiur.asp?id=338.

15. However, there were rabbis who expressed their opinions in related responsa. For instance, in a written online responsum, Rabbi Weitzman, the head of the Ma'alot yeshiva, expressed his view against disobeying orders. At the end of his answer, he wrote: "A soldier should obey the military's orders, unless all the rabbis and all of the people of Israel should arrive at the place being evacuated with the aim of stopping the evacuation, and then he should be part of this group. Enough said." "How to deal with an order to evacuate settlements?" Kipa, accessed February 2013, http://www.kipa.co.il/ask/show.asp?id=5864. This response was given in May 2002. Rabbi Sugarman was quoted in a report from a memorial service for Rabbi Zvi Yehuda Kook as opposing Rabbi Aviner's position (Ben-Haim 2005), but the students interviewed for this study from the Golan yeshiva did not confirm that this was indeed Rabbi Sugarman's opinion.

16. For instance, when asked to identify their rabbis, both Rabbi Sadan and Rabbi Peretz mentioned Rabbi Avigdor Nebenzahl, rabbi of Jerusalem's Old City at the time, who was in favor of disobeying orders. Rabbi Peretz called Rabbi Yehoshua Zuckerman from the Har Ha-Mor yeshiva "my rabbi and teacher" (Peretz, first interview). Some reports in the media claimed that Rabbi Zvi Tau, the head of the Har Ha-Mor yeshiva, was in favor of disobeying orders, although it was unclear if he supported outright or "grey disobedience." See Sheleg 2004.

17. According to the transcript of a lesson by Rabbi Sabato during the Disengagement, he was against disobeying orders, but he did not say so explicitly. This transcript was emailed to the students (Sabato 2005).

18. The exception was one student who would not state his opinion on the matter.

19. Approximately fifteen Gar'in members participated in the Disengagement.

20. He continued to serve in reserve duty and later returned to the IDF for a company commanders' training course.

21. In contrast to Yagil Levy's (2007) claim that Religious Zionism was willing to forgo its demand for disobedience in return for certain social dividends.

22. After the Disengagement, Rabbi Tal underwent a deep ideological transformation. However, in the summer of 2005, he peacefully left the Gaza Strip with his students.

23. Where the most resistance to the evacuation was found.

24. Homesh, a settlement in Samaria, was evacuated during the 2005 Disengagement. However, civilians continued to attempt to return to its ruins, causing the IDF to evacuate them again and again. The soldiers were protesting the fact that they were ordered to participate in these evacuations.

25. See, for example, an anonymous letter written by a student to the popular weekly Torah portion flyer *Olam Katan*, January 2, 2010: 8.

26. Nadav is referring to the fact that Stern is himself religious and enlisted on his own rather than through a study program.

Chapter 9

1. A more stringent level of kashrut with regard to meat products.

2. Joint travel requires any two friends to compromise. In the case of religious and secular friends traveling together, this would also require substantial concessions concerning travel or lack of travel on Shabbat and holidays, food, and so on. Usually it is the secular friend who must make more concessions. Thus, traveling together indicates a stable and deep friendship strong enough to endure significant challenges.

3. Traditionally, the bride and groom are not to be left alone on their wedding day until the ceremony. Usually, the bride and groom each ask a close friend to serve as their companion for the day. To be asked to fill this position is usually indicative of a very close friendship.

4. In the past, this was also Rabbi Amital's policy (at the Har Etzion yeshiva), although as time progressed, his advancing age prevented him from continuing to follow this policy (Amital, first interview).

5. The Kibbutz Movement maintains a committee that acts as a liaison with the IDF and can pressure the IDF regarding its members before and during military service. See the Kibbutz Movement's Security Committee's website, accessed June 2009, http://www.kibbutz.org.il/bitachon/.

6. A high school for girls only with a strong religious curriculum.

7. Students may also turn to written responsa in order to independently find answers to halakhic quandaries.

8. Rabbi Krim himself declined a number of times to be interviewed for this study, and has since returned to military service, serving in the Military Rabbinate.

Chapter 10

1. Notably, Ron-Tal made no reference to Shiluv rabbis.

2. As explained in Chapter 8, education NCOs spend their time teaching soldiers in structured courses. Should a meeting occur during teaching hours—which is usually the case—and if part of the staff is made up of Gar'in members, a substantial portion of the course staff will go to the meeting, leaving their comrades to fill in for missing instructors. Military courses are structured such that a class cannot be canceled.

3. *Torato umanuto*, lit., "Torah is his vocation." A religious man can affirm he is a full-time Torah scholar and therefore be exempt from service.

4. Most of the senior officers interviewed thought that if they did not offer these soldiers special arrangements, they would not enlist, but would follow the ultra-Orthodox sector's example. This idea has been disproven to a large extent. See Rosman-Stollman 2005.

5. Considered the best manpower in the IDF due to the fact that the air force has the right to pick its pilots first out of the general pool of conscripts.

Chapter 11

1. When asked about this, Brigadier General Zamir (first interview), who dealt with this issue as part of his post in the Manpower Division, denied this claim completely. See Rosman-Stollman 2005.

2. In this sense, the changes taking place in the Shiluv program (see Chapter 4) are no less than earth-shattering, since they contradict everything the program has stood for and seem to prove that it is not possible to both study seriously and serve a full enlistment.

3. Jacob ben Asher, also known as Ba'al Ha-Turim, a medieval Rabbinic authority (b. Cologne, Germany, c.1269; d. Toledo, Spain, c.1343).

4. With the exception of Eli students, as described earlier.

5. See the following section in the current chapter.

6. This is an almost verbatim citation of Rabbi Amital. See Amital 2005, 121–122.

7. Concentration and intent to perform a religious obligation.

8. See Chapter 8 for the controversy that arose in Religious Zionist society surrounding the refusal of students from the Har Brakha Hesder yeshiva to participate in a course taught by female instructors and commanded by a woman.

9. A euphemism for stealing another unit's (or soldier's) officially issued military equipment in order to avoid punishment for losing or damaging one's own.

10. Despite these accusations, when comparing the data relating to the number of students attending the Hesder and Mekhinot programs, including data supplied by the Igud, it is quite clear that if there is any damage caused by the Mekhinot to the Hesder program, it is insignificant. See Rosman-Stollman 2005.

11. For further explanation of the program, see the Bnei David site, accessed March 2011, http://www.bneidavid.org/show_item.asp?itemId=80&levelId=62676&itemType=0.

12. This is reminiscent of the Volozhin yeshiva's ambivalent attitude toward secular studies; see Stampfer 2005, 106–108, 176–181.

13. A fair amount of criticism is leveled at Hesder students for using the time they are still on SHALAT to prepare themselves for civilian life. Both Hesder and Mekhina students remarked that it is wrong for students to prepare for the psychometric exam at a time when—based on their agreement with the IDF—they should be dedicating themselves solely to Torah studies. See Rosman-Stollman 2005.

Chapter 12

1. Interestingly, while most Shiluv and Mekhinot students felt their studies were of no practical help during their first year in the IDF, some changed their minds when asked during their second year of service and noted that there were situations where their preservice Torah studies helped them to cope. However, during their third year of service, Shiluv and Mekhinot interviewees returned to their original observation: most felt their studies were not helpful. Moreover, a number of Shiluv students thought their studies actually caused some of their problems: moving back and forth between the yeshiva and the military world—as per the program's structure—was difficult. After their second study period at the yeshiva, they found themselves unable to return to uniform as though nothing had happened. When Shiluv students resumed their service, most of their friends had already been discharged and were beginning their lives as adult civilians. This caused Shiluv interviewees to compare themselves and their stage of life to that of their cohorts, which frustrated them: Their friends were beginning academic studies, traveling, and working, whereas they had another year and a half in uniform ahead of them.

2. This was largely true for male students. Gar'in members, on the other hand, felt a special connection to their specific class. While they felt better about serving with other religious women and members of other Gar'inim, their main affinity was to their own class. Still, students from parallel Gar'inim didn't criticize each others' programs. Perhaps this was because in principle there is no fundamental difference between Be'er, Ma'ayn, and Hadas, ideologically.

3. As noted by S. Cohen, friendships forged in the IDF between religious and secular young people are becoming rarer as religionization tendencies grow stronger in the Religious Zionist camp. This is especially true of Hesder students who serve in homogeneous units. See S. Cohen 1999, 393–394.

4. Naturally, as described above, this is not always how things turn out in practice. However, this is the message Gar'in members wish to convey.

5. See references to this feeling in Tzuriel 2007; Greiner, 2007.

6. As stated by all officers interviewed. A member of a study program is always "marked" as a student, unless he or she chooses to omit the information during the traditional introductory interview every officer conducts with his or her subordinates.

7. A case in point is the words of the then chief of staff (CoS) of the IDF Lieutenant General Dan Halutz, in June 2005. The CoS was quoted in the press saying, "It isn't possible

to sustain a dual system and call upon people to disobey orders while enjoying Hesder terms of service in the IDF [. . .] this will not continue if this turns into a trend" (as quoted in *Haaretz*, June 29, 2005). As discussed in Chapter 8, only a minority of Hesder rabbis advocated disobeying orders. There were also Hesder rabbis who publicly denounced the phenomenon (such as Rabbis Cherlow, Lichtenstein, and Amital). However, the public views expressed by a minority of radical rabbis reflected upon the program as a whole.

8. See S. Cohen 2008, particularly Chapter 6.

9. As described earlier, "part," meaning not the majority. It seems that most of the Religious Zionist sector did not take any part in the protest against the Disengagement, but rather behaved as a "silent bourgeoisie majority," to quote Asher Cohen 2005.

Chapter 13

1. For an explanation of Luckham's model, see Chapter 1.

2. The idea of the "civilization" of the military in Israel, rather than a militarization of society, has already been introduced and delineated by S. Cohen 2005; 2008.

Methodological Appendix

1. In addition, phone interviews were conducted with two more students from Ein Ha-Natziv, who participated in the Disengagement and were not part of the original pool of interviewees. Since no Ma'ayan students from the original pool participated in the Disengagement, I felt it was important to contact at least some students who did participate, in order to understand the situation better. These students received the same promise of confidentiality, were given the same explanations, and gave permission for recordings—as did all other interviewees.

2. Rabbi David Bigman, head of the Kibbutz yeshiva at Ma'ale Gilboa; Rabbi Yoel Bin-Nun, head of the Kibbutz yeshiva at Ein Tzurim; Ms. Tami Biton, head of the Be'er program; Rabbi Eliyahu Blumenzweig, head of the Hesder yeshiva at Yeruham; Rabbi Yuval Cherlow, head of the Hesder yeshiva at Petach Tikva; Rabbi Avraham Davidovitch, head of the Mekhina at Rosh Pina; Rabbi Chaim Drukman, head of the Hesder yeshiva at Or Etzion; Rabbi Moshe Hager-Lau, head of the Mekhina at Yatir; Rabbi Eli Kahan, head of the Ma'ayan program; Rabbi Tzvi Kostiner, head of the Hesder yeshiva at Mitzpe Ramon; Rabbi Aharon Lichtenstein and Rabbi Yehuda Amital, heads of the Hesder yeshiva at Har Ezion; Rabbi Rafi Peretz, then head of the Mekhina at Atzmona and today chief military rabbi; Rabbi Eliezer Rabinovitch, head of the Hesder yeshiva at Ma'ale Adumim; Rabbi Eli Sadan, head of the Mekhina at Eli; Rabbi Eliezer Sheinwald, then a member of the faculty at HaGolan and today, head of the Shesder yeshiva at Modi'in; Ms. Leah Shakdiel, head of the *beit midrash* of Be'er in the past and today a member of the faculty; Rabbi Amnon Sugarman, head of the Hesder yeshiva at HaGolan; Rabbi Ohad Tehar-Lev, head of the Hadas program. All the above individuals are referred to throughout this book by their last name and, when appropriate, their title. When referred to in notes and the bibliography, only the last name and the interview number are listed.

3. Lieutenant Colonel Rabbi Shimon Elmaliach, liaison for the Gari'n program; Major General Yiftach Ron-Tal, then head of Land Forces of the IDF; then Brigadier General Elazar Stern, then chief education officer; Brigadier General Avi Zamir, then head of the Manpower Planning Division in the IDF. These interviewees are referred to by their last name and rank in the book and are cited by last name and interview number only.

4. Rabbi Avraham Brun, then head of the Igud; Brigadier General Yehuda Duvdevani, influential in the creation of the Mekhinot; Eliezer Deutsch, administrative executive at the Igud; Eitan Ozeri, head of the Igud today; Rabbi David Stav, spokesperson for the Igud.

BIBLIOGRAPHY

INTERVIEWS

Heads of Study Programs, Senior Officers, and Administrative Figures

Amital, Rabbi Yehuda (head of the Har Etzion Hesder yeshiva, also known as the Gush), first interview (Jerusalem), October 8, 2002.

Bigman, Rabbi David (head of the Religious Kibbutz yeshiva at Ma'ale Gilboa), first interview (Ma'ale Gilboa), October 23, 2002.

Bin-Nun, Rabbi Yoel (head of the Religious Kibbutz yeshiva at Ein Tzurim), first interview (Ein Tzurim), October 15, 2002.

Biton, Tami (head of the Be'er program), first interview (Yerucham), December 19, 2002; second interview (phone), June 16, 2004.

Blumenzweig, Rabbi Eliyahu (head of the Yerucham Hesder yeshiva), first interview (Yerucham), January 27, 2003.

Brun, Rabbi Avraham (head of the Association of Hesder Yeshivot, or Igud, 1980–2005), first interview (Alon Shvut), May 1, 2003.

Cherlow, Rabbi Yuval (head of the Petach Tikva Hesder yeshiva), first interview (Petach Tikva), October 8, 2002.

Davidovitch, Rabbi Avraham (head of the Rosh Pina Mekhina), first interview (Rosh Pina), March 25, 2003.

Deutsch, Eliezer (administrative executive of the Association of Hesder Yeshivot, or Igud), first interview (phone), December 23, 2007.

Drukman, Rabbi Chaim (head of the Or Etzion Hesder yeshiva), first interview (Jerusalem), November 19, 2002.

Duvdevani, Brigadier General (res.) Yehuda (head of the Youth and NAHAL Department), first interview (Jerusalem), July 25, 2004.

Eliav, David (administrator of Or Etzion Hesder yeshiva), first interview (Merkaz Shapira), May 4, 2004.

Elmaliach, Lieutenant Colonel Rabbi Shimon (liaison for the Gar'inim program), first interview (Ramla), May 13, 2003; second interview (Jerusalem), March 3, 2008.

Hager-Lau, Rabbi Moshe (head of the Yatir Mekhina and head of the Association of Mekhinot), first interview (Bet Yatir), November 6, 2002; second interview (Ramat Gan), September 15, 2010.

Kahan, Rabbi Eli (head of the Ma'ayan program), first interview (Ein Ha-Natziv), October 23, 2002.

Kostiner, Rabbi Tzvi (head of the Midbara ke-Eden Hesder yeshiva, Mitzpe Ramon), first interview (Mitzpe Ramon), February 12, 2003.

Lichtenstein, Rabbi Aharon (head of the Har Etzion Hesder yeshiva, Gush), first interview (Alon Shvut), January 5, 2003.

Ozeri, Eitan (CEO, Association of Hesder Yeshivot, or Igud), first interview (phone), January 2, 2008.

Peretz, Rabbi Rafi (head of the Otzem Mekhina, Atzmona-Yated), first interview (Jerusalem), December 25, 2002; second interview (phone), January 7, 2003.

Rabinovitch, Rabbi Nachum (head of the Birkat Moshe Hesder yeshiva, Ma'ale Adumim), first interview (Ma'ale Adumim), January 12, 2003. (Note: Rabbi Rabinovitch also uses the spelling Rabinowitz.)

Ron-Tal, Major General (res.) Yiftach (head of Ground Command, MAZI), first interview (Tel Aviv), May 2, 2003.

Sadan, Rabbi Eli (head of the Bnei David Mekhina, Eli), first interview (phone), March 11, 2004.

Senior Turkish military source A, first interview (Tel Aviv), November 9, 2004.

Senior Turkish military source B, first interview (Jerusalem), November 14, 2004.

Shakdiel, Leah (former beit midrash head and teacher at the Be'er program), first interview (Yerucham), March 23, 2004.

Sheinwald, Rabbi Eliezer (head of the Modi'in Shesder yeshiva and past member of the faculty at the Golan Hesder yeshiva), first interview (Chispin), May 18, 2004.

Stav, Rabbi David (head of the Petach Tikva Hesder yeshiva and Igud spokesperson), first interview (phone), December 19, 2007.

Stern, Brigadier General (res.) Elazar (chief education officer), first interview (Tel haShomer), June 23, 2003.

Sugarman, Rabbi Amnon (head of the Golan Hesder yeshiva), first interview (Chispin), January 22, 2003.

Tehar-Lev, Rabbi Ohad (head of the Hadas program), first interview (Jerusalem), October 26, 2002; second interview (Jerusalem), November 16, 2006.

Weitzman, Rabbi Yehoshua (head of the Ma'alot Ya'akov, Ma'alot, Hesder yeshiva), first interview (phone), October 20, 2002.

Zamir, Brigadier General (res.) Avi (head of the IDF Manpower Planning Division, TOMKA), first interview (Tel Aviv), January 12, 2004.

Hesder Yeshiva Students Cited (Pseudonyms, in Alphabetical Order)

Amir (Har Etzion student), first interview (Alon Shvut), April 1, 2003; second interview (phone), June 9, 2004; third interview (phone), April 3, 2003; fourth interview (phone), March 25, 2006; fifth interview (phone), April 30, 2007.

Avishai (Ha-Golan student), first interview (Chispin), May 18, 2004; second interview (phone), May 14, 2005; third interview (phone), August 20, 2006; fourth interview (phone), May 18, 2007.

Barkai (Har Etzion student), first interview (Alon Shvut), March 10, 2004; second interview (phone), February 27, 2005; third interview (phone), September 2, 2005; fourth interview (phone), September 17, 2006.

Chagai (Har Etzion alumnus), first interview (Alon Shvut), April 1, 2003.

Chaim (Yerucham alumnus), first interview (Yerucham), January 27, 2003.

Daniel (Yerucham student), first interview (Yerucham), January 27, 2003; second interview (phone), June 25, 2004; third interview (phone), February 27, 2005.

Eli (Or Etzion student), first interview (Merkaz Shapira), January 9, 2003; second interview (phone), June 4, 2004; third interview (phone), April 29, 2005; fourth interview (phone), April 22, 2006.

Elichai (Petach Tikva student), first interview (Petach Tikva), March 2, 2003; second interview (phone), June 4, 2004; third interview (phone), July 8, 2005; fourth interview (phone), May 19, 2006; fifth interview (phone), May 4, 2007.

Gadi (Ha-Golan student), first interview (Chispin), January 22, 2003; second interview (phone), May 29, 2004; third interview (phone), February 27, 2005; fourth interview (phone), March 17, 2006.

Ira (Or Etzion student), first interview (Merkaz Shapira), May 4, 2004; second interview (phone), March 5, 2005; third interview (phone), September 3, 2006.

Lavi (Or Etzion alumnus), first interview (Merkaz Shapira), May 2, 2004.

Lior (Yerucham alumnus), first interview (Yerucham), March 23, 2004.

Liron (Ha-Golan alumnus), first interview (Chispin), May 18, 2004.

Meir (Yerucham alumnus), first interview (Yerucham), January 27, 2003.

Mickey (Birkat Moshe student), first interview (Ma'ale Adumim), October 27, 2004; second interview (phone), May 13, 2005; third interview (phone), August 25, 2006; fourth interview (phone), April 27, 2007.

Nerya (Birkat Moshe student), first interview (Ma'ale Adumim), October 27, 2004; second interview (phone), May 13, 2005; third interview (phone), August 25, 2006; fourth interview (phone), May 13, 2007.

Noam (Har Etzion alumnus), first interview (Alon Shvut), April 1, 2003.

Ron (Petach Tikva student), first interview (Petach Tikva), March 4, 2003; second interview (phone), May 29, 2004; third interview (phone), March 3, 2005; fourth interview (phone), September 10, 2005; fifth interview (phone), May 26, 2006; sixth interview (phone), October 7, 2007.

Ronen (Har Etzion student), first interview (phone), July 18, 2004; second interview (Jerusalem), March 30, 2005; third interview (phone), September 4, 2006.

Sagi (Har Etzion student), first interview (Alon Shvut), April 1, 2003; second interview (phone), June 18, 2004; third interview (Alon Shvut), February 27, 2005; fourth interview (phone), March 17, 2006; fifth interview (phone), April 17, 2007.

Shmuel (Yerucham student), first interview (Yerucham), March 23, 2004; second interview (phone), March 4, 2005; third interview (phone), August 19, 2006; fourth interview (phone), May 13, 2007.

Tomer (Petach Tikva student), first interview (Petach Tikva), March 24, 2004; second interview (phone), April 1, 2005; third interview (phone), August 26, 2005; fourth interview (phone), June 23, 2006.

Tziyon (Birkat Moshe alumnus), first interview (Jerusalem), June 24, 2004.

Tzvi (Ha-Golan alumnus), first interview (Chispin), May 18, 2004.

Yaakov (Petach Tikva alumnus), first interview (Petach Tikva), March 4, 2003.

Yoel (Yerucham student), first interview (Yerucham), March 23, 2004; second interview (phone), April 14, 2005; third interview (phone), May 21, 2006; fourth interview (phone), April 14, 2007.

Yossi (Ha-Golan alumnus), first interview (Chispin), May 18, 2004.

Midrasha Students Cited (Pseudonyms, in Alphabetical Order)

Avital (Ma'ayan student), first interview (Ein Ha-Natziv), January 14, 2003; second interview (Ein Ha-Natziv), May 18, 2004; third interview (Jerusalem), May 2, 2005; fourth interview (phone), February 22, 2006; fifth interview (phone), April 30, 2007.

Basmat (Ma'ayan student), first interview (Ein Ha-Natziv), March 2, 2004; second interview (phone), February 20, 2005; third interview (phone), May 5, 2006; fourth interview (phone), April 17, 2007.

Dafna (Ma'ayan student), first interview (Ein Ha-Natziv), January 14, 2003; second interview (phone), March 13, 2004; third interview (phone), February 5, 2005; fourth interview (phone), February 9, 2006; fifth interview (phone), March 23, 2007.

Dalia (Hadas alumna), first interview (Havat Ha-Shomer), July 15, 2003.

Einat (Ma'ayan student), first interview (Ein Ha-Natziv), January 14, 2003; second interview (phone), May 14, 2004; third interview (phone), February 19, 2005; fourth interview (phone), March 10, 2006; fifth interview (phone), May 7, 2007.

Galit (Hadas student), first interview (Jerusalem), January 1, 2003; second interview (phone), March 22, 2004; third interview (phone), February 18, 2005; fourth interview (phone), February 22, 2006; fifth interview (phone), March 23, 2007.

Hagit (Be'er student), first interview (Yerucham), December 19, 2002; second interview (phone), March 27, 2004; third interview (phone), February 18, 2005; fourth interview (phone), September 2, 2005; fifth interview (phone), May 18, 2006.

Limor (Ma'ayan alumna), first interview (Ein Ha-Natziv), March 2, 2004.

Ma'ayan (Ma'ayan alumna), first interview (Ein Ha-Natziv), March 2, 2004.

Maya (Be'er student), first interview (Yerucham), December 19, 2002; second interview (phone), April 24, 2004; third interview (phone), February 5, 2005; fourth interview (phone), June 9, 2006; fifth interview (phone), March 23, 2007.

Miriam (Be'er student), first interview (Yerucham), March 23, 2004; second interview (phone), February 18, 2005; third interview (phone), September 2, 2005; fourth interview (phone), October 10, 2006; fifth interview (phone), March 23, 2007.

Nava (Be'er student), first interview (Yerucham), December 19, 2002; second interview (phone), March 28, 2004; third interview (phone), May 20, 2005; fourth interview (phone), February 22, 2006; fifth interview (phone), March 25, 2007.

Nili (Ma'ayan alumna), first interview (Ein Ha-Natziv), January 14, 2003.

Noa (Be'er student), first interview (Yerucham), December 19, 2002; second interview (phone), April 16, 2004; third interview (phone), February 6, 2005; fourth interview (phone), May 12, 2006; fifth interview (phone), March 25, 2007.

Noga (Hadas student), first interview (Jerusalem), January 1, 2003; second interview (phone), March 12, 2004; third interview (phone), February 11, 2005; fourth interview (phone), February 22, 2006; fifth interview (phone), March 10, 2007.

Orit (Hadas student), first interview (Jerusalem), January 1, 2003; second interview (phone), March 12, 2004; third interview (phone), February 5, 2005; fourth interview (phone), September 2, 2005; fifth interview (phone), February 22, 2006; sixth interview (phone), April 11, 2007.

Sarit (Ma'ayan alumna), first interview (Ein Ha-Natziv), January 14, 2003.

Sharon (Hadas student), first interview (Jerusalem), January 1, 2003; second interview (phone), August 30, 2004; third interview (phone), May 6, 2005; fourth interview (phone), March 10, 2006.

Tamar (Hadas alumna), first interview (Jerusalem), February 25, 2004.

Ya'ara (Ma'ayan student), first interview (Ein Ha-Natziv), March 2, 2004; second interview (phone), February 4, 2005; third interview (phone), March 27, 2006.

Yael (Hadas student), first interview (Jerusalem), February 25, 2004; second interview (phone), February 13, 2005; third interview (phone), August 27, 2005; fourth interview (phone), April 22, 2006; fifth interview (phone), October 8, 2007.

Mekhinot Students Cited (Pseudonyms, in Alphabetical Order)

Aviad (Eli student), first interview (phone), July 15, 2004; second interview (phone), May 14, 2005.

Avihu (Yatir student), first interview (Beit Yatir), March 17, 2004; second interview (phone), April 14, 2005; third interview (phone), July 7, 2006.

Benny (Atzmona student), first interview (Efrat), July 29, 2003; second interview (Efrat), July 18, 2004; third interview (phone), March 12, 2005; fourth interview (phone), May 12, 2006; fifth interview (phone), October 7, 2007.

Danny (Yatir student), first interview (Beit Yatir), March 17, 2004; second interview (phone), May 13, 2005.

Dor (Atzmona student), first interview (phone), May 15, 2004; second interview (phone), May 7, 2005; third interview (phone), April 9, 2006; fourth interview (phone), May 19, 2007.

Eran (Rosh Pina student), first interview (Rosh Pina), March 16, 2004; second interview (phone), March 11, 2005; third interview (phone), April 7, 2006; fourth interview (phone), June 15, 2007.

Evyatar (Atzmona student), first interview (phone), May 30, 2004; second interview (phone), May 27, 2005; third interview (phone), July 12, 2006.

Matan (Eli alumnus), first interview (Alon Shvut), March 11, 2004.

Micha (Eli student), first interview (phone), August 31, 2003; second interview (phone), June 29, 2004; third interview (phone), March 12, 2005; fourth interview (phone), September 6, 2005; fifth interview (phone), May 7, 2006; sixth interview (phone), June 16, 2007.

Nitai (Eli student), first interview (phone), June 25, 2003; second interview (phone), April 30, 2004; third interview (phone), March 4, 2005; fourth interview (phone), May 12, 2006.

Noach (Yatir student), first interview (Beit Yatir), November 6, 2002; second interview (phone), May 2, 2004.

Ophir (Yatir alumnus), first interview (phone), July 30, 2004.

Refael (Rosh Pina student), first interview (Rosh Pina), March 25, 2003; second interview (phone), May 9, 2004; third interview (phone), March 20, 2006; fourth interview (phone), August 18, 2006; fifth interview (phone), May 11, 2007.

Shachar (Atzmona student), first interview (phone), July 14, 2003; second interview (phone), July 20, 2004; third interview (phone), March 10, 2005; fourth interview (phone), May 14, 2006; fifth interview (phone), August 8, 2007.

Shimon (Yatir student), first interview (Beit Yatir), November 6, 2002; second interview (phone), April 16, 2004; third interview (phone), March 6, 2005; fourth interview (phone), April 10, 2006; fifth interview (phone), May 13, 2007.

Tzur (Eli student), first interview (phone), June 24, 2003; second interview (phone), May 2, 2004; third interview (phone), May 6, 2005; fourth interview (phone), July 1, 2006; fifth interview (phone), December 12, 2007.

Uri (Rosh Pina student), first interview (Rosh Pina), March 16, 2004; second interview (phone), March 18, 2005; third interview (phone), April 10, 2006; fourth interview (phone), May 20, 2007.

Yaniv (Rosh Pina student), first interview (Rosh Pina), March 25, 2003; second interview (phone), April 7, 2004; third interview (phone), March 11, 2005; fourth interview (phone), September 15, 2006.

Yinon (Yatir student), first interview (Beit Yatir), November 6, 2002; second interview (phone), October 22, 2004; third interview (phone), May 27, 2005; fourth interview (phone), April 22, 2006; fifth interview (phone), December 10, 2007.

Yochai (Atzmona alumnus), first interview (phone), August 2, 2003.

Yoni (Eli student), first interview (phone), July 30, 2004; second interview (phone), May 27, 2005; third interview (phone), May 5, 2006; fourth interview (phone), May 13, 2007.

Shiluv Students Cited (Pseudonyms, in Alphabetical Order)

Asaf (Ma'ale Gilboa student), first interview (Ma'ale Gilboa), January 14, 2003; second interview (phone), May 21, 2004; third interview (phone), February 19, 2005; fourth interview (phone), April 15, 2006.

Aviv (Ma'ale Gilboa graduate in uniform), first interview (phone), June 8, 2004.

Carmel (Ma'ale Gilboa alumnus), first interview (Jerusalem), September 14, 2003.

Chen (Ma'ale Gilboa alumnus), first interview (phone), June 8, 2004.

Gadi (Ma'ale Gilboa alumnus), first interview (Ma'ale Gilboa), January 14, 2003.

Gil (Ma'ale Gilboa student), first interview (Ma'ale Gilboa), January 14, 2003; second interview (phone), May 21, 2004; third interview (phone), February 19, 2005.

Idan (Ma'ale Gilboa student), first interview (Ma'ale Gilboa), March 2, 2004; second interview (phone), February 27, 2005; third interview (phone), August 26, 2005; fourth interview (phone), March 17, 2006; fifth interview (phone), July 20, 2007.

Michael (Ma'ale Gilboa student), first interview (Ma'ale Gilboa), January 14, 2003; second interview (phone), May 21, 2004; third interview (phone), February 25, 2005; fourth interview (phone), March 24, 2006; fifth interview (phone), September 20, 2007.

Nadav (Ma'ale Gilboa student), first interview (Ma'ale Gilboa), January 14, 2003; second interview (Efrat), June 4, 2004; third interview (Efrat), February 26, 2005; fourth interview (Jerusalem), July 14, 2006; fifth interview (Jerusalem), August 13, 2007; sixth interview (personal emails), December 2007.

Nir (Ein Tzurim student), first interview (Ein Tzurim), January 9, 2003; second interview (phone), May 15, 2004; third interview (phone), February 21, 2005; fourth interview (phone), August 4, 2006; fifth interview (phone), August 10, 2007.

Ronny (Ma'ale Gilboa alumnus), first interview (Ma'ale Gilboa), March 2, 2004.

Shaul (Ein Tzurim alumnus), during military service, first interview (Ein Tzurim), May 4, 2004.

Tal (Ein Tzurim student), first interview (Ein Tzurim), January 9, 2003; second interview (phone), May 14, 2004; third interview (phone), February 19, 2005; fourth interview (phone), September 4, 2005; fifth interview (phone), March 31, 2006; sixth interview (phone), July 17, 2007.

Yoav (Ein Tzurim student), first interview (Ein Tzurim), January 9, 2003; second interview (phone), May 21, 2004; third interview (phone), March 4, 2005; fourth interview (phone), June 23, 2006; fifth interview (phone), December 13, 2007.

Junior Officers Cited (Pseudonyms, in Alphabetical Order)

Lieutenant Avichai (team commander, MAGLAN [Special Forces unit, infantry]), first interview (phone), October 15, 2004.

Lieutenant Barak (deputy company commander, NAHAL Brigade [infantry]), first interview (phone), July 27, 2003.

Second Lieutenant Chaim (platoon commander, Givati Brigade [infantry]), first interview (phone), August 10, 2003.

Captain David (senior instructor, Education Corps [comparable to a company commander in an infantry unit]), first interview (Havat Ha-Shomer base), July 15, 2003.

Lieutenant Didi (platoon commander, Haruv [infantry]), first interview (phone), July 14, 2003.

Lieutenant Dikla (education officer), first interview (Havat Ha-Shomer base), July 15, 2003.

Corporal Eli (company clerk, Netzach Yehuda Battalion, NAHAL Haredi [infantry]), first interview (phone), May 29, 2005.

Lieutenant Gidon (team commander, NAHAL Reconnaissance Company [infantry]), first interview (phone), July 30, 2004.

Lieutenant Idan (platoon commander, Armored Corps), first interview (phone), July 3, 2004

Second Lieutenant Ido (team commander, MAGLAN [Special Forces unit, infantry]), first interview (phone), July 30, 2004.

Lieutenant Nadav (team commander, NAHAL Reconnaissance Company [infantry]), first interview (phone), May 21, 2003.

Lieutenant Natan (deputy company commander, NAHAL Reconnaissance Company [infantry]), first interview (Jerusalem), September 14, 2003.

Captain Noam (company commander, Armored Corps), first interview (phone), July 12, 2004.

Second Lieutenant Orly (education officer), first interview (Havat Ha-Shomer base), July 1, 2003.

Second Lieutenant Rachamim (platoon commander, Givati Brigade [infantry]), first interview (phone), August 10, 2003; second interview (phone), January 27, 2004.

Sergeant Rami (NCO, squad commander, Netzach Yehuda Battalion, NAHAL Haredi [infantry]), first interview (phone), March 3, 2005.

Lieutenant Shimon (company commander, Netzach Yehuda Battalion, NAHAL Haredi [infantry]), first interview (phone), July 11, 2003.

Second Lieutenant Udi (company commander, Armored Corps), first interview (phone), July 19, 2003.

Sergeant Yehuda (NCO, Netzach Yehuda Battalion, NAHAL Haredi [infantry]), first interview (phone), February 26, 2005.

Lieutenant Yehudit (commander, Training and Command Course, Education Corps), first interview (phone), July 27, 2003.

Captain Yigal (company commander, Armored Corps), first interview (phone), July 25, 2003.

Lieutenant Yishai (team commander, Paratroopers' Reconnaissance Company [infantry]), first interview (phone), May 28, 2004.

DATA AND PERSONAL CORRESPONDENCE

Data

Association of Hesder Yeshivot (Igud), general numbers of all Hesder students during the years 1991–2003; 2003–2007.

Association of Mekhinot, student lists, 1988–2007.

Association of Mekhinot, "Mitzui leKtzuna ulePikud miKerev Bogrei haMekhinot haKdam Tzvaiyot: Mikhtav me-et Udi Drori, Ozer Bakhir leGiyus, Misrad haBitachon, leRashei haMekhinot" (Fulfillment of Officer and NCO Potential of Mekhinot Graduates: A Letter from Udi Drori, Senior Aid for Conscription Matters, Ministry of Defense, to the Heads of the Mekhinot), February 22, 2006.

Birkat Moshe (Ma'ale Adumim), Hesder yeshiva, student lists, 1977–2002.

Ha-Golan (Chispin), Hesder yeshiva, student lists, 1977–2002.

Har Etzion (Alon Shvut), Hesder yeshiva, student lists, 1990–2002.

Ma'alot Ya'akov (Ma'a lot), Hesder yeshiva, student lists, 1977–2003.

Midbara ke-Eden (Mitzpe Ramon), Hesder yeshiva, student lists, 1999–2003.

Midreshet Be'er (Yerucham), *midrasha*, Be'er student list, 2002–2003.

Midreshet haBanot beEin Ha-Natziv (Ein Ha-Natziv), Ma'ayan student lists, 1998–2003.

Midreshet Lindenbaum (Jerusalem), *midrasha*, Hadas student lists, 1998–2003.

Ozem (Atzmona), Mekhina, student lists, 1997–2003.

Petach Tikva, Hesder yeshiva, student lists, 1999–2003.

Yatir (Beit Yatir), Mekhina, student lists, 2000–2004.

Yerucham, Hesder yeshiva, student lists, 1998–2002.

Yeshivat Ha-Kibbutz Ha-Dati (Ein Tzurim), Shiluv student lists, 1986–2003.

Yeshivat Ha-Kibbutz Ha-Dati (Ma'ale Gilboa), Shiluv student lists, 1994–2003.

Personal Correspondence

Hashim, veteran of the Turkish Armed Forces, letter to author, November 1, 2004.

IDF spokesperson's office, letter to author, August 1, 2005.

Kerman, veteran of the Turkish Armed Forces, letter to author, November 10, 2004.

Lisa, wife of a U.S. Navy serviceman, correspondence with author, August 2005.

Military attaché of India in Tel Aviv, Israel, letter to author, June 20, 2005.

Sergeant Daniel, U.S. Air Force, correspondence with author, August 2005.

DOCUMENTS AND OFFICIAL INTERNAL PUBLICATIONS

Americans United for the Separation of Church and State. *Report of Americans United for Separation of Church and State on Religious Coercion and Endorsement of Religion at the United States Air Force Academy*. May 2005, accessed February 2013. http://www.au.org.

Cherlow, Rabbi Yuval. "Mipnei Ma Anu Meshartim Ba-Tzava" (Why Do We Serve in the Military). Petach Tikva yeshiva, n.d.

Drukman, Chaim. Shiur Odot Chilul Shabbat bePinui Chavat Gilad (Class on the Desecration of the Sabbath during the Evacuation of Chavat Gilad). Accessed February 2013. http://shiurim.moreshet.co.il/web/shiur.asp?id=338.

European Court of Human Rights. "Third Section, Partial Decision as to the Admissibility of Application No. 45824/99" by Ziya Çelikates and Others against Turkey. October 3, 2002, accessed February 2013. http://www.echr.coe.int/.

European Court of Human Rights. "Third Section, Final Decision as to the Admissibility of Application no. 45824/99" by Sedat Şen and Others against Turkey. July 8, 2003, accessed February 2013. http://www.echr.coe.int/.

IDF Archive 177/896/03. Lishkat Rosh Agaf Koach Adam, "Sikum Forum—'Ha-Shiluv Ha-Ra'ui'" (Office of Human Resources, "Minutes of the Meeting for the Proper Integration"). March 4, 2001.

IDF Archive 177/896/03. DOCH miYeshivat Segel BAHAD 16, Beit haSefer leChilutz veHatzala im Rashei Yeshivot Ha-Hesder shel Sha'alablim veHaRav haPikudi: "Va'adat Muda'ut Ben haYeshiva, Diyun Mispar 1—Sikum" (The Committee for Awareness [of the Needs] of the Yeshiva Student, Discussion No. 1—Summary). June 11, 2000.

IDF Archive 177/896/03. Yechezkel Ya'akovson. "Sikum Mifgashim Va'adat BENISH BAHAD 16" (Summary of Meetings between the Ben Yeshiva Committee and Instruction Base 16). n.d.

Indian Army. *Additional Directorate General Recruiting and Publicity*. Chapter 31 and Appendix A. Accessed February 2013. http://indianarmy.nic.in/rtg.doc.

Knesset. Protocols of the First Knesset, no. 2 (1949).

Law of the Preservice Preparatory Seminaries (Mekhinot), 2008. Accessed June 2011. shatil.org.il/files/%20תוניכמה%20הקדם%20תויאבצ%202008.doc. And its proposed amendments for the year 2010. Accessed June 2011. www.knesset.gov.il/privatelaw/data/18/2354.rtf.

Ministry of Education and Culture and the Ministry of Defense. *Mekhinot Kdam-Tzvaiyot* (Premilitary Service Preparatory Seminaries). Jerusalem: Ministry of Education, 2002.

Ministry of Education and Culture. Pniya laTzibur beInyan Kavanat Misrad haChinukh haTarbut veHaSport liTmoch beLimud Torani ubePe'ulot Meyuchadot leMosadot Toraniyim (Public Appeal Regarding the Intention of the Ministry for Education, Culture and Sports to Support Torahic Study and Special Programs for Torah Institutions). 2004.

Sabato, Rabbi Chaim. "Sichat Idud Shel haRav Chaim Sabato leTalmidim" (Encouragement from Rabbi Chaim Sabato to Students). Taped and transcribed by Tuvia Ben-David, August 2005.

State of Israel. *Budget for the Year 2000—Ministry for Religious Affairs*. Accessed June 2009. http://www.mof.gov.il/budget2000/.

State of Israel. *Budget for the Year 2003—Ministry for Religious Affairs*. Accessed June 2009. http://147.237.72.152/magic93scripts/mgrqispi93.dll?APPNAME=budget&PRGNAME=doc3&ARGUMENTS=-N2003,-A22.

Stern, Elazar. "Letter from the Head of the Manpower Division to Hesder Conscripts and Soldiers." May 27, 2007, accessed June 2009. IDF website, http://www.aka.idf.il/giyus/general/?CatID=32282&DocID=62402).

Supreme Court of Israel. Leah Shakdiel vs. the Minister for Religious Affairs, Case 153/87 (1987).

Supreme Court of Israel. Alice Miller vs. the Minister of Defense and others, Case 4541/94 (1994).

Supreme Court of Israel. Nishmat vs. the Minister for Religious Affairs, Case 744/95 (1995).

Supreme Court of Israel. Ohr Torah Stone vs. the Minister for Religious Affairs, Case 6318/99 (1999).

Supreme Court of Israel. Laura Milo vs. the Minister of Defense, Case 2383/04 (2004).

Supreme Court of Israel. 63 Students of the Har Brakha Hesder Yeshiva vs. the Minister of Defense, the Hesder Yeshiva's Association (Igud Yeshivot Ha-Hesder). Official Response of the State Attorney Presenting the Position of the Ministry of Defense. Case 2/10 (January 2010).

United Catholic Church. *Military Chaplain Guidelines*. 2002, accessed June 2009. http://usmarrigelaws.com.

United States Department of Defense. *Department of Defense Directive Number 1300.17*. February 3, 1988, certified current as of November 21, 2003.

United States Supreme Court. Goldman vs. Weinberger, 475 U.S. 503 (1986). Accessed June 2009. http://caselaw.lp.findlaw.com/scripts/getcase.pl?court=us&vol=475&invol=503.

Watchtower Information Service. "US Army policy letter regarding Jehovah's Witnesses and blood." July 2002, accessed June 2009. http://www.watchtowerinformationservice.org/milblood.htm.

CIRCULARS AND BULLETINS

Alon Kesher, circular for Ma'ale Adumin Hesder yeshiva students, accessed June 2009, http://www.birkatmoshe.org.il/index.asp?id=106.

Be-Ahava uBe-Emuna, 2001–2005, weekly Tora bulletin.

Daf Kesher, Har Etzion Hesder yeshiva circular, accessed February 2013, http://www.etzion.org.il/dk/other.htm.

El HaMa'ayan, newsletter published for members of the Ma'ayan program.

HaMa'agal HaYarok, circular for Ma'ale Gliboa students, accessed February 2013, http://www.maalegilboa.org/.

Shiluvon, newsletter published for students of the Religious Kibbutz yeshiva at Ein Tzurim, accessed June 2009, http://www.ykd.co.il/hebrew/hebrew.htm.

NEWSPAPERS: DAILIES, WEEKLIES, MONTHLIES, AND ONLINE PAPERS

Amudim, 2000–2005, monthly, the Religious Kibbutz official publication, printed edition.

Arutz Sheva/INN, 2002–2005, daily, online edition.

Besheva, 2002–2010, weekly, printed edition.

De'ot, 2002–2008, monthly, Ne'emani Tora veAvoda official publication, printed edition.

Haaretz, 1999–2011, daily, online, and printed editions.

HaTzofe, 2000–2005, weekly, online, and printed editions.

Ma'ariv/NRG, 1999–2011, daily, printed, and online editions.

Makor Rishon, 2002–2010, weekly, printed, and online editions.

Yediot Aharonot/Ynet, 2000–2011, daily, printed, and online editions.

BOOKS

Amital, Rabbi Yehuda. *veHa'aretz Natan liVnei Adam: Pirkei Hagut veChinukh* (And the Earth He Gave to Man: Jewish Values in a Changing World). Alon Shvut: Mikhlelet Hertzog, 2005.

Aviner, Rabbi Shlomo. *Tzniut beTzava* (Modesty in the Military). Jerusalem: Makhon Ma'arakhot Yisrael, 1999.

———. *miChayil el Chayil: Inyanei Tzava* (From Strength to Strength: Military Matters). Parts I, II. 2nd printing. Bet El: Sifriyat Hava, 2000.

———. *Al Diglo* (On His Flag). Jerusalem: Sifriyat Hava, 2000b.

Bar Ilan, Shaul. *Kaftor haPeleh* (The Magic Button). N.p.: Manhigut Yehudit, 2005.

Barth, Shaul, and Itzchak Barth, eds. *BeSe'arat haAkira* (In the Storm of Eviction). Tel Aviv: Yedioth Ahronoth, 2007.

Baumgarten, Albert I. *The Flourishing of Jewish Sects in the Maccabean Era: An Interpretation.* Leiden: Brill, 1997.

Ben-Shlomo, Rabbi Zekharia. *Nohal Achid* (One Protocol). Sha'albim: Oz, 1986.

Berger, Peter L., and Richard John Neuhaus. *To Empower People: From State to Civil Society.* 2nd ed. Edited by Michael Novak. Washington, DC: AEI Press, 1996.

Binyamin, Moshe, and Yair Cohen. *Maftechot leHilkhot Tzava* (Index of Military Responsa). Atzmona: Mekhina Toranit leTzahal Otzem, 2000.

Blackham, H. J. *Religion in Modern Society.* London: Constable, 1966.

Breuer, Mordechai. *Ohalei Torah: HaYeshiva, Tavnita veTolodtiaha* (Ohalei Torah: The Yeshiva, Its Mode and History). Jerusalem: Merkaz Shazar, 2004.

Carkoğlu, Ali, and Binnaz Toprak. *Religion, Society and Politics in Turkey, 2000.* Istanbul: TESEV, 2000. Accessed June 2009. http://www.tesev.org.tr/eng.

Cohen, Stuart A. *The Scroll or the Sword? Dilemmas of Religion and Military Service in Israel.* Amsterdam: Harwood, 1997.

———. *Israel and its Army: From Cohesion to Confusion.* New York: Routledge, 2008.

Cohen, Tova, and Yisrael Rich. *Etgarim beChinukh habit haDatit caIdan haModerni* (Challenges in the Education of Modern Orthodox Young Women). Discussion Papers, no. 3. Ramat Gan: The Fanya Gottesfeld Heller Center for the Study of Women in Judaism, Stern Institute for the Study and Advancement of Religious Education, Women in Judaism, 2000.

Cohen, Yehezkel. *Giyus kaHalakha: Al Shichrur Talmidei Yeshivot miTZAHAL* (Giyus kaHalakha: On the Exemption of Yeshiva Students from the IDF). Jerusalem: Ne'emanei Torah vaAvoda, 1994.

Colton, Timothy J. *Commissars, Commanders, and Civilian Authority: The Structure of Soviet Military Politics.* Cambridge, MA: Harvard University Press, 1979.

Cordesman, Anthony. *Iran's Military Forces: 1988–1993.* Washington, DC: CSIS, 1994.

Coser, Lewis A. *Greedy Institutions: Patterns of Undivided Commitment.* New York: Free Press, 1974.

Drazin, Israel, and Cecil B. Currey. *For God and Country: The History of a Constitutional Challenge to the Army Chaplaincy.* New Jersey: KTAV, 1995.

Drukman, Rabbi Chaim. *Zeh haYom Asah Hashem!: Berurim beYachas leTrumat Medinat Yisrael uLeMitzvat haHodaya laHashem beChagigot Yom HaAtzmaut* (This Day God Has Made!: On the Contribution of the State of Israel and the Obligation of Giving Thanks to God by Celebrating Independence Day). Merkaz Shapira: The HaMakhon haTorani Or Etzion, HaKeren LePituach Netzrim, 2006.

Eisenstadt, Michael. *Iranian Military Power: Capabilities and Intentions.* Policy Paper #42. Washington, DC: The Washington Institution for Near East Policy, 1996.

Eligur, Banu. *The Mobilization of Political Islam in Turkey.* Cambridge: Cambridge University Press, 2010.

Elor, Tamar. *Ba-Pessach Ha-ba* (Next Pessach: Literacy and Identity of Young Religious Zionist Women). Tel Aviv: Am Oved, 1998.

Gal, Reuven, ed. *Dat, Politika veTzava: HaIm TZAHAL Natun beTahalikhei Hadata?* (Religion, Politics and the Military: Is the IDF undergoing Religionization?). Round table discussion proceedings, Kinneret Center for Society, Security and Peace, April 14, 2010.

Gal, Reuven, and Tamir Libel, eds. *Bein haKipa laKumta: Dat, Politika veTzava beYisrael* (Between the Yarmulke and the Beret: Religion, Politics and the Military in Israel). Ben Shemen: Modan, 2012.

Goffman, Erving. *Asylums: Essays on the Social Situation of Mental Patients and Other Inmates.* New York: Doubleday, 1961.

Goren, Rabbi Shlomo. *Meshiv Milchama: SHOOT beInyanei Tzava, Milchama uBitachon* (Meshiv Milchama: Responsa on Military, War and Security Matters). Vols. 1–3. Jerusalem: HaIdra Raba, 1994–1996.

Grimes, Roland L. *Deeply into the Bone: Re-Inventing Rites of Passage.* Berkley: University of California Press, 2000.

Harel, Amos. *Teda Kol Em Ivriya: Kavim leDmuto shel TZAHAL haChadash* (The Face of the New IDF). Or Yehuda: Kinneret, Zmora-Bitan, Dvir, 2013.

Hassan, Hussein D. *Iran: Ethnic and Religious Minorities.* CRS Reports for Congress, May 27, 2007. Accessed February 2013. http://www.fas.org/sgp/crs/mideast/RL34021.pdf.

Heilman, Samuel C. *Synagogue Life: A Study in Symbolic Interaction.* Chicago: University of Chicago Press, 1973.

———. *The People of the Book: Drama, Fellowship and Religion.* Chicago: University of Chicago Press, 1987.

———. *Defenders of the Faith: Inside Ultra-Orthodox Jewry.* New York: Shocken Books, 1992.

Helman, Sara. "HaSeruv leSharet baTzava keNisayon leHagdara Muchsheet shel Ezrachut" (Refusal to Serve in the Military as a Tangible Attempt to Classify Citizenship). PhD diss., Hebrew University, 1993.

Horowitz, Dan, and Moshe Lissak. *Metzukot Be-Otopiya* (Israel as an Overburdened Polity). Tel Aviv: Am Oved, 1990.

Jenkins, Gareth. *Context and Circumstance: The Turkish Military and Politics.* Adelphi Paper no. 337. London: IISS, 2001.

Kampinsky, Aharon (Roni). "Dat, Tzavaa VeHevra BeYisrael: Tmurot BeItzuvah UVeDarkah Shel HaRabanut HaTzva'it" (Religion, Military and Society in Israel: Changes in the Development of the "Rabanut Tsvait"). PhD diss., Bar Ilan University, 2007.

Kanaaneh, Rhoda Ann. *Surrounded: Palestinian Soldiers in the Israeli Military*. Stanford: Stanford University Press, 2009.

Katzman, Kenneth. *The Warriors of Islam: Iran's Revolutionary Guard*. Boulder, CO: Westview Press, 1993.

Kelner, Yosef. *Pluralism, Fanatisism veKlaliyut: HaKriteryon laEmet, haKriteryon laMusar, Shiurim sheNe-emru beTASHNAT beMekhina haYeshivatit laChayim beEli* (Pluralism, Fanaticism and Generality: Criteria for Truth, Criteria for Ethics, Classes Given During 1999 at the Program for Graduates of Eli). Jerusalem: Netiv haEmuna, 2001.

Kidder, Louise H., and Charles M. Judd. *Research Methods in Social Relations*. New York: Holt, Rinehart and Winston, 1986.

Koffman, Rabbi Itchak. *HaTzava kaHalakha: Hilkhot Michama veTzava* (The Proper Military: Laws of War and Military). Jerusalem: Kol Mevaser, 1994.

Krim, Rabbi Eyal M. *Kishrei Milchama: She'elot beInyanei Halakha baTzava* (Ties of War: Responsa on Matters of Halakha in the Military). Vols. 1–3. Jerusalem: Makhon Ma'arakhot Yisrael, 2000–2001.

Kundu, Arpurba. *Militarism in India: The Army and Civil Society in Consensus*. London: Tauris, 1998.

Lasloi, Avraham, and Yisrael Rich. *Seker Talmidei Kitot Y"B baChinuck haMamlakhti Dati— TASHNAT* (Twelfth Grade Students Survey among Public Religious High Schools: A Research Report). Ramat Gan: Research Institution for the Study of Religious Education, Bar Ilan University, 2001.

Levy, Yagil. *Tzava Akher leYisrael: Militarizm Chomrani beYisrael* (The Other Army of Israel: Materialist Militarism in Israel). Tel Aviv: Yediot Achronot, 2003.

———. *miTzva haAm leTzva haPeriferiyot* (From "People's Army" to "Army of the Peripheries"). Jerusalem: Carmel, 2007.

McCracken, Grant. *The Long Interview*. Newbury Park: Sage, 1988.

Min Ha-Har, Rabbi Shlomo. *Dinei Tzava uMilchama* (Laws of the Military and War). Jerusalem: Haskel, 1972.

Naor, Aryeh. *Eretz Yisrael haShlema: Emuna uMediniyut* (Greater Israel: Belief and Policy). Haifa: University of Haifa, 2001.

Nevo, Baruch, and Yael Shor. *Kvod haAdam beTZAHAL* (Dignity of Man in the Israel Defense Forces). The Army-Society Project of the IDF and the Israel Democracy Center. Jerusalem: Israel Democracy Center, 2001.

———. *Nashim beTZAHAL* (Women in the Israel Defense Forces). The Army-Society Project of the IDF and the Israel Democracy Center. Jerusalem: Israel Democracy Center, 2001b.

———. *haChozeh ben TZAHAL laChevra haYisraelit: Sherut haChova* (The Contract between the IDF and Israeli Society: Conscription). The Army-Society Project of the IDF and the Israel Democracy Center. Jerusalem: Israel Democracy Center, 2002.

———. *Kol ham Tzava?: Sherut haMiluim beYisrael* (The People's Army?: The Reserves in Israel). The Army-Society Project of the IDF and the Israel Democracy Center. Jerusalem: Israel Democracy Center, 2002b.

Novak, Michael, ed. *Democracy and Mediating Structures: A Theological Inquiry*. Washington, DC: American Enterprise Institute for Public Policy Research, 1980.

Peled, Alon. *A Question of Loyalty: Military Manpower Policy in Multiethnic States*. Ithaca: Cornell University Press, 1998.

Peres, Yochanan, and Eliezer Ben-Rafael. *Kirva U-Meriva: Shsai'm Ba-Hevra Ha-Yisraelit* (Cleavages in Israeli Society). Tel Aviv: Am Oved, 2007.

Rabinovitch, Rabbi Nachum Eliezer. *Melumadei Milchama: SHOOT BeInyanei Tzava uBitachon* (Melumadei Milchama: Responsa on Military and Security Matters). Ma'ale Adumim: Maaliyot, 1993.

Ravitzky, Aviezer. *Ha-Ketz Ha-Meguleh Ve-Medinat Ha-Yehudim* (Redemption and the Jewish State). Tel Aviv: Am Oved, 1993.

Rimon, Rabbi Yosef Tzvi. *Tzava kaHalakha* (Proper/Halakhic Military). Alon Shvut: Yeshivat Har Etzion, 2007.

Ronski, Rabbi Avi. *keChitzim beYad Gibor* (As Arrows in the Hands of the Brave). Vols. 1–3. Jerusalem, 1996.

Rosen, Stephen Peter. *Societies and Military Power: India and Its Armies*. Ithaca: Cornell University Press, 1996.

Rosenberg-Friedman, Lilach. *Mehapkhaniyot Be'al Korchan: Nashim uMigdar baTziyonut haDatit biTkufat haYishuv* (Unwilling Revolutionaries: Women and Gender in Religious Zionism in the Yishuv Period). Jerusalem: Yad Ben Zvi, 2005.

Rosman-Stollman, Elisheva. "Tzava veDat keMivnim Tov'aniyim: HaTziyonut haDatit veTZAHAL" (Religion and the Military as Greedy Frameworks: Religious Zionism and the Israel Defense Forces). PhD diss., Bar Ilan University, 2005.

Ross, Tamar. *Expanding the Palace of Torah: Orthodoxy and Feminism*. Waltham, MA.: Brandeis University Press, 2004.

Rubin, Mishael. *haMorim baKeshet* (Teachers of the Bow). Kiryat Arba, 1998.

Sadan, Rabbi Eli. *VeYehi Yadav Emuna: Shiurim beNoseh Chevra, Medina veDemokratiya sheNitnu beBeit haMidrash "Bnei David" beEli* (Teachings on Society, State and Democracy Given at the Bnei David Beit Midrash in Eli). Eli: private publishing house, 2001.

———. *Ne'emanutaynu laTorah velaTzava: Sicha Me'et haRav Eli Sadan SHLITA beDvar haYachas lePkudat Pinui Yeshuvim Yehudiyim* (Our Loyalty to Torah and the Military: A Discussion by Rabbi Eli Sadan Regarding Orders to Evacuate Jewish Settlements). Eli: Makhon Binyan haTorah, 2005.

Sasson-Levy, Orna. *Zehuyot beMadim: Gavriyut veNashiyut baTzava haYisraeli* (Identities in Uniform: Masculinity and Femininity in the Israeli Military). Jerusalem: Magnes, 2006.

Schwartz, Dov. *Ha-Tziyonut Ha-Datit: Ben Higayon Le-Meshihiyut* (Religious Zionism: Between Logic and Messianism). Tel Aviv: Am Oved, 1999.

Shagar, Rabbi. *Kelim Shvurim: Torah veTziyonut Datit beSviva Postmodernit* (Broken Vessels: Torah and Religious Zionism in a Postmodern Environment). Efrat: Yeshivat Siach, 2004.

Shankland, David. *Islam and Society in Turkey*. Cambridgeshire, UK: Eothen Press, 1999.

Sheffer, Gabriel, et al., eds. *Tzava sheYesh Lo Medina?: Mabat Mechodash al Yachasei haTchum haBitchoni vehaEzrachi beYisrael* (An Army that Has a State?: New Approaches to Civil-Security Relations in Israel). Jerusalem: Carmel, 2008.

Sheleg, Yair. *HaDatiyim haChadashim* (The New Religious Jews). Jerusalem: Keter, 2000.

Shilo, Margalit, ed. *Lehiyyot Isha Yehudiya—Divrei haKenes haBen-Leumi haRishon: Isha veYahaduta* (To Be a Jewish Woman—Proceedings of the First International Conference: A Woman and Her Judaism). Jerusalem: Kolech, 2001.

Slomovitz, Albert Isaac. *The Fighting Rabbis*. New York: New York University Press, 1999.

Stampfer, Shaul. *HaYeshiva haLitait beHithavuta* (The Lithuanian Yeshiva during Its Creation). Jerusalem: Merkaz Shazar, 2005.

de Toqueville, Alexis. *Democracy in America*. Vol. 2. New York: Vintage Books, 1990.

Urbach, Uri. *Saba Sheli Haya Rav: Lexikon Dati-Chiloni* (My Grandfather Was a Rabbi: A Religious-Secular Lexicon). Jerusalem: Keter, 2002.

Wahrhaftig, Zerach. *Chuka leYisrael—Dat uMedina* (A Constitution for Israel—Religion and State). Jerusalem: Mesilot, 1988.

Weinberger, Naomi, and Stuart Cohen. *The Right to Protest the Dismantling of Jewish Settlements: Study Guide for Dean's Table Discussion*. New York: Yeshiva College Book Project, 1999.

Weinberger, Sarel, and Amichai Beitner, eds. *HaChazit sheBaOref: Asufat Ma'amarim laChayal sheBeOref haChevra hsYisreelit* (Articles for the Noncombat Soldier in Israeli Society). Bet El: Sifriyat Bet El, 2007.

Wengraf, Tom. *Qualitative Research Interviewing: Biographic Narrative and Semi-Structured Methods*. London: Sage, 2001.

Wolansky, Rabbi Oded. *Even Yisrael*. Part 3. Jerusalem: Hosen Yeshuot, 1997.

Wolff, Kurt H., ed. and trans. *The Sociology of Georg Simmel*. Glencoe, IL: The Free Press, 1950.

Yavuz, M. Hakan. *Islamic Political Identity in Turkey*. Oxford: Oxford University Press, 2003.

Yisraeli, Rabbi Shaul. *Amud haYemini* (The Right-Hand Pillar). 2nd ed. Jerusalem: Eretz Hemdah, 1992.

———. *HaRabanut veHaMedina* (The Rabbinate and the State). Jerusalem: Eretz Hemdah, 2001.

Zabih, Sepher. *The Iranian Military in Revolution and War*. New York: Routledge, 1988.

ARTICLES

Ahituv, Yosef. "From the Book to the Sword: On the Proposed Image of the Israeli Army According to the Torah during the First Years of Statehood." *In Shnei Evrei haGesher: Dat uMedina beReshit Darka shel Yisrael* (Both Sides of the Bridge: Church and State during the First Years of Israel), edited by Mordechai Bar-On and Zvi Tzameret, 414–433. Jerusalem: Yad Ben-Zvi, 2002.

Ahmed, Samina. "Civil-Military Relations in India." *Regional Studies* 10, no. 3 (1992): 3–52.

Ariel, Rabbi Yaakov. "Disobeying Orders Due to a Religious Obligation or Moral Considerations." *Tchumin*, no. 4 (1983): 173–179.

Aviner, Rabbi Shlomo. "A Song of Praise for the Mekhina Student." *Be-Ahava uBe-Emuna* (9 Elul 2002): 7–8.

———. "This Army Is Ours." *Be-Ahava uBe-Emuna* (13 Tishrei 2002b): 10–12.

———. "The Religious Female Soldier." *Be-Ahava uBe-Emuna* (4 Elul 2003): 7–8.

———. "Turning the Mekhinot into Hesder Yeshivot." *Be-Ahava uBe-Emuna* (1 Cheshvan 2004): 7–8.

———. "Stop Pulling the IDF Apart." *Be-Ahava uBe-Emuna* (10 Adar Aleph 2005): 7–8.

———. "An Important Clarification." *Be-Ahava uBe-Emuna* (17 Adar Aleph 2005b): 7–8.

B. (full name withheld by journal). "The Place of Religious Soldiers in Tactical Command Posts in the IDF." *Ma'arachot*, no. 432 (August 2010): 50–57.

Bar Kokhva, Ofer. "No to Disbanding." *Daf Kesher* (Har Etzion's circular), no. 996, Truma (2005). Accessed February 2013. http://www.etzion.org.il.

Bar-Lev, Mordechai. "The Shiluv Yeshiva as a Unique Religious Kibbutz Framework." In *HaChinukh haKibbutzi beSvivato* (Kibbutz Education in Context), edited by Yuval Dror, 105–132. Tel Aviv: University of Tel Aviv, 1997.

Bartov, Hagit. "The Challenge of Bachelorhood." *Deot* 10 (2004): 28–30.

Baruch, Uzi. "A Capable Soldier Must Continue on to Command Posts." *Arutz* 7, online edition (April 21, 2008). Accessed June 2009. http://www.inn.co.il/News/News.aspx/17415.

Becker, Avichai. "The Secular Response: First Cohort." *Haaretz* (March 9, 1998): B2.

Ben-Ari, Eyal, and Edna Levy-Schreiber. "Body Building, Character Building, and Nation Building: Gender and Military Service in Israel." *Tarbut Demikratit*, 4–5 (2001): 99–130.

Ben-Haim, Avishai. "The Father, the Son, and the Battle Spirit." *Ma'ariv: Shabbat Magazine* (February 25, 2005): 25.

Berger, Peter L. "In Praise of Particularity: The Concept of Mediating Structures." *Review of Politics* 38, no. 3 (1976): 399–410.

Biernacki, Patrick, and Dan Waldorf. "Snowball Sampling: Problems and Techniques of Chain Referral Sampling." *Sociological Methods & Research* 10, no. 2 (1981): 141–163.

Bigman, Rabbi David. "Shiluv Celebrates a Decade." *Amudim* (2005): 258–259.

Block, Neil. "The Current State of Jewish Lay Leadership." *Jews in Green* (2005). Accessed June 2009. http://www.jewsingreen.com.

Bruno, Greg, and Jayshree Bajoria. "Iran's Revolutionary Guards." *Council on Foreign Relations* 25 (2007).

Budaie-Hyman, Ranit. "Khaki Skirts: The Religious Feminine Choice to Serve in the IDF." In *Ben HaKipa LeKumta* (Between the Beret and the Skullcap), edited by Reuven Gal and Tamir Libel, 549–573. Ben-Shemen: Kinneret, Modan, 2012.

"Careers." *Islamic Voice* 11–05, no. 124 (1997). Accessed April 2004. http://www.islamicvoice.com/may.97/guidance.htm.

Cherlow, Rabbi Yuval. "The Morality of Yeshiva Study versus Military Service." *Moreshet* (2002). Accessed February 2013. http://www.moreshet.co.il/web/shut/shut2.asp?id=14299.

———. "The Morality of Studying in a Hesder Yeshiva as Opposed to Military Service." *Moreshet* (November 2002b). Accessed July 2009. http://www.moreshet.co.il/web/shut/shut2/asp?id=14299.

———. "Torah Study in Hesder Yeshivot: Trends and Directions." *Shana beShana* 43 (2003): 151–172.

———. "The Obligation to Obey," *Haaretz*, online edition (February 26, 2004).

———. "The Army's Obligation." *HaTzofe*, online edition (October 14, 2004b).

Cizre, Umit. "Problems of Democratic Governance of Civil-Military Relations in Turkey and the European Union Enlargement Zone." *European Journal of Political Research* 43 (2004): 107–125.

Cohen, Asher. "Nothing Is Shattered." *NRG, Ma'ariv* online edition (September 5, 2005).

Cohen, Stuart A. "The Hesder Yeshivot in Israel: A Church-State Military Arrangement." *Journal of Church and State* 35, no. 1 (1993): 113–130.

———. "From Integration to Segregation: The Role of Religion in the Israel Defense Force." *Armed Forces and Society* 25, no. 3 (1999): 393–394.

———. "Dimensions of Tension between Religion and Military Service in Contemporary Israel." *In Military, State and Society in Israel*, edited by Daniel Maman, Eyal Ben-Ari, and Zeev Rosenhek, 186–187. Piscataway, NJ: Transaction Books, 2001.

———. "Dilemmas of Military Service in Israel: The Religious Dimension." *The Torah u-Madda Journal* 12 (2004): 1–23.

———. "Toward an Over-Subordination of the IDF?: A Change in the Relationship between the Civil and Military Echelons in Israel." *Ma'arachot* 404 (2005): 8–21.

———. "The Spiritual World of the Religious Soldier: The Testimony of the Responsa." *Psichologiya Tzvait* (Military Psychology) 5 (2006): 147–196.

"Constitution lies at heart of military supremacy in Turkey." *Yeni Şafak* (January 24, 2010). Accessed February 2003. http://yenisafak.com.tr/English/?i=237505&t=24.01.2010.

Dantes, Edmond. "The Indian Armed Forces." *Asian Defence Journal* 1 (1991): 6–15.

Don Yehiya, Eliezer. "Fundementalism Dati veRadicalizm Politi: HaYeshivot haLeumiyot beYisrael." *In Aztmaut: 50 haShanim haRishonot* (Independence: The First Fifty Years), edited by Anita Shapira, 447–451. Jerusalem: Merkaz Shazar, 1998.

Drori, Rabbi Tzfania. "The Contribution of the Hesder Yeshivot." *Kovetz haTziyonut haDatit* 3 (2001): 762–769.

Edelman, Shmuel. "The Head Is Covered and So Is the Home Front." *Besheva* (April 22, 2004): 26.

Eitam, Noa. "A Mekhina for the Ordinary People." *Musaf HaTzofe*, online edition (January 16, 2004).

Ekstein, Chaim. "Hesder in Graphs." *Olam Katan* (Weekend Torah Circular) 403 (2013): 10–11.

Entessar, Nader. "The Military and Politics in the Islamic Republic of Iran." In *Post-Revolutionary Iran*, edited by Hooshang Amirahmadi and Manoucher Parvin, 56–74. Boulder, CO: Westview Press, 1988

Ettinger, Yair. "The Rabbis Agree on One Thing: The State Is Acting against the Religious Sector." *Haaretz*, online edition (February 7, 2006).

Friedman, Matti. "The Back Page: Everyone needs a corner of their own, but do they need to stay in that corner?" *The Jerusalem Report* (February 21, 2005): 48.

Galili, Lily. "Female Conscientious Objectors Who Wish to Do National Service Face Rejection." *Haaretz*, online edition (July 6, 2004).

Ghose, Jayanti. "In the line of fire." *The Times of India* (September 9, 2002). Accessed June 2009. http://timesofindia.indiatimes.com/articleshow/21650295.cms.

Goldstein, Kenneth. "Getting in the Door: Sampling and Completing Elite Interviews." *Political Science and Politics* 35 (2002): 669–672.

Goodman, Rabbi Mordechai. "Toward a New Model for Hesder Yeshivot." *Tzohar*, no. 8 (Fall 2002): 151–169.

Greenberg, Chanan and Efrat Weiss. "The Chief of Staff Has Decided: The 'Kisufim Disobeyers' Platoon Will Be Disbanded." *YNET, Yediot Ahronot* online edition (August 17, 2005). Accessed June 2009. http://www.ynet.co.il/Ext/App/TalkBack/CdaView OpenTalkBack/1,11382,L-3113899-4,00.html.

Greiner, Eyal. "The Meaning of Service." In *HaChazit sheBaOref: Asufat Ma'amarim laChayal sheBeOref haChevra hsYisreelit* (Articles for the Noncombat Soldier in Israeli Society), edited by Sarel Weinberger and Amichai Beitner, CD-ROM, Part 1. Bet El: Sifriyat Bet El, 2007.

Grizim, Limor. "The IDF Is the Best, Sister." *Musaf HaTzofe*, online edition (January 25, 2004).

Gross, Netty C. "A Hilltop Coming-of-Age." *The Jerusalem Report* (December 2, 2002): 38–40.

Guttel, Nerya. "The Military Rabbinate's Window of Opportunity." *HaTzofe* (October 20, 2000).

Gvaryahu, Amit. "Your Blemish Is Far Worse." *Daf Kesher* (Har Etzion's circular), no. 996, Truma (2005). Accessed June 2009. http://www.etzion.org.il.

Haber, Shmuel. "Hesder From the Onset." Karnei Shomron Hesder Yeshiva website. Accessed April 2004. http://www.geocities.com/hesderks/articles/mikarmey/hesder/hesder.html.

Hager-Lau, Rabbi Moshe. "Presentation at the BESA Conference on Religious and Secular in the Military: The Challenge." Ramat Gan, September 15, 2010.

Haltiner, Karl W. "The Definite End of the Mass Army in Western Europe." *Armed Forces & Society* 25 (1998): 7–36.

Harel, Amos. "The Halakha Battle in the IDF: The Military Rabbinate vs. Mekhinot Rabbis." *Haaretz*, online edition (November 27, 1999).

————. "Make Yourself a Battle." *Haaretz Magazine* (March 10, 2000): 46–50.

————. "The Debate of Desecration of Shabbat Is Overshadowing the Settlers' Violence." *Haaretz*, online edition (October 21, 2002).

————. "Recommendation to Mofaz: Stop Monetary Support for the Extreme Right-Wing Mekhinot. *Haaretz*, online edition (December 30, 2004).

————. "Senior IDF Officers: The Disengagement Has Caused Religious Youth to Avoid Conscription; Increased Requests for Religious Deferments." *Haaretz*, online edition (December 30, 2007).

Harel, Amos and Nadav Shragai. "AKA Head and the Heads of Hesder Yeshivot Discussed the Disbanding of Hesder Units." *Haaretz*, online edition (January 26, 2005).

Hashim, Ahmed S. "Civil-Military Relations in the Islamic Republic of Iran." In *Iran, Iraq and the Arab Gulf States*, edited by Joseph A. Kechichian, 31–53. New York: Palgrave, 2001.

Heilman, Samuel C. "Jewish Sociologist: Native-as-Stranger." *The American Sociologist* 15 (1980): 100–108.

Idan, Yosef. "Too Much Motivation." *NRG, Ma'ariv* online edition (February 14, 2005).

Ilan, Shachar. "Litzman's Coup." *Haaretz*, online edition (April 28, 2005).

Isaiah (Metropolitan). "Guidelines for Greek Orthodox Priests Serving as Chaplains with the US Armed Forces." US Air Force Chaplain Service (2004). Accessed June 2009. http://www.usafhc.af.mil/Attachments/Recruiting/03c.%20Greek%20Orthodox%20Chaplain%20Guidelines.doc.

"Islam in the US Armed Forces." *Renaissance* (February 1999). Accessed April 2004. http://www.renaissance.com.pk.

"Isle Muslims in Military Service Keep Faithful to Their Religion." American Muslim Armed Forces and Veteran Affairs Council (October 2001). Accessed June 2003. http://www.amafandvzc.org/.

Izraeli, Dafna N. "Paradoxes of Women's Service in the Israel Defense Forces." In *Military, State and Society in Israel*, edited by Daniel Maman, Eyal Ben-Ari, and Zeev Rosenhek, 203–238. Piscataway, NJ: Transaction Books, 2001.

Jacobs, G. "India's Army." *Asian Defence Journal* 9 (1985): 4–27.

Kahan, Eli. "The Intensifying Fountainhead." *Amudim* (1998): 8–12.

Kampinsky, Aharon (Roni). "Religion and the Military and Security in Israel." PhD diss., Bar Ilan University (2007).

Kashti, Or, and Nadav Shragai. "Heads of the Mekhinot: The Minister of Education Is Not Protecting Us." *Haaretz*, online edition (August 13, 2007).

Kehat, Chana. "Women's Status and the Study of Torah in Orthodox Society." In *HaTishma Koli: Yetzugim shel Nashim baTarbut haYisraelit* (Will You Listen to My Voice? Representations of Women in Israeli Culture), edited by Yael Atzmon, 355–364. Jerusalem: Van Leer Institute, 2001.

Keren, Rachel. "Scholarly Women: From Where and Where To?" In *To Be a Jewish Woman*, edited by Margalit Shilo, 77–78. Jerusalem: Kolech, 2001.

———. Lecture, Shazar Center Conference, Yeshivot veBatei Midrashot, Jerusalem, January 7, 2004.

Khalidi, Omar. "Ethnic Group Recruitment in the Indian Army: The Contrasting Cases of Sikhs, Muslims, Gurkhas and Others." *Pacific Affairs* 74, no. 4 (2001–2002): 529–552.

Kimmerling, Baruch. "Militarism in Israeli Society." *Teoria uBikoret* 4 (1994): 123–140.

Kook, Rabbi Zvi Yehuda. "Responsa." *Tchumin* 3 (1982): 387.

Krechmer-Raziel, Yoel. "A Letter to Our Soldiers." *The Shiluvon* (Tamuz 2005).

Leech, Beth L. "Asking Questions: Techniques for Semistructured Interviews." *Political Science and Politics* 35 (2002): 665–668.

Lichtenstein, Rabbi Aharon. "The Ideology of Hesder." In *Darka shel haYeshiva: Kovetz Ma'amarim miToch Bitonei Yeshivat Har Etzion* (The Yeshiva's Road: Selected Articles from the Har Etzion Yeshiva's Publications). Alon Shvut: Yeshivat Har Etzion, 2002.

Liebman, Charles S. "Extremism as a Religious Norm." *Journal for the Scientific Study of Religion* 22, no.1 (1983): 75–86.

———. "Religion and the Chaos of Modernity: The Case of Contemporary Judaism." In *Take Judaism for Example: Studies Toward the Comparison of Religions*, edited by Jacob Neusner, 147–164. Chicago: University of Chicago Press, 1983b.

Lijphart, Arend. "Consociational Democracy." *World Politics* 21, no. 2 (1969): 207–225.

Lissak, Moshe. "The Civil Components of Israel's National Security Doctrine." *Iyunim beTkumat Yisrael* 1 (1991): 191–210.

Luckham, A. R. "A Comparative Typology of Civil-Military Relations." *Government and Opposition* 6, no. 1 (1971): 5–35.

Malin, Don. "Military Chaplains and Religious Pluralism." *Watchman Fellowship of Alabama* (2004). Accessed June 2009. http://www.wfial.org/index.cfm?fuseaction=artGeneral.article_6.

"Many Faiths, One Army." *India Express* (1999). Accessed April 2004. http://www.financialexpress.com/ie/daily/19990825/iex25056p.html.

Melamed, Rabbi Eliezer. "The Military and the Mitzva." *Besheva* (August, 15 2002): 8.

———. "Disobeying Orders Strengthens the IDF." *Besheva* (February 24, 2005): 19.

———. "The Responsibility of Disobeying Orders." *Besheva* (March 15, 2005b): 18.

———. "The Most Important Part Is Missing from the Report." *Besheva* (February 7, 2008): 32.

Melamed, Rabbi Zalman. "Great Torah Scholars—This Is a National Need." *Tchumin* 7 (1986): 330–334.

Michaelson, Menachem. "The Military Rabbinate." In *TZAHAL beChaylo* (The IDF and Its Layout), edited by Ilan Kfir and Yaakov Erez, 83–101. Tel Aviv: Revivim, 1982.

Min Ha-Har, Rabbi Shlomo. "Women in Obligatory War." *Tchumin* 4 (1983): 68–78.

Nir, Tomer. "Hesder Shiluvim Begins." *Srugim* (November 22, 2010). Accessed February 2011. http://www.srugim.co.il/.

Perry, Tony. "Muslim Chaplains Play Key Role." *The Detroit News* (2001). http://www.beliefnet.com/story/89/story_8950.html.

Porat, Amitai, and Na'ama Una. "Alamot." *Amudim* (Tamuz 2003): 22.

Rappaport, Amir. "The IDF Presents: The Modesty Patrol." *NRG, Ma'ariv* online edition (March 15, 2005).

———. "The End of the Arrangement." *Ma'ariv: Weekend Magazine* 28 (January 28, 2005b): 12–13.

———. "Is Stern Folding?" *NRG, Ma'ariv* online edition (February 10, 2005c).

Reichner, Elyashiv. "A Loudmouth, Aggressive Zionism." *NRG, Ma'ariv* online edition (June 12, 2004).

Reid, T. R. "Air Force Removes Chaplain from Post." *The Washington Post* (May 13, 2005). Accessed June 2009. http://www.washingtonpost.com.

"Religious Orientation of Muslim Soldiers in the United States Armed Forces." *Defence Journal* (June 1999). Accessed April 2004. http://defencejournal.com/jun99/orientation.htm.

Rose, Gregory F. "The Post Revolutionary Purge of Iran's Armed Forces: A Revisionist Assessment." *Iranian Studies* 17, no. 2–3 (1984): 153–194.

Rosen, Rabbi Yisrael. "From Military Rabbinate to a Religious Council in Uniform." *Shabbat beShabato* 968, Chukat Portion (July 5, 2003).

Rosenberg, Esti. "To Dive into the World of Torah: An Unobstructed Encounter between the Young Woman and the World of Torah." In *Etgarim beChinukh habit haDatit caIdan haModerni* (Challenges in the Education of Modern Orthodox Young Women). Discussion Papers, no. 3, edited by Tova Cohen and Yisrael Rich, 21–29. Ramat Gan: The Fanya Gottesfeld Heller Center for the Study of Women in Judaism, Stern Institute for the Study and Advancement of Religious Education, Women in Judaism, 2000.

———. "Yeshivot veBatei Midrashot." Lecture, Merkaz Shazar Conference, Jerusalem, January 7, 2004.

Rosman-Stollman, Elisheva. "The 'Shiluv' Program: Between Church and State—A Religious-Zionist Solution to the Dilemma of Conscription in Israel." *Iyunim beTkumat Israel* 10 (2000): 59–297.

Rosner, Rivka. "We Need Serious Judaism, Not Symposia: An Interview With Rabbi Avia HaCohen." *Deot* 40, online edition (2008). Accessed February 2013. http://toravoda.org.il/node/952.

Ross, Tamar. "Yeshivot veBatei Midrashot." Lecture, Merkaz Shazar Conference, Jerusalem, January 7, 2004.

Rotem, Tamar. "Master of Impossible Connections." *Haaretz*, online edition (September 18, 2003).

Rotenberg, Hagit. "Judgment Day for the Mekhinot." *Besheva* (February 10, 2005): 33.

———. "The Usual Spin—Closing Mekhinot." *Besheva* (February 3, 2005b): 38.

Sasson-Levy, Orna. "Subversion in Oppression: Gender Identity of Female Soldiers in 'Male' Military Roles." In *HaTishma Koli: Yetzugim shel Nashim baTarbut haYisraelit* (Will You Listen to My Voice? Representations of Women in Israeli Culture), edited by Yael Atzmon, 151–172. Jerusalem: Van Leer Institute, 2001.

Schiff, Shaul. "Sod Seiach." *HaTzofe*, online edition (May 14, 2004).

Schild, E. O. "On the Meaning of Military Service in Israel." In *Israel: Social Structure and Change*, edited by Michael Curtis and Mordecai S. Chertoff, 419–432. Piscataway, NJ: Transaction Books, 1973.

Segal, Mady Wechsler. "The Military and the Family as Greedy Institutions." *Armed Forces and Society* 13, no. 1 (1986): 9–38.

Sela, Yifat. "Serving in Faith: Religious Female Soldiers and the IDF." In *Ben HaKipa LeKumta* (Between the Beret and the Skullcap), edited by Reuven Gal and Tamir Libel, 529–548. Ben-Shemen: Kinneret, Modan, 2012.

Selengut, Charles. "By Torah Alone: Yeshiva Fundamentalism in Jewish Life." In *Accounting for Fundamentalism*, edited by Martin E. Marty and R. Scott Appleby, vol. 4, 237. Chicago: University of Chicago Press, 1994.

"Serving Allah and America: Muslims in the military strive to reconcile religion." AMAF and VAC site (November 12, 2002). Accessed June 2009. http://www.amafandvac.org.

Sezgin, Yüksel. "Can the Israeli Status Quo Model Help Post-February 28 Turkey Solve Its Problems?" *Turkish Studies* 4, no. 3 (2003): 47–70.

Shakdiel, Leah. "An Army of Women Learning Torah." Paper presented at the Militarism and Education Conference at the Hebrew University in Jerusalem, May 30, 2001.

Sharon, Ro'i. "Stern to Hesder Units: Enlist and Say Thank You." *NRG, Ma'ariv* online edition (May 10, 2007).

Shavit, Ari. "What? Don't You Remember How Dangerous Sharon Is?" *Haaretz* (January 28, 2005): 17–20.

Shaviv, Rabbi Yehuda. "Women in Obligatory War." *Tchumin* 4 (1994): 79–89.

Shelach, Ofer. "A Small Story, a Huge Shame." *NRG, Ma'ariv* online edition (September 29, 2007).

Sheleg, Yair. "The Letter, What Was Written, and the Rabbi's Deputy." *Haaretz* (February 22, 1999): B3.

———. "The IDF Must Decide: Women Combat Soldiers or Hesder Soldiers." *Haaretz* (January 21, 2001): A11.

———. "On the Brink of a Rift in Religious Zionism." *Haaretz* (March 27, 2002).

———. "Elite—It's Time to Use the Word without Embarrassment." *Haaretz* (May 6, 2003): B6.

———. "The 'Grey' Refusal of Rabbi Tau." *Haaretz* (September 15, 2004): B5.

———. "Yeshivot Hesder, The Feminine Version." *Haaretz*, online edition (June 10, 2004b).

Shetach, Shmuel. "It's Possible without Going to Jail." *Besheva* (April 10, 2008): 28.

Shilat, Rabbi Yitzchak. "Hesder Yeshivot—Values and Educational Trends." *Ma'aliyot* 10 *Ma'ale heAsor* (1988): 43–51.

Shragai, Nadav. "In Ma'aleh Adumim the Question Is Not Whether to Refuse Orders, But How." *Haaretz*, online edition (October 20, 2004).

———. "On the Eve of Independence Day, Religious Zionist Rabbis Affirm Allegiance to the State—But Only Conditionally." *Haaretz*, online edition (May 11, 2005).

Singh, Pushpindar. "The Indian Army Today: Colour and Firepower." *Asian Defence Journal*, no. 4 (April 1987): 4–27.

Tadmor, Erez. "There Is Fear in the Religious Sector." *Makor Rishon—Dyukan* (October 21, 2005): 14–15.

Tesler, Itzchak. "Rabbi David Stav: Rabbi Melamed Caused a Desecration of God's Name." *NRG, Ma'ariv* online edition (July 27, 2010).

Timm, Angelika. "Israeli Civil Society Facing New Challenges." *Israeli Studies Forum* 17, no. 1 (2001): 47–68.

Toprak, Binnaz. "The State, Politics, and Religion in Turkey." In *State Democracy and the Military: Turkey in the 1980s*, edited by Metin Heper and Ahmet Evin, 119–136. New York: Walter de Gruyter, 1988.

Toprak, Binnaz. "Islam and Democracy in Turkey." *Turkish Studies* 6, no. 2 (2005): 167–186.

Tor-Paz, Moshe. "When Modern Orthodoxy Enlisted." Ne'emanei Tora Va-Avoda website (February 2005). http://toravoda.org.il/army_hebrew.html.

Tzuriel, Moshe. "Words of Encouragement for the Noncombat Soldier." In *HaChazit sheBaOref: Asufat Ma'amarim laChayal sheBeOref haChevra hsYisreelit* (Articles for the Noncombat Soldier in Israeli Society), edited by Sarel Weinberger and Amichai Beitner, 282–292. Bet El: Sifriyat Bet El, 2007.

Tzviran, Guy. "Letter from the Field: On Coping with Secular Society in the Military." *Daf Kesher leTalmidei haYeshiva beTZAHAL* (Newsletter for the Yeshiva's Students in the IDF). Har Etzion, newsletter 1013, Korach Portion (Sivan 2005).

Vaner, Semih. "The Army." In *Turkey in Transition: New Perspectives*, edited by Irvin C. Schick and Ertugrul Ahmet Tonak, 236–265. New York: Oxford University Press, 1987.

"War Chaplains." *Religion and Ethics Newsweekly* (March 28, 2003). Accessed June 2003. http://www.pbs.org/wnet/religionandethics/week630/p-cover.html.

Wolman, Yisrael. "I Will Instruct My Students: Carry Out the Order." *Yedioth Ahronot: Shabbat Magazine* (October 22, 2004): 6–7, 26.

Wolvier, Laura R. "Ethical Dilemmas in Personal Interviewing." *Political Science and Politics* 35 (2002): 677–678.

Yochanan, Yiftach. "A Movement in Movement: Security Department." *Amudim* (Tishrei 2003): 49–50.

Yoffie, Eric H. "Torah Study and Army Service in the State of Israel: Ambiguous Sources, Unexpected Conclusions." *Central Conference of American Rabbis* (Summer 1991): 49–61.

Yuval-Davis, Nira. "The Israeli Example." In *Loaded Questions: Women in the Military*, edited by Wendy Chapkis, 73–77. Amsterdam: Transnational Institute, 1981.

INTERNET SITES

Ateret Cohanim Yeshiva, accessed June 2009, http://www.ateret.org.il/hebrew/library.php?id=767.

American Muslims Armed Forces and Veterans Affairs Council, accessed January 2010, http://www.amafandvac.org.

Bnei David Eli Mekhina, accessed February 2003, http://www.bneidavid.org/.

Beit Yatir (Yatir) Mekhina, accessed February 2003, http://www.yatir.org/.

Bemidbar Midrasha, accessed February 2003, http://www.bamidbar.org/index.html.

Birkat Moshe (Ma'ale Adumim) Hesder Yeshiva, accessed February 2003, http://www.birkatmoshe.org.il/index.asp?id=152.

Catholic Chaplains of the Australian Military, accessed June 2009, http://www.military.catholic.org.au/index.htm.

Catholic Chaplains of the French Military, accessed June 2009, http://catholique-diocese-aux-armees.cef.fr.

Chemdat Yehuda Mekhina, accessed June 2009, http://www.chemdat.org.il/index.php.

Department of Torah Culture, Ministry of Education, Israel, accessed June 2009, http://cms.education.gov.il.

Ein Tzurim Religious Kibbuta Yeshiva, accessed June 2009, http://www.ykd.co.il/.

Elon Moreh Hesder Yeshiva, accessed June 2009, http://www.mideorayta.org/.

Ha-Golan Hesder Yeshiva, accessed June 2009, http://www.golan.org.il/yeshiva/.

Har Etzion Hesder Yeshiva, accessed June 2009, http://www.haretzion.org/.

Jewish Welfare Board, accessed June 2009, http://www.jcca.org/JWB/.

Jews in Green, accessed February 2013, http://www.jewsingreen.com/.

Karnei Shomron Hesder Yeshiva, accessed June 2009, http://www.geocities.com/hesderks/index.html?20053.

Kerem Be-Yavneh Hesder Yeshiva, accessed February 2013, http://www.kby.org.il/.

Kipa, accessed February 2013, http://kipa.co.il.

Indian Military, unofficial site, accessed June 2009, http://www.bharat-rakshak.com/LAND-FORCES/Army/Reg-Inf.htm.

Ma'ale Gilboa Religious Kibbutz Yeshiva, accessed June 2009, http://www.maalegilboa.org/.

Ma'alot Ya'akov Hesder Yeshiva, accessed June 2009, http://www.yesmalot.co.il/tei.html.

Meir Haerl, Shesder Yeshiva in Modi'in, http://www.meirharel.org/page.asp?id=1123/.

Midrashot Forum, accessed June 2010, http://www.midrashot.net/list.asp.

Ministry of Defense, India, accessed June 2009, http://mod.nic.in/rec&training/body.htm.

Ministry of Education, Turkey, accessed June 2009, http://www.yok.gov.tr/webeng/histedu/part3_4.html.

Moriya, accessed June 2009, http://www.moriya.org.il/.

Moreshet, accessed June 2009, http://www.moreshet.co.il/.

Moreshet Ya'akov Hesder Yeshiva, accessed February 2013, http://muni.tik-tak.co.il/subweb/web/index.asp.

Office of the Chief of Chaplains, U.S. military, accessed June 2009, http://www.chapnet.army.mil/.

Official Indian Army site, accessed November 2013, http://www.joinindianarmy.nic.in.

Otniel Hesder Yeshiva, accessed February 2013, http://www.otniel.org.

Shilo Hesder Yeshiva, accessed February 2013, http://www.yshilo.co.il/.

Tekoa Hesder Yeshiva, accessed June 2009, http://www.yeshivatekoa.org.il/.

The Jewish Soldier (U.S. military lay leaders' site), accessed June 2009, http://www.thejewishsoldier.com/.

Yehudi Lo Megaresh Yehudi (A Jew Doesn't Expel a Fellow Jew), accessed April 2006, http://www.seruv.co.il/?page=23.

Yom Pkuda, accessed April 2006, http://www.yom-pkuda.org/.

Yeshiva, accessed February 2013, http://yeshiva.org.il/.

INDEX

www.ingramcontent.com/pod-product-compliance
Ingram Content Group UK Ltd.
Pitfield, Milton Keynes, MK11 3LW, UK
UKHW010315240525
458861UK00003B/457